Optimizing C++

ISBN 0-13-977430-0

90000

Optimizing C++

Steve Heller

Prentice Hall, PTR
Upper Saddle River, New Jersey 07458
http://www.phptr.com

Library of Congress Cataloging-in-Publication Data

Heller, Steve.
    Optimizing C++ / Steve Heller.
        p.   cm.
    Includes index.
    ISBN 0-13-977430-0
    1. C++ (Computer program language)   I. Title.
QA76.73.C153H4545   1999
005.13'3--dc21   98-24381
                                                                 CIP

Editorial/Production Supervision: Craig Little
Acquisitions Editor: Jeffrey Pepper
Editorial Assistant: Kristy Schaak
Manufacturing Manager: Alexis R. Heydt
Marketing Manager: Kaylie Smith
Cover Design Director: Jerry Votta
Cover Design: Anthony Gemmellaro/Design Source

© 1999 by Prentice Hall PTR
Prentice-Hall Inc.
A Simon & Schuster Company
Upper Saddle River, NJ 07458

All rights reserved. No part of this book may be
reproduced, in any form or by any means, without
permission in writing from the publisher.

All product names mentioned herein are the trademarks or registered trademarks of their respective owners.

Prentice Hall books are widely used by corporations and government agencies for training, marketing, and resale.

The publisher offers discounts on this book when ordered in bulk quantities.
For more information, contact: Corporate Sales Department at 800-382-3419, fax: 201-236-7141,
email: corpsales@prenhall.com or write Corporate Sales Department, Prentice Hall PTR, One Lake Street,
Upper Saddle River, New Jersey 07458.

Printed in the United States of America
10 9 8 7 6 5 4 3 2 1

ISBN   0-13-977430-0

Prentice-Hall International (UK) Limited, *London*
Prentice-Hall of Australia Pty. Limited, *Sydney*
Prentice-Hall Canada Inc., *Toronto*
Prentice-Hall Hispanoamericana, S.A., *Mexico*
Prentice-Hall of India Private Limited, *New Delhi*
Prentice-Hall of Japan, Inc., *Tokyo*
Simon & Schuster Asia Pte. Ltd., *Singapore*
Editora Prentice-Hall do Brasil, Ltda., *Rio de Janeiro*

Contents

Chapter 3: A Mailing List System   67

Chapter 6: Heavenly Hash: A Dynamic Hashing Algorithm 265

Chapter 7: Zensort: A Sorting Algorithm for Limited Memory 309

Figures

This book is dedicated to Susan Patricia Caffee Heller, the light of my life. Without her, this book would not be what it is; even more important, I would not be what I am: a happy man.

Acknowledgements

I'd like to thank all those readers who have provided feedback on the first two editions of this book, especially those who have posted reviews on Amazon.com; their contributions have made this a better book.

I'd also like to thank Jeff Pepper, my editor at Prentice-Hall, for his support and encouragement. Without him, this third edition would never have been published.

Finally, I would like to express my appreciation to John P. Linderman at AT&T Labs Research for his help with the code in the chapter on sorting immense files.

Preface

Imagine that you are about to finish a relatively large program, one that has taken a few weeks or months to write and debug. Just as you are putting the finishing touches on it, you discover that it is either too slow or runs out of memory when you feed it a realistic set of input data. You sigh, and start the task of optimizing it.

But why optimize? If your program doesn't fit in memory, you can just get more memory; if it is too slow, you can get a faster processor.

I have written *Optimizing C++* because I believe that this common attitude is incorrect, and that a knowledge of optimization is essential to a professional programmer. One very important reason is that we often have little control over the hardware on which our programs are to be run. In this situation, the simplistic approach of adding more hardware is not feasible.

Optimizing C++ provides working programmers and those who intend to be working programmers with a practical, real-world approach to program optimization. Many of the optimization techniques presented are derived from my reading of academic journals that are, sadly, little known in the programming community. This book also draws on my nearly 30 years of experience as a programmer in diverse fields of application, during which I have become increasingly concerned about the amount of effort spent in reinventing optimization techniques rather than applying those already developed.

The first question you have to answer is whether your program needs optimization at all. If it does, you have to determine what part of the program is the culprit, and what resource is being overused. Chapter 1 indicates a method of attack on these problems, as well as a real-life example.

All of the examples in this book were compiled with both Microsoft's Visual C++ 5.0 and the DJGPP compiler, written and copyrighted by DJ Delorie. The latter compiler, along with all the source code for the examples, is on the CD in the back of this book. The CD also includes RHIDE, an integrated development environment for the DJGPP compiler, written and copyrighted by Robert Hoehne.

All of the timings and profiling statistics, unless otherwise noted, were the result of running the corresponding program compiled with Visual C++ 5.0 on my Pentium II 233 Megahertz machine with 64 megabytes of memory.

I am always happy to receive correspondence from readers. If you wish to contact me, the best way is to visit my WWW page. At the moment, you can reach my page by going to any of the following addresses:

http://www.dos32.com/heller/heller.htm
http://ourworld.compuserve.com/homepages/steve_heller
http://www.koyote.com/users/stheller

If none of these addresses gets you to my page, or you have questions that aren't answered by it, you can email me at:

steve_heller@compuserve.com

Finally, if you don't have email access either, you can write to me care of my publishers at the following address:

Steve Heller
c/o Prentice-Hall, Inc.
One Lake Street
Upper Saddle River, NJ 07548

In the event that you enjoy this book and would like to tell others about it, you might want to write an on-line review on Amazon.com, which you can do by visiting my home page and following the links to the "readers reviews" on Amazon.

I should also tell you how the various typefaces are used in the book. HelveticaNarrow is used for program listings, for terms used in programs, and for words defined by the C++ language. *Italics* are used primarily for technical terms that are found in the glossary, although they are also used for emphasis in some places. The first time that I use a particular technical term that you might not know, it is in **bold** face.

Chapter 1

Prologue

Introduction to Optimization

What is optimization anyway? Clearly, we have to know this before we can discuss how and why we should optimize programs.

Definition

Optimization is the art and science of modifying a working computer program so that it makes more efficient use of one or more scarce resources, primarily memory, disk space, or time.

This definition has a sometimes overlooked but very important corollary (The First Law of Optimization): The speed of a nonworking program is irrelevant.

Algorithms Discussed

Radix40 Data Representation, Lookup Tables[1]

---

[1] If you don't have the time to read this book in its entirety, you can turn to Figures 8.1-8.4 in Chapter 8 to find the algorithms best suited to your problem.

Deciding Whether to Optimize

Suppose you have written a program to calculate mortgage payments; the yearly run takes ten minutes. Should you spend two hours to double its speed? Probably not, since it will take twenty-four years to pay back the original investment of time at five minutes per year.[2] On the other hand, if you run a program for three hours every working day, even spending thirty hours to double its speed will pay for itself in only twenty working days, or about a month. Obviously the latter is a much better candidate for optimization. Usually, of course, the situation is not nearly so unambiguous: even if your system is overloaded, it may not be immediately apparent which program is responsible.[3]

My general rule is not to optimize a program that performs satisfactorily. If you (or the intended users) don't become impatient while waiting for it to finish, don't bother. Of course, if you just feel like indulging in some recreational optimization, that's another matter.

Why Optimization Is Necessary

Assuming that our programs are too big, or too slow, why don't we just add more memory or a faster processor? If that isn't possible today, then the next generation of processors should be powerful enough to spare us such concerns.

Let's examine this rather widely held theory. Although the past is not an infallible guide to the future, it is certainly one source of information about what happens when technology changes. A good place to start is to compare the computers of the late 1970's with those of the late 1990's.

The first diskette-based computer I ever owned was a Radio Shack TRS-80 Model III™, purchased in 1979.[4] It had a 4 MHz Z80™

---

2. Actually, you will never be ahead; five minutes saved 23 years from now is not as valuable as five minutes spent now. This is analogous to the lottery in which you win a million dollars, but the prize is paid as one dollar a year for a million years!

3. This is especially true on a multiuser system.

4. My previous computer was also a Radio Shack computer, but it had only a cassette recorder/player for "mass storage"!

processor, 48 Kbytes of memory, and Basic™ in ROM. The diskettes held about 140 Kbytes apiece. Among the programs that were available for this machine were word processors, assemblers, debuggers, data bases, and games. While none of these were as advanced as the ones that are available today on 80x86 or 680x0 machines, most of the basic functions were there.

The Pentium II™ machines of today have at least 1000 times as much memory and 20000 times as much disk storage and are probably 1000 times as fast. Therefore, according to this theory, we should no longer need to worry about efficiency.

Recently, however, several of the major microcomputer software companies have had serious performance problems with new software releases of both application programs and system programs, as they attempted to add more and more features to those available in the previous versions.[5] This illustrates what I call the Iron Law of Programming: whenever more resources are made available, a more ambitious project is attempted. This means that optimal use of these resources is important no matter how fast or capacious the machine.

Why Optimization Is Often Neglected

In view of this situation, why has optimization of application programs not gained more attention? I suspect that a major reason is the tremendous and continuing change in the relative costs of programming time and computer hardware. To illustrate this, let us examine two situations where the same efficiency improvement is gained, but the second example occurs after twenty years of technological improvement.

In the early 1970's a programmer's starting salary was about $3 per hour, and an hour of timesharing connect time cost about $15. Therefore, if a program originally took one hour to run every day, and the programmer spent a week to reduce this time by 20%, in about eight weeks the increased speed would have paid for the programmer's time.

---

5. Microsoft is the most prominent example at the moment; the resource consumption of Windows NT™ is still a matter of concern to many programmers, even though the machines that these programmers own have increased in power at a tremendous rate.

In the late 1990's, the starting salary is in the vicinity of $15 per hour, and if we assume that the desktop computer costs $2500 and is amortized over three years, the weekly cost of running the unoptimized program is about $2.00. Holding the other assumptions constant, the optimization payback time is about 30 years![6]

This long-term trend seems to favor hardware solutions for performance problems over the investment of programming effort. However, the appropriate strategy for performance improvement of a program depends on how much control you have over the hardware on which the program will run. The less control you have over the hardware, the greater the advantage of software solutions to performance problems, as illustrated by the situations below.

Considering a Hardware Solution

While every optimization problem is different, here are some general guidelines that can help you decide whether adding hardware to help you with your performance problems makes sense.

1.   If you are creating a system that includes both software and hardware, and you can improve the functioning of the program, ease maintenance, or speed up development at a small additional expense for extra hardware resources, you should almost certainly do so.

A few years ago, I was involved in a classic example of this situation. The project was to create a point-of-sale system, including specialized hardware and programs, that tied a number of terminals into a common database. Since the part of the database that had to be accessed rapidly could be limited to about 1 1/2 megabytes, I suggested that we put enough memory in the database server machine to hold the entire database. That way, the response time would be faster than even a very good indexing system could provide, and the programming effort would be greatly reduced. The additional expense came to about $150 per system, which was less

---

6. This example is actually quite conservative. The program that took one hour to run on a timesharing terminal would probably take much less than that on a current desktop computer; we are also neglecting the time value of the savings, as noted above.

than 3% of the price of the system. Of course, just adding hardware doesn't always mean that no software optimization is needed. In this case, as you will see below, adding the hardware was only the beginning of the optimization effort.

2.   If you are writing programs for your own use on one computer, and you can afford to buy a machine powerful enough to perform adequately, then you might very well purchase such a machine rather than optimizing the program.[7]

3.   If you are writing a program that will be running on more than one computer, even if it is only for internal use at your company, the expense and annoyance of requiring the other users to upgrade their computers may outweigh the difficulty of optimization.

4.   If your program is to run on many computers at your company, it is almost always a good idea to try to optimize it rather than to require all those users to upgrade their hardware.

5.   If your program is to be sold in the open market to run on standard hardware, you must try to optimize it. Otherwise, the users are likely to reject the program.

An excellent example of what happens when you try to make a number of users upgrade their computers is the relatively disappointing sales record (as of this writing) of the Windows NT™ operating system.

In order to get any reasonable performance under version 4.0 of Windows NT (the latest extant as of this writing), you need at least 64 megabytes of memory and a Pentium II/233 processor. Since almost the only people who have such machines are professional software developers, the sales of this program to other users have been much smaller than expected.

---

7. Of course, if your old machine is more than two or three years old, you might want to replace it anyway, just to get the benefit of the improved technology available today.

Categories of Optimization

There are two broad categories of optimization: using a better algorithm, and improving the implementation of the algorithm we are already using. Generally, we should replace an algorithm by a better one as soon as possible, as this usually does not hinder understanding or later modification of the program. An example is the use of a distribution counting sort (see Chapter 3) in preference to Quicksort. Of course, if we employ these efficient algorithms from the start of our programming effort, then we are not optimizing in the strict sense of our definition (changing a working program to make it more efficient). However, the end result is still a better program than we would have obtained otherwise.[8]

The second category of optimization is the modification of the implementation of an existing algorithm to take advantage of peculiarities of the environment in which it is running or of the characteristics of the data to which it is applied. This type of modification often has the unfortunate side effect of making the algorithm much harder to understand or modify in the future; it also impairs portability among different hardware and software architectures. Therefore, such an optimization should be postponed until the last possible moment, in order to reduce its negative effects on the development and maintenance of the program. This is an application of the First Law of Optimization: don't try to optimize a program (in the strict sense of modifying an existing program) until it is working correctly.

Finding the Critical Resource

It may seem obvious that, before you can optimize a program, you have to know what is making it inefficient. Of course, if you run out of memory or disk space while executing the program, this determination becomes much simpler.

Depending on which language and machine you are using, there may be "profiling" tools available which allow you to determine where your program is spending most of its time. These, of course,

---

8. Perhaps this could be referred to as optimizing the design.

are most useful when the problem is CPU time, but even if that is not the problem, you may still be able to find out that, e.g., your program is spending 95% of its time in the disk reading and/or writing routines. This is a valuable clue to where the problem lies.

However, even if no profiler is available for your system, it isn't hard to gather some useful information yourself. One way to do this is to insert a call to a system timer routine (such as clock() in ANSI C) at the beginning of the segment to be timed and another call at the end of the segment and subtract the two times. Depending on the resolution of the timer, the length of the routine, and the speed of your processor, you may have to execute the segment more than once to gather any useful information. This is illustrated in the real-life example below.

Determining How Much Optimization Is Needed

Sometimes your task is simply to make the program run as fast (or take as little memory) as possible. In this case, you must use the most effective optimization available, regardless of the effort involved. However, you often have (or can get) a specific target, such as a memory budget of 1.4 megabytes for your data. If you can achieve this goal by relatively simple means, it would be a waste of your time to try to squeeze the last few kilobytes out of the data by a fancier compression algorithm. In fact, it may be worse than a waste of time; the simpler algorithm may also have other desirable characteristics (other than its raw performance).

A good example of such a simple algorithm is the Radix40 data compression method (see Chapter 2, Figures 2.16 through 2.19), which is, on average, considerably less effective at reducing the size of a data file than a number of other data compression algorithms. On the other hand, it is quite fast, requires very little storage, and always produces the same amount of output for the same amount of input, which means that its compression efficiency can be calculated exactly in advance. The (statistically) more effective routines such as those using arithmetic coding take more memory and more time, and they generally produce different amounts of output for a given amount of input (depending on what has gone before), so that their compression efficiency cannot be predicted exactly. (In fact, in rare circumstances, they produce output that is larger than the input.) This context dependence also means that they are more difficult to use in applications where random access to compressed data is needed.

The moral is that you should use the simplest algorithm that will meet your needs. If you can define your needs precisely, you probably won't have to implement as sophisticated an algorithm to solve your problem, which will leave you more time to work on other areas that need improvement.

A Real-Life Example

The point-of-sale database program I mentioned earlier is an excellent example of the fact that optimization rarely follows a straight-line path. The first problem was the speed of access to the database by multiple users. Since the software is supplied with specialized hardware, it was reasonable to solve this problem by adding enough memory to hold the portion of the database that requires rapid access. My employer determined that 15,000 invoice records and 5000 customer records would be sufficient, resulting in a memory requirement of about 1.25 megabytes. The expense of this amount of memory was within reason.

Unfortunately, that part of memory (**conventional** memory) which allows normal program access is limited to 640 kilobytes on IBM-compatible systems running the MS-DOS operating system, the environment in which this program operated. While our actual hardware allowed for more memory, it could be referenced only as **expanded** memory, which cannot be allocated as simply as conventional memory.

Luckily, the problem of using expanded memory for data storage has been addressed by libraries of routines which allow any particular 16 Kbyte "page" of expanded memory to be loaded when the data in it are required. Storing the records in expanded memory solved the speed problem by eliminating excessive disk I/O.

However, the amount of expanded memory required was very close to the total available. In the very likely event of adding even a single field to the record definition, there would not be enough room for all the records. Therefore, I had to consider ways to reduce the space taken by these records.

The makeup of the database is important to the solution of this new problem. It consists almost entirely of 15,000 invoice records of approximately 35 bytes each and 5000 customer records of approximately 145 bytes each. Fortunately, the majority of the fields in the customer record contained only uppercase alphabetic characters, numeric digits, a few special characters (".", ",", and "-"), and spaces. This limited character set allows the use of Radix40 compression, which packs three characters into two bytes. (See Chapter 2 for more details on this algorithm).

However, the time required to convert these fields from ASCII to Radix40 representation seemed excessive. Some testing disclosed that converting 5000 records containing 6 fields of 12 characters each from ASCII to Radix40 on a 33 MHz i386 took about 40 seconds![9] Although the most common operations in this system do not require wholesale conversion, it is required in such cases as importing an old-style database into this new system, and such inefficiency was unacceptable. So my space problem had become a speed problem again.

I resolved to improve the speed of this conversion (from 1300 microseconds/12 character string) as much as was practical, before proposing further hardware upgrades to the system. The first problem was to determine which operation was consuming the most CPU time. Examination of the code (Figure 1.1), disclosed that the toupper function was being called for every character in the string, every time the character was being examined). This seemed an obvious place to start.

Figure 1.1: First version of ascii_to_Radix40 routine (from intro\ascrad1.cpp)

```
int ascii_to_radix40_1(radix40_data,ascii_data,max_chars)
unsigned *radix40_data;
unsigned char *ascii_data;
int max_chars;
/* this routine converts a null-terminated ascii character string */
```

---

9. This is worse than it may sound; the actual hardware on which the system runs is much slower than the i386 development machine I was using at the time.

```
/* to radix 40 representation.  The allowable characters are: */
/* A-Z, 0-9, period, comma, hyphen, and space.  If any illegal characters */
/* are detected, they will be converted to hyphens, and the return value */
/* will be S_ILLEGAL. */
/* Lowercase letters will be upper-cased without error indication. */
/* The radix40 value will be padded with blanks to a multiple of three */
/* characters. If the number of characters in the ascii string is > max_chars */
/* only max_chars will be converted, and the return value will be S_ILLEGAL. */
/* If no error is detected, the return value will be S_OKAY. */
{
        int i;
        int j;
        int ascii_length;
        int result;
        int conversion_status;
        int words_to_convert;
        int words_to_clear;
        int cycle;
        unsigned current_word_index;

        result = S_OKAY;
        ascii_length = strlen((char *)ascii_data);
        if (ascii_length > max_chars)
                {
                ascii_length = max_chars;
                result = S_ILLEGAL;
                }

        words_to_convert = ascii_length / 3;
        if (ascii_length % 3 != 0)
                words_to_convert ++;

        words_to_clear = max_chars / 3;
        if (max_chars % 3 != 0)
                words_to_clear ++;

        for (i = 0; i < words_to_clear; i ++)
                radix40_data[i] = 0; /* this blanks out the output string */

        current_word_index = -1;
        cycle = 0;
        for (i = 0; i < ascii_length; i ++)
                {
                if (cycle == 0)
                        current_word_index ++;
                conversion_status = 0;
                for (j = 0; j < 40; j ++)
                        if (legal_chars[j] == toupper(ascii_data[i]))
```

```
                    {
                    conversion_status = 1;
                    break;
                    }
        if (conversion_status == 0)
            {
            result = S_ILLEGAL;
            j = HYPHEN; /* code for hyphen */
            }
        radix40_data[current_word_index] += weights[cycle] * j;
        cycle = (cycle + 1) % 3;
        }

    return(result);
}
```

The purpose of writing the loop in this way was to avoid making changes to the input string; after all, it was an input variable. However, a more efficient way to leave the input string unaltered was to make a copy of the input string and convert the copy to uppercase, as indicated in Figure 1.2. This reduced the time to 650 microseconds/12 character string, but I suspected that more savings were possible.

Figure 1.2: Second version of ascii_to_Radix40 routine (from intro\ascrad2.cpp)

```
int ascii_to_radix40_2(radix40_data,ascii_data,max_chars)
unsigned *radix40_data;
unsigned char *ascii_data;
int max_chars;
/* this routine converts a null-terminated ascii character string */
/* to radix 40 representation.  The allowable characters are: */
/* A-Z, 0-9, period, comma, hyphen, and space.  If any illegal characters */
/* are detected, they will be converted to hyphens, and the return value */
/* will be S_ILLEGAL. */
/* Lowercase letters will be upper-cased without error indication. */
/* The radix40 value will be padded with blanks to a multiple of three */
/* characters. If the number of characters in the ascii string is > max_chars */
/* only max_chars will be converted, and the return value will be S_ILLEGAL. */
/* If no error is detected, the return value will be S_OKAY. */
{
    int i;
    int j;
```

```
int ascii_length;
int result;
int conversion_status;
int words_to_convert;
int words_to_clear;
int cycle;
unsigned current_word_index;
unsigned char *temp_ascii_data;

result = S_OKAY;
ascii_length = strlen((char *)ascii_data);
if (ascii_length > max_chars)
        {
        ascii_length = max_chars;
        result = S_ILLEGAL;
        }

temp_ascii_data = malloc(ascii_length+1);
for (i = 0; i < ascii_length+1; i ++)
        temp_ascii_data[i] = toupper(ascii_data[i]);

words_to_convert = ascii_length / 3;
if (ascii_length % 3 != 0)
        words_to_convert ++;

words_to_clear = max_chars / 3;
if (max_chars % 3 != 0)
        words_to_clear ++;

for (i = 0; i < words_to_clear; i ++)
        radix40_data[i] = 0; /* this blanks out the output string */

current_word_index = -1;
cycle = 0;
for (i = 0; i < ascii_length; i ++)
        {
        if (cycle == 0)
                current_word_index ++;
        conversion_status = 0;
        for (j = 0; j < 40; j ++)
                if (legal_chars[j] == temp_ascii_data[i])
                        {
                        conversion_status = 1;
                        break;
                        }
        if (conversion_status == 0)
                {
                result = S_ILLEGAL;
```

```
            j = HYPHEN; /* code for hyphen */
            }
        radix40_data[current_word_index] += weights[cycle] * j;
        cycle = (cycle + 1) % 3;
        }

    free(temp_ascii_data);
    return(result);
}
```

Another possible area of improvement was to reduce the use of dynamic string allocation to get storage for the copy of the string to be converted to uppercase. In my application, most of the strings would be less than 100 characters, so I decided to allocate room for a string of 99 characters (plus the required null at the end) on the stack and to call the dynamic allocation routine only if the string was larger than that. However, this change didn't affect the time significantly, so I removed it.

I couldn't see any obvious way to increase the speed of this routine further, until I noticed that if the data had about the same number of occurrences of each character, the loop to figure out the code for a single character would be executed an average of 20 times per character! Could this be dispensed with?

Yes, by allocating 256 bytes for a table of conversion values.[10] Then I could index into the table rather than searching the string of legal values (see Figure 1.3). Timing this version revealed an impressive improvement: 93 microseconds/12 character string. This final version is 14 times the speed of the original.[11]

Figure 1.3: Fourth version of ascii_to_Radix40 routine (from intro\ascrad4.cpp)

```
int ascii_to_radix40_4(radix40_data,ascii_data,max_chars)
unsigned *radix40_data;
unsigned char *ascii_data;
int max_chars;
/* this routine converts a null-terminated ascii character string */
/* to radix 40 representation.  The allowable characters are: */
```

---

10. This table of conversion values can be found in Figure 2.16.

11. I also changed the method of clearing the result array to use memset rather than a loop.

```
/* A-Z, 0-9, period, comma, hyphen, and space.  If any illegal characters */
/* are detected, they will be converted to hyphens, and the return value */
/* will be S_ILLEGAL. */
/* Lowercase letters will be upper-cased without error indication. */
/* The radix40 value will be padded with blanks to a multiple of three */
/* characters. If the number of characters in the ascii string is > max_chars */
/* only max_chars will be converted, and the return value will be S_ILLEGAL. */
/* If no error is detected, the return value will be S_OKAY. */
{
        int i;
        int j;
        int ascii_length;
        int result;
        int words_to_convert;
        int words_to_clear;
        int cycle;
        unsigned current_word_index;

        result = S_OKAY;
        ascii_length = strlen((char *)ascii_data);
        if (ascii_length > max_chars)
                {
                ascii_length = max_chars;
                result = S_ILLEGAL;
                }

        words_to_convert = ascii_length / 3;
        if (ascii_length % 3 != 0)
                words_to_convert ++;

        words_to_clear = max_chars / 3;
        if (max_chars % 3 != 0)
                words_to_clear ++;

        memset(radix40_data,0,words_to_clear*sizeof(Radix40));

        current_word_index = -1;
        cycle = 0;
        for (i = 0; i < ascii_length; i ++)
                {
                if (cycle == 0)
                        current_word_index ++;
                j = lookup_chars[ascii_data[i]];
                if (j & 0x80)
                        {
                        j = j & 0x7f;
                        result = S_ILLEGAL;
                        }
```

```
        radix40_data[current_word_index] += weights[cycle] * j;
        cycle = (cycle + 1) % 3;
        }

    return(result);
}
```

The use of a profiler would have reduced the effort needed to determine the major causes of the inefficiency. Even without such an aid, attention to which lines were being executed most frequently enabled me to remove the major bottlenecks in the conversion to Radix40 representation. It is no longer a significant part of the time needed to access a record.

Summary

In this chapter, I have given some guidelines and examples of how to determine whether optimization is required and how to apply your optimization effort effectively. In the next chapter we will start to examine the algorithms and other solutions that you can apply once you have determined where your program needs improvement.

Chapter 2

A Supermarket Price Lookup System

Introduction

In this chapter we will use a supermarket price lookup system to illustrate how to save storage by using a restricted character set and how to speed up access to records by employing **hash coding** (or "scatter storage") and **caching** (or keeping copies of recently accessed records in memory). We will look items up by their UPC (Universal Product Code), which is printed in the form of a "bar code" on virtually all supermarket items other than fresh produce. We will emphasize rapid retrieval of prices, as maintenance of such files is usually done after hours, when speed would be less significant.

Algorithms Discussed

Algorithms discussed: Hash Coding, Radix40 Data Representation, BCD Data Representation, Caching

Up the Down Staircase

To begin, let us assume that we can describe each item by the information in the structure definition in Figure 2.1.

Figure 2.1: Item information

```
typedef struct {
    char upc[10];
    char description[21];
    float price;
    } ItemRecord;
```

One solution to our price-retrieval problem would be to create a file with one record for each item, sorted by UPC code. This would allow us to use a binary search to locate the price of a particular item. How long would it take to find a record in such a file containing 10,000 items?

To answer this question, we have to analyze the algorithm of the binary search in some detail. We start the search by looking at the middle record in the file. If the key we are looking for is greater than the key of the middle record, we know that the record we are looking for must be in the second half of the file (if it is in the file at all). Likewise, if our key is less than the one in the middle record, the record we are looking for must be in the first half of the file (again, if it is there at all). Once we have decided which half of the file to examine next, we look at the middle record in that half and proceed exactly as we did previously. Eventually, either we will find the record we are looking for or we will discover that we can no longer divide the segment we are looking at, as it has only one record (in which case the record we are looking for is not there).

Probably the easiest way to figure out the average number of accesses that would be required to find a record in the file is to start from the other end of the problem: how many records could be found with one access? Obviously, only the middle record. With another access, we could find either the record in the middle of the first half of the file or the record in the middle of the second half. The next access adds another four records, in the centers of the first, second, third, and fourth quarters of the file. In other words, each added access doubles the number of added records that we can find.

Figure 2.2: Binary search statistics

Number of accesses		Number of newly accessible records	Total accesses to find all records	Total records accessible
1	X	1	1	1
2	X	2	4	3
3	X	4	12	7
4	X	8	32	15
5	X	16	80	31
6	X	32	192	63
7	X	64	448	127
8	X	128	1024	255
9	X	256	2304	511
10	X	512	5120	1023
11	X	1024	11264	2047
12	X	2048	24576	4095
13	X	4096	53248	8191
14	X	1809	25326	10000
		10000	123631	

Average number of accesses per record = 12.3631 accesses/record

Figure 2.2 shows the calculation of the average number of accesses for a 10,000 item file. Notice that each line represents twice the number of records as the one above, with the exception of line 14. The entry for that line (1809) is the number of 14-access records needed to reach the capacity of our 10,000 record file. As you can see, the average number of accesses is approximately 12.4 per record. Therefore, at a typical hard disk speed of 10 milliseconds per access, we would need almost 125 milliseconds to look up an average record using a binary search. While this lookup time might not seem excessive, remember that a number of checkout terminals would probably be attempting to access the database at the same time, and the waiting time could become noticeable. We might also be concerned about the amount of wear on the disk mechanism that would result from this approach.

Some Random Musings

Before we try to optimize our search, let us define some terms. There are two basic categories of storage devices, distinguished by the access they allow to individual records. The first type is **sequential access**;[1] in order to read record 1000 from a sequential device, we must read records 1 through 999 first, or at least skip over them. The second type is **direct access**; on a direct access device, we can read record 1000 without going past all of the previous records. However, only some direct access devices allow nonsequential accesses without a significant time penalty; these are called **random access** devices.

Unfortunately, disk drives are direct access devices, but not random access ones. The amount of time it takes to get to a particular data record depends on how close the read/write head is to the desired position; in fact, sequential reading of data may be more than ten times as fast as random access.

Is there a way to find a record in a large file with an average of about one nonsequential access? Yes; in fact, there are several such methods, varying in complexity. They are all variations on **hash coding**, or address calculation; as you will see, such methods actually can be implemented quite simply, although for some reason they have acquired a reputation for mystery.

Hashing It Out

Let's start by considering a linear or sequential search. That is, we start at the beginning of the file and read each record in the file until we find the one we want (because its key is the same as the key we are looking for). If we get to the end of the file without finding a record with the key we are looking for, the record isn't in the file. This is certainly a simple method, and indeed is perfectly acceptable for a very small file, but it has one major drawback: the average time it takes to find a given record increases every time we add another record. If the file gets twice as big, it takes twice as long to find a record, on the average. So this seems useless.

---

1. Tape drives are the most commonly used sequential access devices.

Divide and Conquer

But what if, instead of having one big file, we had many little files, each with only a few records in it? Of course, we would need to know which of the little files to look in, or we wouldn't have gained anything. Is there any way to know that?

Let's see if we can find a way. Suppose that we have 1000 records to search through, keyed by telephone number. To speed up the lookup, we have divided the records into 100 subfiles, averaging 10 numbers each. We can use the last two digits of the telephone number to decide which subfile to look in (or to put a new record in), and then we have to search through only the records in that subfile. If we get to the end of the subfile without finding the record we are looking for, it's not in the file. That's the basic idea of hash coding.

But why did we use the last two digits, rather than the first two? Because they will probably be more evenly distributed than the first two digits. Most of the telephone numbers on your list probably fall within a few telephone exchanges near where you live (or work). For example, suppose my local telephone book contained a lot of 758 and 985 numbers and very few numbers from other exchanges. Therefore, if I were to use the first two digits for this hash coding scheme, I would end up with two big subfiles (numbers 75 and 98) and 98 smaller ones, thus negating most of the benefit of dividing the file. You see, even though the average subfile size would still be 10, about 90% of the records would be in the two big subfiles, which would have perhaps 450 records each. Therefore, the average search for 90% of the records would require reading 225 records, rather than the five we were planning on. That is why it is so important to get a reasonably even distribution of the data records in a hash-coded file.

Unite and Rule

It is inconvenient to have 100 little files lying around, and the time required to open and close each one as we need it makes this implementation inefficient. But there's no reason we couldn't combine all of these little files into one big one and use the hash code to tell us where we should start looking in the big file. That is, if we have a capacity of 1000 records, we could use the last two digits of the telephone number to tell us which "subfile" we need of the 100 "subfiles" in the big file (records 0-9, 10-19 ... 980-989, 990-999). To help visualize this, let's look at a smaller example: 10 subfiles having a capacity of four telephone numbers each and a hash code consisting of just the last digit of the telephone number (Figure 2.3).

Figure 2.3: Hashing with subfiles, initialized file

Subfile #

0	I 0000000	I 0000000	I 0000000	I 0000000
1	I 0000000	I 0000000	I 0000000	I 0000000
2	I 0000000	I 0000000	I 0000000	I 0000000
3	I 0000000	I 0000000	I 0000000	I 0000000
4	I 0000000	I 0000000	I 0000000	I 0000000
5	I 0000000	I 0000000	I 0000000	I 0000000
6	I 0000000	I 0000000	I 0000000	I 0000000
7	I 0000000	I 0000000	I 0000000	I 0000000
8	I 0000000	I 0000000	I 0000000	I 0000000
9	I 0000000	I 0000000	I 0000000	I 0000000

In order to use a big file rather than a number of small ones, we have to make some changes to our algorithm. When using many small files, we had the end-of-file indicator to tell us where to add records and where to stop looking for a record; with one big file subdivided into small subfiles, we have to find another way to handle these tasks.

Knowing When to Stop

One way is to add a "valid-data" flag to every entry in the file, which is initialized to "I" (for invalid) in the entries in Figure 2.3, and set each entry to "valid" (indicated by a "V" in that same position) as we store data in it. Then if we get to an invalid record while looking up a record in the file, we know that we are at the end of the subfile and therefore the record is not in the file (Figure 2.4).

Figure 2.4: Hashing with distinct subfiles

Subfile #

0	I 0000000	I 0000000	I 0000000	I 0000000
1	V 9876541	V 2323231	V 9898981	I 0000000
2	V 2345432	I 0000000	I 0000000	I 0000000
3	I 0000000	I 0000000	I 0000000	I 0000000
4	I 0000000	I 0000000	I 0000000	I 0000000
5	I 0000000	I 0000000	I 0000000	I 0000000
6	I 0000000	I 0000000	I 0000000	I 0000000
7	I 0000000	I 0000000	I 0000000	I 0000000
8	I 0000000	I 0000000	I 0000000	I 0000000
9	I 0000000	I 0000000	I 0000000	I 0000000

For example, if we are looking for the number "9898981", we start at the beginning of subfile 1 in Figure 2.4 (because the number ends in 1), and examine each record from there on. The first two entries have the numbers "9876541" and "2323231", which don't match, so we continue with the third one, which is the one we are looking for. But what if we were looking for "9898971"? Then we would go through the first three entries without finding a match. The fourth entry is "I 0000000", which is an invalid entry. This is the marker for the end of this subfile, so we know the number we are looking for isn't in the file.

Now let's add another record to the file with the phone number "1212121". As before, we start at the beginning of subfile 1, since the number ends in 1. Although the first three records are already in use, the fourth (and last) record in the subfile is available, so we store our new record there, resulting in the situation in Figure 2.5.

Figure 2.5: Hashing with merged subfiles

Subfile #

0	I 0000000	I 0000000	I 0000000	I 0000000
1	V 9876541	V 2323231	V 9898981	V 1212121
2	V 2345432	I 0000000	I 0000000	I 0000000
3	I 0000000	I 0000000	I 0000000	I 0000000
4	I 0000000	I 0000000	I 0000000	I 0000000
5	I 0000000	I 0000000	I 0000000	I 0000000
6	I 0000000	I 0000000	I 0000000	I 0000000
7	I 0000000	I 0000000	I 0000000	I 0000000
8	I 0000000	I 0000000	I 0000000	I 0000000
9	I 0000000	I 0000000	I 0000000	I 0000000

However, what happens if we look for "9898971" in the above situation? We start out the same way, looking at records with phone numbers "9876541", "2323231", "9898981", and "1212121". But we haven't gotten to an invalid record yet. Can we stop before we get to the first record of the next subfile?

Handling Subfile Overflow

To answer that question, we have to see what would happen if we had added another record that belonged in subfile 1. There are a number of possible ways to handle this situation, but most of them are appropriate only for memory-resident files. As I mentioned above, reading the next record in a disk file is much faster than reading a record at a different place in the file. Therefore, for disk-based data, the most efficient place to put "overflow" records is in the next open place in the file, which means that adding a record with phone number "1234321" to this file would result in the arrangement in Figure 2.6.[2]

Figure 2.6: Hashing with overflow between subfiles

Subfile #

0	I 0000000	I 0000000	I 0000000	I 0000000
1	V 9876541	V 2323231	V 9898981	V 1212121
2	V 2345432	V 1234321	I 0000000	I 0000000
3	I 0000000	I 0000000	I 0000000	I 0000000
4	I 0000000	I 0000000	I 0000000	I 0000000
5	I 0000000	I 0000000	I 0000000	I 0000000
6	I 0000000	I 0000000	I 0000000	I 0000000
7	I 0000000	I 0000000	I 0000000	I 0000000
8	I 0000000	I 0000000	I 0000000	I 0000000
9	I 0000000	I 0000000	I 0000000	I 0000000

So the answer is that we can't stop before the beginning of the next subfile, because the record we are looking for might have overflowed to the next subfile, as "1234321" just did. Where can we stop? Well, we know that the record we are looking for is somewhere between the beginning of the subfile it belongs in and the next invalid record, since we go to the next subfile only when the one we are trying to use is filled up. Therefore, if we get to an invalid record, we know that the record could not be stored later in the file, since the current subfile is not filled up yet; this means that we can stop looking when we get to the first invalid record.

---

2. In general, the "next open place" is not a very good place to put an overflow record if the hash table is kept in memory rather than on the disk; the added records "clog" the table, leading to slower access times. A linked list approach is much better for tables that are actually memory resident. Warning: this does not apply to tables in virtual memory, where linked lists provide very poor performance. For more discussion on overflow handling, see the dynamic hashing algorithm in Chapter 6.

Some Drawbacks of Hashing

This points out one of the drawbacks of standard disk-based hashing (SDBH). We cannot delete a record from the file simply by setting the invalid flag in that record; if we did, any record which overflowed past the one we deleted would become inaccessible, as we would stop looking when we got to the invalid record. For this reason, invalid records must be only those that have never been used and therefore can serve as "end-of-subfile" markers.

While we're on the topic of drawbacks of SDBH, we ought to note that as the file gets filled up, the maximum length of a search increases, especially an unsuccessful search. That is because adding a record to the end of a subfile that has only one invalid entry left results in "merging" that subfile and the next one, so that searches for entries in the first subfile have to continue to the next one. In our example, when we added "1212121" to the file, the maximum length of a search for an entry in subfile 1 increased from four to seven, even though we had added only one record. With a reasonably even distribution of hash codes (which we don't have in our example), this problem is usually not serious until the file gets to be about 80% full.

While this problem would be alleviated by increasing the capacity of the file as items are added, unfortunately SDBH does not allow such incremental expansion, since there would be no way to use the extra space; the subfile starting positions can't be changed after we start writing records, or we won't be able to find records we have already stored. Of course, one way to overcome this problem is to create a new file with larger (or more) subfiles, read each record from the old file and write it to the new one. What we will do in our example is simply to make the file 25% bigger than needed to contain the records we are planning to store, which means the file won't get more than 80% full.

Another problem with SDBH methods is that they are not well suited to storage of variable-length records; the address calculation used to find a "slot" for a record relies on the fact that the records are of fixed length.

Finally, there's the ever-present problem of coming up with a good hash code. Unfortunately, unless we know the characteristics of the input data precisely, it's theoretically possible that all of the records will generate the same hash code, thus negating all of the performance advantages of hashing. Although this is unlikely, it makes SDBH an inappropriate algorithm for use in situations where a maximum time limit on access must be maintained.

When considering these less-than-ideal characteristics, we should remember that other search methods have their own disadvantages, particularly in speed of lookup. All in all, the disadvantages of such a simply implemented access method seem rather minor in comparison with its benefits, at least for the current application. In addition, recent innovations in hashing have made it possible to improve the flexibility of SDBH methods by fairly simple changes. For example, the use of "last-come, first-served" hashing, which stores a newly added record exactly where the hash code indicates, greatly reduces the maximum time needed to find any record; it also makes it possible to determine for any given file what that maximum is, thus removing one of the barriers to using SDBH in a time-critical application.[3]

Even more recently, a spectacular advance in the state of the art has made it possible to increase the file capacity incrementally, as well as to delete records efficiently. Chapter 6 provides a C++ implementation of this remarkable innovation in hashing.

Caching out Our Winnings

Of course, even one random disk access takes a significant amount of time, from the computer's point of view. Wouldn't it be better to avoid accessing the disk at all?

While that would result in the fastest possible lookup, it would require us to have the entire database in memory, which is usually not feasible. However, if we had some of the database in memory, perhaps we could eliminate some of the disk accesses.

A **cache** is a portion of a large database that we want to access, kept in a type of storage that can be accessed more rapidly than the type used to store the whole database. For example, if your system has an optical disk which is considerably slower than its hard disk, a portion of the database contained on the optical disk may be kept on

---

3. For a description of "last-come, first-served" hashing, see Patricio V. Poblete and J. Ian Munro, "Last-Come-First-Served Hashing", in *Journal of Algorithms* 10, 228-248, or my article "Galloping Algorithms", in *Windows Tech Journal*, 2(February 1993), 40-43.

the hard disk. Why don't we just use the hard disk for the whole database? The optical disk may be cheaper per megabyte or may have more capacity, or the removability and long projected life span of the optical diskettes may be the major reason. Of course, our example of a cache uses memory to hold a portion of the database that is stored on the hard disk, but the principle is the same: memory is more expensive than disk storage, and with certain computers, it may not be possible to install enough memory to hold a copy of the entire database even if price were no object.

If a few items account for most of the transactions, the use of a cache speeds up access to those items, since they are likely to be among the most recently used records. This means that if we keep a number of the most recently accessed records in memory, we can reduce the number of disk accesses significantly. However, we have to have a way to locate items in the cache quickly: this problem is very similar to a hash-coded file lookup, except that we have more freedom in deciding how to handle overflows, where the entry we wish to use is already being used by another item. Since the cache is only a copy of data that is also stored elsewhere, we don't have to be so concerned about what happens to overflowing entries; we can discard them if we wish to, since we can always get fresh copies from the disk.

The simplest caching lookup algorithm is a direct-mapped cache. That means each key corresponds to one and only one entry in the cache. In other words, overflow is handled by overwriting the previous record in that space with the new entry. The trouble with this method is that if two (or more) commonly used records happen to map to the same cache entry, only one of them can be in the cache at one time. This requires us to go back to the disk repeatedly for these conflicting records. The solution to this problem is to use a multiway associative cache. In this algorithm, each key corresponds to a **cache line**, which contains more than one entry. In our example, it contains eight entries. Therefore, if a number of our records have keys that map to the same line, up to eight of them can reside in the cache simultaneously. How did I decide on an eight-way associative cache? By trying various cache sizes until I found the one that yielded the greatest performance.

The performance of a disk caching system is defined by its hit ratio, or the proportion of accesses to the disk that are avoided by using the cache. In order to estimate the performance of this caching algorithm, we have to quantify our assumptions. I have written a program called stestgen.cpp to generate test keys in which 20% of the items account for 80% of the database accesses (Figure 2.7), along with another called supinit.cpp that initializes the database (Figure 2.8), and a third called supert.cpp to read the test keys and look them up (Figure 2.9). The results of this simulation indicated that, using an eight-way associative cache, approximately 44% of the disk accesses that would be needed in a noncached system could be eliminated.

Figure 2.7: Test program for caching (superm\stestgen.cpp)

```
/*TITLE generates test code file */

/****keyword-flag*** "%v %f %n" */
/* "4 20-Mar-98,20:14:08 STESTGEN.CPP" */

#include <stdio.h>
#include <stdlib.h>
#include "superm.h"

void process(FILE *in_file, FILE *out_file);

int main(int argc, char *argv[])
{
        FILE *in_file;
        FILE *out_file;

        if (argc < 3)
                {
                printf("Usage: stestgen in_code_file out_code_file\n");
                exit(1);
                }

        in_file = fopen(argv[1],"r+");
        out_file = fopen(argv[2],"w+");

        process(in_file,out_file);

        fclose(in_file);
        fclose(out_file);

        return 0;
}
```

```c
void process(FILE *in_file,FILE *out_file)
{
      unsigned record_number;
      char *ascii_code_number[FILE_CAPACITY];
      int i;
      char *result;
      int selection_range;
      char temp_code_number[100];
      int random_value;
      int file_capacity;

      for (i = 0; i < FILE_CAPACITY; i ++)
            {
            ascii_code_number[i] = (char*)malloc(ASCII_KEY_SIZE+1);
            result = fgets(temp_code_number,100,in_file);
            if (result == NULL)
                  break;
            temp_code_number[ASCII_KEY_SIZE] = 0;
            strcpy(ascii_code_number[i],temp_code_number);
            }

      file_capacity = FILE_CAPACITY; /* for easier debugging */

      for (i = 0; i < FILE_CAPACITY; i ++)
            {
            random_value = rand();
            random_value = random_value % file_capacity;
            if (random_value < file_capacity * 80 / 100)
                  {
                  /* usually pick one in first 20% */
                  selection_range = file_capacity * 20 / 100;
                  record_number = rand() % selection_range;
                  }
            else
                  {
                  selection_range = file_capacity * 80 / 100;
                  record_number = rand() % selection_range +
                  file_capacity * 20 / 100;
                  }
            fputs(ascii_code_number[record_number],out_file);
            fputs("\n",out_file);
            }
}
```

Figure 2.8: Database initialization program for caching
(superm\supinit.cpp)

```
/*TITLE supermarket pricing file initialization */

/****keyword-flag*** "%v %f %n" */
/* "9 20-Mar-98,20:14:10 SUPINIT.CPP" */

#include <stdio.h>
#include <stdlib.h>
#include "superm.h"

PriceFile* initialize(char *price_file_name);
void process(PriceFile* price_file,char *source_file_name, char *list_file_name);
void terminate(PriceFile* price_file);

int main(int argc, char *argv[])
{
      PriceFile* price_file;

      if (argc < 4)
            {
            printf("Usage: supinit source_file price_file list_file\n");
            exit(1);
            }

      price_file = initialize(argv[2]);

      process(price_file,argv[1],argv[3]);

      terminate(price_file);

      return 0;
}


#define MAX_DESCRIPTIONS 100
#define MAX_DESC_LENGTH 100

PriceFile* initialize(char *price_file_name)
{
      PriceFile *price_file;
      FILE *dos_file_stream;
      ItemRecord **temp_cache_ptr;
      ItemRecord *temp_cache_data;
      unsigned i;
      ItemRecord dummy_record;
```

```
    unsigned *temp_record_number_ptr;

    price_file = (PriceFile *)malloc(sizeof(PriceFile));

    memset(&dummy_record,0,sizeof(ItemRecord));
    dummy_record.upc[0] = (unsigned char)INVALID_BCD_VALUE;

    dos_file_stream = fopen(price_file_name,"w+b");
    if (dos_file_stream == NULL)
        {
        printf("Can't open price file %s.\n",price_file_name);
        exit(1);
        }

    price_file->dos_file_stream = dos_file_stream;

    temp_cache_ptr = (ItemRecord **)calloc(CACHE_SIZE, sizeof(ItemRecord *));
    temp_cache_data = (ItemRecord *)calloc(CACHE_SIZE, sizeof(ItemRecord));

    for (i = 0; i < CACHE_SIZE; i ++)
        {
        temp_cache_ptr[i] = temp_cache_data ++;
        *(temp_cache_ptr[i]) = dummy_record;
        }

    price_file->item_cache = temp_cache_ptr;

    temp_record_number_ptr = (unsigned *)calloc(CACHE_SIZE, sizeof(unsigned));

    for (i = 0; i < CACHE_SIZE; i ++)
        temp_record_number_ptr[i] = (unsigned)-1;

    price_file->file_record_number = temp_record_number_ptr;

    return(price_file);
}


void process(PriceFile* price_file,char *source_file_name, char *list_file_name)
{
    unsigned i;
    int j;
    int k;
    unsigned record_number;
    FILE *source_file_stream;
    FILE *list_file_stream;
    char *item_description[MAX_DESCRIPTIONS];
    char description[MAX_DESC_LENGTH];
```

```
char *desc_status;
int desc_count;
ItemRecord dummy_record;
FILE *dos_file_stream;
char ascii_code_number[ASCII_KEY_SIZE+1];
char *lf_pos;
int status;

dos_file_stream = price_file->dos_file_stream;

memset(&dummy_record,0,sizeof(ItemRecord));
dummy_record.upc[0] = (unsigned char)INVALID_BCD_VALUE;

for (i = 0; i < FILE_SIZE; i ++)
      {
      position_record(price_file,i);
      fwrite(&dummy_record,1,sizeof(ItemRecord),dos_file_stream);
      }

source_file_stream = fopen(source_file_name,"r");
if (source_file_stream == NULL)
      {
      printf("Can't open source file %s.\n",source_file_name);
      exit(1);
      }

list_file_stream = fopen(list_file_name,"w");
if (list_file_stream == NULL)
      {
      printf("Can't open list file %s.\n",list_file_name);
      exit(1);
      }

for (i = 0; i < MAX_DESCRIPTIONS; i ++)
      {
      desc_status = fgets(description,MAX_DESC_LENGTH,source_file_stream);
      if (desc_status == NULL)
            break;
      item_description[i] = (char *)malloc(strlen(description)+1);
      lf_pos = strchr(description,'\n');
      *lf_pos = 0;
      strcpy(item_description[i],description);
      }

desc_count = i;

for (i = 0; i < FILE_CAPACITY; i ++)
      {
```

```
        j = i % desc_count;
        k = i / desc_count;

        sprintf(description,"%s #%d",item_description[j],k);
        ascii_to_radix40(&dummy_record.description[0],(unsigned char*)description,
        DESCRIPTION_CHARS);

        sprintf(ascii_code_number,"%010ld",(long)rand()+i);
        ascii_to_BCD(&dummy_record.upc[0],ascii_code_number,ASCII_KEY_SIZE);

        fprintf(list_file_stream,"%s %s\n",ascii_code_number,description);

        dummy_record.price = 100*j+k;

        status = lookup_record_number(price_file,ascii_code_number,
        &record_number);

        if (status == NOT_IN_FILE)
            {
            position_record(price_file,record_number);
            fwrite(&dummy_record,1,sizeof(ItemRecord),dos_file_stream);
            }
        else if (status == FILE_FULL)
            {
            printf("Cannot add entry for item #%s to file\n",ascii_code_number);
            break;
            }
        else if (status == FOUND)
            printf("Item #%s already in file\n",ascii_code_number);
        }

    fclose(dos_file_stream);

}


void terminate(PriceFile* price_file)
{
    FILE *dos_file_stream;

    dos_file_stream = price_file->dos_file_stream;
    fclose(dos_file_stream);
}
```

Figure 2.9: Retrieval program for caching (superm\supert.cpp)

```
/*TITLE supermarket pricing main program */

/****keyword-flag*** "%v %f %n" */
/* "10 20-Mar-98,20:14:10 SUPERT.CPP" */

#include <stdio.h>
#include <stdlib.h>
#include "superm.h"

void process(PriceFile* price_file, FILE *UPC_file);

extern long lookup_count;
extern long hit_count;

int main(int argc, char *argv[])
{
      PriceFile* price_file;
      FILE *UPC_file;

      if (argc < 3)
            {
            printf("Usage: supert price_file code_file\n");
            exit(1);
            }

      price_file = initialize_price_file(argv[1],KEEP_FILE);
      UPC_file = fopen(argv[2],"r+");

      setvbuf(UPC_file,NULL,_IOFBF,32000);

      process(price_file,UPC_file);

      terminate_price_file(price_file);

      fclose(UPC_file);
      printf("Hit rate: %3.2f\n",((float)hit_count/(float)lookup_count));

    return 0;
}



void process(PriceFile* price_file,FILE *UPC_file)
{
      ItemRecord *item_record_ptr;
```

```
char ascii_code_number[100];
int status;
char upc[11];
char description[100];
int i;
char *result;

for (i = 0; ; i ++)
        {
        result = fgets(ascii_code_number,100,UPC_file);
        if (result == NULL)
                break;
        ascii_code_number[10] = 0;
        status = lookup_record(price_file,ascii_code_number,
                &item_record_ptr);
        if (status == FOUND)
                {
                BCD_to_ascii(upc,&item_record_ptr->upc[0],ASCII_KEY_SIZE);
                radix40_to_ascii((unsigned char*)description,
                &item_record_ptr->description[0], DESCRIPTION_CHARS);
/*              printf("%s:%s:%u\n",upc,description,item_record_ptr->price); */
                }
        else if (status == NOT_IN_FILE)
                printf("Item #%s not found\n",ascii_code_number);
        }

}
```

Figure 2.10 shows the results of my experimentation with various line sizes.

Figure 2.10: Line size effects

Line size	Hit ratio
1	.34[4]
2	.38
4	.42
8	.44
16	.43

---

4. This is a direct-mapped cache.

The line size is defined by the constant MAPPING_FACTOR in superm.h (Figure 2.11).

Figure 2.11: Header file for supermarket lookup system (superm\superm.h)

```
/*TITLE supermarket pricing include file */

/****keyword-flag*** "%v %f %n" */
/* "11 20-Mar-98,20:29:58 SUPERM.H" */

#include <string.h>
#include <minmax.h>
#include "radix40.h"
#include "bcdconv.h"

const int DESCRIPTION_WORDS = 7;
const int DESCRIPTION_CHARS = (CPW*DESCRIPTION_WORDS);

const int FILE_CAPACITY = 1000;
const unsigned FILE_SIZE = ((unsigned)(FILE_CAPACITY*1.25));
const int BCD_KEY_SIZE = 5;
const int ASCII_KEY_SIZE = (BCD_KEY_SIZE*2);

const unsigned char INVALID_BCD_VALUE = 0xFF;
const unsigned char DELETED_BCD_VALUE = 0xFE;

const unsigned INVALID_RECORD_NUMBER = 0xFFFF;

const int MAPPING_FACTOR = 8;  /* how many slots can be used by any one record */

const double CACHE_FACTOR = .20;

const int APPROXIMATE_CACHE_SIZE =
   (max(int(FILE_CAPACITY*CACHE_FACTOR),MAPPING_FACTOR));

const unsigned CACHE_SIZE =
   ((unsigned)(APPROXIMATE_CACHE_SIZE/MAPPING_FACTOR)*MAPPING_FACTOR);

typedef struct // ItemRecord struct
{
   BCD upc[BCD_KEY_SIZE];
   Radix40 description[DESCRIPTION_WORDS];
   unsigned price;
} ItemRecord;

typedef struct // PriceFile struct
```

```
{
    FILE *dos_file_stream;
    ItemRecord **item_cache;
    unsigned *file_record_number;
} PriceFile;

const int QUESTIONABLE = 0;
const int FOUND = 1;
const int NOT_IN_FILE = 2;
const int FILE_FULL = 3;

const int INPUT_MODE = 0;
const int LOOKUP_MODE = 1;

const int CLEAR_FILE = 0;
const int KEEP_FILE = 1;

unsigned compute_hash(char *key_value);

unsigned compute_file_hash(char *key_value);

unsigned compute_cache_hash(char *key_value);

int lookup_record(PriceFile* price_file, char *ascii_key_value,
ItemRecord **item_record);

int lookup_record_number(PriceFile* price_file, char *ascii_key_value,
unsigned *record_number);

int write_record(PriceFile* price_file, ItemRecord new_record);

unsigned compute_starting_cache_hash(unsigned cache_index);

unsigned compute_ending_cache_hash(unsigned cache_index);

PriceFile* initialize_price_file(char *price_file_name, int file_mode);

void terminate_price_file(PriceFile* price_file);

void position_record(PriceFile* price_file, unsigned record_number);

int lookup_record_and_number(PriceFile* price_file, char *ascii_key_value,
ItemRecord **item_record, unsigned *record_number);
```

Heading for The Final Lookup

Now that we have added a cache to our optimization arsenal, only three more changes are necessary to reach the final lookup algorithm that we will implement. The first is to shrink each of the subfiles to one entry. That is, we will calculate a record address rather than a subfile address when we start trying to add or look up a record. This tends to reduce the length of the search needed to find a given record, as each record (on average) will have a different starting position, rather than a number of records having the same starting position, as is the case with longer subfiles.

The second change is that, rather than having a separate flag to indicate whether a record position in the file is in use, we will create an "impossible" key value to mean that the record is available. Since our key will consist only of decimal digits (compressed to two digits per byte), we can set the first digit to 0xf (the hex representation for 15), which cannot occur in a genuine decimal number. This will take the place of our "invalid" flag, without requiring extra storage in the record.

Finally, we have to deal with the possibility that the search for a record will encounter the end of the file, because the last position in the file is occupied by another record. In this case, we will wrap around to the beginning of the file and keep looking. In other words, position 0 in the file will be considered to follow immediately after the last position in the file.

Saving Storage

Now that we have decided on our lookup algorithm, we can shift our attention to reducing the amount of storage required for each record in our supermarket price lookup program. Without any special encoding, the disk storage requirements for one record would be 35 bytes (10 for the UPC, 21 for the description, and 4 for the price). For a file of 10,000 items, this would require 350 Kbytes; allowing 25% extra space to prevent the hashing from getting too slow means that the file would end up taking up about 437 Kbytes. For this application, disk storage space would not be a problem; however, the techniques we will use to reduce the file size are useful in many other applications as well. Also, searching a smaller file is likely to be faster, because the heads have to move a shorter distance on the average to get to the record where we are going to start our search.

If you look back at Figure 2.1, you will notice that the upc field is ten characters long. Using the ASCII code for each digit, which is the usual representation for character data, takes one byte per digit or 10 bytes in all. I mentioned above that we would be using a limited character set to reduce the size of the records. UPC codes are limited to the digits 0 through 9; if we pack two digits into one byte, by using four bits to represent each digit, we can cut that down to five bytes for each UPC value stored. Luckily, this is quite simple, as you will see when we discuss the BCD (binary-coded decimal) conversion code below. The other data compression method we will employ is to convert the item descriptions from strings of ASCII characters, limited to the sets 0-9, A-Z, and the special characters comma, period, minus, and space, to Radix40 representation, mentioned in Chapter 1. The main difference between Radix40 conversions and those for BCD is that in the former case we need to represent 40 different characters, rather than just the 10 digits, and therefore the packing of data must be done in a slightly more complicated way than just using four bits per character.

The Code

Now that we have covered the optimizations that we will use in our price lookup system, it's time to go through the code that implements these algorithms. This specific implementation is set up to handle a maximum of FILE_CAPACITY items, defined in superm.h (Figure 2.11).[5] Each of these items, as defined in the ItemRecord structure in the same file, has a price, a description, and a key, which is the UPC code. The key would be read in by a bar-code scanner in a real system, although our test program will read it in from the keyboard.

---

5. Increasing the maximum number of records in the file by increasing FILE_CAPACITY would also increase the amount of memory required for the cache unless we reduced the cache size as a fraction of the file size by reducing the value .20 in the calculation of APPROXIMATE_CACHE_SIZE.

Some User-Defined Types

Several of the fields in the ItemRecord structure definition require some explanation, so let's take a closer look at that definition, shown in Figure 2.12.

Figure 2.12: ItemRecord struct definition (from superm\superm.h)

```
typedef struct
{
    BCD upc[BCD_KEY_SIZE];
    Radix40 description[DESCRIPTION_WORDS];
    unsigned price;
} ItemRecord;
```

The upc field is defined as a BCD (binary-coded decimal) value of ASCII_KEY_SIZE digits (contained in BCD_KEY_SIZE bytes). The description field is defined as a Radix40 field DESCRIPTION_WORDS in size; each of these words contains three Radix40 characters.

A BCD value is stored as two digits per byte, each digit being represented by a four-bit code between 0000(0) and 1001(9). Function ascii_to_BCD in bcdconv.cpp (Figure 2.13) converts a decimal number, stored as ASCII digits, to a BCD value by extracting each digit from the input argument and subtracting the code for '0' from the digit value; BCD_to_ascii (Figure 2.14) does the reverse.

Figure 2.13: ASCII to BCD conversion function (from superm\bcdconv.cpp)

```
BCD *ascii_to_BCD(BCD *bcd_value, char *ascii_value, int ascii_length)
{
    int i;
    int j;
    int temp_bcd;
    int temp_ascii_digit;

    j = 0;
    for (i = 0; i < ascii_length/2; i ++)
```

```
        {
        temp_ascii_digit = ascii_value[j++];
        if (temp_ascii_digit < '0' || temp_ascii_digit > '9')
                {
                printf("Invalid ascii to BCD conversion: input char = %c\n",
                temp_ascii_digit);
                exit(1);
                }
        temp_bcd = (temp_ascii_digit & 15) << 4;

        temp_ascii_digit = ascii_value[j++];
        if (temp_ascii_digit < '0' || temp_ascii_digit > '9')
                {
                printf("Invalid ascii to BCD conversion: input char = %c\n",
                temp_ascii_digit);
                exit(1);
                }
        temp_bcd += temp_ascii_digit & 15;
        bcd_value[i] = temp_bcd;
        }

    return(bcd_value);
}
```

Figure 2.14: BCD to ASCII conversion function (from
superm\bcdconv.cpp)

```
char *BCD_to_ascii(char *ascii_value, BCD *bcd_value, int ascii_length)
{
    int i;
    int j;
    int temp_bcd;
    int temp_digit;

    j = 0;
    for (i = 0; i < ascii_length/2; i ++)
            {
            temp_bcd = bcd_value[i];
            temp_digit = temp_bcd >> 4;
            ascii_value[j++] = temp_digit + '0';
            temp_digit = temp_bcd & 15;
            ascii_value[j++] = temp_digit + '0';
            }
    ascii_value[ascii_length] = 0;
    return(ascii_value);
```

}

A UPC code is a ten-digit number between 0000000000 and 9999999999, which unfortunately is too large to fit in a long integer of 32 bits. Of course, we could store it in ASCII, but that would require 10 bytes per UPC code. So BCD representation saves five bytes per item compared to ASCII.

A Radix40 field, as mentioned above, stores three characters (from a limited set of possibilities) in 16 bits. This algorithm (like some other data compression techniques) takes advantage of the fact that the number of bits required to store a character depends on the number of distinct characters to be represented.[6] The BCD functions described above are an example of this approach. In this case, however, we need more than just the 10 digits. If our character set can be limited to 40 characters (think of a Radix40 value as a "number" in base 40), we can fit three of them in 16 bits, because 40^3 is less than 2^{16}.

Let's start by looking at the header file for the Radix40 conversion functions, which is shown in Figure 2.15.

Figure 2.15: The header file for Radix40 conversion (superm\radix40.h)

```
/*TITLE include file for Radix40 routines */

/****keyword-flag*** "%v %f %n" */
/* "5 20-Mar-98,20:29:58 RADIX40.H" */

const int CPW = 3; /* characters per word in Radix40 code */

const int S_OKAY = 0;
const int S_ILLEGAL = 1;

const char HYPHEN = 2;
const char ILLEGAL = char(0x80);
const char IL = (HYPHEN|ILLEGAL);
/* this is the code for a -, but with the illegal flag set */
/* it is used in the conversion table to indicate that a character is invalid */
```

---

6. The arithmetic coding data compression algorithm covered in Chapter 4, however, does not restrict the characters that can be represented; rather, it takes advantage of the differing probabilities of encountering each character in a given situation.

```
typedef unsigned Radix40;

int radix40_to_ascii(unsigned char *ascii_data, Radix40 *radix40_data,int max_chars);

int ascii_to_radix40(Radix40 *radix40_data, unsigned char *ascii_data, int max_chars);
```

The legal_chars array, shown in Figure 2.16 defines the characters that can be expressed in this implementation of Radix40.[7] The variable weights contains the multipliers to be used to construct a two-byte Radix40 value from the three characters that we wish to store in it.

Figure 2.16: The legal_chars array (from superm\radix40.cpp)

```
char legal_chars[41] = " ,-.0123456789ABCDEFGHIJKLMNOPQRSTUVWXYZ";
```

As indicated in the comment at the beginning of the ascii_to_radix40 function (Figure 2.17), the job of that function is to convert a null-terminated ASCII character string to Radix40 representation. After some initialization and error checking, the main loop begins by incrementing the index to the current word being constructed, after every third character is translated. It then translates the current ASCII character by indexing into the lookup_chars array, which is shown in Figure 2.18. Any character that translates to a value with its high bit set is an illegal character and is converted to a hyphen; the result flag is changed to S_ILLEGAL if this occurs.

Figure 2.17: The ascii_to_radix40 function (from superm\radix40.cpp)

```
int ascii_to_radix40(Radix40 *radix40_data, unsigned char *ascii_data, int max_chars)
/* this routine converts a null-terminated ascii character string */
/* to radix 40 representation.  The allowable characters are: */
/* A-Z, 0-9, period, comma, hyphen, and space.  If any illegal characters */
/* are detected, they will be converted to hyphens, and the return value */
/* will be S_ILLEGAL. */
/* Lowercase letters will be upper-cased without error indication. */
/* The radix40 value will be padded with blanks to a multiple of three */
/* characters. If the number of characters in the ascii string is > max_chars */
```

---

7. Note that this legal_chars array must be kept in synchronization with the lookup_chars array, shown in Figure 2.18.

```
/* only max_chars will be converted, and the return value will be S_ILLEGAL. */
/* If no error is detected, the return value will be S_OKAY. */
{
      int i;
      unsigned char j;
      int ascii_length;
      int result;
      int words_to_convert;
      int words_to_clear;
      int cycle;
      unsigned current_word_index;

      result = S_OKAY;
      ascii_length = strlen((char *)ascii_data);
      if (ascii_length > max_chars)
            {
            ascii_length = max_chars;
            result = S_ILLEGAL;
            }

      words_to_convert = ascii_length / 3;
      if (ascii_length % 3 != 0)
            words_to_convert ++;

      words_to_clear = max_chars / 3;
      if (max_chars % 3 != 0)
            words_to_clear ++;

      memset(radix40_data,0,words_to_clear*sizeof(Radix40));

      current_word_index = unsigned(-1);
      cycle = 0;
      for (i = 0; i < ascii_length; i ++)
            {
            if (cycle == 0)
                  current_word_index ++;
            j = lookup_chars[ascii_data[i]];
            if (j & ILLEGAL)
                  {
                  j = HYPHEN ; /* make it a hyphen */
                  result = S_ILLEGAL; /* and remember that it was illegal */
                  }
            radix40_data[current_word_index] += weights[cycle] * j;
            cycle = (cycle + 1) % 3;
            }

      return(result);

}
```

Figure 2.18: The lookup_chars array (from superm\radix40.cpp)

```
char lookup_chars[256] =
{IL, IL, IL, IL, IL, IL, IL, IL,/* 00 */
IL, IL, IL, IL, IL, IL, IL, IL, /* 08 */
IL, IL, IL, IL, IL, IL, IL, IL, /* 10 */
IL, IL, IL, IL, IL, IL, IL, IL, /* 18 */
 0, IL, IL, IL, IL, IL, IL, IL, /* 20 */
IL, IL, IL, IL,  1,  2,  3, IL, /* 28 */
 4,  5,  6,  7,  8,  9, 10, 11, /* 30 */
12, 13 ,IL, IL, IL, IL, IL, IL, /* 38 */
IL, 14, 15, 16, 17, 18, 19, 20, /* 40 */
21, 22, 23, 24, 25, 26, 27, 28, /* 48 */
29, 30, 31, 32, 33, 34, 35, 36, /* 50 */
37, 38, 39, IL, IL, IL, IL, IL, /* 58 */
IL, 14, 15, 16, 17, 18, 19, 20, /* 60 */
21, 22, 23, 24, 25, 26, 27, 28, /* 68 */
29, 30, 31, 32, 33, 34, 35, 36, /* 70 */
37, 38, 39, IL, IL, IL, IL, IL, /* 78 */
IL, IL, IL, IL, IL, IL, IL, IL, /* 80 */
IL, IL, IL, IL, IL, IL, IL, IL, /* 88 */
IL, IL, IL, IL, IL, IL, IL, IL, /* 90 */
IL, IL, IL, IL, IL, IL, IL, IL, /* 98 */
IL, IL, IL, IL, IL, IL, IL, IL, /* A0 */
IL, IL, IL, IL, IL, IL, IL, IL, /* A8 */
IL, IL, IL, IL, IL, IL, IL, IL, /* B0 */
IL, IL, IL, IL, IL, IL, IL, IL, /* B8 */
IL, IL, IL, IL, IL, IL, IL, IL, /* C0 */
IL, IL, IL, IL, IL, IL, IL, IL, /* C8 */
IL, IL, IL, IL, IL, IL, IL, IL, /* D0 */
IL, IL, IL, IL, IL, IL, IL, IL, /* D8 */
IL, IL, IL, IL, IL, IL, IL, IL, /* E0 */
IL, IL, IL, IL, IL, IL, IL, IL, /* E8 */
IL, IL, IL, IL, IL, IL, IL, IL, /* F0 */
IL, IL, IL, IL, IL, IL, IL, IL  /* F8 */
};
```

In the line radix40_data[current_word_index] += weights[cycle] * j;, the character is added into the current output word after being multiplied by the power of 40 that is appropriate to its position. The first character in a word is represented by its position in the legal_chars string. The second character is represented by 40 times that value and the third by 1600 times that value, as you would expect for a base-40 number.

The complementary function radix40_to_ascii (Figure 2.19) decodes each character unambiguously. First, the current character is extracted from the current word by dividing by the weight appropriate to its position; then the current word is updated so the next character can be extracted. Finally, the ASCII value of the character is looked up in the legal_chars array.

Figure 2.19: The radix40_to_ascii function (from superm\radix40.cpp)

```
int radix40_to_ascii(unsigned char *ascii_data, Radix40 *radix40_data,int max_chars)
/* this routine converts a radix 40 character string */
/* to ascii representation.  Trailing blanks will be deleted. */
{
        int i;
        int ascii_length;
        int new_ascii_length;
        int words_to_convert;
        int cycle;
        unsigned current_word_index;
        unsigned current_word;
        unsigned current_char;

        ascii_length = max_chars;

        words_to_convert = ascii_length / 3;
        if (ascii_length % 3 != 0)
                words_to_convert ++;

        memset(ascii_data,0,max_chars+1);

        current_word_index = unsigned(-1);
        cycle = 0;
        for (i = 0; i < ascii_length; i ++)
                {
                if (cycle == 0)
                        {
                        current_word_index ++;
                        current_word = radix40_data[current_word_index];
                        }
                current_char = current_word / weights[cycle];
                current_word -= current_char * weights[cycle];
                ascii_data[i] = legal_chars[current_char];
                cycle = (cycle + 1) % 3;
                }
```

```
new_ascii_length = strlen((char*)ascii_data);
for (i = new_ascii_length - 1; i >= 0; i --)
        {
        if (ascii_data[i] != ' ')
                break;
        ascii_data[i] = 0;
        }

return(S_OKAY);
}
```

Preparing to Access the Price File

Now that we have examined the user-defined types used in the
ItemRecord structure, we can go on to the PriceFile structure, which is
used to keep track of the data for a particular price file.[8] The best
way to learn about this structure is to follow the program as it
creates, initializes, and uses it. The function main, which is shown in
Figure 2.20, after checking that it was called with the correct number
of arguments, calls the initialize_price_file function (Figure 2.21) to set
up the PriceFile structure.

Figure 2.20: The main function (from superm\superm.cpp)

```
void main(int argc, char *argv[])
{
        PriceFile* price_file;
        char price_file_name[100];
        char answer[100];
        int file_mode;

        if (argc < 2)
                {
                printf("Usage: superm price_file\n");
                exit(1);
                }

        strcpy(price_file_name,argv[1]);
```

---

8. While we could theoretically have more than one of these files active at a time, our example
program uses only one such file.

```
      printf("Do you want to clear the file?\n");
      gets(answer);
      if (toupper(answer[0]) == 'Y')
            file_mode = CLEAR_FILE;
      else
            file_mode = KEEP_FILE;

      price_file = initialize_price_file(price_file_name,file_mode);

      process(price_file);

      terminate_price_file(price_file);
}
```

Figure 2.21: The initialize_price_file function (from superm\suplook.cpp)

```
PriceFile* initialize_price_file(char *price_file_name, int file_mode)
{
      PriceFile *price_file;
      FILE *dos_file_stream;
      ItemRecord **temp_cache_ptr;
      ItemRecord *temp_cache_data;
      unsigned i;
      ItemRecord dummy_record;
      unsigned *temp_record_number_ptr;

      price_file = (PriceFile *) malloc(sizeof(PriceFile));

      dos_file_stream = fopen(price_file_name,"r+b");
      if (dos_file_stream == NULL)
            dos_file_stream = fopen(price_file_name,"w+b");
      if (dos_file_stream == NULL)
            {
            printf("Can't open price file %s.\n",price_file_name);
            exit(1);
            }

      price_file->dos_file_stream = dos_file_stream;

      temp_cache_ptr = (ItemRecord **)calloc(CACHE_SIZE, sizeof(ItemRecord *));
      temp_cache_data = (ItemRecord *)calloc(CACHE_SIZE, sizeof(ItemRecord));

      memset(&dummy_record,0,sizeof(ItemRecord));
      dummy_record.upc[0] = (unsigned char)INVALID_BCD_VALUE;

      for (i = 0; i < CACHE_SIZE; i ++)
```

```
        {
        temp_cache_ptr[i] = temp_cache_data ++;
        *(temp_cache_ptr[i]) = dummy_record;
        }

    price_file->item_cache = temp_cache_ptr;

    temp_record_number_ptr = (unsigned *)calloc(CACHE_SIZE, sizeof(unsigned));

    for (i = 0; i < CACHE_SIZE; i ++)
        temp_record_number_ptr[i] = INVALID_RECORD_NUMBER;

    price_file->file_record_number = temp_record_number_ptr;

    if (file_mode == CLEAR_FILE)
        {
        for (i = 0; i < FILE_SIZE; i ++)
            {
            position_record(price_file,i);
            fwrite(&dummy_record,1,sizeof(ItemRecord),dos_file_stream);
            }
        }

    return(price_file);
}
```

The initialize_price_file function allocates storage for and initializes
the PriceFile structure, which is used to control access to the price file.
This structure contains pointers to the file, to the array of cached
records that we have in memory, and to the array of record numbers
of those cached records. As we discussed earlier, the use of a cache
can reduce the amount of time spent reading records from the disk by
maintaining copies of a number of those records in memory, in the
hope that they will be needed again. Of course, we have to keep track
of which records we have cached, so that we can tell whether we
have to read a particular record from the disk or can retrieve a copy
of it from the cache instead.

When execution starts, we don't have any records cached;
therefore, we initialize each entry in these arrays to an "invalid" state
(the key is set to INVALID_BCD_VALUE). If file_mode is set to CLEAR_FILE,
we write such an "invalid" record to every position in the price file as
well, so that any old data left over from a previous run is erased.

Now that access to the price file has been set up, we can call the process function (Figure 2.22). This function allows us to enter items and/or look up their prices and descriptions, depending on mode.

Figure 2.22: The process function (from superm\superm.cpp)

```
void process(PriceFile* price_file)
{
    ItemRecord *item_record_ptr;
    ItemRecord new_record;
    char ascii_code_number[100];
    int status;
    char upc[11];
    char description[100];
    double temp_price;
    unsigned price;
    int i;
    int mode;
    int old_mode;
    char temp_string[100];
    char temp2[100];
    int field_length;

    mode = INPUT_MODE;
    old_mode = LOOKUP_MODE;

    for (i = 0; ; i ++)
        {
        if (mode == INPUT_MODE)
            {
            if (old_mode != INPUT_MODE)
                {
                printf("Now in INPUT mode.\n");
                old_mode = INPUT_MODE;
                }
            printf("Please enter code number,\n");
            printf("ENTER to switch to lookup mode,\n");
            printf("or * to terminate the program.\n");
            gets(temp_string);
            if (strcmp(temp_string,"*") == 0)
                break;
            if (strlen(temp_string) == 0)
                {
                mode = LOOKUP_MODE;
                continue;
```

```
        }
field_length = strlen(temp_string);
if (field_length > ASCII_KEY_SIZE)
        {
        printf("UPC code is a maximum of %d characters\n",
                ASCII_KEY_SIZE);
        continue;
        }
else if (field_length < ASCII_KEY_SIZE)
        {
        memset(temp2,0,ASCII_KEY_SIZE+1);
        memset(temp2,'0',ASCII_KEY_SIZE-field_length);
        strcat(temp2,temp_string);
        strcpy(temp_string,temp2);
        }
ascii_to_BCD(new_record.upc,temp_string,ASCII_KEY_SIZE);

printf("Please enter description: ");
gets(temp_string);
field_length = strlen(temp_string);
if (field_length > DESCRIPTION_CHARS)
        {
        printf("Description is a maximum of %d characters\n",
        DESCRIPTION_CHARS);
        continue;
        }
ascii_to_radix40((unsigned int *)new_record.description,
(unsigned char *)temp_string, DESCRIPTION_CHARS);

printf("Please enter price: ");
gets(temp_string);
temp_price = atof(temp_string);
if (temp_price > 655.35)
        {
        printf("Price too large - limit is $655.35\n");
        continue;
        }
new_record.price = (unsigned)(100*temp_price);

status = write_record(price_file,new_record);
if (status == FILE_FULL)
        {
        printf("Cannot add entry for item #%s to file\n",
        new_record.upc);
        break;
        }
else if (status == FOUND)
        printf("Item #%s already in file\n",new_record.upc);
```

```
                    }
            else
                {
                if (old_mode != LOOKUP_MODE)
                        {
                        printf("Now in LOOKUP mode.\n");
                        old_mode = LOOKUP_MODE;
                        }
                printf("Please enter code number: ");
                gets(temp_string);
                if (strcmp(temp_string,"*") == 0)
                        break;
                if (strlen(temp_string) == 0)
                        {
                        mode = INPUT_MODE;
                        continue;
                        }
                field_length = strlen(temp_string);
                if (field_length > ASCII_KEY_SIZE)
                        {
                        printf("UPC code is a maximum of %d characters\n",
                                ASCII_KEY_SIZE);
                        continue;
                        }
                else if (field_length < ASCII_KEY_SIZE)
                        {
                        memset(temp2,0,ASCII_KEY_SIZE+1);
                        memset(temp2,'0',ASCII_KEY_SIZE-field_length);
                        strcat(temp2,temp_string);
                        strcpy(temp_string,temp2);
                        }
                strcpy(ascii_code_number,temp_string);
                status = lookup_record(price_file,ascii_code_number,
                        &item_record_ptr);
                if (status == FOUND)
                        {
                        BCD_to_ascii(upc,&item_record_ptr->upc[0],ASCII_KEY_SIZE);
                        radix40_to_ascii((unsigned char *)description,
                        &item_record_ptr->description[0], DESCRIPTION_CHARS);
                        price = item_record_ptr->price;
                        printf("%s:%s:%u\n",upc,description,price);
                        }
                else if (status == NOT_IN_FILE)
                        printf("Item #%s not found\n",ascii_code_number);
                }

        }
```

First, let's look at entering a new item (INPUT_MODE). We must get the UPC code, the description, and the price of the item. The UPC code is converted to BCD, the description to Radix40, and the price to unsigned. Then we call write_record (Figure 2.23) to add the record to the file.

Figure 2.23: The write_record function (from superm\suplook.cpp)

```
int write_record(PriceFile* price_file, ItemRecord new_record)
{
        FILE *dos_file_stream;
        int status;
        unsigned record_number;
        char ascii_key_value[ASCII_KEY_SIZE+1];

        BCD_to_ascii(ascii_key_value,new_record.upc,ASCII_KEY_SIZE);

        status = lookup_record_number(price_file,ascii_key_value,&record_number);

        if (status == FILE_FULL || status == FOUND)
                return(status);

        dos_file_stream = price_file->dos_file_stream;

        position_record(price_file,record_number);
        fwrite(&new_record,1,sizeof(ItemRecord),dos_file_stream);

        return(NOT_IN_FILE);
}
```

In order to write a record to the file, write_record calls lookup_record_number (Figure 2.24) to determine where the record should be stored so that we can retrieve it quickly later. The lookup_record_number function does almost the same thing as lookup_record (Figure 2.25), except tha the latter returns a pointer to the record rather than its number. Therefore, they are implemented as calls to a common function: lookup_record_and_number (Figure 2.26).

Figure 2.24: The lookup_record_number function (from superm\suplook.cpp)

```
int lookup_record_number(PriceFile* price_file, char *ascii_key_value,
unsigned *record_number)
{
    int status;
    ItemRecord *item_record;

    status = lookup_record_and_number(price_file, ascii_key_value,
    &item_record, record_number);

    return(status);
}
```

Figure 2.25: The lookup_record function (from superm\suplook.cpp)

```
int lookup_record(PriceFile* price_file, char *ascii_key_value,
ItemRecord **item_record)
{
    int status;
    unsigned record_number;

    status = lookup_record_and_number(price_file, ascii_key_value,
    item_record, &record_number);

    return(status);
}
```

Figure 2.26: The lookup_record_and_number function (from superm\suplook.cpp)

```
int lookup_record_and_number(PriceFile* price_file, char *ascii_key_value,
ItemRecord **item_record, unsigned *record_number)
{
    unsigned starting_cache_index;
    ItemRecord *temp_cache_data;
    ItemRecord temp_file_data;
    int status;
    unsigned starting_file_index;
    FILE *dos_file_stream;
    unsigned current_file_index;
    unsigned start_looking_in_cache;
```

```
          unsigned stop_looking_in_cache;
          unsigned i;
          unsigned cache_replace_index;
          BCD *bcd_key_value;
static unsigned longest_search = 0;
          unsigned current_search;

          bcd_key_value = (BCD *)malloc(strlen(ascii_key_value));

          lookup_count ++;

          dos_file_stream = price_file->dos_file_stream;

          starting_cache_index = compute_cache_hash(ascii_key_value);

          ascii_to_BCD(bcd_key_value,ascii_key_value,ASCII_KEY_SIZE);

          status = QUESTIONABLE;

          start_looking_in_cache = compute_starting_cache_hash(starting_cache_index);
          stop_looking_in_cache = compute_ending_cache_hash(starting_cache_index);
          for (i = start_looking_in_cache; i < stop_looking_in_cache; i ++)
               {
               temp_cache_data = price_file->item_cache[i];
               if (memcmp(&temp_cache_data->upc,bcd_key_value,BCD_KEY_SIZE) == 0)
                    {
                    status = FOUND;
                    hit_count ++;
                    break;
                    }
               }

          if (status == FOUND)
               {
               *item_record = temp_cache_data;
               *record_number = price_file->file_record_number[i];
               free(bcd_key_value);
               return(status);
               }

          cache_replace_index = start_looking_in_cache +
          (lookup_count % MAPPING_FACTOR);

          for (i = start_looking_in_cache; i < stop_looking_in_cache; i ++)
               {
               temp_cache_data = price_file->item_cache[i];
               if (temp_cache_data->upc[0] == INVALID_BCD_VALUE)
                    {
```

```
                    cache_replace_index = i; /* use an invalid entry, if there is one */
                    break;
                    }
            }

starting_file_index = compute_file_hash(ascii_key_value);

for (current_file_index = starting_file_index;
current_file_index < FILE_SIZE; current_file_index ++)
        {
        position_record(price_file,current_file_index);
        fread(&temp_file_data,1,sizeof(ItemRecord),dos_file_stream);
        if (temp_file_data.upc[0] == INVALID_BCD_VALUE)
                {
                status = NOT_IN_FILE;
                break;
                }
        if (memcmp(&temp_file_data.upc,bcd_key_value,BCD_KEY_SIZE) == 0)
                {
                status = FOUND;
                break;
                }
        }

current_search = current_file_index - starting_file_index;
if (current_search > longest_search)
        longest_search = current_search;

temp_cache_data = price_file->item_cache[cache_replace_index];

if (status == FOUND)
        {
        memcpy(temp_cache_data,&temp_file_data,sizeof(ItemRecord));
        price_file->file_record_number[cache_replace_index] =
        current_file_index;
        *item_record = temp_cache_data;
        *record_number = current_file_index;
        free(bcd_key_value);
        return(status);
        }
else if (status == NOT_IN_FILE)
        {
        price_file->file_record_number[cache_replace_index] =
        current_file_index;
        *item_record = temp_cache_data;
        *record_number = current_file_index;
        free(bcd_key_value);
        return(NOT_IN_FILE);
```

```
        }
for (current_file_index = 0; current_file_index < starting_file_index;
current_file_index ++)
        {
        position_record(price_file,current_file_index);
        fread(&temp_file_data,1,sizeof(ItemRecord),dos_file_stream);
        if (temp_file_data.upc[0] == INVALID_BCD_VALUE)
                {
                status = NOT_IN_FILE;
                break;
                }
        if (memcmp(&temp_file_data.upc,bcd_key_value,BCD_KEY_SIZE) == 0)
                {
                status = FOUND;
                break;
                }
        }

if (status == FOUND)
        {
        memcpy(temp_cache_data,&temp_file_data,sizeof(ItemRecord));
        price_file->file_record_number[cache_replace_index] =
        current_file_index;
        *item_record = temp_cache_data;
        *record_number = current_file_index;
        free(bcd_key_value);
        return(status);
        }
else if (status == NOT_IN_FILE)
        {
        price_file->file_record_number[cache_replace_index] =
        current_file_index;
        *item_record = temp_cache_data;
        *record_number = current_file_index;
        free(bcd_key_value);
        return(NOT_IN_FILE);
        }
else
        {
        free(bcd_key_value);
        return(FILE_FULL);
        }
}
```

After a bit of setup code, lookup_record_and_number determines whether the record we want is already in the cache, in which case we don't have to search the file for it. To do this, we call compute_cache_hash (Figure 2.27), which in turn calls compute_hash (Figure 2.28) to do most of the work of calculating the hash code.

Figure 2.27: The compute_cache_hash function (from superm\suplook.cpp)

```
unsigned compute_cache_hash(char *key_value)
{
        unsigned hash_code;
        unsigned cache_index;

        hash_code = compute_hash(key_value);

        cache_index = hash_code % CACHE_SIZE;

        return(cache_index);
}
```

Figure 2.28: The compute_hash function (from superm\suplook.cpp)

```
unsigned compute_hash(char *key_value)
{
        int i;
        unsigned hash_code;

        hash_code = 0;
        for (i = 0; i < ASCII_KEY_SIZE; i ++)
            {
            hash_code = ((hash_code * 10) + (hash_code / HASH_DIVISOR));
            hash_code += (key_value[i] & 15);
            }

        return(hash_code);
}
```

This may look mysterious, but it's actually pretty simple. After clearing the hash code we are going to calculate, it enters a loop that first shifts the old hash code one (decimal) place to the left, end around, then adds the low four bits of the next character from the key to the result. When it finishes this loop, it returns to the caller, in this case compute_cache_hash. How did I come up with this algorithm?

Making a Hash of Things

Well, as you will recall from our example of looking up a telephone number, the idea of a hash code is to make the most of variations in the input data, so that there will be a wide distribution of "starting places" for the records in the file. If all the input values produced the same hash code, we would end up with a linear search again, which would be terribly slow. In this case, our key is a UPC code, which is composed of decimal digits. If each of those digits contributes equally to the hash code, we should be able to produce a fairly even distribution of hash codes, which are the starting points for searching through the file for each record. As we noted earlier, this is one of the main drawbacks of hashing: the difficulty of coming up with a good hashing algorithm. After analyzing the nature of the data, you may have to try a few different algorithms with some test data, until you get a good distribution of hash codes. However, the effort is usually worthwhile, since you can often achieve an average of slightly over one disk access per lookup (assuming that several records fit in one physical disk record).

Meanwhile, back at compute_cache_hash, we convert the result of compute_hash, which is an unsigned value, into an index into the cache. This is then returned to lookup_record_number as the starting cache index. As mentioned above, we are using an eight-way associative cache, in which each key can be stored in any of eight entries in a **cache line**. This means that we need to know where the line starts, which is computed by compute_starting_cache_hash (Figure 2.29) and where it ends, which is computed by compute_ending_cache_hash (Figure 2.30).[9]

Figure 2.29: The compute_starting_cache_hash function (from superm\suplook.cpp)

```
unsigned compute_starting_cache_hash(unsigned cache_index)
{
      return((cache_index/MAPPING_FACTOR)*MAPPING_FACTOR);
}
```

9. This function actually returns one more than the index to the last entry in the line because the standard C loop control goes from the first value up to one less than the ending value.

Figure 2.30: The compute_ending_cache_hash function (from superm\suplook.cpp)

```
unsigned compute_ending_cache_hash(unsigned cache_index)
{
    return((cache_index/MAPPING_FACTOR)*MAPPING_FACTOR+MAPPING_FACTOR);
}
```

After determining the starting and ending positions where the key might be found in the cache, we compare the key in each entry to the key that we are looking for, and if they are equal, we have found the record in the cache. In this event, we set the value of the record_number argument to the file record number for this cache entry, and return with the status set to FOUND.

Otherwise, the record isn't in the cache, so we will have to look for it in the file; if we find it, we will need a place to store it in the cache. So we pick a "random" entry in the line (cache_replace_index) by calculating the remainder after dividing the number of accesses we have made by the MAPPING_FACTOR. This will generate an entry index between 0 and the highest entry number, cycling through all the possibilities on each successive access, thus not favoring a particular entry number.

However, if the line has an invalid entry (where the key is INVALID_BCD_VALUE), we should use that one, rather than throwing out a real record that might be needed later. Therefore, we search the line for such an empty entry, and if we are successful, we set cache_replace_index to its index.

Next, we calculate the place to start looking in the file, via compute_file_hash, (Figure 2.31), which is very similar to compute_cache_hash except that it uses the FILE_SIZE constant in superm.h (Figure 2.11) to calculate the index rather than the CACHE_SIZE constant, as we want a starting index in the file rather than in the cache.

Figure 2.31: The compute_file_hash function (from superm\suplook.cpp)

```
unsigned compute_file_hash(char *key_value)
{
     unsigned hash_code;
     unsigned file_index;

     hash_code = compute_hash(key_value);

     file_index = hash_code % FILE_SIZE;

     return(file_index);
}
```

As we noted above, this is another of the few drawbacks of this hashing method: the size of the file must be decided in advance, rather than being adjustable as data is entered. The reason is that to find a record in the file, we must be able to calculate its approximate position in the file in the same manner as it was calculated when the record was stored. The calculation of the hash code is designed to distribute the records evenly throughout a file of known size; if we changed the size of the file, we wouldn't be able to find records previously stored. Of course, different files can have different sizes, as long as we know the size of the file we are operating on currently: the size doesn't have to be an actual constant as it is in our example, but it does have to be known in advance for each file.

Searching the File

Now we're ready to start looking for our record in the file at the position specified by starting_file_index. Therefore, we enter a loop that searches from this starting position toward the end of the file, looking for a record with the correct key. First we set the file pointer to the first position to be read, using position_record (Figure 2.32), then read the record at that position.

Figure 2.32: The position_record function (from superm\suplook.cpp)

```
void position_record(PriceFile* price_file, unsigned record_number)
{
    FILE *dos_file_stream;

    dos_file_stream = price_file->dos_file_stream;
    fseek(dos_file_stream,sizeof(ItemRecord)*(long)record_number,SEEK_SET);
}
```

If the key in that record is the one we are looking for, our search is successful. On the other hand, if the record is invalid, then the record we are looking for is not in the file; when we add records to the file, we start at the position given by starting_file_index and store our new record in the first invalid record we find.[10] Therefore, no record can overflow past an invalid record, as the invalid record would have been used to store the overflow record.

In either of these cases, we are through with the search, so we break out of the loop. On the other hand, if the entry is neither invalid nor the record we are looking for, we keep looking through the file until either we have found the record we want, we discover that it isn't in the file by encountering an invalid record, or we run off the end of the file. In the last case we start over at the beginning of the file.

If we have found the record, we copy it to the cache entry we've previously selected and copy its record number into the list of record numbers in the cache so that we'll know which record we have stored in that cache position. Then we return to the calling function, write_record, with the record we have found. If we have determined that the record is not in the file, then we obviously can't read it into the cache, but we do want to keep track of the record number where we stopped, since that is the record number that will be used for the record if we write it to the file.

To clarify this whole process, let's make a file with room for only nine records by changing FILE_SIZE to 6 in superm.h (Figure 2.11). After adding a few records, a dump looks like Figure 2.33.

---

10. Of course, we might also find a record with the same key as the one we are trying to add, but this is an error condition, since keys must be unique.

Figure 2.33: Initial condition

Position Key   Data
   0. INVALID
   1. INVALID
   2. 0000098765:MINESTRONE:245
   3. 0000121212:OATMEAL, 1 LB.:300
   4. INVALID
   5. INVALID
   6. 0000012345:JELLY BEANS:150
   7. INVALID
   8. 0000099887:POPCORN:99

Let's add a record with the key "23232" to the file. Its hash code turns out to be 3, so we look at position 3 in the file. That position is occupied by a record with key "121212", so we can't store our new record there. The next position we examine, number 4, is invalid, so we know that the record we are planning to add is not in the file. (Note that this is the exact sequence we follow to look up a record in the file as well). We use this position to hold our new record. The file now looks like Figure 2.34.

Figure 2.34: After adding "milk" record

Position Key   Data
   0. INVALID
   1. INVALID
   2. 0000098765:MINESTRONE:245
   3. 0000121212:OATMEAL, 1 LB.:300
   4. 0000023232:MILK:128
   5. INVALID
   6. 0000012345:JELLY BEANS:150
   7. INVALID
   8. 0000099887:POPCORN:99

Looking up our newly added record follows the same algorithm. The hash code is still 3, so we examine position 3, which has the key

"121212". That's not the desired record, and it's not invalid, so we continue. Position 4 does match, so we have found our record. Now let's try to find some records that aren't in the file.

If we try to find a record with key "98789", it turns out to have a hash code of 8. Since that position in the file is in use, but with a different key, we haven't found our record. However, we have encountered the end of the file. What next?

Wrapping Around at End-of-File

In order to continue looking for this record, we must start over at the beginning of the file. That is, position 0 is the next logical position after the last one in the file. As it happens, position 0 contains an invalid record, so we know that the record we want isn't in the file.[11]

In any event, we are now finished with lookup_record_and_number. Therefore, we return to lookup_record_number, which returns the record number to be used to write_record (Figure 2.23), along with a status value of FILE_FULL, FOUND, or NOT_IN_FILE (which is the status we want). FILE_FULL is an error, as we cannot add a record to a file that has reached its capacity. So is FOUND, in this situation, as we are trying to add a new record, not find one that alreadys exists. In either of these cases, we simply return the status to the calling function, process, (Figure 2.22), which gives an appropriate error message and continues execution.

However, if the status is NOT_IN_FILE, write_record continues by positioning the file to the record number returned by lookup_record_number, writing the record to the file, and returns the status NOT_IN_FILE to process, which continues execution normally.

That concludes our examination of the input mode in process. The lookup mode is very similar, except that it uses the lookup_record function (Figure 2.25) rather than lookup_record_number, since it wants the record to be returned, not just the record number. The lookup mode, of course, also differs from the entry mode in that it expects the record to be in the file, and displays the record data when found.

After process terminates when the user enters "*" instead of a code number to be looked up or entered, main finishes up by calling

---

11. If we were adding a new record with this key rather than trying to find one, we would use position 0.

terminate_price_file (Figure 2.35) , which closes the price file and returns. All processing complete, main exits to the operating system.

Figure 2.35: The terminate_price_file function (from superm\suplook.cpp)

```
void terminate_price_file(PriceFile* price_file)
{
    FILE *dos_file_stream;

    dos_file_stream = price_file->dos_file_stream;
    fclose(dos_file_stream);
}
```

Summary

In this chapter, we have covered ways to save storage by using a restricted character set and to gain rapid access to data by an exact key, using hash coding and caching. In the next chapter we will see how to use bitmaps and distribution sorting to aid in rearranging information by criteria that can be specified at run-time.

Problems

1. What modifications to the program would be needed to support:

    a. Deleting records?

    b. Handling a file that becomes full, as an off-line process?

    c. Keeping track of the inventory of each item?

2. How could hash coding be applied to tables in memory?

3. How could caching be applied to reduce the time needed to look up an entry in a table in memory?

(You can find suggested approaches to problems in Chapter 8).

Chapter 3

A Mailing List System

Introduction

In this chapter we will use a selective mailing list system to illustrate rapid access to and rearrangement of information selected by criteria specified at run time. Our example will allow us to select certain customers of a mail-order business whose total purchases this year have been within a particular range and whose last order was within a certain time period. This would be very useful for a retailer who wants to send coupons to lure back the (possibly lost) customers who have spent more than $100 this year but who haven't been in for 30 days. The labels for the letters should be produced in ZIP code order, to take advantage of the discount for presorted mail.

Algorithms Discussed

The Distribution Counting Sort, Bitmaps

A First Approach

To begin, let us assume that the information we have about each customer can be described by the structure definition in Figure 3.1.

Figure 3.1: Customer information

```
typedef struct
    {
    char last_name[LAST_NAME_LENGTH+1];
    char first_name[FIRST_NAME_LENGTH+1];
    char address1[ADDRESS1_LENGTH+1];
    char address2[ADDRESS2_LENGTH+1];
    char city[CITY_LENGTH+1];
    char state[STATE_LENGTH+1];
    char zip[ZIP_LENGTH+1];
    int date_last_here;
    int dollars_spent;
    } DataRecord;
```

A straightforward approach would be to store all of this information in a disk file, with one DataRecord record for each customer. In order to construct a selective mailing list, we read through the file, testing each record to see whether it meets our criteria. We extract the sort key (ZIP code) for each record that passes the tests of amount spent and last transaction date, keeping these keys and their associated record numbers in memory. After reaching the end of the file, we sort the keys (possibly with a heapsort or Quicksort) and rearrange the record numbers according to the sort order, then reread the selected records in the order of their ZIP codes and print the address labels.

It may seem simpler just to collect records in memory as they meet our criteria. However, the memory requirements of this approach might be excessive if a large percentage of the records are selected. The customer file of a mail-order business is often fairly large, with 250000 or more 100-byte records not unheard of; in this situation a one-pass approach might require as much as 25 megabytes of memory for storing the selected records.

However, if we keep only the keys of the selected records in memory and print the label for each customer as his record is reread on the second pass, we never have to have more than one record in memory at a time. In our example, the length of the key (ZIP code) is nine bytes and the record number is two bytes long, so that 250000 selected records would require only 2.75 megabytes. This is a much more reasonable memory budget, considering that our program might not be the only one running, especially under an operating system like Windows™.

Even so, there is no reason to allocate all the storage we might ever need in advance, and every reason not to. We'd like the program to run in the minimum memory possible, so that it would be useful even on a machine with limited memory or one that is loaded up with network drivers and memory-resident utilities.

A linked list is a fairly simple way to allocate memory as needed, but we must be careful to use this method efficiently. Allocating a new block of storage for each record that matches our criteria would be very wasteful, as extra control storage is needed to keep track of each allocation. In MS-DOS, each allocation requires at least 16 bytes of control storage, so 250000 allocations would use about 4 megabytes just for the control storage! This problem is easy to solve; we will allocate storage for a number of records at once, 1000 in our example, which reduces that 4 megabyte overhead to 4 kilobytes.[1]

Saving Storage with Bitmaps

Let's start our optimization by trying to reduce the memory we need for each selected record during this first pass through the file. One possibility is to convert the ZIP codes to Radix40 representation to save memory. Unfortunately, such data is not suitable for sorting.

However, there is another way for us to save memory during the first pass: using a **bitmap** to keep track of the records that match our criteria. A bitmap is an array of bits that can be used to record one characteristic of a number of items, as long as that characteristic can be expressed as yes/no, true/false, present/absent or some similar pair of opposites. In this case, all we want to remember is whether each record was selected. So if we allocate a bitmap with one bit for each possible record number, we can clear the whole bitmap at the start (indicating we haven't selected any records yet) and then set the bit for each record number we select. When we get done with the selection, we will know how many records were selected, so we can allocate storage for the record numbers we need to sort. Then we can

---

1. 250 blocks of 1000 records, at 16 bytes of overhead per block, yields an overhead of 250*16, or 4000 bytes.

go through the bitmap, and every time we find a bit that is set, we will add the corresponding record number to the end of the list to be passed to the sort.

Of course, we could use an array of bytes, one per record, instead of a bitmap, which would not require us to write bit access functions. However, the bitmap requires only one-eighth as much as storage as an array of bytes, which can result in considerable savings with a big array. In our example, with a 250000-record file, a bitmap with one bit per record would occupy only about 31 KB, whereas an equivalent byte array would occupy 250 KB. While this difference may not be significant in the present case, larger files produce proportionally larger savings.

As with almost everything, there is a drawback to the use of bitmaps; they usually require more time to access than byte arrays. This is especially true for those machines (such as the 80x86) that do not have an instruction set designed for easy or efficient access to individual bits. Even on machines like the 68020 and its successors, which do have good bit manipulation instructions, compiler support for these functions may be poor. However, since CPU time is unlikely to be the limiting factor while we are reading records from our input file, this extra processing time is probably unimportant in our case.

Increasing Processing Speed

Now that we have reduced the memory requirements for the first pass, is there any way to speed up the program? In my tests with large numbers of selected records, it turns out that the disk reading and writing time are a small part of the entire elapsed time required to run the program, at least when we are using a standard sorting function. In such a case, by far the greatest proportion of the time is spent in sorting the keys, so that's where we'll focus our attention next.

Sorting Speed

Which sort should we use? Surely we can't improve on the standard sort supplied with the C++ compiler we're using (typically Quicksort) or one of its relatives such as heapsort. After all, the conventional wisdom is that even the fastest sorting algorithm takes time proportional to $n*\log(n)$. That is, if sorting 1000 items takes 1 second, sorting 1,000,000 items would take at least 2000 seconds, using an optimal sorting algorithm. Since these commonly used algorithms all have average times proportional to this best case, it seems that all we have to do is select the one best suited for our particular problem.

This is a common misconception: in fact, only sorts that require comparisons among keys have a lower bound proportional to $n*\log(n)$. The distribution counting sort we are going to use takes time proportional to n, not $n*\log(n)$, so that if it takes 1 second to sort 1000 items, it would take 1000 seconds to sort 1,000,000 items, not 2000 seconds.[2] Moreover, this sort is quite competitive with the commonly used sorts even for a few hundred items, and it is easy to code as well. For some applications, however, its most valuable attribute is that its timing is data independent. That is, the sort takes the same amount of time to execute whether the data items are all the same, all different, already sorted, in reverse order, or randomly shuffled. This is particularly valuable in real-time applications, where knowing the average time is not sufficient.[3]

Actually, this sort takes time proportional to the number of keys multiplied by the length of each key. The reason that the length of the keys is important is that a distribution counting sort actually treats each character position of the sort keys as a separate "key"; these keys are used in order from the least to the most significant. Therefore, this method actually takes time proportional to $n*m$, where n is the number of keys and m is the length of each key.

---

2. A description of this sort can be found in Donald Knuth's book *The Art of Computer Programming*, vol. 3. Reading, Massachusetts: Addison-Wesley, 1968. Every programmer should be aware of this book, since it describes a great number of generally applicable algorithms. As I write this, a new edition of this classic work on algorithms is about to be published.

3. However, distribution counting is **not** suitable for use where the data will be kept in virtual memory. See my article "Galloping Algorithms", in *Windows Tech Journal*, 2(February 1993), 40-43, for details on this limitation.

However, in most real-world applications of sorting, the number of items to be sorted far exceeds the length of each item, and additions to the list take the form of more items, not lengthening of each one. If we had a few very long items to sort, this sort would not be as appropriate.

You're probably wondering how fast this distribution sort really is, compared to Quicksort. According to the results of my tests, which sorted several different numbers of records between 23480 and 234801 on 5-digit ZIP codes using both Microsoft's implementation of the Quicksort algorithm (qsort) in version 5.0 of their Visual C++ compiler and my distribution counting sort, which I call "Megasort", there's no contest.[4] The difference in performance ranged from approximately 43 to 1 at the low end up to an astonishing 316 to 1 at the high end! Figures 3.15 and 3.16, near the end of this chapter, show the times in seconds when processing these varying sets of records.

Now let's see how such increases in performance can be achieved with a simple algorithm.

The Distribution Counting Sort

The basic method used is to make one pass through the keys for each character position in the key, in order to discover how many keys have each possible ASCII character in the character position that we are currently considering, and another pass to actually rearrange the keys. As a simplified example, suppose that we have ten keys to be sorted and we want to sort only on the first letter of each key.

The first pass consists of counting the number of keys that begin with each letter. In the example in Figure 3.2, we have three keys that begin with the letter 'A', five that begin with the letter 'B', and two that begin with the letter 'C'. Since 'A' is the lowest character we have seen, the first key we encounter that starts with an 'A' should be the first key in the result array, the second key that begins with an 'A' should be the second key in the result array, and the third 'A' key

---

4. As is standard in C and C++ library implementations, this version of qsort requires the user to supply the address of a function that will compare the items to be sorted. While this additional overhead biases the comparison slightly against qsort, this small disadvantage is not of the same order of magnitude as the difference in inherent efficiency of the two algorithms.

should be the third key in the result array, since all of the 'A' keys should precede all of the 'B' keys.

Figure 3.2: Unsorted keys

1	bicycle
2	airplane
3	anonymous
4	cashier
5	bottle
6	bongos
7	antacid
8	competent
9	bingo
10	bombardier

The next keys in sorted order will be the ones that start with 'B'; therefore, the first key that we encounter that starts with a 'B' should be the fourth key in the result array, the second through fifth 'B' keys should be the fifth through eighth keys in the result array, and the 'C' keys should be numbers nine and ten in the result array, since all of the 'B' keys should precede the 'C' keys. Figure 3.3 illustrates these relationships among the keys.

Figure 3.3: Counts and pointers

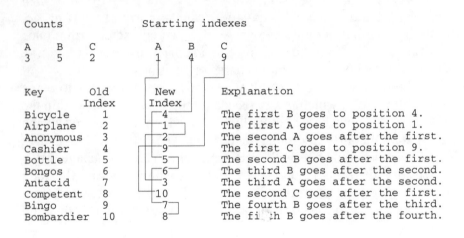

```
Counts                Starting indexes

A     B     C         A     B     C
3     5     2         1     4     9


Key          Old      New      Explanation
             Index    Index
Bicycle       1        4       The first B goes to position 4.
Airplane      2        1       The first A goes to position 1.
Anonymous     3        2       The second A goes after the first.
Cashier       4        9       The first C goes to position 9.
Bottle        5        5       The second B goes after the first.
Bongos        6        6       The third B goes after the second.
Antacid       7        3       The third A goes after the second.
Competent     8       10       The second C goes after the first.
Bingo         9        7       The fourth B goes after the third.
Bombardier   10        8       The fifth B goes after the fourth.
```

If we rearrange the keys in the order indicated by their new indexes, we arrive at the situation shown in Figure 3.4:

Figure 3.4: After the sort on the first character

Index	Unsorted Keys	Sorted Keys
1	Bicycle	Airplane
2	Airplane	Anonymous
3	Anonymous	Antacid
4	Cashier	Bicycle
5	Bottle	Bottle
6	Bongos	Bongos
7	Antacid	Bingo
8	Competent	Bombardier
9	Bingo	Cashier
10	Bombardier	Competent

Multicharacter Sorting

Of course, we usually want to sort on more than the first character. As we noted earlier, each character position is actually treated as a separate key; that is, the pointers to the keys are rearranged to be in order by whatever character position we are currently sorting on. With this in mind, let's take the case of a two character string; once we can handle that situation, the algorithm doesn't change significantly when we add more character positions.

We know that the final result we want is for all the A's to come before all the B's, which must precede all the C's, etc., but within the A's, the AA's must come before the AB's, which have to precede the AC's, etc. Of course, the same applies to keys starting with B and C: the BA's must come before the BB's, etc. How can we manage this?

We already know that we are going to have to sort the data separately on each character position, so let's work backward from what the second sort needs as input. When we are getting ready to do the second (and final) sort, we need to know that all the AA's precede all the AB's, which precede all the AC's, etc., and that all the BA's precede the BB's, which precede the BC's. The same must be true for the keys starting with C, D, and any other letter. The reason that the second sort will preserve this organization of its input data is that it moves keys with the same character at the current character position from input to output in order of their previous position in the input data. Therefore, any two keys that have the same character in the current position (both A's, B's, C's, etc.) will maintain their relative order in the output. For example, if all of the AA's precede all of the AB's in the input, they will also do so in the output, and similarly for the BA's and BB's. This is exactly what we want. Notice that we don't care at this point whether the BA's are behind or ahead of the AB's, as arranging the data according to the first character is the job of the second sort (which we haven't done yet). But how can we ensure that all the AA's precede the AB's, which precede the AC's, etc. in the input? By sorting on the second character position first!

For example, suppose we are sorting the following keys: AB, CB, BA, BC, CA, BA, BB, CC. We start the sort by counting the number of occurrences of each character in the second position of each key (the less significant position). There are three A's, three B's, and two C's. Since A is the character closest to the beginning of the alphabet, the first key that has an A in the second position goes in the first slot of the output. The second and third keys that have an A in the second position follow the first one. Those that have a B in the second position are next, in output positions 4, 5, and 6. The C's bring up the rear, producing the situation in Figure 3.5.

After this first sort (on the second character position), all of the keys that have an A in the second position are ahead of all of the keys that have a B in the second position, which precede all those that have a C in the second position. Therefore, all AA keys precede all AB keys, which precede all AC keys, and the same is true for BA, BB, BC and CA, CB, and CC as well. This is the exact arrangement of input needed for the second sort.

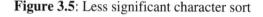

Figure 3.5: Less significant character sort

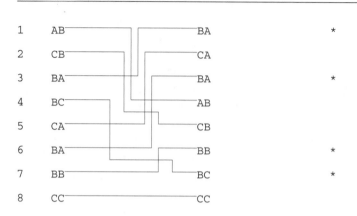

Now we are ready for the second, and final, sorting operation. We start by counting the number of occurrences of each character in the first, or more significant, position. There is one A in this position, along with four B's, and three C's. Starting with the lowest character value, the key that has an A in this position ends up in the first slot of the output. The B's follow, starting with the second slot. Remember that the keys are already in order by their second, or less significant, character, because of our previous sort. This is important when we consider the order of keys that have the same first character. For example, in Figure 3.5, the asterisks mark the keys that start with B.[5] They are in order by their second character, since we have just sorted on that character. Therefore, when we rearrange the keys by their first character position, those that have the same first character will be in order by their second character as well, since we always move keys from the input to the output in order of their position in the input. That means that the B records have the same order in the output that they had in the input, as you can see in Figure 3.6.

This may seem like a lot of work to sort a few strings. However, the advantage of this method when we have many keys to be sorted is that the processing for each pass is extremely simple, requiring only a few machine instructions per byte handled (less than 30 on the 80x86 family).

---

5. Of course, we could just as well have used the keys that start with any other character.

Figure 3.6: More significant character sort

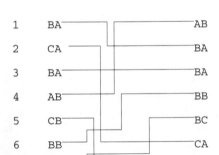

1	BA	AB
2	CA	BA
3	BA	BA
4	AB	BB
5	CB	BC
6	BB	CA
7	BC	CB
8	CC	CC

On the Home Stretch

Having finished sorting the keys, we have only to retrieve the records we want from the input file in sorted order and write them to the output file. In our example, this requires reading the desired records and writing them into an output file. But how do we know which records we need to read and in what order?

The sort function requires more than just the keys to be sorted. We also have to give it a list of the record numbers to which those keys correspond, so that it can rearrange that list in the same way that it rearranges the keys. Then we can use the rearranged list of record numbers to retrieve the records in the correct order, which completes the task of our program.

The Code

Let's start our examination of the mailing list program by looking at the header file that defines its main constants and structures, which is shown in Figure 3.7.

Figure 3.7: The main header file for the mailing list program (mail\mail.h)

```c
/*TITLE mailing list include file */

/****keyword-flag*** "%v %f %n" */
/* "7 21-Mar-98,6:56:06 MAIL.H" */

#include <string.h>

#define DATA_FIELD_COUNT 6
#define BATCH_SIZE 100

// the result of multiplying the next two entries
// must be greater than or equal to the number of
// records to be processed
#define ZIP_BLOCK_COUNT 3000
#define ZIP_BLOCK_ENTRIES 1000

#define MAX_ASCII_FIELD_LENGTH 15

#define LAST_NAME_LENGTH 15
#define FIRST_NAME_LENGTH 9
#define ADDRESS1_LENGTH 15
#define ADDRESS2_LENGTH 15
#define CITY_LENGTH 12
#define STATE_LENGTH 2
#define ZIP_LENGTH 9

#define ASCII_DATE_LENGTH 10
#define ASCII_CENTS_LENGTH 10

#define BINARY_DATE_LENGTH 2
#define BINARY_DOLLARS_LENGTH 2

typedef struct
{
    char last_name[LAST_NAME_LENGTH+1];
    char first_name[FIRST_NAME_LENGTH+1];
    char address1[ADDRESS1_LENGTH+1];
    char address2[ADDRESS2_LENGTH+1];
    char city[CITY_LENGTH+1];
    char state[STATE_LENGTH+1];
} DataRecord;

typedef struct
{
    char zip[ZIP_LENGTH+1];
```

```
        int date_last_here;
        int dollars_spent;
} KeyRecord;

typedef struct
{
        int min_spent;
        int max_spent;
        int min_date;
        int max_date;
} CustomerSelection;

typedef struct
{
        char zip[ZIP_LENGTH+1];
} ZipRecord;

void Megasort(unsigned char **PtrArray, unsigned *RecNums, int KeyLength,
unsigned ArraySize);
```

Now we're ready to look at the implementation of these algorithms, starting with function main (Figure 3.8).

Figure 3.8: main function definition (from mail\mail.cpp)

```
int main(int argc, char *argv[])
{
        start_timing();

        FILE *customer_data_file;
        FILE *customer_list_file;
        char customer_data_file_name[100];
        char customer_list_file_name[100];
        CustomerSelection customer_selection;

        if (argc < 6)
                {
                printf("Usage: mailx customer_file min max start end [override]\n");
                exit(1);
                }

        if (argc < 7)
                override = 0;
        else
                override = atoi(argv[6]);
```

```
strcpy(customer_data_file_name,argv[1]);
strcat(customer_data_file_name,".dat");

strcpy(customer_list_file_name,argv[1]);
strcat(customer_list_file_name,".lst");

customer_data_file = fopen(customer_data_file_name,"rb");

if (customer_data_file == NULL)
    {
    printf("Cannot open file %s.\n",customer_data_file_name);
    exit(1);
    }

customer_list_file = fopen(customer_list_file_name,"w");

if (customer_list_file == NULL)
    {
    printf("Cannot open file %s.\n",customer_list_file_name);
    exit(1);
    }

setvbuf(customer_list_file, NULL, _IOFBF, 32000);

customer_selection = initialize(argv[2],argv[3],argv[4],argv[5]);

process(customer_data_file, customer_list_file, customer_selection);

terminate(customer_data_file, customer_list_file);

end_timing();

return 0;
}
```

This function begins by checking the number of arguments with
which it was called, and exits with an informative message if there
aren't enough. Otherwise, it constructs the output file name and
opens the file for binary input. Then it calls the initialize function
(Figure 3.9), which sets up the selection criteria according to input
arguments 3 through 6 (minimum spent, maximum spent, earliest
last-here date, and latest last-here date). Now we are ready to call
process (Figure 3.10), to select the records that meet those criteria.

Figure 3.9: initialize function definition (from mail\mail.cpp)

```cpp
CustomerSelection initialize(char *min,char *max,char *start,char *end);

void process(FILE *customer_data_file, FILE *customer_list_file,
CustomerSelection customer_selection);

void terminate(FILE *customer_data_file, FILE *customer_list_file);

static int override;

int main(int argc, char *argv[])
{
        start_timing();

        FILE *customer_data_file;
        FILE *customer_list_file;
        char customer_data_file_name[100];
        char customer_list_file_name[100];
        CustomerSelection customer_selection;

        if (argc < 6)
                {
                printf("Usage: mailx customer_file min max start end [override]\n");
                exit(1);
                }

        if (argc < 7)
                override = 0;
        else
                override = atoi(argv[6]);

        strcpy(customer_data_file_name,argv[1]);
        strcat(customer_data_file_name,".dat");

        strcpy(customer_list_file_name,argv[1]);
        strcat(customer_list_file_name,".lst");

        customer_data_file = fopen(customer_data_file_name,"rb");

        if (customer_data_file == NULL)
                {
                printf("Cannot open file %s.\n",customer_data_file_name);
                exit(1);
                }

        customer_list_file = fopen(customer_list_file_name,"w");
```

```
    if (customer_list_file == NULL)
        {
        printf("Cannot open file %s.\n",customer_list_file_name);
        exit(1);
        }

    setvbuf(customer_list_file, NULL, _IOFBF, 32000);

    customer_selection = initialize(argv[2],argv[3],argv[4],argv[5]);

    process(customer_data_file, customer_list_file, customer_selection);

    terminate(customer_data_file, customer_list_file);

    end_timing();

    return 0;
}
```

Figure 3.10: process function definition (from mail\mail.cpp)

```
void process(FILE *customer_data_file, FILE *customer_list_file,
CustomerSelection customer_selection);

void terminate(FILE *customer_data_file, FILE *customer_list_file);

static int override;

int main(int argc, char *argv[])
{
    start_timing();

    FILE *customer_data_file;
    FILE *customer_list_file;
    char customer_data_file_name[100];
    char customer_list_file_name[100];
    CustomerSelection customer_selection;

    if (argc < 6)
        {
        printf("Usage: mailx customer_file min max start end [override]\n");
        exit(1);
        }

    if (argc < 7)
        override = 0;
```

```
else
      override = atoi(argv[6]);

strcpy(customer_data_file_name,argv[1]);
strcat(customer_data_file_name,".dat");

strcpy(customer_list_file_name,argv[1]);
strcat(customer_list_file_name,".lst");

customer_data_file = fopen(customer_data_file_name,"rb");

if (customer_data_file == NULL)
      {
      printf("Cannot open file %s.\n",customer_data_file_name);
      exit(1);
      }

customer_list_file = fopen(customer_list_file_name,"w");

if (customer_list_file == NULL)
      {
      printf("Cannot open file %s.\n",customer_list_file_name);
      exit(1);
      }

setvbuf(customer_list_file, NULL, _IOFBF, 32000);

customer_selection = initialize(argv[2],argv[3],argv[4],argv[5]);

process(customer_data_file, customer_list_file, customer_selection);

terminate(customer_data_file, customer_list_file);

end_timing();

return 0;
}
```

The first order of business in process is to set up the buffering for the list (output), and data files. It is important to note that we are using a large buffer for the list file and for the first pass through the data file, but are changing the buffer size to the size of 1 record for the second pass through the data file. What is the reason for this change?

Determining the Proper Buffer Size

On the first pass through the data file, we are going to read every record in physical order, so a large buffer is useful in reducing the number of physical disk accesses needed.

This analysis, however, does not apply to the second pass through the data file. In this case, using a bigger buffer for the data file would actually reduce performance, since reading a large amount of data at once is helpful only if you are going to use the data that you are reading.[6] On the second pass, we will read the data records in order of their ZIP codes, forcing us to move to a different position in the data file for each record rather than reading them consecutively. Using a big buffer in this situation would mean that most of the data in the buffer would be irrelevant.

Preparing to Read the Key File

Continuing in process, we calculate the number of records in the data file, which determines how large our record selection bitmap should be. Then we call the macro allocate_bitmap, which is defined in bitfunc.h (Figure 3.11), to allocate storage for the bitmap.

Figure 3.11: The header file for the bitmap functions (mail\bitfunc.h)

```
/*TITLE bitmap header file */

/****keyword-flag*** "%v %f %n" */
/* "2 12-May-92,19:23:14 BITFUNC.H" */


int setbit(char *bitmap,unsigned long element);
int clearbit(char *bitmap,unsigned long element);
int testbit(char *bitmap,unsigned long element);

#define allocate_bitmap(x) calloc((unsigned)(x/8+1),1)
```

---

6. There are some situations where this is not strictly true. For example, suppose we want to read a large fraction of the records in a file in physical order, and the records are only a few hundred bytes or less. In that case, it is almost certainly faster to read them all with a big buffer and skip the ones we aren't interested in. The gain from reading large chunks of data at once is likely to outweigh the time lost in reading some unwanted records.

Of course, each byte of a bitmap can store eight bits, so the macro divides the number of bits we need by eight and adds one byte to the result. The extra byte is to accommodate any remainder after the division by eight.

Now that we have allocated our bitmap, we can read through the data file and select the records that meet our criteria. After initializing our counts of "items read" and "found" to zero, we are ready to start reading records. Of course, we could calculate the number of times through the loop rather than continue until we run off the end of the input file, since we know how many records there are in the file. However, since we are processing records in batches, the last of which is likely to be smaller than the rest, we might as well take advantage of the fact that when we get a short count of items_read, the operating system is telling us that we have reached the end of the file.

Reading the Key File

The first thing we do in the "infinite" loop is to read a set of processing_batch records (to avoid the overhead of calling the operating system to read each record). Now we are ready to process one record at a time in the inner loop. Of course, we want to know whether the record we are examining meets our selection criteria, which are whether the customer has spent at least min_spent, no more than max_spent, and has last been here between min_date and max_date (inclusive). If the record fails to meet any of these criteria, we skip the remainder of the processing for this record via "continue". However, let's suppose that a record passes these four tests.

In that case, we increment items_found. Then we want to set the bit in the found bitmap that corresponds to this record. To do this, we need to calculate the current record number, by adding the number of records read before the current processing batch (total_items_read) and the entry number in the current batch (i). Now we are ready to call setbit (Figure 3.12).

Figure 3.12: setbit function definition (from mail\bitfunc.cpp)

```
int setbit(char *bitmap,unsigned long element)
{
      unsigned bytenumber;
      int bitnumber;
      int byte;
      int mask;

      bytenumber = (unsigned)(element / 8);

      bitnumber = (unsigned)(element % 8);

      byte = bitmap[bytenumber];

      mask = 1 << bitnumber;

      bitmap[bytenumber] |= mask;

      if (mask & byte)
            return(1);
      else
            return(0);
}
```

Setting a Bit in a Bitmap

The setbit function is quite simple. Since there are eight bits in a byte, we have to calculate which byte we need to access and which bit within that byte. Once we have calculated these two values, we can retrieve the appropriate byte from the bitmap.

In order to set the bit we are interested in, we need to create a "mask" to isolate that bit from the others in the same byte. The statement that does this, mask = 1 << bitnumber;, may seem mysterious, but all we are doing is generating a value that has a 1 in the same position as the bit we are interested in and 0 in all other positions. Therefore, after we perform a "logical or" operation of the mask and the byte from the bitmap, the resulting value, stored back into the bitmap, will have the desired bit set.

This setbit function also returns a value indicating the value of the bit before we set it. Thus, if we want to know whether we have actually changed the bit from off to on, we don't have to make a call to testbit before the call to setbit; we can use the return value from setbit to determine whether the bit was set before we called setbit. This would be useful, for example, in an application where the bitmap was being used to allocate some resource, such as a printer, which cannot be used by more than one process at a time. The function would call setbit and, if that bit had already been set, would return an error indicating that the resource was not available.

Now we have a means of keeping track of which records have been selected. However, we also need to save the ZIP code for each selected record for our sort. Unfortunately, we don't know how many records are going to be selected until we select them. This is easily dealt with in the case of the bitmap, which is so economical of storage that we can comfortably allocate a bit for every record in the file; ZIP codes, which take ten bytes apiece, pose a more difficult problem. We need a method of allocation which can provide storage for an unknown number of ZIP codes.

Allocate as You Go

Of course, we could use a simple linked list. In that approach, every time we found a record that matches our criteria, we would allocate storage for a ZIP code and a pointer to the next ZIP code. However, this consumes storage very rapidly, as additional memory is required to keep track of every allocation of storage. When very small blocks of ten bytes or so are involved, the overhead can easily exceed the amount of storage actually used for our purposes, so that allocating 250000 14-byte blocks can easily take 7.5 megabytes or more, rather than the 3.5 megabytes that we might expect.

To avoid this inefficiency, we can allocate larger blocks that can accommodate a number of ZIP codes each, and keep track of the addresses of each of these larger blocks so that we can retrieve individual ZIP codes later. That is the responsibility of the code inside the if statement that compares current_zip_entry with ZIP_BLOCK_ENTRIES.[7]

To understand how this works, let's look back at the lines in process that set current_zip_block to -1 and current_zip_entry to

---

7. Please note that there is a capacity constraint in this program relating to the total number of ZIP entries that can be processed. See Figure 3.7 for details on this constraint.

ZIP_BLOCK_ENTRIES. This initialization ensures that the code in the "if" will be executed for the first selected record. We start by incrementing current_zip_block (to zero, in this case) and setting current_zip_entry to zero, to start a new block. Then we allocate storage for a new block of ZIP codes (zip_block) and set up pointers to each one (temp_zip_pointer) so that we can copy the ZIP codes from the keys as we select each record.

Once that bookkeeping is out of the way, we can copy the ZIP code for the current record into the ZIP block via the temp_zip_pointer pointer array and increment which pointer in the array will be used next (current_zip_entry).

Now we're at the end of the processing for one record in a processing batch. Once all the records in the batch have been processed, we fall off the end of the inner loop. At this point, we can add the number of items we have read in this batch to total_items_read. If we have read less than a full batch, we must have reached the end of the file, so we are finished with this phase of processing.

Getting Ready to Sort

Now that we have all the information needed to sort the keys so that we will be able to read the records in ZIP code order on the second pass. However, the sort function, Megasort (Figure 3.13) requires that same information in a different form, so we have some preparation to do before we can call it.

Figure 3.13: The Megasort function (mail\megac.cpp)

```
/*TITLE distribution sorting program*/

/****keyword-flag*** "%v %f %n" */
/* "8 21-Mar-98,17:44:20 MEGAC.CPP" */

#include <stdio.h>
#include <stdlib.h>
#include <string.h>

void Megasort(unsigned char **PtrArray, unsigned *RecNums, int KeyLength,
unsigned ArraySize)
```

```
{
     unsigned char      m;
     int      cum;
     int i;
     unsigned j;

     int      BucketCount [ 256 ];
     int      BucketPosition[ 256 ];
     unsigned char      **TempPtrArray;
     unsigned *TempRecNums;

/* either 0 or 1 element means no sorting required */
     if (ArraySize < 2)
           return;

     TempPtrArray = (unsigned char **) malloc ( sizeof(unsigned char *) * ArraySize);
     if ( TempPtrArray == NULL )
           {
           printf( "out of memory\n" );
           exit( 1 );
           }
     TempRecNums = (unsigned *) malloc ( sizeof(unsigned) * ArraySize );

     if (TempRecNums  == NULL )
           {
           printf( "out of memory\n" );
           exit( 1 );
           }

     for (i = KeyLength-1; i >= 0; i-- )
           {
           memset(BucketCount,0,256*sizeof(int));

           for (j = 0; j < ArraySize; j++ )
                 {
                 m = PtrArray[ j ][ i ];
                 ++BucketCount[m];
                 }

           BucketPosition[0] = 0;
           for (cum = 1; cum < 256; cum++ )
                 BucketPosition[ cum ] = BucketCount[ cum-1 ] + BucketPosition[ cum-1 ];

           for (j = 0; j < ArraySize; j++ )
                 {
                 m = PtrArray[j][i];
                 TempPtrArray[BucketPosition[m]] = PtrArray[j];
                 TempRecNums[BucketPosition[m]] = RecNums[j];
```

```
        ++BucketPosition[m];
        }

    memcpy(PtrArray,TempPtrArray,ArraySize*sizeof(unsigned char *));
    memcpy(RecNums,TempRecNums,ArraySize*sizeof(int));
    }

free(TempPtrArray);
free(TempRecNums);
}
```

Looking at the parameters for this function, we see that the data to be sorted are described by an array of string pointers (unsigned char **PtrArray), whereas what we have is a number of blocks of ZIP codes. The record numbers, which the sort function will rearrange according to the order of the ZIP codes, must be passed as an array of unsigned values (unsigned *RecNums), rather than as the bitmap in which they are stored by our search function.

To set up the first argument to Megasort, we need to produce an array of pointers to each of the ZIP codes we have stored in the blocks, which we do in the portion of Figure 3.10 between the function call that reports the "Pass 1 time" and the call to the Megasort function.

We start by allocating a block of ZIP code pointers (zip_pointer) that can hold all the pointers we will need (items_found). Then, for each block of ZIP codes we have created (zip_block[i]), we calculate the address of each ZIP code in the block and store it in an entry of our zip_pointer array.

That takes care of the pointers to the ZIP codes. Now we have to turn the bitmap into an array of record numbers to be rearranged. First we allocate the array of unsigned values, with items_found entries. Then we call testbit (Figure 3.14).

Figure 3.14: The testbit function definition (from mail\bitfunc.cpp)

```
int testbit(char *bitmap,unsigned long element)
{
        unsigned bytenumber;
        int bitnumber;
        int byte;
        int mask;
```

```
bytenumber = (unsigned)(element / 8);

bitnumber = (unsigned)(element % 8);

byte = bitmap[bytenumber];

mask = 1 << bitnumber;

if (mask & byte)
        return(1);
else
        return(0);
}
```

We call testbit once for every record number in the file, and every time we find a bit set, we store that record number in the next available space in the record_number array. The testbit function is very similar to setbit, described above. The difference is that we don't want to set the bit, but to find out whether it is already set; therefore, we don't modify the bitmap array. Now we are finally ready to call Megasort (Figure 3.13).

The Megasort Function

The main variables involved are the BucketCount array, which keeps track of the number of strings that have each character in the current sorting position (the number of A's, B's, etc.), and the BucketPosition array, which maintains the current position in the output array for each possible character (where the next A string should go, the next B string, etc.). We also have to allocate storage to the TempPtrArray variable for a copy of the pointers to the strings, and to the TempRecNums variable for a copy of the record numbers to be rearranged. All of this setup code having been executed, the main sorting loop is ready to go.

You may be surprised to see how few lines of code are involved in the main loop. If we disregard blank lines and those that contain only a starting or ending brace, only 17 lines contain any executable code. Yet in many common applications this simple algorithm will outperform all of the complex methods favored by the computer science textbooks.

The outer loop is executed once for each character position in the sort. That is, if we are sorting a number of ten-character strings, it will be executed ten times. Its role is to select which character of the strings to be sorted will be used in the current pass through the strings. The reason that the loop index i decreases for each pass through the loop was discussed above: each character position is treated as a separate "key", so we have to sort on the least significant "key" first and work our way up to the most significant one. Each pass of this sort leaves strings in the same order as they were in before the current pass if they have the same character in the current position.

The first operation in the main loop is to use the memset function to clear the BucketCount array, which maintains the counts for each possible ASCII character code. In the first pass through the input data, we step through PtrArray, selecting the ith character as the current character to be sorted from each element of the array. The ASCII value of that character, m, is used to select the element of BucketCount to be incremented, so that when we reach the end of the pointer array, we will know the number of strings that have that character in the current position being sorted.

Once all the counts have been accumulated, we can use that information to fill in the BucketPosition array, which indicates the next available slot for each possible character position. This serves the function of directing traffic from the input pointer array PtrArray to the output one, TempPtrArray. Each element in the BucketPosition array corresponds to the next output position to be used in TempPtrArray for a given character. For example, suppose that the lowest character in the current position of the array to be sorted is 'A', and there are five strings that have an 'A' in the current position. In that case, the initial value of BucketPosition['A'] would be 0, and the initial value of BucketPosition['B'] would be 5, since the first 'A' key should go into output slot 0 and the first 'B' key should go into output slot 5.

After filling in the BucketPosition array, we are ready to rearrange the pointers to the keys by copying these pointers into the temporary array TempPtrArray. That is done in the second inner loop through all the keys. First, we calculate the appropriate index into the BucketPosition array by retrieving the character from the input string, as in the first inner loop above. Then we use that index to retrieve the appropriate element of the BucketPosition array, which we will use to copy both the key pointer and the record number of the current record into the output arrays, TempPtrArray and TempRecNums, respectively.

Then we increment the element of BucketPosition that we have used, because the next key that has that particular character in the current position should go in the next position of the output. In our example, after the first 'A' key has been copied into the output array, BucketPosition['A'] would be incremented to 1, meaning that the next 'A' key should go into output slot 1. Similarly, after the first 'B' key has been copied into the output array, BucketPosition['B'] would be incremented to 6, meaning that the next 'B' key should go into output slot 6.

After copying all of the pointers from PtrArray into TempPtrArray, and all of the record numbers from RecNums into TempRecNums in sorted order, we copy them back into the original arrays for use in the next sorting pass, if there is one, or as the final result if we are done.

Finishing Up

When we are done with the sort, we can return the sorted keys and record numbers to process (Figure 3.10), so that it can retrieve and print the first and last name and the ZIP code for each customer in order by their ZIP codes. We then free the dynamic storage used in the function and return to the main program, which calls terminate to close the files, then exits.

Performance

You may be wondering how much performance improvement we have obtained by using distribution sorting in our example program, mail.cpp. In order to answer this question, I have created another program called mailx.cpp that is identical to mail.cpp except that mailx.cpp uses qsort rather than the distribution counting sort. I've included calls to timing functions in both versions and have run each of them four times with different numbers of keys to see how they perform; Figures 3.15 and 3.16 summarize the results of those runs.

Figure 3.15: Performance figures for mailx.cpp (mail\promailx.out)

```
Pass 1 time:    0.55
Sorting time:    9.39
Pass 2 time:    1.71
Total records selected: 23480
Total time:   11.65

Pass 1 time:    0.54
Sorting time:   38.67
Pass 2 time:    3.41
Total records selected: 46960
Total time:   42.67

Pass 1 time:    0.66
Sorting time: 282.48
Pass 2 time:    8.68
Total records selected: 117400
Total time: 291.82

Pass 1 time:    1.32
Sorting time: 1147.23
Pass 2 time:   17.52
Total records selected: 234801
Total time: 1166.24
```

Figure 3.16: Performance figures for mail.cpp (mail\promail.out)

```
Pass 1 time:    0.50
Sorting time:    0.22
Pass 2 time:    1.65
Total records selected: 23480
Total time:    2.37

Pass 1 time:    0.55
Sorting time:    0.39
Pass 2 time:    3.40
Total records selected: 46960
Total time:    4.34

Pass 1 time:    0.66
Sorting time:    2.03
Pass 2 time:    8.57
Total records selected: 117400
Total time:   11.32

Pass 1 time:    0.94
Sorting time:    3.62
Pass 2 time:   17.41
Total records selected: 234801
Total time:   22.14
```

While the improvement in performance increases with the number of elements, even at the low end, we've multiplied the performance of the sorting part of the task by about 42 times. At the high end, the difference in the sorting speed is a phenomenal 316 to 1, and the overall performance in that case is more than 50 times what it is using qsort. Is optimization always that simple?

This would be a good time for me to mention an attempted optimization that actually did not help performance in the final analysis: the idea of "strip mining", which can most simply be described as dividing a file into two parts, one of which is the "key" portion and the other the "data" portion. Theoretically, it should be faster to read just the keys on the first pass of our mailing list program, then read the data on the second pass only for those records that have been selected. Unfortunately, when I tried this "optimization", it actually slowed the program down. I found this quite surprising, because in earlier tests on other machines, it did help somewhat. However, it doesn't help on my current machine, so I've omitted it.

Moral Support

Is there a moral to this real-life optimization story that summarizes both its successes and failures?

I think there are several. First, we've seen that a very simple algorithm can grossly out-perform a standard library function from a well-known compiler vendor. Second, and more important, optimization is a tricky business. The common thread of these lessons is that no matter how carefully you plan a programming task, the unexpected is very likely to occur. You have to be willing to examine all your preconceptions and discard them if necessary in the face of new evidence. Perhaps this willingness, along with the ability to handle the unexpected when it occurs, is the difference between a novice and an expert.

A Cautionary Tale

Before we leave this chapter, I should mention that the programs described here do not work properly when compiled with the DJGPP compiler on the CD in the back of the book, but produce general protection faults at apparently random times during their execution. This is quite surprising, because they work perfectly with the Microsoft C++ version 5 compiler. Unfortunately, I have discovered this problem too late in the production process to be able to track down and eliminate it; however, at least I can tell you about the problem before you discover it for yourself. As to the cause of the problem: I can only guess that it is caused by bugs in the most recent release of DJGPP.

Summary

In this chapter, we have covered the use of a bitmap to keep track of one attribute of a number of records, sorting via the distribution counting sort, and how to gain rapid access to data according to criteria specified at run time. In the next chapter we will examine the arithmetic coding method of data compression.

Problems

What modifications to the distribution counting sort would:

1. Arrange the output in descending order rather than ascending order?

2. Make only one pass through the data for each character position, rather than two as at present?

3. Add the ability to handle integer or floating-point data rather than character data?

4. Add the ability to handle variable-length strings as keys?

(You can find suggested approaches to problems in Chapter 8).

Chapter 4

Cn U Rd Ths (Qkly)? A Data Compression Utility

Introduction

In this chapter we will examine the Huffman coding and arithmetic coding methods of data compression and develop an implementation of the latter algorithm. The arithmetic coding algorithm allows a tradeoff among memory consumption and compression ratio; our emphasis will be on minimum memory consumption, on the assumption that the result would eventually be used as embedded code within a larger program.

Algorithms Discussed

Huffman Coding, Arithmetic Coding, Lookup Tables

Huffman Coding

Huffman coding is widely recognized as the most efficient method of encoding characters for data compression. This algorithm is a way of encoding different characters in different numbers of bits, with the most common characters encoded in the fewest bits. For example, suppose we have a message made up of the letters 'A', 'B', and 'C', which can occur in any combination. Figure 4.1 shows the relative frequency of each of these letters and the Huffman code assigned to each one.

Figure 4.1: Huffman code table

Letter	Frequency	Huffman Code	Fixed-length Code
A	1/4	00	00
B	1/4	01	01
C	1/2	1	10

The codes are determined by the frequencies: as mentioned above, the letter with the greatest frequency, 'C', has the shortest code, of one bit. The other two letters, 'A' and 'B', have longer codes. On the other hand, the simplest code to represent any of three characters would use two bits for each character. How would the length of an encoded message be affected by using the Huffman code rather than the fixed-length one?

Let's encode the message "CABCCABC" using both codes. The results are shown in Figure 4.2.

Figure 4.2: Huffman vs. fixed-length coding

Letter	Huffman Code	Fixed-length Code
C	1	10
A	00	00
B	01	10
C	1	10
C	1	01
A	00	00
B	01	01
C	1	10
Total bits used	12	16

Here we have saved one-fourth of the bits required to encode this message; often, the compression can be much greater. Since we ordinarily use an eight-bit ASCII code to represent characters, if one of those characters (such as carriage return or line feed) accounts for a large fraction of the characters in a file, giving it a short code of two or three bits can reduce the size of the file noticeably.

Let's see how arithmetic coding[1] would encode the first three characters of the same message, "CAB".

Figure 4.3: One-character messages

Message	Freq.	Cum. Freq.	Codes	Previous Output	Current Output	Output So Far
A	16	16	000000(0)-001111(15)	None	00	00
B	16	32	010000(16)-011111(31)	None	01	01
* C	32	64	100000(32)-111111(63)	None	1	1

Figure 4.3 is the first of several figures which contain the information needed to determine how arithmetic coding would encode messages of up to three characters from an alphabet consisting of the letters 'A', 'B', and 'C', with frequencies of 1/4, 1/4, and 1/2, respectively. The frequency of a message composed of three characters chosen independently is the product of the frequencies of those characters. Since the lowest common denominator of these three fractions is 1/4, the frequency of any three-character message will be a multiple of $(1/4)^3$, or 1/64. For example, the frequency of the message "CAB" will be (1/2)*(1/4)*(1/4), or 1/32 (=2/64). For this reason, we will express all of the frequency values in terms of 1/64ths.

Thus, the "Freq." column signifies the expected frequency of occurrence of each message, in units of 1/64; the "Cum. Freq." column accumulates the values in the first column; the "Codes" column indicates the range of codes that can represent each message[2]; the "Previous Output" column shows the bits that have

---

1. I. H. Witten, R. M. Neal, and J. G. Cleary. "Arithmetic Coding for Data Compression". Commun. ACM 30(6), 520-540 (June 1987).

2. This column is derived from the "Cum. Freq." column; it represents the range of codes that has been allocated to messages that begin with the characters in the "Message So Far" column. For example, messages beginning with the character 'A' have a cumulative frequency of 16/64. This means that messages that start with that letter have codes between the cumulative frequency of the previous message (in this case 0, since this is the first message) and 15/64. Similarly, since messages beginning with the letter 'B' have a cumulative frequency of 32/64, codes for such messages must lie between 16/64, which is the cumulative frequency of the previous entry, and 31/64.

been output before the current character was encoded; the "Current Output" column indicates what output we can produce at this point in the encoding process; and the "Output So Far" column shows the cumulative output for that message, starting with the first character encoded.

As the table indicates, since the first character happens to be a 'C', then we can output "1", because all possible messages starting with 'C' have codes starting with a "1". Let's continue with Figure 4.4 to see the encoding for a two-character message.

Figure 4.4: Two-character messages

Message	Freq.	Cum. Freq.	Codes	Previous Output	Current Output	Output So Far
AA	4	4	000000(00)-000011(03)	00	00	0000
AB	4	8	000100(04)-000111(07)	00	01	0001
AC	8	16	001000(08)-001111(15)	00	1	001
BA	4	20	010000(16)-010011(19)	01	00	0100
BB	4	24	010100(20)-010111(23)	01	01	0101
BC	8	32	011000(24)-011111(31)	01	1	011
* CA	8	40	100000(32)-100111(39)	1	00	100
CB	8	48	101000(40)-101111(47)	1	01	101
CC	16	64	110000(48)-111111(63)	1	1	11

After encoding the first two characters of our message, "CA", our cumulative output is "100", since the range of codes for messages starting with "CA" is from "100000" to "100111"; all these codes start with "100". The whole three-character message is encoded as shown in Figure 4.5.

We have generated exactly the same output from the same input as we did with Huffman coding. So far, this seems to be an exercise in futility; is arithmetic coding just another name for Huffman coding?

These two algorithms provide the same compression efficiency only when the frequencies of the characters to be encoded happen to be representable as integral powers of 1/2, as was the case in our examples so far; however, consider the frequency table shown in Figure 4.6.

Figure 4.5: Three-character messages

Message	Freq.	Cum. Freq.	Codes	Previous Output	Current Output	Output So Far
AAA	1	1	000000(00)-000000(00)	0000	00	000000
AAB	1	2	000001(01)-000001(01)	0000	10	000001
AAC	2	4	000010(02)-000011(03)	0000	1	00001
ABA	1	5	000100(04)-000100(04)	0001	00	000100
ABB	1	6	000101(05)-000101(05)	0001	01	000101
ABC	2	8	000110(06)-000111(07)	0001	1	00011
ACA	2	10	001000(08)-001001(09)	001	00	00100
ACB	2	12	001010(10)-001011(11)	001	01	00101
ACC	4	16	001100(12)-001111(15)	001	1	0011
BAA	1	17	010000(16)-010000(16)	0100	00	010000
BAB	1	18	010001(17)-010001(17)	0100	01	010001
BAC	2	20	010010(18)-010011(19)	0100	1	01001
BBA	1	21	010100(20)-010100(20)	0101	00	010100
BBB	1	22	010101(21)-010101(21)	0101	01	010101
BBC	2	24	010110(22)-010111(23)	0101	1	01011
BCA	2	26	011000(24)-011001(25)	011	00	01100
BCB	2	28	011010(26)-011111(27)	011	01	01101
BCC	4	32	011100(28)-011111(31)	011	1	0111
CAA	2	34	100000(32)-100001(33)	100	00	10000
* CAB	2	36	100010(34)-100011(35)	100	01	10001
CAC	4	40	100100(36)-100111(39)	100	1	1001
CBA	2	42	101000(40)-101001(41)	101	00	10100
CBB	2	44	101010(42)-101011(43)	101	01	10101
CBC	4	48	101100(44)-101111(47)	101	1	1011
CCA	4	52	110000(48)-110011(51)	11	00	1100
CCB	4	56	110100(52)-110111(55)	11	01	1101
CCC	8	64	110000(56)-111111(63)	11	1	111

Figure 4.6: Suboptimal Huffman code table

Letter	Frequency	Huffman Code	Fixed-length Code
A	3/4	0	0
B	1/4	1	1

Using Huffman coding, there is no way to assign theoretically optimal codes to characters with such a frequency distribution.[3] Since the shortest possible Huffman code is one bit, the best we can do is to assign a one-bit code to each character, although this does not reflect the difference in their frequencies. In fact, Huffman

---

3. For that matter, a similar problem occurs when we have three characters of equal frequency; the characters have to end up with different code lengths in a Huffman code, even though their frequencies are equal.

coding can never provide any compression at all with a two-character alphabet.

However, such a situation is handled very well indeed by arithmetic compression. To see how, we will start by asking a fundamental question: what is a bit?

Half a Bit Is Better than One

A bit is the amount of information required to specify an alternative that has a frequency of 50%; two bits can specify alternatives that have a frequency of 25%, and so forth. For example, the toss of a coin can result in either heads or tails, each of which can be optimally represented by a one-bit code; similarly, if a chance event has four equally likely outcomes, we can express each possible result most economically with two bits. On the other hand, as we have seen in our discussion of Huffman codes, we can have a number of alternatives that are not equally likely; in that case, we assign longer codes for those alternatives that are less likely. However, the shortest possible code in Huffman coding is one bit, which is assigned to an outcome with a frequency of one-half.

The general formula for the optimal length of a code specifying a particular outcome with frequency f is "$\log_2(1/f)$". In our previous examples, an outcome with a frequency of .5 should have a code length of $\log_2(1/(1/2))$ or 1 bit. Similarly, if an outcome has a frequency of .25 it should have a code length of $\log_2(1/(1/4))$, or two bits.

But what if one of the possible outcomes has a frequency greater than one-half? Logically, we should use less than one bit to specify it. For example, if we have a data file in which 84% of the characters are spaces, we can calculate the appropriate number of bits in the code for that character as $\log_2(1/(.84))$, or approximately .25 bits. If the remaining 255 characters all have equal frequencies, each of these frequencies is .0627%, so that our formula reduces to $\log_2(1/(.0627))$, or approximately 10.63 bits each. This would result in an average code length of $(.84)*(.25) + (.16)*10.63$, or 1.91 bits per character. By contrast, a Huffman code would require $(.84)*1 + (.16)*9$, or 2.28 bits per character. If we were compressing a 250-Kbyte file with such characteristics, using Huffman codes would produce a 71-Kbyte file, whereas arithmetic coding would result in a

60-Kbyte file, about a 20% difference between these two approaches.[4]

Getting a Bit Excited

Of course, we can't output a code of less than one bit. However, we can use a set of one or more bits to represent more than one character in the same message. This is why the statement that Huffman coding is the most efficient way to represent characters is true, but misleading; if our messages contain more than one character each, we may be able to combine the codes for a number of characters while consuming a fractional number of bits for some characters.

To make this clearer, let's go through the encoding of a three-character message, "ABA", from a two-character alphabet in which the letter 'A' accounts for three-fourths of all the characters and the letter 'B' the remaining one-fourth. The situation after we see the first character is shown in Figure 4.7.

Figure 4.7: The first character

Message So Far	Freq.	Cum. Freq.	Codes	Previous Output	Current Output	Output So Far
* A	48	48	000000(0)-101111(47)	None	None	None
B	16	64	110000(48)-111111(63)	None	11	11

If the first character were a 'B', then we could output "11", because all possible messages starting with 'B' have codes starting with those two bits. However, what can we output when the first character is an 'A'?

Nothing! We don't know whether the first bit of our encoded message will be a 0 or a 1; that depends on what happens next. Remember, messages starting with the letter 'A' can have codes

4. As we will see later, there are commonly occurring situations which have even more lopsided distributions than this, when the context in which each character is seen is taken into account; for example, following a carriage return in a DOS-formatted text file, the next character is almost certain to be a line feed. In such cases, we can use much less than one-fourth of a bit to represent a line feed character following a carriage return and gain far more efficiency compared to Huffman coding.

starting with 00 through 10, or three-fourths of all possible codes. An 'A' gives us somewhat less than 1/2 bit of information, not nearly enough to produce any output by itself. Now let's look at Figure 4.8 for the information needed to encode the next character.

Figure 4.8: The second character

Message So Far	Freq.	Cum. Freq.	Codes	Previous Output	Current Output	Output So Far
AA	36	36	000000(0)-100011(35)	None	None	None
* AB	12	48	100100(36)-101111(47)	None	10	10
BA	12	60	110000(48)-111011(59)	11	None	11
BB	4	64	111100(60)-111111(63)	11	11	1111

We have two bits of output, since all the codes for messages starting with "AB" have the initial bits "10".[5] Let's continue with Figure 4.9 for the third (and last) character of our message.

Figure 4.9: The third character

Message So Far	Freq.	Cum. Freq.	Codes	Previous Output	Current Output	Output So Far
AAA	27	27	000000(0)-011010(26)	None	0	0
AAB	9	36	011011(27)-100011(35)	None	None	None
* ABA	9	45	100100(36)-101100(44)	10	None	10
ABB	3	48	101101(45)-101111(47)	10	11	1011
BAA	9	57	110000(48)-111000(56)	11	None	11
BAB	3	60	111001(57)-111011(59)	11	10	1110
BBA	3	63	111100(60)-111110(62)	1111	None	1111
BBB	1	64	111111(63)-111111(63)	1111	11	111111

We have still produced only two bits of output from our three character message, "ABA". The best we could do with Huffman coding is three bits. However, this is not the extreme case; if we were encoding the most frequent message, "AAA", we would have only a "0" bit.[6]

---

5. Notice that if we were encoding "AA", we still wouldn't have even the first bit!

6. The second most frequent message, "AAB", is a special case, which we will see again later. Although it occupies only nine of the 64 possible message positions, some of those nine start with a 0 and some with a 1; therefore, we don't know the first bit to be output. However, we

A Character Study

This algorithm will work nicely if we happen to know in advance what the frequencies of all the possible characters will be. But how do we acquire this information? If our program reads an input file and writes an output file, we can go through the input file once, counting the number of times a given character appears, build the table of frequencies, and then make a second pass using this table to do the actual encoding. However, this is not possible when we are compressing data as it is being generated, as there is then no input file to be analyzed. This might seem to be an insurmountable obstacle.

Luckily, it is not; calculating the character frequencies as we encode yields about the same compression efficiency as precalculation, and in some cases even better efficiency! The reason for this surprising result is that most files (or sets of data) are not uniform throughout, but rather exhibit local variations in the frequency of a given character or set of characters. Calculating the frequencies on the fly often produces a better match for these changing characteristics.

Therefore, our approach is as follows. Every character is initially assumed to have the same frequency of occurrence. After each character is read and encoded, its entry in the table of frequencies is increased to reflect our having seen it. The next time we encode it, its encoding will account for the fact that we have seen it before.

That may seem quite simple for the sender, but not for the receiver. If the encoding table is being modified as we go, how does the receiver keep in step?

The receiver has the same initial table as the transmitter; each character has the same expected frequency of occurrence. Then, as the receiver decodes each character, it updates its copy of the frequency table. This also explains why we increase a character's frequency after we encode it, rather than before; until the receiver

---

do know that the code for messages beginning with "AAB" starts with either "011" or "100"; as we continue encoding characters, eventually we will have enough information to decide which. At that point, we will be able to output at least those first three bits.

decodes the character, it cannot update the frequency of that character's occurrence.[7]

Keeping It in Context

In our implementation, we achieve a large improvement in compression efficiency by using the context in which a character occurs when estimating its frequency of occurrence. It should be apparent that the frequency of a given character appearing in a message at a given point is quite dependent on the previous context. For example, in English text, a "Q" is almost certain to be followed by a "u", at least if we exclude articles about software such as DESQview! Ideally, therefore, the amount of information needed to encode a "u" following a "q" should be very small. The same principle, of course, applies to the encoding of a line feed following a carriage return in text files where this is a virtual certainty.

On the other hand, the amount of storage required to keep track of a large amount of previous context can become excessive.[8] Even one character of previous context requires the construction of 256 tables of frequencies, one for each possible previous character. A direct extension of the approach given in the reference in footnote 8 would require over 300 KB of storage for these tables.

We will apply a number of space-saving methods to reduce the above storage requirement by about 90%, to approximately 35 KB, while still achieving good data-compression performance in most cases.

Conspicuous Nonconsumption

In order to achieve such a reduction in memory consumption, we must avoid storing anything that can be recalculated, such as the

---

7. A consequence of this approach is that we cannot decompress data in any order other than the one in which it was compressed, which prevents direct access to records in compressed files. This limitation is the subject of one of the problems at the end of this chapter.

8. A. Moffat. "Word-Based Text Compression". *Software -- Practice and Experience*, 19(2), 185-198 (February 1989).

cumulative frequencies of all possible characters.[9] We must also dispense with the use of a self-organizing table that attempts to speed up encoding and decoding by moving more frequently used characters toward the front of the table, as is done in the reference in footnote 1.

However, we must provide as large a dynamic range of frequencies as possible: the larger the ratio between the highest frequency and the lowest, the greater the possible efficiency. The greatest dynamic range is needed when one character always occurs in a particular context, such as line feed after carriage return. Assuming that we must be able to encode any of the 256 possible one-byte values, the algorithm limits the possible dynamic range to approximately one-fourth of the range of an unsigned value.[10] For maximum compression efficiency we therefore need 256 tables of 256 two-byte entries each, consuming a total of 128 KB.[11] When I first implemented this algorithm, I saw no way to reduce this significantly.

Then early one morning, I woke up with the answer. We need some very large frequency values and some very small ones, but surely not every one in between. Why not use a code to represent one of a number of frequency values? These values would be spaced out properly to get as close as possible to optimal compression efficiency, but each would be represented by a small index, rather than literally.

How small an index? First I considered using an eight-bit index. But that still would require 64 KB for a complete 256x256 table. Maybe a smaller index would help. But wouldn't that impose an unreasonable processing time penalty?

Amazingly enough, we can use a four-bit index with no time penalty: in fact, processing is actually faster than with a byte index! This seemingly magical feat is accomplished by one of my favorite time-saving methods: the lookup table.

---

9. This is the column labeled "Cum. Freq." in Figures 4.3-4.5 and 4.7-4.9.

10. For compilers which produce two-byte unsigneds, the maximum cumulative frequency is 16,383 if we wish to avoid the use of long arithmetic. This limits the dynamic range to 16,128 for the one common character and 1 for each of the other characters.

11. Theoretically, we could use 14 bits per entry, but the CPU time required to encode or decode would be greatly increased by packing and unpacking frequencies stored in that way.

You see, a significant amount of the CPU time needed to encode a symbol is spent in a loop that computes the necessary portion of the cumulative frequency table for the current context. If each frequency value occupied one byte, we would have to execute that loop once for every index in the table up to the ASCII value of the character whose cumulative frequency we are trying to compute. However, since we have packed two indexes into one byte, we can accumulate two indexes worth of frequency values with one addition, thus reducing the number of times the loop has to be executed by approximately 50%.

Each execution of the loop translates a pair of indexes contained in one byte into a total frequency value that is the sum of their individual frequency values by using the byte as an index into a 256-word table, which has one entry for each possible combination of two indexes. This table (the both_weights table) is calculated once at the start of the program.

Once we have determined the frequency of occurrence assigned to the character to be encoded, we can decide how many bits we can send and what their values are.

Receiving the Message

The receiver uses almost the same code as the sender, with two main exceptions. First, the receiver reads the input one bit at a time and outputs each character as soon as it is decoded, just the reverse of the sender. Second, rather than knowing how many frequency entries we have to accumulate in advance as the sender does, we have to accumulate them until we find the one that corresponds to the range we are trying to interpret. The latter situation reduces the efficiency of our loop control, which accounts for much of the difference in speed between encoding and decoding.

The Code

Let's start at the beginning, with the main function in encode.cpp (Figure 4.10).

Figure 4.10: Main program for encoding (compress\encode.cpp)

```
/*TITLE encoding main module */

/****keyword-flag*** "%v %f %n" */
/* "8.2 12-May-92,18:01:10 ENCODE.C" */

#include <stdio.h>
#include <stdlib.h>
#include "model.h"

FILE *infile;
FILE *outfile;

main(int argc, char *argv[])
{
    unsigned oldch;
    unsigned ch;

    if (argc < 3)
        {
        printf("Usage: encode original compressed.\n");
        exit(1);
        }

    infile = fopen(argv[1],"rb");
    outfile = fopen(argv[2],"wb");
    setvbuf(infile,NULL,_IOFBF,32000);
    setvbuf(outfile,NULL,_IOFBF,32000);

    start_model();
    start_outputing_bits();
    start_encoding();
    oldch = 0;
    for (;;)
        {
        ch = fgetc(infile);
        if (ch == (unsigned)EOF)
            break;
        encode_symbol(ch,oldch);
        update_model(ch,(unsigned char)oldch);
        oldch = ch;
        }
    encode_symbol(EOF_SYMBOL,oldch);
    done_encoding();
    done_outputing_bits();
    fclose(infile);
```

```
        fclose(outfile);

        return 0;
}
```

This function opens the input and output files and sets up buffers to speed up input and output, then calls start_model (Figure 4.11).

Figure 4.11: start_model function (from compress\adapt.cpp)

```
start_model()
{
        int i;
        int j;
        double temp_threshold;

        for (i = 0; i < TRANSLATE_SIZE - 1; i ++)
                {
                temp_threshold = 256*(1-(double)translate[i]/(double)translate[i+1]);
                upgrade_threshold[i] = (unsigned char)temp_threshold;
                }

        upgrade_threshold[TRANSLATE_SIZE-1] = 255;
        char_total = 0;

        for (i = 0; i < TRANSLATE_SIZE; i ++)
                for (j = 0; j < TRANSLATE_SIZE; j ++)
                        both_weights[TRANSLATE_SIZE*i+j] = translate[i] + translate[j];

        for (i = 0; i < NO_OF_CHARS; i ++)
                {
                frequency_info[i] = &frequency_info_data[i];
                for (j = 0; j < (NO_OF_SYMBOLS+1+1)/2; j ++)
                        frequency_info[i]->freq[j] = 0;
                frequency_info[i]->total_freq = translate[0] * (NO_OF_SYMBOLS + 1);
                }

        for (i = 0; i < NO_OF_CHARS; i ++)
                char_translation[symbol_translation[i]] = i;

        return(0);
}
```

This function starts out by initializing the upgrade_threshold array, which is used to determine when to promote a character to the next higher frequency index value. As noted above, these values are not consecutive, so that we can use a four-bit index rather than literal values; this means that we have to promote a character only once in a while rather than every time we see it, as we would do with literal frequency values. How do we decide when to do this?

A pseudorandom approach seems best: we can't use a genuine random number to tell us when to increment the index, because the receiver would have no way of reproducing our decisions when decoding the message. My solution is to keep a one-byte hash total of the ASCII codes for all the characters that have been sent (char_total) and to increment the index in question whenever char_total is greater than the corresponding value stored in the upgrade_threshold array. That threshold value is calculated so that the probability of incrementing the index is inversely proportional to the gap between frequency values in the translation table.[12] If, for example, each frequency value in the translation table were twice the previous value, there would be a 1/2 probability of incrementing the index each time a character was encountered. After we finish initializing the upgrade_threshold array, we set char_total to 0, in preparation for accumulating our hash total.

The next operation in start_model is to generate the both_weights table. As we discussed above, this table allows us to translate from a pair of frequency values (or weights) to the total frequency to which they correspond. We calculate it by generating every possible pair and adding them together to fill in the corresponding table entry. The values in the translate table are defined in Figure 4.12, in the line that starts with #define TRANSLATE_TABLE. How did I generate these values?

Figure 4.12: Header file for translation table constants and variables
(compress\model.h)

```
/*TITLE translation table coding constants and variables */

/****keyword-flag*** "%v %f %n" */
/* "9 12-May-92,17:46:24 MODEL.H" */
```

---

12. The last entry in the upgrade_threshold array is set to 255, which prevents the index from being increased beyond 15, the maximum value that can be stored in a four-bit value; char_total, being an unsigned char variable, cannot exceed 255.

```
#define NO_OF_CHARS 256
#define EOF_SYMBOL (NO_OF_CHARS+1)

#define NO_OF_SYMBOLS (NO_OF_CHARS+1)

#define MAX_FREQUENCY 16383

typedef struct
{
    unsigned total_freq;
    unsigned char freq[(NO_OF_SYMBOLS+1+1)/2];
} FrequencyInfo;

extern FrequencyInfo frequency_info_data[NO_OF_CHARS];
extern FrequencyInfo *frequency_info[NO_OF_CHARS];

extern unsigned translate[16];

extern unsigned both_weights[256];

extern unsigned symbol_translation[NO_OF_CHARS];

extern unsigned char_translation[NO_OF_CHARS];

#define HIGH_MASK 240 /* the high four bits */
#define LOW_MASK 15   /* the low four bits */

#define HIGH_INCREMENT 16 /* the difference between two high values */
#define LOW_INCREMENT 1 /* the difference between two low values */

#define HIGH_SHIFT 4 /* how much to shift a high nibble */
#define LOW_SHIFT 0 /* how much to shift a low nibble */

#define UPPER_INDEX 15 /* how high is the last table index */

#define TRANSLATE_SIZE 16

#define TRANSLATE_TABLE {1,16,22,30,42,58,79,109,150,\
   207,285,392,540,744,1024,16000}

int start_inputing_bits(void);
int start_model(void);
int update_model(int symbol,unsigned char oldch);
int start_decoding(void);
unsigned decode_symbol(unsigned oldch);
int input_bit(void);
int output_0(void);
int output_1(void);
int done_outputing_bits(void);
```

```
int start_outputing_bits(void);
int done_encoding(void);
int start_encoding(void);
int encode_symbol(unsigned symbol, unsigned oldch);
```

A Loose Translation

It wasn't easy. I knew that I wanted to allow the largest possible dynamic range, which means that the lowest value has to be 1 and the highest value has to be close to the maximum that can be accommodated by the algorithm (16,128). The reason I chose a top value lower than that maximum value is that if the highest value were 16,128, then the occurrence of any character other than the preferred one would cause the total frequency to exceed the allowable maximum, with the result that the table of frequencies would be recalculated to reduce the top value to the next lower step. This would greatly reduce the efficiency of the compression for this case. That accounts for the lowest and highest values. What about the ones in between?

Initially, I decided to use a **geometric progression**, much like the tuning of a piano; in such a progression, each value is a fixed multiple of the one before it. However, I found that I achieved better compression on a fairly large sample of files by starting the progression with the second value at 16 and ending with the next to the last at 1024. Why is this so?

The reason for leaving a big gap between the lowest frequency and the second lowest one is that many characters never occur in a particular situation. If they occur once, they are likely to recur later. Therefore, setting the next-to-the-lowest frequency to approximately one-tenth of 1% of the maximum value improves the efficiency of the compression. I have also found through experimentation that the compression ratio is improved if the first time a character is seen, it is given a frequency of about six-tenths of 1%, which requires an initial index of 7. Lower initial frequencies retard adaptation to popular new characters, and higher ones overemphasize new characters that turn out to be unpopular in the long run.

The reason to leave a large gap between the next-to-highest frequency and the highest one is that most of the time, a very skewed distribution has exactly one extremely frequent character. It is rare to find several very high-frequency characters that have about the same frequency. Therefore, allowing the highest frequency to approach the theoretical maximum produces the best results.

Of course, these are only empirical findings. If you have samples that closely resemble the data that you will be compressing, you can try modifying these frequency values to improve the compression.

Getting in on the Ground Floor

Continuing in start_model (Figure 4.11), we initialize NO_OF_CHARS frequency_info tables, one for every possible character. Each of these tables will store the frequencies for characters that follow a particular character. If we start to encode the string "This is a test", the first character, 'T' will be encoded using the table for character 0 (a null); this is arbitrary, since we haven't seen any characters before this one. Then the 'h' will be encoded using the table for 'T'; the 'i' will be encoded with the table for 'h', and so forth. This approach takes advantage of the context dependence of English text; as we noted before, after we see a 'q', the next character is almost certain to be a 'u', so we should use a very short code to represent a 'u' in that position.

However, our initialization code contains no information about the characteristics of English text (or any other kind of data for that matter). We assign the same frequency (the lowest possible) to every character in every frequency table. As discussed above, the encoding program will learn the appropriate frequencies for each character in each table as it processes the input data. At the end of the initialization for each table, we set its total_freq value to the translation of the lowest frequency, multiplied by the number of index pairs in the table. This value is needed to calculate the code that corresponds to each character, and recalculating it every time we access the table would be time-consuming.

The last operation in start_model initializes the char_translation array, which is used to translate the internal representation of the characters being encoded and decoded to their ASCII codes.[13] Then we return to encode.cpp.

---

13. Although this array is not used in the initial version of our program, we will see near the end of this chapter how it contributes to our optimization effort.

Gentlemen, Start Your Output

The next operation in main is to call start_outputing_bits (Figure 4.13).

Figure 4.13: start_outputing_bits function (from compress\arenc.cpp)

```
int start_outputing_bits()
{
    buffer = 0;
    bits_to_go = 8;
    return(0);
}
```

Of course, we can't send individual bits to the output file; we have to accumulate at least one byte's worth. Whenever we have some bits to be output, we will store them in buffer; since we haven't encoded any characters yet, we set it to 0. In order to keep track of how many more bits we need before we can send buffer to the output file, we set bits_to_go to eight; then we return to main.

The next thing we do in main is to call start_encoding (Figure 4.14).

Figure 4.14: start_encoding function (from compress\arenc.cpp)

```
int start_encoding()
{
    low = 0;
    high = (unsigned)TOP_VALUE;
    bits_to_follow = 0;
    return(0);
}
```

This is a very short function, but it initializes some of the most important variables in the program; low, high, and bits_to_follow. The first two of these keep track of the range of codes for the current message; at this point we know nothing about the message, so they are set to indicate the widest possible range of messages, from 0 to TOP_VALUE, which is defined in arith.h (Figure 4.15).

Figure 4.15: Header file for arithmetic coding constants (compress\arith.h)

```
/*TITLE arithmetic coding constants */

/****keyword-flag*** "%v %f %n" */
/* "5 13-Sep-91,7:20:08 ARITH.H" */

#define CODE_VALUE_BITS 16
typedef long code_value;

#define TOP_VALUE     (((long)1<<CODE_VALUE_BITS)-1)

#define FIRST_QTR     (TOP_VALUE/4+1)
#define HALF          (2*FIRST_QTR)
#define THIRD_QTR     (3*FIRST_QTR)
```

In our current implementation, with 16-bit code values, TOP_VALUE evaluates to 65535.[14] The third variable, bits_to_follow, keeps track of the number of bits that have been deferred for later output. This is used where the range of possible codes for the current message includes codes that start with 0 and some that start with 1; as we have seen already, in such a situation we're not ready to send out any bits yet. After initializing these variables, we return to main.

The Main Loop

Upon returning to main, we need to do one more initialization before we enter the main loop of our program, which is executed once for each character in the input file; namely, setting oldch to 0. This variable controls the context in which we will encode each character. Since we haven't seen any characters as yet, it doesn't really matter which frequency table we use, as long as the decoding program selects the same initial table.

The first operation in the main loop is to get the character to be encoded, via getc. If we have reached the end of the file, we break out of the loop. Otherwise, we call encode_symbol (Figure 4.16) to place the representation of the current character in the output stream.

---

14. To fully understand the function of low and high, we must wait until we examine encode_symbol (Figure 4.16). For now, let's just say that they indicate the current state of our knowledge about the message being encoded; the closer together they are, the more bits we are ready to output.

Figure 4.16: encode_symbol function (from compress\arenc.cpp)

```
int encode_symbol(unsigned symbol, unsigned oldch)
{
    long range;
    unsigned i;
    unsigned cum;
    unsigned prev_cum;
    unsigned char *freq_ptr;
    int current_pair;
    unsigned char high_half;
    unsigned high_half_weight;
    unsigned total_pair_weight;
    unsigned total_freq;
    FrequencyInfo *temp_freq_info;

    temp_freq_info = frequency_info[oldch];
    freq_ptr = temp_freq_info->freq;
    total_freq = temp_freq_info->total_freq;
    prev_cum = 0;
    for (i = 0; i < symbol/2; i ++)
        {
        current_pair = *(freq_ptr++);
        total_pair_weight = both_weights[current_pair];
        prev_cum += total_pair_weight;
        }
    if (symbol % 2 == 0)  /* if even, prev cum is ok, update cum */
        {
        current_pair = *freq_ptr;
        high_half = (unsigned char)((current_pair & HIGH_MASK) >> HIGH_SHIFT);
        high_half_weight = translate[high_half];
        cum = prev_cum + high_half_weight;
        }
    else /* if odd, update both */
        {
        current_pair = *freq_ptr;
        total_pair_weight = both_weights[current_pair];
        cum = prev_cum + total_pair_weight;
        high_half = (unsigned char)((current_pair & HIGH_MASK) >> HIGH_SHIFT);
        high_half_weight = translate[high_half];
        prev_cum += high_half_weight;
        } /* end updating */

    range = (long)(high-low)+1;
    high = low + (unsigned)((range * cum)/total_freq-1);
    low = low + (unsigned)((range * prev_cum)/total_freq);
```

```
for (;;)
    {
    if (high < HALF)
            bit_plus_follow_0
    else if (low >= HALF)
            {
            bit_plus_follow_1
            low -= (unsigned)HALF;
            high -= (unsigned)HALF;
            }
    else if (low >= FIRST_QTR && high < THIRD_QTR)
            {
            bits_to_follow ++;
            low -= (unsigned)FIRST_QTR;
            high -= (unsigned)FIRST_QTR;
            }
    else
            break;

    low <<= 1;
    high <<= 1;
    high ++;
    } /* end of bit output loop */

    return 0;
}
```

This function takes two parameters: ch, the character to be encoded, and oldch, which determines the frequency table to be used for this encoding. As we have noted above, selecting a frequency table based upon the previous character encoded provides far better compression efficiency, as the frequency of occurrence of a particular character is greatly affected by the preceding character.

encode_symbol

Although encode_symbol is a short function, it is the subtlest function in this chapter; fortunately, you can use this algorithm effectively without going through the explanation below. The version here closely follows the reference in footnote 1; if you are really interested in the details of operation of this function, I strongly advise you to study that reference very carefully in conjunction with the explanation here.

To clarify this algorithm, we will work through a somewhat simplified example as we examine the code. For ease in calculation, we will set TOP_VALUE to 255, or 11111111 binary, rather than 65535 as in the actual program; as a result, high will start out at 255 as well. We will also use a single, constant frequency table (Figure 4.17) containing only four entries rather than selecting a 256-entry table according to the previous character and modifying it as we see each character, so our translate and both_weights tables (Figures 4.18 and 4.19, respectively) will be adjusted correspondingly. Instead of ASCII, we will use the codes from 0 (for 'A') to 3 (for 'D') in our example message.

Figure 4.17: Sample frequency table

Character Frequency code
   A,B   00010011 (1,3)
   C,D   00000010 (0,2)

Figure 4.18: Sample translate table

Index	Value
0	1
1	2
2	8
3	52

Figure 4.19: Sample both_weights table

First Index	Second Index			
	0	1	2	3
0	2	3	9	53
1	3	4	10	54
2	9	10	16	60
3	53	54	60	104

As we begin encode_symbol, we establish temp_freq_info as a pointer to the structure containing the current frequency table. Next, we set freq_ptr to the address of the frequency table itself and total_freq to the stored total frequency in the frequency structure; as we will see shortly, total_freq is used to determine what fraction of the frequency range is accounted for by the particular character being encoded. The final operation before entering the frequency accumulation loop is to set prev_cum to 0. This variable is used to keep track of the cumulative frequency of all characters up to but not including the one being encoded; this is used to determine the position of the character being encoded as a part of the entire range of possibilities.

On the Right Frequency

Now we are ready to enter the frequency accumulation loop, which is shown in Figure 4.20.

Figure 4.20: The frequency accumulation loop (from compress\arenc.cpp)

```
for (i = 0; i < symbol/2; i ++)
    {
    current_pair = *(freq_ptr++);
    total_pair_weight = both_weights[current_pair];
    prev_cum += total_pair_weight;
    }
```

The reason we need this loop is that, as we saw before, we cannot afford to keep the cumulative frequency tables in memory; they would occupy hundreds of kilobytes of memory. Instead, we calculate the cumulative frequency for each character being encoded, as we need it. The total_freq variable, however, we do maintain from one encoding to the next; recalculating it would require us to go all the way through the frequency table for each character, even if we are encoding a character with a low ASCII code. Since we are saving the total frequency with the table, we have to accumulate the frequencies only up to the ASCII code of the character we are encoding.

Let's see how this loop accumulates the frequencies of all the characters up to the character we want to encode. The first interesting item is that the loop executes only half as many times as the value of the character being encoded, since we are packing two 4-bit indexes into each byte of the frequency table. So the first statement in the loop retrieves one of these pairs of indexes from the frequency table and increments the pointer to point to the next pair. Then we index into the both_weights table with the index pair we just retrieved and set total_pair_weight to that entry in the table. The both_weights table is the key to translating two 4-bit indexes into a total frequency. Each entry in the table is the sum of the frequency values that correspond to the two indexes that make up the byte we use to index into the table. Finally, we add total_pair_weight to prev_cum, which is accumulating all of the frequencies.

> In our example, the first letter of our message is 'D', which has a symbol value of 3. Using the frequency table in Figure 4.17, we execute the statements in the loop once. First, we set current_pair to the first entry in the frequency table, 00010011, which indicates that the frequency code for 'A' is 1 (0001 binary) and the frequency code for 'B' is 3 (0011 binary). Then we set total_pair_weight to entry (1,3) from the both_weights table, the sum of the frequencies to which this pair of indexes corresponds; its value is 54. The last statement in the loop adds this value to prev_cum, which was set to 0 before the loop was started.

The next section of code, shown in Figure 4.21, finishes the accumulation of the cumulative frequencies of the character to be encoded and the previous character, for both of the possible alignments of the character we are encoding and the previous character.

Figure 4.21: Finishing the accumulation (from compress\arenc.cpp)

```
if (symbol % 2 == 0)  /* if even, prev cum is ok, update cum */
    {
    current_pair = *freq_ptr;
    high_half = (unsigned char)((current_pair & HIGH_MASK) >> HIGH_SHIFT);
    high_half_weight = translate[high_half];
    cum = prev_cum + high_half_weight;
    }
else /* if odd, update both */
```

```
{
current_pair = *freq_ptr;
total_pair_weight = both_weights[current_pair];
cum = prev_cum + total_pair_weight;
high_half = (unsigned char)((current_pair & HIGH_MASK) >> HIGH_SHIFT);
high_half_weight = translate[high_half];
prev_cum += high_half_weight;
} /* end updating */
```

If the target character has an even ASCII code, we already have the correct value for prev_cum; to calculate cum, the frequency accumulation for the current character, we need the first index from the next byte, which is stored in the high half of the byte. So we pick up current_pair, shift its high index down, and use it to retrieve the corresponding weight from the both_weights table. Then we add that frequency value to prev_cum to calculate cum.

On the other hand, if the target character has an odd ASCII code, we need to update both prev_cum and cum. First, we add the total weights for the last two characters to prev_cum, which results in cum. Then we translate the high half of the current_pair and add that to prev_cum.

> In our example, the code of the first character is 3, so we need to update both prev_cum and cum. The value of current_pair is (0,2). Looking in the both_weights table, we set total_pair_weight to the translation of that pair, which is 9. Then cum is calculated as the sum of prev_cum and total_pair_weight, or 63. Then we extract the high part of current_pair, 0, which translates to 1; we add this amount to prev_cum, setting it to 55. This means that the code range associated with character "D" starts at 55 and ends slightly before 64, a range of 9 positions out of the total of 64. This will allow us to send out slightly less than three bits for this character, as we will narrow the range by a factor of more than 7.

Home on the Range

Now that we have calculated the cumulative frequencies of the current character and the previous character, we are ready to narrow the range of frequencies that correspond to our message, as shown in Figure 4.22.

Figure 4.22: Narrowing the range of frequencies (from compress\arenc.cpp)

```
range = (long)(high-low)+1;
high = low + (unsigned)((range * cum)/total_freq-1);
low = low + (unsigned)((range * prev_cum)/total_freq);
```

The first line of this section of code calculates the previous range of frequencies for our message. Then the other lines calculate the new range of the message.

The purpose of low and high is to delimit the frequency interval in which the current message falls; range is just the size of the frequency interval extending from the old value of low to the old value of high, inclusive.

In our example, the old value of low is 0 and the old value of high is 255. Therefore, the formula for range, (long)(high-low)+1, produces 256, which is its maximum value. This makes sense, as we have not yet used the information from the first character of our message.

The new values of low and high represent the narrowing of the previous range due to the frequency of the new character. We calculate the new value of high, which represents the high end of the new range of frequencies for our message after the most recent character is added to the message.[15]

Similarly, the new value of low represents the low end of the range of frequencies for our message after the most recent character is added to the message.

In our example, low is still 0, range is 256, cum is 63, and total_freq is 63. The expression to calculate high is low + (range * cum) / total_freq - 1. Therefore, high is calculated as 0+(256*63)/63-1, or 255. This means that the new range of frequencies for our message ends slightly below 256. Next, we recalculate low. Its value is still 0 so far, range is 256, prev_cum is 55, and total_freq is 63. The expression to calculate low is low + (range * prev_cum)/total_freq. Therefore, we calculate the new value of low as 0+(256*55)/63, or 223. This means that the new range of frequencies for our message begins at 223.

---

15. Actually, the top end of the range of frequencies for the message is just below high+1; even the authors of the reference in footnote 1, which is the source of the original version of this algorithm, admit that this is confusing!

A Bit of All Right

Now we are finally ready to start sending bits out. The loop shown in Figure 4.23 extracts as many bits as possible from the encoding of the message so far, and widens the range correspondingly to allow the encoding of more characters.

Figure 4.23: The bit output loop (from compress\arenc.cpp)

```
for (;;)
    {
    if (high < HALF)
            bit_plus_follow_0
    else if (low >= HALF)
            {
            bit_plus_follow_1
            low -= (unsigned)HALF;
            high -= (unsigned)HALF;
            }
    else if (low >= FIRST_QTR && high < THIRD_QTR)
            {
            bits_to_follow ++;
            low -= (unsigned)FIRST_QTR;
            high -= (unsigned)FIRST_QTR;
            }
    else
            break;

    low <<= 1;
    high <<= 1;
    high ++;
    } /* end of bit output loop */
```

In order to understand this code, we need to look at the table of possible initial bits of high and low, which is given in Figure 4.24.

The entries in this table could use some explanation. The first two columns contain all the possible combinations of the first two bits of low and high; we know that low cannot be greater than high, since these two values delimit the range of codes for the message being compressed. If low ever became greater than high, it would be impossible to encode any further characters. The "Action" column indicates what, if anything, we can output now. Clearly, if low and high have the same first bit, we can output that bit. The entries labeled "Next" indicate that since the separation between the values of low and high is at least one-fourth of the total range of values (0-TOP_VALUE), we can encode at least one more character now; this is the reason for the limit on the total frequency of all characters.

Figure 4.24: Possible initial code bits

Low	High	Action
00	00	0
00	01	0
00	10	Next
00	11	Next
01	01	0
01	10	Defer
01	11	Next
10	10	1
10	11	1
11	11	1

The entry "Defer" means that we can't do any output now; however, when we do have output, we will be able to emit at least the first two bits of the result, since we know already that these bits are either "01" or "10". As we will see shortly, this condition is indicated by a nonzero value for bits_to_follow.

Testing: One, Two, Three

The first test determines whether the highest frequency value allocated to our message is less than one-half of the total frequency range. If it is, we know that the first output bit is 0, so we call the bit_plus_follow_0 macro (Figure 4.25) to output that bit. Let's take a look at that macro.

First we call output_0, which adds a 0 bit to the output buffer and writes it out if it is full. Then, in the event that bits_to_follow is greater than 0, we call output_1 and decrement bits_to_follow until it reaches 0. Why do we do this?

Figure 4.25: The bit_plus_follow_0 macro (from compress\arenc.cpp)

```
#define bit_plus_follow_0 \
{ \
     output_0(); \
     while (bits_to_follow > 0) \
          { \
          output_1(); \
          bits_to_follow --; \
          } \
}
```

The reason is that bits_to_follow indicates the number of bits that could not be output up till now because we didn't know the first bit to be produced ("deferred" bits). For example, if the range of codes for the message had been 011 through 100, we would be unable to output any bits until the first bit was decided. However, once we have enough information to decide that the first bit is 0, we can output three bits, "011". The value of bits_to_follow would be 2 in that case, since we have two deferred bits. Of course, if the first bit turns out to be 1, we would emit "100" instead. The reason that we know that the following bits must be the opposite of the initial bit is that the only time we have to defer bits is when the code range is split between codes starting with 0 and those starting with 1; if both low and high started with the same bit, we could send that bit out.

> The values of HALF, FIRST_QTR, and THIRD_QTR are all based on TOP_VALUE (Figure 4.15). In our example, FIRST_QTR is 64, HALF is 128, and THIRD_QTR is 192. The current value of high is 255, which is more than HALF, so we continue with our tests.

Assuming that we haven't obtained the current output bit yet, we continue by testing the complementary condition. If low is greater than or equal to HALF, we know that the entire frequency range allocated to our message so far is in the top half of the total frequency range; therefore, the first bit of the message is 1. If this occurs, we output a 1 via bit_plus_follow_1. The next two lines reduce high and low by HALF, since we know that both are above that value.

> In our example, low is 223, which is more than HALF. Therefore, we can call bit_plus_follow_1 to output a 1 bit. Then we adjust both low and high by

subtracting HALF, to account for the 1 bit we have just produced; low is now 95 and high is 127.

If we haven't passed either of the tests to output a 0 or a 1 bit, we continue by testing whether the range is small enough but in the wrong position to provide output at this time. This is the situation labeled "Defer" in figure 4.24. We know that the first two bits of the output will be either 01 or 10; we just don't know which of these two possibilities it will be. Therefore, we defer the output, incrementing bits_to_follow to indicate that we have done so; we also reduce both low and high by FIRST_QTR, since we know that both are above that value. If this seems mysterious, remember that the encoding information we want is contained in the differences between low and high, so we want to remove any redundancy in their values.[16]

If we get to the break statement near the end of the loop, we still don't have any idea what the next output bit(s) will be. This means that the range of frequencies corresponding to our message is still greater than 50% of the maximum possible frequency; we must have encoded an extremely frequent character, since it hasn't even contributed one bit! If this happens, we break out of the output loop; obviously, we have nothing to declare.

In any of the other three cases, we now have arrived at the statement low <<= 1; with the values of low and high guaranteed to be less than half the maximum possible frequency.[17] Therefore, we shift the values of low and high up one bit to make room for our next pass through the loop. One more detail: we increment high after shifting it because the range represented by high actually extends almost to the next frequency value; we have to shift a 1 bit in rather than a 0 to keep this relationship.

> In our example, low is 95 and high is 127, which represents a range of frequencies from 95 to slightly less than 128. The shifts give us 190 for low and 255 for high, which represents a range from 190 to slightly less than 256. If we hadn't added 1 to high, the range would have been from 190 to slightly less than 255.

---

16. In our example, we don't execute this particular adjustment.

17. The proof of this is left to the reader as an exercise; see the problems at the end of the chapter.

Round and Round and Round It Goes

Since we have been over the code in this loop once already, we can continue directly with the example. We start out with low at 190 and high at 255. Since high is not less than HALF (128), we proceed to the second test, where low turns out to be greater than HALF. So we call bit_plus_follow_1 again as on the first loop and then reduce both low and high by HALF, producing 62 for low and 127 for high. At the bottom of the loop, we shift a 0 into low and a 1 into high, resulting in 124 and 255, respectively.

On the next pass through the loop, high is not less than HALF, low isn't greater than or equal to HALF, and high isn't less than THIRD_QTR (192), so we hit the break and exit the loop. We have sent two bits to the output buffer.

We are finished with encode_symbol for this character. Now we will start processing the next character of our example message, which is 'B'. This character has a symbol value of 1, as it is the second character in our character set. First, we set prev_cum to 0. The frequency accumulation loop in Figure 4.20 will not be executed at all, since symbol/2 evaluates to 0; we fall through to the adjustment code in Figure 4.21 and select the odd path after the else, since the symbol code is odd. We set current_pair to (1,3), since that is the first entry in the frequency table. Then we set total_pair_weight to the corresponding entry in the both_weights table, which is 54. Next, we set cum to 0 + 54, or 54. The high part of the current pair is 1, so high_half_weight becomes entry 1 in the translate table, or 2; we add this to prev_cum, which becomes 2 as well.

Now we have reached the first line in Figure 4.22. Since the current value of low is 124 and the current value of high is 255, the value of range becomes 131. Next, we recalculate high as 124 + (131*54)/63 - 1, or 235. The new value of low is 124 + (131*2)/63, or 128. We are ready to enter the output loop.

First, high is not less than HALF, so the first test fails. Next, low is equal to HALF, so the second test succeeds. Therefore, we call bit_plus_follow_1 to output a 1 bit; it would also output any deferred bits that we might have been unable to send out before, although there aren't any at present. We also adjust low and high by subtracting HALF, to account for the bit we have just sent; their new values are 0 and 107, respectively.

Next, we proceed to the statements beginning at low <<= 1;, where we shift low and high up, injecting a 0 and a 1, respectively; the new values are 0 for low and 215 for high. On the next pass through the loop we will discover that these values are too far apart to emit any more bits, and we will break out of the loop and return to the main function.

We could continue with a longer message, but I imagine you get the idea. So let's return to the main function (Figure 4.10).[18]

update_model

The next function called is update_model (Figure 4.26), which adjusts the frequencies in the current frequency table to account for having seen the most recent character.

Figure 4.26: The update_model function (from compress\adapt.cpp)

```
update_model(int symbol,unsigned char oldch)
{
        int i;
        int index;
        unsigned char *freq_ptr;
        unsigned char freq;
        int old_weight_code;
        unsigned weight_gain;
        unsigned char temp_freq;
        long temp_total_freq;
        FrequencyInfo *temp_freq_info;
        unsigned char low_symbol;

        low_symbol = (unsigned char)(symbol_translation[symbol] & 255);

        char_total = (unsigned char)(char_total + low_symbol);

        old_weight_code = -1;
        temp_freq_info = frequency_info[oldch];
        freq_ptr = temp_freq_info->freq;
```

---

18. You may be wondering what happened to the remaining information contained in low and high. Rest assured that it will not be left twisting in the wind; there is a function called done_encoding that makes sure that all of the remaining information is encoded in the output stream.

```
index = symbol/2;
if (symbol % 2 == 0) /* if a high symbol */
    {
    temp_freq =
         (unsigned char)((freq_ptr[index] & HIGH_MASK) >> HIGH_SHIFT);
    if (temp_freq == 0)
         {
         freq_ptr[index] += INIT_INDEX << HIGH_SHIFT;
         temp_freq_info->total_freq +=
         translate[INIT_INDEX] - translate[0];
         }
    else if (char_total > upgrade_threshold[temp_freq])
         {
         old_weight_code = temp_freq;
         freq_ptr[index] += HIGH_INCREMENT; /* bump it */
         }
    }
else /* if a low one */
    {
    temp_freq = (unsigned char)((freq_ptr[index] & LOW_MASK) >> LOW_SHIFT);
    if (temp_freq == 0)
         {
         freq_ptr[index] += INIT_INDEX << LOW_SHIFT;
         temp_freq_info->total_freq +=
         translate[INIT_INDEX] - translate[0];
         }
    else if (char_total > upgrade_threshold[temp_freq])
         {
         old_weight_code = temp_freq;
         freq_ptr[index] += LOW_INCREMENT; /* bump it */
         }
    }

if (old_weight_code != -1) /* if there was an adjustment of weight */
    {
    weight_gain = translate[old_weight_code+1] - translate[old_weight_code];
    temp_freq_info->total_freq += weight_gain;
    }

temp_total_freq = temp_freq_info->total_freq;
while (temp_total_freq > MAX_FREQUENCY)
    {
    temp_total_freq = 0;
    freq_ptr = temp_freq_info->freq;
    for (i = 0; i < (NO_OF_SYMBOLS+1)/2; i ++)
         {
         if (*freq_ptr == 0) /* if this is at the bottom, forget it */
             temp_total_freq += BOTH_WEIGHTS_ZERO;
```

```
            else /* if it needs to be updated */
                {
                freq = *freq_ptr;
                if ((freq & HIGH_MASK) != 0)
                    {
                    /* if the top is not at the lowest value*/
                    *freq_ptr -= HIGH_INCREMENT; /* decrement it */
                    }
                if ((freq & LOW_MASK) != 0)
                    {
                    /* if the low is not at the lowest value*/
                    *freq_ptr -= LOW_INCREMENT; /* decrement it */
                    }
                temp_total_freq += both_weights[*freq_ptr];
                }
            freq_ptr ++;
            }
        }
    temp_freq_info->total_freq = (unsigned)temp_total_freq;
    return(0);
}
```

The arguments to this function are symbol, the internal value of the character just encoded, and oldch, the previous character encoded, which indicates the frequency table that was used to encode that character. What is the internal value of the character? In the current version of the program, it is the same as the ASCII code of the character; however, near the end of the chapter we will employ an optimization that involves translating characters from ASCII to an internal code to speed up translation.

This function starts out by adding the character's ASCII code to char_total, a hash total which is used in the simple pseudorandom number generator that we use to help decide when to upgrade a character's frequency to the next frequency index code. We use the symbol_translation table to get the ASCII value of the character before adding it to char_total; this is present for compatibility with our final version which employs character translation.

The next few lines initialize some variables: old_weight_code, which we set when changing a frequency index code or "weight code", so that we can update the frequency total for this frequency table; temp_freq_info, a pointer to the frequency table structure for the current character; and freq_ptr, the address of the frequency table itself.

Next, we compute the index into the frequency table for the weight code we want to examine. If this index is even, that means that this symbol is in the high part of that byte in the frequency table. In this case, we execute the code in the true branch of the if statement "if (symbol % 2 == 0)". This starts by setting temp_freq to the high four bits of the table entry. If the result is 0, this character has the lowest possible frequency value; we assume that this is because it has never been encountered before and set its frequency index code to INIT_INDEX. Then we update the total_freq element in the frequency table.

However, if temp_freq is not 0, we have to decide whether to upgrade this character's frequency index code to the next level. The probability of this upgrade is inversely proportional to the ratio of the current frequency to the next frequency; the larger the gap between two frequency code values, the less the probability of the upgrade. So we compare char_total to the entry in upgrade_threshold; if char_total is greater, we want to do the upgrade, so we record the previous frequency code in old_weight_code and add HIGH_INCREMENT to the byte containing the frequency index for the current character. We have to use HIGH_INCREMENT rather than 1 to adjust the frequency index, since the frequency code for the current character occupies the high four bits of its byte.

Of course, the character is just as likely to be in the low part of its byte; in that case, we execute the code in the false branch of that if statement, which corresponds exactly to the above code. In either case, we follow up with the if statement whose condition is "(old_weight_code != -1)", which tests whether a frequency index code was incremented. If it was, we add the difference between the new code and the old one to the total_freq entry in the current frequency table, unless the character previously had a frequency index code of 0; in that case, we have already adjusted the total_freq entry.

Over the Top

The last operation in update_symbol is to make sure that the total of all frequencies in the frequency table does not exceed the limit of MAX_FREQUENCY; if that were to happen, more than one character might map into the same value between high and low, so that unambiguous decoding would become impossible. Therefore, if temp_total_freq exceeds MAX_FREQUENCY, we have to reduce the frequency indexes until this is no longer the case. The while loop whose continuation expression is "(temp_total_freq > MAX_FREQUENCY)" takes care of this problem in the following way.

First, we initialize temp_total_freq to 0, as we will use it to accumulate the frequencies as we modify them. Then we set freq_ptr to the address of the first entry in the frequency table to be modified. Now we are ready to step through all the bytes in the frequency table; for each one, we test whether both indexes in the current byte are 0. If so, we can't reduce them, so we just add the frequency value corresponding to the translation of two 0 indexes (BOTH_WEIGHTS_ZERO) to temp_total_freq.

Otherwise, we copy the current index pair into freq. If the high index is nonzero, we decrement it. Similarly, if the low index is nonzero, we decrement it. After handling either or both of these cases, we add the translation of the new index pair to temp_total_freq. After we have processed all of the index values in this way, we retest the while condition, and when temp_total_freq is no longer out of range, we store it back into the frequency table and return to the main program.

The Home Stretch

Finally, we have returned to the main function (Figure 4.10), where we copy ch to oldch, so that the current character will be used to select the frequency table for the next character to be encoded; then we continue in the main loop until all characters have been processed.

When we reach EOF in the input file, the main loop terminates; we use encode_symbol to encode EOF_SYMBOL, which tells the receiver to stop decoding. Then we call done_encoding (Figure 4.27) and done_outputing_bits (Figure 4.28) to flush any remaining information to the output file. Finally, we close the input and output files and exit.

Figure 4.27: The done_encoding function (from compress\arenc.cpp)

```
int done_encoding()
{
    bits_to_follow ++;
```

```
        if (low < FIRST_QTR)
                bit_plus_follow_0
        else
                bit_plus_follow_1
        return(0);
}
```

Figure 4.28: The done_outputing_bits function (from compress\arenc.cpp)

```
int done_outputing_bits()
{
        fputc(buffer>>bits_to_go,outfile);
        return(0);
}
```

Finding the Bottlenecks

Now that we have developed a working version of our program, let's see how much more performance we can get by judicious optimization in the right places. The first step is to find out where those places are. Therefore, I ran the program under Microsoft's profiler on a file of approximately 11 KB, compressing it to a little less than 5 KB (a compression ratio of 2.3 to 1). This didn't take very long, as you can see from the profile in Figure 4.29.

Figure 4.29: Profile of encode.exe before optimization

Total time: 167.100 milliseconds

```
    Func
    Time  %       Function
-------------------------
80.010 49.0   encode_symbol(unsigned int,unsigned int) (arenc.obj)
29.139 17.9   _main (encode.obj)
18.717 11.5   output_1(void) (arenc.obj)
17.141 10.5   output_0(void) (arenc.obj)
15.957  9.8   update_model(int,unsigned char) (adapt.obj)
 2.234  1.4   start_model(void) (adapt.obj)
```

The majority of the CPU time is spent in the encode_symbol function, so that's where we'll look first. As I mentioned in the discussion of the algorithm, a significant amount of the CPU time needed to encode a symbol is spent in the loop shown in Figure 4.20. Accordingly, we should be able to increase the speed of our implementation by using a more efficient representation of the characters to be encoded, so that the accumulation loop will be executed fewer times in total. While we cannot spare the space for self-organizing tables of character translations, a fixed translation of characters according to some reasonable estimate of their likelihood in the text is certainly possible. Let's see how that would affect our performance.

A Bunch of Real Characters

After analyzing a number of (hopefully representative) text files, I used the results to produce a list of the characters in descending order of number of occurrences. This information is stored in the symbol_translation table (Figure 4.30), which is used during decoding to translate from the internal code into ASCII.

Figure 4.30: The symbol_translation table (from compress\adapt.cpp)

```
unsigned symbol_translation[NO_OF_CHARS] = {32,101,116,111,97,105,110,114,115,
104,108,100,13,10,99,117,109,112,103,121,102,46,98,119,44,94,118,107,78,84,
```

The inverse transformation, used by the encoder, is supplied by the char_translation table, which is initialized near the end of the start_model function (Figure 4.11).

To use these new values for each character when encoding and decoding, we have to make some small changes in the encoding and decoding main programs. Specifically, in main, we have to use the translated character rather than the ASCII code as read from the input file when we call the encode_symbol function. The new version of the main program for encoding is shown in Figure 4.31.

Figure 4.31: The new main encoding program (compress\encode1.cpp)

```
/*TITLE encoding main module */

/****keyword-flag*** "%v %f %n" */
/* "11 12-May-92,18:01:10 ENCODE1.C" */

#include <stdio.h>
#include <stdlib.h>
#include "model.h"

FILE *infile;
FILE *outfile;

main(int argc, char *argv[])
{
    unsigned oldch;
    unsigned ch;
    unsigned symbol;

    if (argc < 3)
        {
        printf("Usage: encode original compressed.\n");
        exit(1);
        }

    infile = fopen(argv[1],"rb");
    outfile = fopen(argv[2],"wb");
    setvbuf(infile,NULL,_IOFBF,32000);
    setvbuf(outfile,NULL,_IOFBF,32000);

    start_model();
    start_outputing_bits();
    start_encoding();
    oldch = char_translation[0];
    for (;;)
        {
        ch = fgetc(infile);
        if (ch == (unsigned)EOF)
            break;
        symbol = char_translation[ch];
        encode_symbol(symbol,oldch);
        update_model(symbol,(unsigned char)oldch);
        oldch = symbol;
        }
    encode_symbol(EOF_SYMBOL,oldch);
    done_encoding();
```

```
        done_outputing_bits();
        fclose(infile);
        fclose(outfile);

        return 0;
}
```

Of course, corresponding changes have to be made to the main function in the decoding program, which then looks like Figure 4.32.

Figure 4.32: The new main decoding program (compress\decode1.cpp)

```
/*TITLE decoding main module */

/****keyword-flag*** "%v %f %n" */
/* "9 12-May-92,18:01:12 DECODE1.C" */

#include <stdio.h>
#include <stdlib.h>
#include "model.h"

FILE *infile;
FILE *outfile;

main(int argc, char *argv[])
{
        unsigned oldch;
        unsigned ch;
        unsigned symbol;

        if (argc < 3)
            {
            printf("Usage: decode compressed original.\n");
            exit(1);
            }

        infile = fopen(argv[1],"rb");
        outfile = fopen(argv[2],"wb");
        setvbuf(infile,NULL,_IOFBF,8000);
        setvbuf(outfile,NULL,_IOFBF,8000);

        start_model();
        start_inputing_bits();
        start_decoding();
        oldch = 0;
```

```
    for (;;)
        {
        symbol = decode_symbol(oldch);
        if (symbol == EOF_SYMBOL)
                break;
        ch = symbol_translation[symbol];
        fputc(ch,outfile);
        update_model(symbol,oldch);
        oldch = ch;
        }

    return(0);
}
```

Figure 4.33 shows the speed improvement resulting from this modification.

Figure 4.33: Profile of encode1.exe, after character translation

---

Total time: 145.061 millisecond

```
    Func
    Time  %     Function
    (msec)
----------------------------
58.980 41.8   encode_symbol(unsigned int,unsigned int) (arenc.obj)
25.811 18.3   _main (encode1.obj)
18.964 13.4   output_0(void) (arenc.obj)
18.586 13.2   output_1(void) (arenc.obj)
16.565 11.7   update_model(int,unsigned char) (adapt.obj)
 2.213  1.6   start_model(void) (adapt.obj)
```

This speed improvement of about 15% took a total of about an hour, mostly to write and debug the character counting program and run it on a number of sample files. However, this change isn't helpful in all cases. It will speed up the handling of files that resemble those used to calculate the translation tables, but will have much less impact on those having a significantly different mix of data characters. In the worst case, it might even slow the program down noticeably; for example, a file containing many nulls, or 0 characters, might be compressed faster without translation, as encoding the most common character would then require no executions of the accumulation loop. This is an example of the general rule that knowing the makeup of the data is important in deciding how to optimize the program.

Summary

In this chapter, we have seen an example of how intelligent encoding of information can pack a lot of data into a relatively small amount of memory. In the next chapter, we will see how quantum files allow us to gain efficient random access to a large volume of variable-length textual data.

Problems

1. How could arithmetic coding be used where each of a number of blocks of text must be decompressed without reference to the other blocks?

2. If we knew that the data to be compressed consisted entirely of characters with ASCII codes 0 through 127, could we reduce the memory requirements of this algorithm further? If so, how much and how?

(You can find suggested approaches to problems in Chapter 8).

Chapter 5

Free at Last: An Efficient Method of Handling Variable-Length Records

Introduction

In this chapter we will develop an algorithm that uses the quantum file access method to handle a file containing a large number of records each of which can vary dynamically in size. In order to appreciate the power of this access method, we will start by considering the much simpler problem of access to fixed-length records.

Algorithm Discussed

The Quantum File Access Method

A Harmless Fixation

Let us suppose that we want to access a number of fixed-length customer records by their record numbers.[1] Given the record number,

---

1. Obviously, this is a simplification: normally, we would want to be able to find a customer's record by his name or other salient characteristic. However, that part of the problem can be handled by, for example, a hash coded lookup from the name into a record number, as we will

we can locate that customer's record by multiplying the record number by the length of a record, which gives us the offset into the file where that record will be found. We can then read or write that record as needed.

Of course, a real application needs to reuse records of customers who have become inactive, to prevent the customer file from growing indefinitely. To handle this problem, we could set a limit on the file size and, when it is reached, start reusing records that haven't been referenced for a long time, making sure to correct or delete any records in other files that refer to the deleted customer.

This fixed-length record system is not very difficult to implement, but it has significant drawbacks; address fields, for example, tend to vary greatly in length, with some records needing 25 or 30 characters for a city name or street address and others needing only 10. If we allocate enough storage for the extreme case, the records become much longer than if we had to handle only the average case. However, allocating enough for only the average case will leave those customers whose names or addresses won't fit into the allotted space quite unhappy, as I know from personal experience as a software developer! The obvious solution is to allow the fields (and therefore the records) to vary in length as necessary.

Checking Out of the Hotel Procrustes

Unfortunately, variable-length records are much more difficult to deal with than fixed-length ones. The most obvious reason, as discussed above, is that determining where fixed-length records are stored requires only a simple calculation; this is not true of variable-length records. However, we could remedy this fairly easily by maintaining a **record index** consisting of an array of structures containing the starting location and length of each record, as depicted in Figure 5.1.[2]

---

see in the next chapter. Here we are concerned with what happens after we know the record number.

2. This figure could just as easily be considered a layout for a single record with variable-length fields; however, the explanation is valid either way.

Figure 5.1: A sample record index array and data for variable-length records

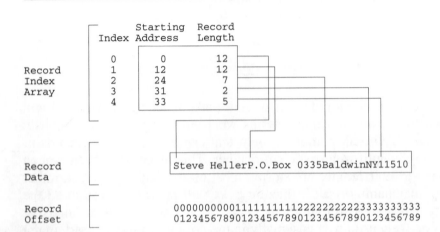

We encounter a more serious difficulty when we want to delete a record and reuse the space it occupied.[3] In some situations we can sidestep the problem by adding the new version of the record to the end of the file and changing the record pointer to refer to the new location of the record; however, in the case of an actively updated file such an approach would cause the file to grow rapidly.

But how can we reuse the space vacated by a deleted record of some arbitrary size? The chances of a new record being exactly the same size as any specific deleted one are relatively small, especially if the records average several hundred bytes each, as is not at all unusual in customer data files. A possible solution is to keep a separate free list for each record size and reuse a record of the correct size. However, there is a very serious problem with this approach: a new record may need 257 bytes, for example, and there may be no available record of exactly that size. Even though half of the records in the file might be deleted, none of them could be reused, and we would still be forced to extend the file. The attempt to solve this difficulty by using a record that is somewhat larger than necessary leads to many unusably small areas being left in the file (a situation known as fragmentation).

---

3. The problem of changing the length of an existing record can be handled by deleting the old version of the record and adding a new version having a different length.

However, there is a relatively unknown way to make variable-length records more tractable: the quantum file access method.[4] The key is to combine them into groups of fixed length, which can then be allocated and deallocated in an efficient manner.

The Quantum File Access Method

Before the following discussion will make much sense to you, I will need to explain in general terms what we're trying to accomplish: building a virtual memory system that can accommodate records of varying lengths in an efficient manner. This means that even though at any given time, we are storing most of our data on the disk rather than maintaining it all in memory, we will provide access to all the data as though it were in memory. To do this, we have to arrange that any actively used data is actually in memory when it is needed. In the present application, our data is divided into fixed-size blocks called **quanta** (plural of **quantum**),[5] so the task of our virtual memory system is to ensure that the correct blocks are in memory as needed by the user.[6]

The quanta in the file are generally divided into a number of addressable units called **items**.[7] When adding a record to the file, we search a free space list, looking for a quantum with enough free space for the new record. When we find one, we add the record to that quantum and store the record's location in the **item reference array**, or IRA, which replaces the record index in Figure 5.1; this array consists of entries of the form "quantum number, item number".[8] The **item number** refers to an entry in the **item index** stored at the

---

4. I am indebted for this extremely valuable algorithm to its inventor, Henry Beitz, who generously shared it with me in the mid-1970's.

5. In general, I use the terms "quantum" and "block" interchangeably; in the few cases where a distinction is needed, I will note it explicitly.

6. In the current implementation, the default block size is 16K. However, it is easy to change that size in order to be able to handle larger individual items or to increase storage efficiency.

7. Some blocks used to store internal tables such as the free space list are not divided into items, but consist of an array of fixed-size elements, sometimes preceded by a header structure describing the array.

8. For simplicity, in our sample application each user record is stored in one item; however, since any one item must fit within a quantum, applications dealing with records that might exceed the size of a quantum should store each potentially lengthy field as a separate item.

beginning of the quantum; the items are stored in the quantum in order of their item index entries, which allows the size of an item to be calculated rather than having to be stored.

For example, if we were to create an array of variable-length strings, some of its item references might look like those illustrated in Figure 5.2.

Figure 5.2: Sample IRA, item index, and data, before deletions

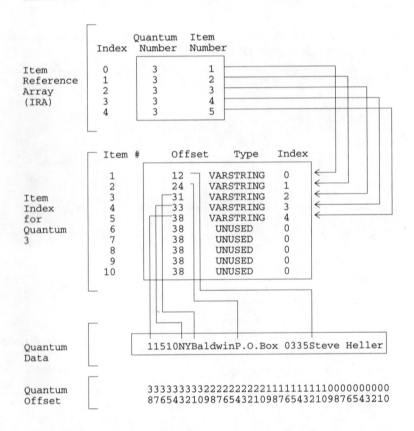

When we delete an item from a quantum, we have to update the free space list entry for that quantum to reflect the amount freed, so the space can be reused the next time an item is to be added to the file. We also have to slide the remaining items in the quantum together so that the free space is in one contiguous block, rather than in slivers scattered throughout the quantum. With a record index like the one in Figure 5.1, we would have to change the record index entries for all the records that were moved. Since the records that were moved might be anywhere in the record index, this could impose unacceptable overhead on deletions; to avoid this problem, we will leave the item index entry for a deleted item empty rather than sliding the other entries down in the quantum, so that the IRA is unaffected by changes in the position of records within a quantum. If we delete element 1 from the array, the resulting quantum looks like Figure 5.3.

Figure 5.3: Sample IRA, item index, and data

	Index	Quantum Number	Item Number
Item Reference Array (IRA)	0	3	1
	1	NONE	0
	2	3	3
	3	3	4
	4	3	5

	Item #	Offset	Type	Index
Item Index for Quantum 3	1	12	VARSTRING	0
	2	12	UNUSED	0
	3	19	VARSTRING	2
	4	21	VARSTRING	3
	5	26	VARSTRING	4
	6	38	UNUSED	0
	7	38	UNUSED	0
	8	38	UNUSED	0
	9	38	UNUSED	0
	10	38	UNUSED	0

Quantum Data

11510NYBaldwinSteve Heller

Quantum Offset

```
33333333322222222222111111111110000000000
87654321098765432109876543210987654321 0
```

Note that we set the offset value of the deleted item equal to the offset of the item before it so that its length can be calculated as zero. Now let us add a new street address of "123 Main Street". After this change, our data structures look like those in Figure 5.4.

Figure 5.4: Sample IRA, item index, and data, after field change

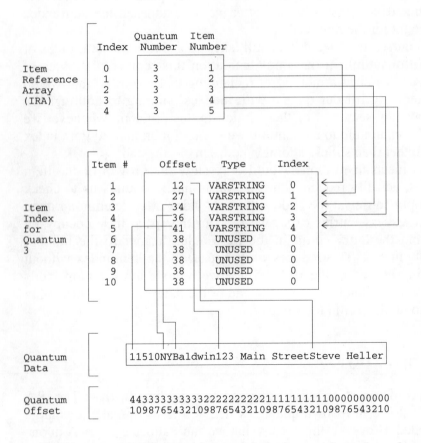

This is the actual mechanism used to change the value of an item: we delete the old item and add the new one. Of course, an item that increases in size may no longer fit in the same quantum, in which case we have to move it to a different quantum. Keeping track of such changes is not difficult as long as we always use the standard method of finding the address of an item: look it up in the IRA to get its quantum number and item number, then use its quantum number and item number to look it up in the item index. This allows us to move the item to a new quantum and change only its entries in the IRA and affected item indexes.

For example, if an item was originally in quantum 3 but now no longer fits there, we might move it to quantum 6. In order to do this, we first delete it from quantum 3 and then add it to quantum 6. As before, all the other IRA entries for items in quantum 3 still refer to the same data items as before, after we have adjusted the item index to account for the removed data.

Of course, the deleted item still takes up a slot in the item index of the old quantum; in our implementation this requires 10 bytes of storage.[9] We need a method of reclaiming that space, so that we do not gradually fill our quanta with indexes pointing to nothing. We have already seen part of the solution to this problem: whenever we are adding an item to a quantum, we search for an unused item index entry rather than simply adding a new entry at the end.

This mechanism alone would only slow the growth of the item indexes; actually reducing the size of an index requires us to check for empty entries at the end of the item index after deleting an item. If such excess entries exist, we reclaim the space they occupy by reducing the entry count in the item index header to the number actually in use. This reduces wasted space in the item index without affecting entries in the IRA. Since we remove unused item index entries only when they are at the end of the index, no IRA entries can refer to items later in the same quantum.

A Large Array

Our records are stored in the quanta pointed to by our IRA. The IRA will be stored in its own quanta, which allows us to make it as large as needed. However, this means that we can't allocate the IRA in one piece. Since a quantum has a fixed size, we will have to break up our IRA into segments that will fit in a quantum; these segments will be

---

9. Four of these bytes are used to hold the index in the IRA to which this item corresponds; this information would be very helpful in reconstructing as much as possible of the file if it should become corrupted. Another two bytes are used to keep track of the type of the item. These entries are for error trapping and file reconstruction if the file should somehow become corrupted.

collectively referred to as the **little pointer array**. We'll also need some way to find the segment that we need for a particular element in the IRA, which will be the responsibility of the **big pointer array**.

Figure 5.5 shows the relationship between the big pointer array and the IRA segments.

Figure 5.5: From the big pointer array to the IRA

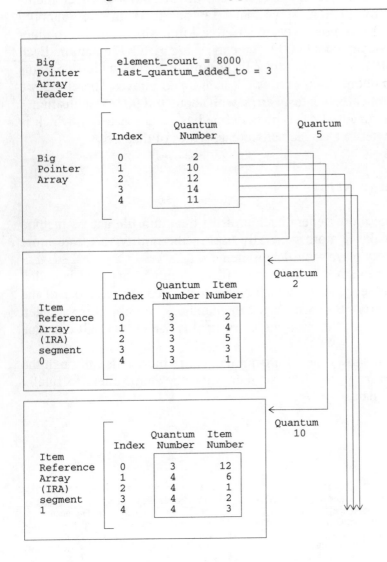

Each IRA segment in the real program, of course, holds more than five entries: with a 16 KB quantum, about 4000 entries will fit in one quantum. However, the segmentation of the IRA works in the same way as this example. The segment number can be determined by dividing the element number by the number of elements in each IRA segment; the index into the IRA segment is the remainder of that division.

The big pointer array sets a limit on the number of elements referenced by an IRA, since that array has to fit in one quantum. However, this is not a very restrictive limit, since one big pointer array can contain about 4000 elements, using a 16 KB quantum. Each of these elements points to a little pointer array, which contains pointers to about 4000 entries, as mentioned above. Therefore, we could theoretically create an array with about 16,000,000 items in it.

Because our ArrayIndex type is defined as an unsigned long, which is usually 4 bytes, we can actually create arrays of that size.[10]

Many Large Arrays

There is one more generalization of the quantum file access method that will make it more generally useful: the ability to create more than one array of variable-length items.

The mechanism by which we will accomplish this goal is called the "main object index", which contains the quantum number of the big pointer array for each object; the number of an object is set when the object is created, by a directory facility which we will examine later.

Figure 5.6 shows the path from the main object index through the big pointer array, the IRA segment, and the item index, to finally arrive at the data.

---

10. Of course, this assumes that we have set the parameters of the quantum file to values that allow us to expand the file to a size large enough to hold that much data. The header file "blocki.h" contains the constants BlockSize and MaxFileQuantumCount, which together determine the maximum size of a quantum file. The beginning of that file also contains a number of other constants and structures related to this issue; you should be able to modify the capacity and space efficiency of a quantum file fairly easily after examining that header file.

Figure 5.6: From the main object index to the data

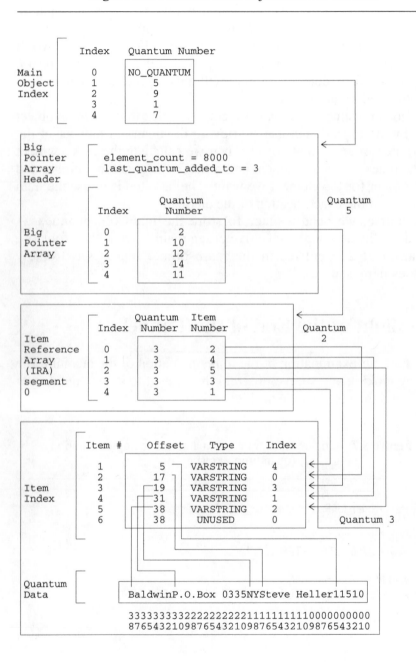

We might use this facility to keep track of both customer records and inventory records, each of which would be logically separate although they may be stored in the same quantum file. In order to facilitate reconstruction of the file if part of the IRA is lost, we won't use the same quantum for items from two different arrays; as a result, the space freed by deleting an item will only be reused when an item is to be added to the same array.

To find an element in a main object, we index into the main object index by the object's number, retrieving the quantum number of the big pointer array for that object. Then we calculate the IRA segment and the index into that segment and retrieve the quantum number and item number for the element we want. The last step is to use the item index to find the exact location of the element.

Of course, we need a place to store the main object index. A normal application might have five or ten main objects; therefore, our allocation of 256 entries in the main object index is extremely generous in most cases.[11]

The Light at the End of the Tunnel

Let's start our examination of the implementation of the quantum file code by looking at a simple program that uses it to store a number of strings and then retrieve them (Figure 5.7).

Figure 5.7: Initial test program for quantum file implementation
(quantum\flextest.cpp)

```
/*TITLE test program for FlexArray and QuantumFile classes*/

/****keyword-flag*** "%v %f %n" */
/* "2 10-May-98,10:37:08 FLEXTEST.CPP" */

/****keyword-flag*** "%v %f %n" */
char FlexTestVersionInfo[] = "2 10-May-98,10:37:08 FLEXTEST.CPP";

extern "C" {
```

---

11. The limit is 256 so that an object number can fit into one byte; this reduces the size of the free space list, as we will see later.

```
#include <time.h>
}

#include <strstrea.h>
#include "common.h"

int main(int argc, char *argv[])
{
        ArrayIndex i;
        String Buf;
        ArrayIndex Size;

//      remove("flextest.qnt");

        FlexArray TestArray;
        FlexArray TestDir;
            String Name;

        QuantumFile QF;
        QF.Open("flextest.qnt");

        TestArray.Open(&QF,"TestArray");
        TestDir.Open(&QF,"Directory");

        Size = TestDir.GetSize();


        for (i = 0; i < Size; i ++)
            {
                    Name = TestDir[i];
                    if (Name != "")
                      cout << i << ": " << TestDir[i] << endl;
            }

        for (i = 0; i < 100; i ++)
            {
            strstream Temp;
            Temp << i;
            Temp >> Buf;
            TestArray[i] = Buf;
            }
#if 0
        for (i = 0; i < 100; i ++)
            {
            cout << TestArray[i] << ' ';
            }
#endif
```

```
        return 0;
}
```

Possibly the most striking feature of this program is how simple it appears, which is a direct consequence of the power of C++. Writing a similar program in C would require much greater knowledge of the implementation of the quantum file algorithm. However, in C++ all we have to know is which header file to include, how to open the quantum file, and how to create a FlexArray object, which behaves like a variable-sized array of variable-sized strings. Once we have dealt with this small set of prerequisites, we can use this extremely powerful and flexible data type in virtually the same way we would use a built-in type.

Let's take a detailed look at exactly how we set up and use a quantum file in this program. First, we have a couple of statements that declare a temporary buffer variable which we'll use to construct data to store in the quantum file and delete any previous version of the quantum file itself. Next, we create a QuantumFile object called QF via the default constructor of the QuantumFile class. Then we call an Open function on that object, supplying the name of the quantum file to be created.

The next statement creates a FlexArray object called TestArray. The arguments to this constructor are a pointer to the QuantumFile object that we'll use to store the data for TestArray, and a name by which we could reuse this same FlexArray object in another program or another execution of this program.

Now we're up to the loop where we will start to use the TestArray object. The loop steps through the first 100 elements of TestArray, assigning each element a String consisting of digits corresponding to the position of that element in the TestArray object. The strstream named Temp is used to format the numeric values of the loop variable i into String values that can be stored in a FlexArray object.

Finally, after we've put the values into TestArray, the second loop displays the values in the TestArray object.

Pay No Attention to the Man Behind the Curtain

At this point, I wouldn't be at all surprised if you had come to the conclusion that I have something up my sleeve ... and you would be right. Underneath this apparent simplicity is a wonderland of complex programming, which I hope I will be able to explain in an understandable way. Let's begin by examining some of these data types we've just seen, in enough detail to demystify them.

The first of these data types is the String. As it happens, this is actually a typedef for a more general type called SVector, so we'll start with the question of exactly what an SVector might be.

An SVector is very much like an array, with the following exceptions:

1. If you try to store something beyond the end of an SVector, you will get an error message rather than a mysterious crash.
2. You can find out how many elements an SVector has, by calling its size member function.
3. You can change the size of an SVector after it has been created, by calling its resize member function.
4. You can assign one SVector of a particular type to another SVector of the same type.
5. You can create an SVector by copying from another SVector of the same type.

While these are very useful characteristics for any type of SVector, they are even more important in one particular type of SVector: the String, which is an SVector of chars. As a specialization of the SVector type, the String has all of the characteristics of any other SVector, but has additional abilities as well. Primary among these is its ability to be read or written using the standard C++ input/output stream functions. This String type, or one very much like it, is one of the most obvious improvements in C++ over C, whose corresponding char* type is notoriously error-prone. In this program, we will use the String data type in much the same way as we would use the char* data type in a C program. Unfortunately, we will not be able to go into detail on the implementation of either the SVector or String classes in this book; we will just use their facilities as described immediately above.

A Very Useful typedef

Another "type" used in this simple test program is ArrayIndex. This is also a typedef, but for a much simpler underlying type: unsigned long.

In this case, the reason I didn't just use the underlying type was to enhance portability. The original version of this program was implemented on a 16-bit compiler, where the definition of ArrayIndex was unsigned short, primarily because it was impossible to create an array or SVector having more than 64K elements. When I ported this program to a 32-bit compiler, I changed the definition of ArrayIndex and several other similar typedefs and recompiled.

I would like to be able to tell you that the program worked without further changes, but that would be a lie: it actually took me a couple of days to get it working again. However, considering the size of the source code for the classes (over 100KB), I was quite happy to take such a short time to port it.

If I had used the explicit type unsigned short everywhere, it would have taken me much longer to figure out which occurrences of that type should be changed to unsigned long and which should remain as they were. As it was, I found a few places where I did not use a typedef or used the wrong one and ran into trouble as a result. Overall, though, I did a pretty good job in using appropriate types originally, which saved me a lot of trouble later.

A Quantum Leap

Now let's start our journey into the interior of the quantum file implementation, starting with the QuantumFile class itself, whose header file is shown in Figure 5.8.

Figure 5.8: Header file for QuantumFile class (quantum\block.h)

```
/*TITLE declarations for block classes*/

/****keyword-flag*** "%v %f %n" */
/* "16 14-Apr-98,22:48:30 BLOCK.H" */

class QuantumFile
```

```
{
public:
QuantumFile();
void Open(String p_FileName="", ArrayIndex p_BufferCount=DefaultBufferCount);
void Flush();
void Close();
long GetReadCount() {return m_ReadCount;}
long GetWriteCount() { return m_WriteCount;}
~QuantumFile();

public:
//used by implementation classes only
 ObjectNumber GetMainObjectCount() {return m_MainObjectCount;}
 ArrayIndex GetMainObjectBlockCount();
 ArrayIndex QGetFreeSpaceListCount() {return m_FreeSpaceListCount;}
 ArrayIndex QGetFreeSpaceListBlockCount();
 void SetFreeSpace(ArrayIndex p_QuantumNumber,
     QFreeSpaceEntry p_FreeSpaceEntry);
 QFreeSpaceEntry QGetFreeSpace(ArrayIndex p_QuantumNumber);
 QuantumNumber FindEmptyBlock();
 QuantumNumber FindSpaceForItem(ObjectNumber p_ObjectNumber,
     ArrayIndex p_ItemSize);
 ArrayIndex GetQuantumNumberAdjustment() {return m_QuantumStartingBlock-1;}
 FreeSpaceBlockPtr MakeFreeSpaceBlockPtr(ArrayIndex p_Index);
 MainObjectBlockPtr MakeMainObjectBlockPtr(ArrayIndex p_Index);
 BigPointerBlockPtr MakeBigPointerBlockPtr(ArrayIndex p_Index);
 LittlePointerBlockPtr MakeLittlePointerBlockPtr(ArrayIndex p_Index);
 LeafBlockPtr MakeLeafBlockPtr(ArrayIndex p_Index);
 Block *MakeBlockResident(ArrayIndex p_BlockNumber);
 void SetModified(ArrayIndex p_BlockNumber);

private:
SVector<Block *> m_Block;
SVector<ArrayIndex> m_BlockNumber;
SVector<char> m_BufferModified;
SVector<ArrayIndex> m_TimeStamp;
String m_FileName;
FILE * m_DosFilePtr;
BlockNumber m_CurrentLowestFreeBlock;
BlockNumber m_MainObjectStartingBlock;
BlockNumber m_FreeSpaceListStartingBlock;
BlockNumber m_QuantumStartingBlock;
ObjectNumber m_MainObjectCount;
ArrayIndex m_FreeSpaceListCount;
ArrayIndex m_Counter;
FreeSpaceArrayPtr *m_FreeSpaceArray;
MainObjectArrayPtr *m_MainObjectArray;
long m_ReadCount;
```

```
long m_WriteCount;

void Position(ArrayIndex p_BlockNumber);
void Write(ArrayIndex p_BlockNumber);
void Read(ArrayIndex p_BlockNumber);
QuantumFile(const QuantumFile&);
QuantumFile& operator=(const QuantumFile&);
};
```

I can't say that I'm completely happy with the design of this class. Ideally, the user of any class should not have to worry about any member data or member variables that the user cannot or should not use. Unfortunately, this is not easily accomplished in C++. I believe it is worthwhile to digress slightly here to discuss the reasons why this is so.

First, let's examine the difficulty of "hiding" private and protected member variables from the class user. The technical problem here is that the compiler cannot allocate space for a variable unless its size is known. This implies that you cannot create a variable of a given class without access to its interface definition, which must in turn include the definitions of all of its member variables.

This does not allow the class user to use those member variables unless they are public, so we don't have to worry about non-member functions accidentally altering member variables. However, it does mean that the user of a class must ensure that all of the data types needed in the declaration of a class are available when the header for that class is compiled, and that the names of those data types do not conflict with any previously defined names. This can be a source of considerable difficulty when trying to use a fairly large library in a context other than the one in which it was developed, which of course reduces the payoff that such reuse would otherwise provide.

The other problem with the design of this class is that it defines a number of functions that application programmers have no need for. These functions are intended for use by other classes that contribute to the functionality of the quantum file implementation. You might think that I could simply make these functions private to prevent their being called by outside classes. Unfortunately, I wasn't able to do that with Microsoft Visual C++ 5.0, one of the compilers with which this code must work, as that compiler apparently cannot understand friend declarations that specify classes that are nested within other classes, as some of mine are. Even if this did work, I'd still prefer to spare the application programmer the details of these functions.

Is there a solution to either or both of these problems? Yes, in fact both of these can be remedied. Let's start with the data problem.

Data Hiding

The standard solution to avoid exposing member variables to the application programmer is to create a secondary data structure that contains the actual data for the object, and include only a pointer to such a structure in the main object. Because the compiler knows the size of a pointer to a structure without having to see the definition of the structure itself, the header file that defines this secondary structure can be included only when needed in the implementation of the class. This frees the application programmer from any concern about the representation of the data.

Function Hiding

What about those functions that the application programmer doesn't need to (and shouldn't) call? This can be solved in much the same way as the data problem. In this case, however, the pointer in the visible class points to an object of a class that supplies the additional functions needed by the other implementation classes. Because the client program would not include the header file that defines this secondary class, it could not access those additional functions. Of course, the other implementation classes would include that header file so that they could access the additional functions as needed.

The Real World Intrudes

Why didn't I implement either of these solutions (or better yet, both)? Because doing so would have required wholesale changes to the implementation, and I ran out of time. Of course, had I considered these issues when I was first creating these classes, they would have been fairly simple to solve, but I didn't think of them at that time.

In any event, the design is usable as it stands, even if it could be improved, so let's move on to how we can use it in its present form. We'll start with the functions that are needed by client programs such as our test program flextest.cpp. Figure 5.9 shows the first of these functions, QuantumFile::QuantumFile().

Figure 5.9: The default constructor for the QuantumFile class (from quantum\block.cpp)

```
QuantumFile::QuantumFile():
m_Block(ArrayIndex(0)),
m_BlockNumber(ArrayIndex(0)),
m_BufferModified(ArrayIndex(0)),
m_TimeStamp(ArrayIndex(0)),
m_FileName(""),
m_DosFilePtr(0),
m_CurrentLowestFreeBlock(0),
m_MainObjectStartingBlock(0),
m_FreeSpaceListStartingBlock(0),
m_QuantumStartingBlock(0),
m_MainObjectCount(0),
m_FreeSpaceListCount(0),
m_Counter(0),
m_FreeSpaceArray(0),
m_MainObjectArray(0)
{
}
```

As you can see, this function's implementation consists entirely of initialization expressions in the member initialization list. We'll look at each of the member variables of this class in detail when we get to the functions that use them. For now, I'll just mention that they are all needed to keep track of the status of the quantum file and the buffers that maintain parts of its data in memory.

Next, let's take a look at Figure 5.10, which shows the first "regular member function" in this class, QuantumFile::Open. This is a good place to start, since we can't do anything to a quantum file until we open it, as with any other file.

Figure 5.10: The Open function for the QuantumFile class (from quantum\block.cpp)

```cpp
void QuantumFile::Open(String p_FileName, ArrayIndex p_BufferCount)
{
    QuantumFileHeaderStruct QFHS;
    char *TempBlock;
    QuantumNumber *TempMainObjectBlock;
    QFreeSpaceEntry *TempFreeSpaceBlock;
    ArrayIndex i;
    int FileCreation;
    QFreeSpaceEntry TempFreeSpaceEntry;
    int ProgramVersion;
    int FileVersion;

    m_ReadCount = 0;
    m_WriteCount = 0;
    m_Block.SetSize(p_BufferCount);
    m_BlockNumber.SetSize(p_BufferCount);
    m_BufferModified.SetSize(p_BufferCount);
    m_TimeStamp.SetSize(p_BufferCount);

    if (p_FileName == "")
        {
        m_DosFilePtr = 0;
        return;
        }

    m_DosFilePtr = fopen(p_FileName,"r+b");

    if (m_DosFilePtr == NULL) /* file does not exist */
        {
        FileCreation = TRUE;
        m_DosFilePtr = fopen(p_FileName,"w+b"); /* create it */

        TempBlock = new char[BlockSize];
        TempMainObjectBlock = (QuantumNumber *)TempBlock;
        TempFreeSpaceBlock = (QFreeSpaceEntry *)TempBlock;

        memset((void *)&QFHS,0,sizeof(QuantumFileHeaderStruct));
        QFHS.main_object_index_count = MainObjectIndexCount;
        QFHS.free_space_list_count = MaxFileQuantumCount;
        strcpy(QFHS.quantum_version_info,program_version_info);

        QFHS.main_object_index_offset = BlockSize;
        QFHS.free_space_list_offset = QFHS.main_object_index_offset+
            BlockSize*((MainObjectIndexCount-1)/MainObjectEntriesPerBlock+1);
```

```
QFHS.starting_quantum_offset = QFHS.free_space_list_offset+
    BlockSize*((MaxFileQuantumCount-1)/FreeSpaceEntriesPerBlock+1);

fseek(m_DosFilePtr,0,SEEK_SET);
memset(TempBlock,0,BlockSize);
fwrite(TempBlock,1,BlockSize,m_DosFilePtr); // clear block 0

fseek(m_DosFilePtr,0,SEEK_SET);
fwrite(&QFHS,1,sizeof(QuantumFileHeaderStruct), m_DosFilePtr);

/* clear the main object index */
memset(TempMainObjectBlock,0,BlockSize);
TempMainObjectBlock[0] = NoQuantum;
fseek(m_DosFilePtr,QFHS.main_object_index_offset,SEEK_SET);
fwrite(TempMainObjectBlock,BlockSize,1,m_DosFilePtr);

/* clear the free space list */
TempFreeSpaceEntry.m_FreeSpaceCode = AvailableQuantum;
TempFreeSpaceEntry.m_ObjectNumber = 0;
for (i = 0; i < FreeSpaceEntriesPerBlock; i ++)
    TempFreeSpaceBlock[i] = TempFreeSpaceEntry;
TempFreeSpaceBlock[0].m_FreeSpaceCode = 0; /* Q #0 doesn't exist */
ArrayIndex FreeSpaceCount = (QFHS.free_space_list_count-1)/
    FreeSpaceEntriesPerBlock+1;
for (i = 0; i < FreeSpaceCount; i ++)
    {
    fseek(m_DosFilePtr,QFHS.free_space_list_offset+i*BlockSize,SEEK_SET);
    fwrite(TempFreeSpaceBlock,sizeof(QFreeSpaceEntry),
    FreeSpaceEntriesPerBlock,m_DosFilePtr);
    TempFreeSpaceBlock[0].m_FreeSpaceCode = AvailableQuantum;
    }
delete [] TempBlock;
}
else
    {
    FileCreation = FALSE;
    fread(&QFHS,1,sizeof(QuantumFileHeaderStruct),m_DosFilePtr);
    ProgramVersion = atoi(program_version_info);
    FileVersion = atoi(QFHS.quantum_version_info);
    if (ProgramVersion != FileVersion)
        {
        printf("Program version %d does not match file version %d.\n",
        ProgramVersion,FileVersion);
//      exit(1);   // file is newer than program, so forget it
        }
    }

m_MainObjectStartingBlock = QFHS.main_object_index_offset / BlockSize;
```

```
    m_FreeSpaceListStartingBlock = QFHS.free_space_list_offset / BlockSize;
    m_QuantumStartingBlock = QFHS.starting_quantum_offset / BlockSize;
    m_MainObjectCount = QFHS.main_object_index_count;
    m_FreeSpaceListCount = QFHS.free_space_list_count;

    for (i = 0; i < p_BufferCount; i ++)
        {
        m_Block[i] = new Block;
        m_BlockNumber[i] = BadBlockNumber;
        m_BufferModified[i] = FALSE;
        m_TimeStamp[i] = 0;
        }

    m_FreeSpaceArray = new FreeSpaceArrayPtr(this);
    m_MainObjectArray = new MainObjectArrayPtr(this);

    if (FileCreation == TRUE) // set up main object name object
        (*m_MainObjectArray)->CreateMainObject("Directory", MainObjectDirectory,
            MainObjectIndexCount,MainObjectIndexCount);
}
```

After declaring a number of variables, this function initializes the variables that keep track of the number of physical read and write operations for benchmarking purposes (m_ReadCount and m_WriteCount, respectively). Then it resizes the SVectors that keep track of the block buffers (m_Block), which quantum is in each block buffer (m_BlockNumber), whether each block buffer has been modified and therefore needs to be written back to the disk (m_BufferModified), and the "time stamp" for each block buffer that indicates how recently it has been accessed (m_TimeStamp). We'll see how each of these variables is used in the program as we go through the code.

The next few lines check whether the caller has supplied a non-null file name for the quantum file. If not, we bail out, because we need a valid file name to use when we open the file to store our data.

Assuming that we do have some sort of file name, we try to open the file for reading, to see whether it is already there. If fopen returns NULL, indicating that the file doesn't exist yet, we create the file, clear the QuantumFileHeaderStruct structure called QFHS, set the main_object_index_count and free_space_list_count to their default values, and copy the current program_version_info into the quantum_version_info structure element.

The next operation is to initialize the member variables of QFHS that keep track of the offsets in the file where the main_object_index, the free_space_list, and the quantum file data area begin, so that these areas of the file can be located when we open the file again.

Since we haven't created any main objects yet, our next task is to clear the main object index, setting it to zeros (which indicates available entries, as quantum number zero is not used), except for the entry for object number zero, which is set to NoQuantum; we will not allow a main object number zero, for better error control. We also write the header block to the file at this point.

The last operation in the new file initialization is to set up the free space list to indicate that all quanta have the maximum available free space, except of course for quantum zero, which is not used.

Of course, the process of opening an already existing quantum file starts differently; we have to read in the quantum file header and check whether it was created by the same version of the program. The current program simply tests whether the version of the program that created the file is different from the one reading it and aborts if they are different. A production program would use this information to determine whether the versions were compatible, so that if we changed the program in a way that makes old files unusable, we could warn the user that the file is of an old type and should be converted. Alternatively, we might automatically convert it to a new format; in either case, it is essential that we know what version of our program created the file. After we have taken care of this detail, the rest of the code for opening either an old or a new file is the same.

We are almost done with the initialization, but there are a few more data structures to handle. First, we have to calculate the block numbers where the main object list, the free space list, and the data area start. Then we initialize the member variables that keep track of the current number of main objects and the number of elements in the free space list. Then we initialize the SVectors of block buffers, block numbers, modified flags, and time stamps. Next, we initialize variables that will allow us to access the free space list and main object list; we'll get into exactly how that works later.

Finally, if we have created a new quantum file (as opposed to opening one that already existed), we create a main object called "Directory", which we will use to keep track of the names of the main objects that the user will create.

Now let's take a look at Figure 5.11, which shows the next user function, QuantumFile::Flush. This function is used to ensure that all data written to the quantum file has actually been stored on the disk. It's a good idea to call Flush whenever you have finished with a logical portion of your data updating, to make sure that a power failure or other crash doesn't lose data.

Figure 5.11: The Flush function for the QuantumFile class (from quantum\block.cpp)

```
void QuantumFile::Flush()
{
    if (m_DosFilePtr)
        {
        for (ArrayIndex i=0; i < m_Block.GetSize(); i ++)
            {
            if (m_BufferModified[i])
                Write(i);
            }
        }
}
```

This isn't a very complicated function, but it does show how the m_BufferModified SVector is used: Each buffer whose flag in that SVector is TRUE is written to the disk via the Write member function. Any buffer whose flag is not TRUE has not been modified since it was last read from the disk, so there is no reason to write it back to the disk. Avoiding unnecessary writes is very helpful in reducing disk I/O and improving the speed of the program. The Write function resets the flag for any buffer it writes, so if we called Flush twice in a row, no buffers would be written out on the second execution.[12]

The final function that we're going to cover in this class at this point is Close (Figure 5.12). As its name suggests, this function closes the quantum file and takes care of all the housekeeping required at that time. However, you generally won't call this function explicitly, because it is called automatically when the QuantumFile object is destroyed at the end of its scope, as you can see by looking at the QuantumFile destructor (Figure 5.13).

---

12. By the way, there is a possible optimization that could be employed here: sorting the buffers to be rewritten to the disk in order of their quantum numbers (i.e., their positions in the file). This could improve performance in systems where the hard disk controller doesn't already provide this service; however, most (if not all) modern disk systems take care of this for us, so sorting by quantum number would not provide any benefit.

Figure 5.12: The Close function for the QuantumFile class (from quantum\block.cpp)

```
void QuantumFile::Close()
{
    Flush();

    fclose(m_DosFilePtr);
    m_DosFilePtr = 0;

    delete m_FreeSpaceArray;
    delete m_MainObjectArray;

    for (ArrayIndex i = 0; i < m_Block.GetSize(); i ++)
        delete m_Block[i];
}
```

Figure 5.13: The destructor for the QuantumFile class (from quantum\block.cpp)

```
QuantumFile::~QuantumFile()
{
    Close();
}
```

Allowing the destructor to close the file automatically is easier and (more important) safer than closing the file explicitly, because it's not always easy to determine when all of the objects in the quantum file are inactive. Hence, I recommend allowing the compiler to take care of closing the file.

Flexible Flying

Now that we've taken a look at the member functions of the QuantumFile class that user programs are concerned with, let's do the same with the FlexArray class. In the process, we'll start to delve into the underlying layers of the quantum file implementation in more detail. Let's start with the interface for the FlexArray class, which is shown in Figure 5.14.

Figure 5.14: The interface for the FlexArray class (from quantum\newquant.h)

```
class FlexArrayRef;

class FlexArray
{
protected:
      MainObjectArrayPtr m_MOA;
      ObjectNumber m_MOAIndex;
      ArrayIndex m_ElementCount;
      ArrayIndex m_MaxElementCount;
public:
      FlexArray();

      FlexArray(QuantumFile *p_QF, ModifiableElement p_ArrayName,
      ArrayIndex p_ElementCount=1, ArrayIndex p_MaxElementCount=UINT_MAX-1);

      FlexArray(MainObjectArrayPtr p_MOA, ObjectNumber p_MOAIndex);

      FlexArrayRef operator[](ArrayIndex p_ElementIndex);

      void Open(QuantumFile *p_QF, ModifiableElement p_ArrayName,
      ArrayIndex p_ElementCount=1, ArrayIndex p_MaxElementCount=UINT_MAX-1);

      ArrayIndex GetSize() {return m_ElementCount;}
};
```

As before, we'll postpone discussion of the member variables of this class until we see how they are used in the member functions. We'll start with the normal constructor for the FlexArray class, which is shown in Figure 5.15.

Figure 5.15: The normal constructor for the FlexArray class (from quantum\newquant.cpp)

```
FlexArray::FlexArray(QuantumFile *p_QF, ModifiableElement p_ArrayName,
      ArrayIndex p_ElementCount, ArrayIndex p_MaxElementCount)
{
      Open(p_QF,p_ArrayName,p_ElementCount,p_MaxElementCount);
}
```

As you can see, this function simply calls an Open function in the same class to do all of the actual work. The purpose of this handoff is to allow the user to create a FlexArray via the default FlexArray constructor before opening the quantum file and fill in the details later via an explicit Open call. Now that I've cleared that up, let's take a look at the function that actually does the work, which is shown in Figure 5.16.

Figure 5.16: The Open function for the FlexArray class (from quantum\newquant.cpp)

```
void FlexArray::Open(QuantumFile *p_QF, ModifiableElement p_ArrayName,
    ArrayIndex p_ElementCount, ArrayIndex p_MaxElementCount)
{
    m_MOA = MainObjectArrayPtr(p_QF);

    m_MOAIndex = m_MOA->FindObjectByName(p_ArrayName);

    if (m_MOAIndex == NoObject)
        {
        m_MOAIndex = m_MOA->FindAvailableObject();
        m_MOA->CreateMainObject(p_ArrayName,m_MOAIndex,
            p_ElementCount, p_MaxElementCount);
        }

    m_ElementCount = m_MOA->GetMainObjectElementCount(m_MOAIndex);
    m_MaxElementCount = m_MOA->GetMainObjectMaxElementCount(m_MOAIndex);
}
```

The header for this function shouldn't be too alarming. The first argument is simply the address of the quantum file object in which the FlexArray will be created. The second argument is the name under which the FlexArray will be stored in the quantum file's directory, which will make it accessible to another program or a later run of this program. The ModifiableElement type is just another name for a String, left over from a previous incarnation of that type. The third argument is the initial number of elements that the FlexArray will contain, and the last argument is the maximum number of elements to which the FlexArray will expand if necessary. If you look at the interface for this class, you'll notice that these last two arguments have default values of 1 and UINT_MAX-1 elements, respectively. Therefore, if you don't have any idea how large a FlexArray might need to be, you can omit these arguments and it will expand as needed.

Now we're up to the first statement inside the function, which appears innocent enough. It assigns a value to a member variable called m_MOA, which stands for "Main Object Array". This member variable can then be used to look up the name of the FlexArray in the quantum file directory, as well as to access a number of other attributes of the quantum file. But what is the type of m_MOA, and how does it give us access to the quantum file attributes?

To answer these questions, we're going to have to get into some fairly complex implementation and language issues. We'll start this excursion with a look at the interface for the MainObjectArrayPtr class, shown in Figure 5.17.

Figure 5.17: The interface for the MainObjectArrayPtr class (from quantum\newquant.h)

```
class MainObjectArrayPtr
{
protected:
class MainObjectArray
{
friend MainObjectArrayPtr;
protected:
QuantumFile *m_QuantumFile;
SVector<MainObjectBlockPtr> m_BlockPtr;
ObjectNumber m_MainObjectCount;
ArrayIndex m_MainObjectBlockCount;
ArrayIndex m_CurrentLowestFreeObject;
int m_ReferenceCount;

public:
MainObjectArray();
MainObjectArray(QuantumFile *p_QuantumFile);
~MainObjectArray();

MainObjectEntry Get(ArrayIndex p_Index);

void Set(ArrayIndex p_Index, MainObjectEntry p_Entry);

ObjectNumber FindAvailableObject();

ObjectNumber GetMainObjectCount() {return m_MainObjectCount;}

ModifiableElement GetModifiableElement(ArrayIndex p_MainObjectNumber,
```

```
            ArrayIndex p_ElementIndex);

    AccessVector<Ulong> GetAccessVectorUlong(
            ArrayIndex p_MainObjectNumber, ArrayIndex p_ElementIndex);

    void SetModified(ArrayIndex p_MainObjectNumber,
            ArrayIndex p_ElementIndex);

    int PutElement(ObjectNumber p_MainObjectNumber,
            ArrayIndex p_ElementIndex, ModifiableElement p_Element);

    void CreateMainObject(ModifiableElement p_ObjectName,
            ObjectNumber p_ObjectNumber, ArrayIndex p_ElementCount=100,
            ArrayIndex p_MaxElementCount=UINT_MAX-1);

    ArrayIndex GetMainObjectElementCount(ArrayIndex p_MainObjectNumber);

    ArrayIndex GetMainObjectMaxElementCount(ArrayIndex p_MainObjectNumber);

    ObjectNumber FindObjectByName(ModifiableElement p_ObjectName);

    ArrayIndex GrowMainObject(ObjectNumber p_ObjectNumber, ArrayIndex
    p_NewElementCount);
    };

    MainObjectArray *m_MOA;

    public:
    MainObjectArrayPtr();
    MainObjectArrayPtr(const MainObjectArrayPtr& p_MOAP);
    MainObjectArrayPtr(QuantumFile *p_QuantumFile);
    MainObjectArray *operator->();
    MainObjectArrayPtr& operator=(const MainObjectArrayPtr& p_MOAP);
    ~MainObjectArrayPtr();
    }; // end of MainObjectArray
```

You will notice that this class has an embedded class called MainObjectArray defined within it, and that the embedded class has quite a few member functions. You may also notice that the MainObjectArrayPtr class itself has only a few member functions, most of which are the standard "structural" member functions — the normal and default constructors, the destructor, and the assignment operator. One of the constructors is the conversion function that constructs a MainObjectArrayPtr object from a QuantumFile pointer (used in the FlexArray Open function), and the others are the default constructor and copy constructor. However, there is one member function that is anything but standard: operator->. Why would we want to redefine that operator, and what can a custom version of operator-> do?

All Hope Abandon, Ye Who Enter Here?

Before we get through with this question, we will have entered a realm of C++ where relatively few have trespassed. I don't believe in adding complexity for the sake of complexity, so why would I use a feature of C++ that most C++ programmers have never dealt with?

Because we need this feature to improve the ease of use and reliability of programs using this quantum file access method implementation. A little history lesson is appropriate here so you can see that I'm not speaking from a solely theoretical perspective.

The first edition of this book included an implementation of the quantum file access method written in C.[13] It had many of the features that the current implementation has, but it was much harder to use. The main problem was that the user program had to deal with memory allocation issues, including remembering to free memory for variables whose storage was assigned inside the quantum file code. In addition, the syntax of a quantum file "array" was much less convenient than dealing with a built-in array. It was obvious to me that resolving all of these issues so that the user could ignore the inner workings of the quantum file would greatly improve the usability of this algorithm.

Unfortunately, this isn't possible in C; however, a major impetus behind the creation of C++ was to make it possible for class library designers to provide such facilities. Since the quantum file access method would benefit greatly from such an approach, I decided to rewrite it in C++.

Rewriting History

Why am I using the word "rewrite", rather than "convert", "translate", or other euphemisms? Judging from the number of ads for "C/C++ programmers" I see in the newspapers, some employers have the

---

13. The second edition also included this C implementation along with an earlier, less capable, version of the C++ implementation we're examining here.

notion that switching to C++ can be accomplished by changing source file extensions to ".cpp" and recompiling. After removing some syntax errors revealed by the stricter type checking of the C++ compiler, the program compiles and runs as it did before. What's so difficult about object-oriented programming?

If you are one of these employers, or you have tried the above experiment yourself and now believe that you are a "C++ programmer", let me break the news to you gently: all you have accomplished is to switch to the C subset of C++, which has nothing to do with object-oriented programming. Virtually none of the code or design from the original quantum file implementation has survived the transition to object orientation unscathed, despite the fact that, according to an expert on object-oriented design, that original C implementation was "object-oriented"!

However, my loss (if that's what it was) can be your gain: I am going to break a long-standing tradition of object-oriented design literature by disclosing not only the final design but also many of the missteps, errors, and difficulties that ensued from my original determination to tackle this rather complex project. So, with no further ado, let's begin with an often neglected concept which is at the core of the implementation of this project: operator overloading.

Warning: Overload!

One of the most powerful mechanisms for hiding the details of implementation from the class user in C++ is operator overloading, which means defining (or in some cases redefining) the semantics of one or more of the standard operators +, -, =, and so forth, as they apply to class objects. For better or worse, the semantics of these operators cannot be changed as they apply to "intrinsic" data types, so the calculation 2+2 is always going to result in 4; this restriction is probably necessary, as the potential confusion could be horrendous.[14]

---

14. Another restriction in C++ operator overloading is that it's impossible to make up your own operators. According to Bjarne Stroustrup, this facility has been carefully considered by the standards committee and has failed of adoption due to difficulties with operator precedence and binding strength. Apparently, it was the exponentiation operator that was the deciding factor; it's the first operator that users from the numerical community usually want to define, but its mathematical properties don't match the precedence and binding rules of any of the "normal" C++ operators.

A good example of the most common type of use for this facility is the implementation of +, -, etc., for manipulating Complex class objects, following the rules of complex arithmetic. The ability to provide this sort of intuitive operation to the number-crunching user is starting to make C++ (with the proper class libraries, of course) a viable alternative to FORTRAN, long the dominant language for such users.

Hello, Operator?

As usual, it's probably best to start with a relatively simple example: in this case, we'll look at an example of overloading operator-.[15] Consider the program in Figure 5.18.

Figure 5.18: Overloading operator-

```
#include <math.h>
#include <stdio.h>

class Point
{
protected:
double m_xValue;
double m_yValue;

public:
Point(double p_xValue=0, double p_yValue=0)
{
        m_xValue = p_xValue;
        m_yValue = p_yValue;
};

double operator-(const Point& p_Point)
{
        double xDiff;
        double yDiff;

        xDiff = m_xValue - p_Point.m_xValue;
        yDiff = m_yValue - p_Point.m_yValue;

        return sqrt(xDiff*xDiff + yDiff*yDiff);
```

15. I'm not claiming this is a good use for overloading; it's only for tutorial purposes.

```
};

};

main()
{

Point x(1,1);
Point y(4,5);

printf("%g\n",x-y);
}
```

As you can see, I've created a very simplified version of the
dreaded Point class, used in innumerable textbooks to represent a point
on the Euclidean plane. The result of running our sample program is
5, which is the distance between the Point (1,1) and the Point (4,5),
calculated by the normal Euclidean calculation:

```
Distance = sqrt(xdiff*xdiff + ydiff*ydiff)
```

where xdiff is the difference between the x coordinates of the two
Points, and ydiff is the difference between their y coordinates; sqrt, of
course, represents the square root function.

The "magic" is in the definition of operator-, which is the syntax for
redefining an operator; in this case it's the subtraction operator.
When the compiler sees the expression x-y, it looks for a definition of
operator- that is specified for class Point, taking an argument which is
also of class Point. Since there is such a definition, the compiler
generates a call to the code specified in that definition. Had there not
been such a definition, a syntax error would have resulted, since the
compiler doesn't have any built-in knowledge of how to subtract two
Points.

The Mask of Arrow

Operator overloading doesn't have to be terribly complicated, as that
example illustrates. However, there's a trick to the overloading of
operator->. When we overload other operators, such as our earlier
example of operator-, our code takes over the implementation of the
operator completely. That is, the result of calling our operator is

whatever we say it is; in the operator- example, it's the double result of the Euclidean distance formula. However, this is not true with operator->; in that case alone, a different scheme is followed by the compiler. Figure 5.19 shows some code derived from an early version of the project. How does the compiler interpret it?[16]

Figure 5.19: Dangerous operator-> overloading

```
class BlockPtr
{
protected:
char *m_BlockData;
char *MakeBlockResident();

public:
BlockPtr();
BlockPtr *operator->();
char Get(int p_Index);
};

BlockPtr::BlockPtr()
{
      m_BlockData = 0;
}

BlockPtr *BlockPtr::operator->()
{
      m_BlockData = MakeBlockResident();
      return this;
}

char *BlockPtr::MakeBlockResident()
{
      return new char[1000];
}

char BlockPtr::Get(int p_Index)
{
      return m_BlockData[p_Index];
}

main()
```

---

16. Warning: do not compile and execute the program in Figure 5.19. Although it will compile, it reads from random locations, which may cause a core dump on some systems.

```
{
    BlockPtr X;
    BlockPtr *Y;

    X->Get(1);
    Y->Get(1);
    X.Get(1);
}
```

The line X->Get(1); will be compiled as follows:
1. Since X is not a pointer to any type, its class definition is examined for a definition of operator->.
2. Since this definition is found, a call to that code is inserted in the function being compiled.
3. Then the return value of the operator-> code is examined. Since it is a pointer type (BlockPtr *, to be exact), the compiler continues by generating code to call BlockPtr->Get(int) with this equal to the result returned by operator->, which is the same BlockPtr that we started with.

Type-Safety First

So far, this is doing exactly what we wanted it to do. However, there is one serious problem with this method of implementing operator->, which is illustrated by what happens when the line Y->Get(1); is compiled.

Unlike our previous example, Y *is* a pointer (to a BlockPtr); therefore, the compiler doesn't look for a definition of operator->, but merely generates code to call BlockPtr->Get(int) with this equal to Y. As a result, our overloaded operator is never called.

Much the same problem will occur when the line X.Get(1); is compiled. The compiler is happy to generate a call to BlockPtr.Get(int) with this being equal to the address of X; again, though, our custom operator-> code won't be executed.

The reason for this problem is that the compiler stops looking for operator-> overloading whenever an actual pointer is found. After all, if you already have a pointer in a place where a pointer is needed, you must have what you want! Obviously, we're going to have to come up with a type-safe solution, so we can't accidentally use the wrong syntax and end up with a nasty bug.[17]

The solution is to have not one, but two classes involved in the virtual memory mechanism, an "outer" (or *handle*) class and an "inner" (or *body*) class.[18] The handle class has two primary functions: the initializing of a body class object and the overloading of operator-> to return a pointer to that body class object, which actually does the work. Figure 5.20 presents this solution.

Figure 5.20: Type-safe operator-> overloading

```
class BlockPtr
{
class Block
{
friend BlockPtr;
protected:
char *m_BlockData;
char *MakeBlockResident();
Block();

public:
char Get(int p_Index);
};

protected:
Block m_Block;

public:
Block *operator->();
BlockPtr();
};


BlockPtr::Block::Block()
```

---

17. By the way, this isn't just a theoretical problem: it happened to me during the development of this program.

18. This is an example of the "handle/body" class paradigm, described in *Advanced C++: Programming Styles and Idioms*, by James O. Coplien (Addison-Wesley Publishing Company, Reading, Massachusetts, 1992). Warning: as its title indicates, this is **not** an easy book; however, it does reward careful study by those who already have a solid grasp of C++ fundamentals. For a kinder, gentler introduction to several advanced C++ idioms of wide applicability, see my *Who's Afraid of More C++?* (AP Professional, San Diego, California, 1998).

```
{
     m_BlockData = 0;
}

BlockPtr::Block *BlockPtr::operator->()
{
     m_Block.m_BlockData = m_Block.MakeBlockResident();
     return &m_Block;
}

char *BlockPtr::Block::MakeBlockResident()
{
     return new char[1000];
}

char BlockPtr::Block::Get(int p_Index)
{
     return m_BlockData[p_Index];
}

main()
{
     BlockPtr X;
     BlockPtr *Y;
     BlockPtr::Block Z; // illegal; the constructor is protected

     X->Get(1); // okay; goes through operator-> to Block object
     Y->Get(1); // won't compile, since BlockPtr doesn't have Get
     X.Get(1);  // won't compile, for the same reason
}
```

One interesting thing about this program is that the main program refers to the Get function in exactly the same way as it did before: in fact, the only difference visible to the class user is that the compiler is now able to prevent him (and us) from compiling the incorrect references as we did before.

However, there are some changes to the internals that deserve comment. First of all, in the class definition, the previous BlockPtr class has been renamed to Block and made a nested class of a new BlockPtr class. The reason for the renaming is to prevent unnecessary changes to the user's code; that was successful, as noted above. Another design decision whose justification is not quite as obvious is the use of a nested class rather than a freestanding class. Why is this appropriate?

Hidden Virtues

Since the purpose of the nested Block class is solely to add type safety, rather than to provide any visible functionality, nesting it inside the BlockPtr class reduces "name space pollution". That is, if the user needs a Block class for some other purpose, its name won't conflict with this one. Such potential conflicts are going to become more serious as the use of class libraries increases; we should do our part to "preserve the environment" when possible.[19]

The fact that the Block class is visible only to members of its enclosing class, BlockPtr, is responsible for the somewhat odd appearance of the member function declarations in Figure 5.20. For example, what are we to make of the declaration "char BlockPtr::Block::Get(int p_Index);"?

Of course, we C++ programmers are used to "qualified" function names, such as Block::Get. But why do we need two qualifiers? Because the compiler knows the meaning of Block only in the context of BlockPtr; that's what prevents the global name pollution that would ensue if Block were declared outside of BlockPtr. This means that we could, for example, have another class called Block nested inside another enclosing class called NewBlockPtr. If that Block class had a Get member function, we could declare it as "char NewBlockPtr::Block::Get(int p_Index);", and the compiler would have no problem telling which Block::Get we meant. Similarly, an unadorned "Block::Get(int p_Index);" would be yet another completely distinct function.[20]

One more safety feature in this new arrangement is worthy of note: the constructor for Block is protected, so that the user can't accidentally create one and use it instead of referencing it through a BlockPtr object the way we intend. This isn't very likely anyway, since the user would have to specify BlockPtr::Block as the type, which isn't easy to do by accident; however, according to the principles of object-oriented programming, it is best to hide the internals of our classes whenever possible, so that class user code can't depend on those internals. That

---

19. In order to solve this problem in a more general way, the ANSI standards committee for C++ has approved the addition of "namespaces", which allow the programmer to specify the library from which one or more functions are to be taken in order to prevent name conflicts.

20. Of course, there are other ways to accomplish the goal of protecting the class user from concern about internals of a given class, as we've discussed briefly in the sections titled "Data Hiding" and "Function Hiding".

restriction makes it possible for us to improve the implementation of our classes without breaking user code.

Polite Pointing

Now that we've investigated the notion of redefining operator->, let's return to the MainObjectArrayPtr class that we were discussing a little while ago. We'll start with Figure 5.21, which shows the code for the normal constructor for that class.

Figure 5.21: The normal constructor for MainObjectArrayPtr (from quantum\newquant.cpp)

```
MainObjectArrayPtr::MainObjectArrayPtr(QuantumFile *p_QuantumFile)
{
    m_MOA = new MainObjectArray(p_QuantumFile);
    m_MOA->m_ReferenceCount = 1;
}
```

This function is fairly simple. It creates a new MainObjectArray object using the normal constructor for that class. This is the "body" object that will actually do the work of both of these classes. Then it sets the *reference count* of that object to 1, indicating that there is one MainObjectArray "handle" object using that "body" object.

The general idea of reference counting is fairly simple, as most great ideas are (after you understand them, at least). It's inefficient to copy a lot of data whenever we set one variable to the same value as another; on the other hand, copying a pointer to the data is much easier. However, we have to consider how we will know when we can delete the data being pointed to, which will be when no one needs the data anymore.

One way to share data safely in such a situation is to write the constructor(s), destructor, and assignment operator to keep track of the number of objects that are using a particular body object, and when there are no more users of that object, to delete it.[21] We'll see

---

21. If we had any functions that could change the contents of a shared object, they would also have to be modified to prevent undesirable interactions between "separate" handle objects that share data. However, we don't have any such functions in this case.

how this works in the case of the MainObjectArray body class and its MainObjectArrayPtr handle class; the implementation is much the same in the other handle/body classes in this program.

However, right now we're more interested in how we can use operator-> in the FlexArray::Open function (Figure 5.16). After creating a member variable called m_MOA via the normal constructor of the MainObjectArrayPtr class, the next line in the Open function invokes MainObjectArrayPtr::operator-> (Figure 5.22).

Figure 5.22: MainObjectArrayPtr::operator-> (from quantum\newquant.cpp)

```
MainObjectArrayPtr::MainObjectArray *MainObjectArrayPtr::operator->()
{
    return m_MOA;
}
```

Given the definition of operator-> in Figure 5.22, how will the compiler interpret the expression m_MOA->FindObjectByName, which is used in the function FlexArray::Open?

1. Since m_MOA is not a pointer to any type, the interface of its class (MainObjectArrayPtr) is examined for a definition of operator->.
2. Since there is such a definition, a call to that code is inserted in the function being compiled.
3. Then the return value of the operator-> code is examined. Since it is a pointer type (MainObjectArray *, to be exact), the compiler continues by generating code to call MainObjectArray->FindObjectByName with this equal to the result returned by operator->, which is the address of the body object of the MainObjectArrayPtr that we started with. Of course, the same analysis applies to the other uses of the m_MOA object in the Open function as well as the other functions that use handle objects.

Now let's continue with the analysis of the Open function in the FlexArray class. The statement we've just examined calls a function called FindObjectByName, which returns an index into the main object array. If the name supplied in the call was in fact the name of an existing object in the main object array, then the returned value will be the element number of that object in the main object array. On the other hand, if the specified name was not found in the main object array, the returned value will be the special value NoObject. In that case, Open will use another member function of MainObjectArray, namely FindAvailableObject, to locate a free element in the main object array. Then it will call the CreateMainObject function to create a new main object which will use that free element.

At this point in the function, we have a valid index into the main object array for our FlexArray, whether it existed previously or was just created. Finally, we retrieve the current and maximum element counts for the FlexArray object.

Now that we have covered the Open function in the FlexArray class, there's only one other function in that class that could use a significant amount of explanation: the implementation of operator []. However, I'm going to postpone coverage of that function until the next chapter, where we'll be examining the somewhat complex task of making one of our data types look as much like an array as possible.

In the meantime, we should go over the rest of the member functions of the MainObjectArrayPtr class, so you can see how this typical handle class works.

The MainObjectArrayPtr class

We'll start with the default constructor (Figure 5.23), which is pretty simple. In fact, it's exactly like the normal constructor (Figure 5.21), except that it uses the default constructor of its body class to create its body object rather than the normal constructor of the body class.

Figure 5.23: The default constructor for MainObjectArrayPtr (from quantum\newquant.cpp)

```
MainObjectArrayPtr::MainObjectArrayPtr()
{
    m_MOA = new MainObjectArray;
    m_MOA->m_ReferenceCount = 1;
}
```

The MainObjectArrayPtr **Copy Constructor**

The copy constructor (Figure 5.24) isn't much more complicated. It copies the pointer to the main object array (body) object from the existing object to the same member variable in the newly created object. Then it increments the reference count because there is now one more user of that body object.

Figure 5.24: The copy constructor for MainObjectArrayPtr (from quantum\newquant.cpp)

```
MainObjectArrayPtr::MainObjectArrayPtr(const MainObjectArrayPtr& p_MOAP)
{
    m_MOA = p_MOAP.m_MOA;
    m_MOA->m_ReferenceCount++;
}
```

The MainObjectArrayPtr::operator = **Function**

The next function, MainObjectArrayPtr::operator = (Figure 5.25), is a bit more complicated than the previous ones, because it has to account for the reference counts in both the current object and the right-hand object being copied from.

Figure 5.25: MainObjectArrayPtr::operator= (from quantum\newquant.cpp)

```
MainObjectArrayPtr& MainObjectArrayPtr::operator=(const MainObjectArrayPtr& p_MOAP)
{
    m_MOA->m_ReferenceCount--;
    if (m_MOA->m_ReferenceCount <= 0 && m_MOA != p_MOAP.m_MOA)
        delete m_MOA;
    m_MOA = p_MOAP.m_MOA;
    m_MOA->m_ReferenceCount ++;
    return *this;
}
```

We start by decrementing the reference count of the current body object, because we won't be pointing to it after this operation (unless the right-hand object happens to point to the same body object as ours does). Then we check whether the reference count is less than or equal to 0, in which case we can (and will) delete the current body object.[22] After taking care of that issue, we copy the right-hand object's main object array pointer to the corresponding member variable in our object and increment the reference count for that main object array. Finally, we return our object to the caller.

The MainObjectArrayPtr **Destructor**

The final function in the MainObjectArrayPtr class is the destructor (Figure 5.26).

Figure 5.26: The destructor for the MainObjectArrayPtr class (from quantum\newquant.cpp)

```
MainObjectArrayPtr::~MainObjectArrayPtr()
{
    m_MOA->m_ReferenceCount --;
    if (m_MOA->m_ReferenceCount <= 0)
        delete m_MOA;
}
```

This shouldn't seem at all mysterious after our analysis of the operator = function, as its operation is basically a subset of what that function does. That is, it decrements the reference count of its body object; if the resulting reference count is less than or equal to 0, it deletes the body object.

Now that we're through with the MainObjectArrayPtr class, we'll examine its body class, MainObjectArray, so we can see how this fundamental data type of the quantum file algorithm works.[23]

---

22. Actually, the reference count should never be less than 0, but I'm engaging in some defensive programming here.

23. To reduce the length of the function names in this class, I'm going to omit the MainObjectArrayPtr qualifier at the beginning of those names.

The MainObjectArrayPtr::MainObjectArray class

We'll skip over the default constructor and destructor, as these functions don't do anything particularly interesting. However, the normal constructor for this class does some initialization that we should pay attention to, as shown in Figure 5.27.

Figure 5.27: The normal constructor for the MainObjectArray class (from quantum\newquant.cpp)

```
MainObjectArrayPtr::MainObjectArray::MainObjectArray(QuantumFile *p_MRU)
{
    ArrayIndex i;

    if (p_MRU)
        {
        m_QuantumFile = p_MRU;
        m_MainObjectCount = p_MRU->GetMainObjectCount();
        m_MainObjectBlockCount = p_MRU->GetMainObjectBlockCount();
        m_CurrentLowestFreeObject = 0;
        m_BlockPtr.SetSize(m_MainObjectCount);
        for (i = 0; i < m_BlockPtr.GetSize(); i ++)
            m_BlockPtr[i] = p_MRU->MakeMainObjectBlockPtr(i);
        }
}
```

As you can see, this constructor begins by checking whether its argument is non-null; if so, it continues by initializing a member variable to the quantum file pointer provided by that argument. Then it uses that quantum file pointer to retrieve the number of main objects in the quantum file as well as the number of blocks that the main object list occupies. Then it resizes its block pointer list to that count and initializes each of the elements in the list to the appropriate block pointer. We'll see exactly how those block pointers work when we get back to the QuantumFile class, but for now we'll just assume that they allow access to the individual blocks that make up the main object list.

The MainObjectArray::Get **Function**

Now let's take a look at the Get function in this class (Figure 5.28).

Figure 5.28: The MainObjectArray::Get function (from quantum\newquant.cpp)

```
MainObjectEntry MainObjectArrayPtr::MainObjectArray::Get(ArrayIndex p_Index)
{
    ArrayIndex Block;
    ArrayIndex Element;
    MainObjectEntry Result;

    if (p_Index >= m_MainObjectCount)
        return(NoObject); // say there's no space here

    Block = p_Index / MainObjectEntriesPerBlock;
    Element = p_Index % MainObjectEntriesPerBlock;
    Result = m_BlockPtr[Block]->Get(Element);

    return Result;
}
```

This function is reasonably straightforward. It begins by checking the index of the element in the main object array that the caller wants to retrieve. If it is out of range, the return value is NoObject, indicating an error. However, assuming that the index is valid, the function calculates which block and element within that block corresponds to the requested entry. It then retrieves that element via the MainObjectBlock::Get function, which is called for the m_BlockPtr variable for that block.[24] Finally, the result of the Get function, which is the quantum number of the big pointer quantum of the object in question, is returned to the calling function.

The MainObjectArray::Set **Function**

The next function we'll cover, MainObjectArray::Set (Figure 5.29), is the counterpart to Get.

---

24. We'll see exactly how this block access works when we cover the MainObjectBlock class, but for now it's sufficient to note that the main object array is potentially divided into blocks which are accessed via the standard virtual memory system.

Figure 5.29: The MainObjectArray::Set function (from quantum\newquant.cpp)

```
void MainObjectArrayPtr::MainObjectArray::Set(ArrayIndex p_Index,
   MainObjectEntry p_Entry)
{
    ArrayIndex Block;
    ArrayIndex Element;

    if (p_Index >= m_MainObjectCount)
        return; // can't store off the end

    Block = p_Index / MainObjectEntriesPerBlock;
    Element = p_Index % MainObjectEntriesPerBlock;
    m_BlockPtr[Block]->Set(Element, p_Entry);
    if ((p_Entry == NoObject) && (p_Index < m_CurrentLowestFreeObject))
        m_CurrentLowestFreeObject = p_Index;

    return;
}
```

This function takes two arguments, the element number in the main object array and the quantum number of that object's big pointer quantum. After checking that the element number is valid, it calculates the block number and element number in which the desired entry will be found, then calls the MainObjectBlock::Set function for the m_BlockPtr variable of the appropriate block in the main object array. Finally, if the entry being stored is equal to NoObject and the element number of this element is less than the current "lowest free object", then we update that variable to indicate that we should start looking at this place in the main object array the next time we are searching for a free object.

The MainObjectArray::FindAvailableObject **Function**

The next function we'll cover, MainObjectArray::FindAvailableObject (Figure 5.30), is used to find an available entry in the main object array when we want to create a new object.

Figure 5.30: The MainObjectArray::FindAvailableObject function (from quantum\newquant.cpp)

```
ObjectNumber MainObjectArrayPtr::MainObjectArray::FindAvailableObject()
{
    ArrayIndex Block;
    ArrayIndex Element;
    ObjectNumber Result = NoObject;

    Block = m_CurrentLowestFreeObject / MainObjectEntriesPerBlock;
    Element = m_CurrentLowestFreeObject % MainObjectEntriesPerBlock;
    for (; Block < m_MainObjectBlockCount; Block ++)
        {
        for (; Element < MainObjectEntriesPerBlock; Element ++)
            {
            if (m_BlockPtr[Block]->Get(Element) == NoObject)
                {
                Result = (ObjectNumber)
                    (Block * MainObjectEntriesPerBlock + Element);
                break;
                }
            }
        if (Result != NoObject)
            break;
        }
    m_CurrentLowestFreeObject = Result;

    return Result;
}
```

This isn't terribly complicated either. It searches the main object list block by block, starting with the entry corresponding to the last known value of the "lowest free object" variable and continuing until it finds an empty entry (i.e., one whose value is NoObject). Once it finds such an entry, it calculates the corresponding element number in the main object array and returns it as the result after storing it in the "lowest free object" variable.[25]

---

25. Actually, the name of the "lowest free object" variable should be something like m_StartLookingHere, but I doubt it will cause you too much confusion after you see how it is used.

The MainObjectArray::GetModifiableElement **Function**

The next function we'll cover, MainObjectArray::GetModifiableElement (Figure 5.31), is used to retrieve a ModifiableElement value from a main object.

Figure 5.31: The MainObjectArray::GetModifiableElement function (from quantum\newquant.cpp)

```
ModifiableElement MainObjectArrayPtr::MainObjectArray::GetModifiableElement(
    ArrayIndex p_MainObjectNumber, ArrayIndex p_ElementIndex)
{
    MainObjectEntry BPAQuantumNumber;
    BigPointerBlockPtr BigPointerBlock;
    LittlePointerBlockPtr LittlePointerBlock;
    LeafBlockPtr ElementBlock;
    ArrayIndex BigPointerIndex;
    ArrayIndex LittlePointerIndex;
    QuantumNumber LPAQuantumNumber;
    ItemReference ElementRef;
    ModifiableElement Element;

    BPAQuantumNumber = Get(p_MainObjectNumber);

    BigPointerBlock =
        m_QuantumFile->MakeBigPointerBlockPtr(BPAQuantumNumber);

    BigPointerIndex = p_ElementIndex / ItemReferencesPerBlock;

    LPAQuantumNumber =
        BigPointerBlock->GetBigArrayElement(BigPointerIndex);

    LittlePointerBlock =
        m_QuantumFile->MakeLittlePointerBlockPtr(LPAQuantumNumber);

    LittlePointerIndex = p_ElementIndex % ItemReferencesPerBlock;
    ElementRef = LittlePointerBlock->GetLittleArrayElement(LittlePointerIndex);

    if (ElementRef.IsReference())
        {
        ElementBlock =
            m_QuantumFile->MakeLeafBlockPtr(ElementRef.GetQuantumNumber());

        Element =
            ElementBlock->GetModifiableItem(ElementRef.GetItemNumber());
```

```
        }
    else
        Element = ModifiableElement();

    return Element;
}
```

Among its many uses, GetModifiableElement is the function that a FlexArray uses to retrieve values, so it is quite important to the functioning of our test program. Although it is somewhat longer than most of the other functions we've seen so far, it's really not too complicated, and it will serve as a good introduction to the more complex functions in this class.

We start by using the Get member function to look up the big pointer array quantum number for the object in which the element is contained. Once we have that quantum number, we call the function QuantumFile::MakeBigPointerBlockPtr to create a handle object that will allow us to access that quantum as a big pointer array. Next, we calculate which big pointer array entry contains the quantum number of the little pointer block that contains the element reference that we'll use to access the actual data. Once we know that, we can call the BigPointerBlock::GetBigArrayElement function to retrieve the quantum number for that little pointer block. Then we call the function QuantumFile::MakeLittlePointerBlockPtr to create a handle object that will allow us to access that quantum as a little pointer array. Once we have done that, we calculate which element in the little pointer array is the element reference to the element we are interested in, and retrieve that element reference from the little pointer array.

Now we're ready to access the element itself, assuming that it actually exists. First, though, we have to account for the possibility that it is a null item, that is, one that contains no data. If this is the case, we return an empty (i.e., default-constructed) ModifiableElement. Why have I handled this case separately, rather than storing a zero-length ModifiableElement in the leaf block?

Some Ado about Nothing

A null item is an optimization: we could treat items containing no data like all other items. However, special handling for this case is worthwhile, since it is very common. For example, a word processor might store each line of a file as a string, removing the trailing null from each string before storing it; with that approach, strings consisting only of a trailing null would be stored as null items. The advantage of using null items is that, rather than occupying an item index slot indicating a length of zero, they are represented by item references that contain a special quantum number called NO_QUANTUM and a special item number called NULL_ITEM_NUMBER, neither of which can appear in a real item reference. This means that a null item does not occupy any space in a item index, and that we can avoid loading a quantum to retrieve its value.

However, let us suppose that the element reference is not null. In that case, we call QuantumFile::MakeLeafPointerBlockPtr to create a handle object that will allow us to access items in the quantum containing the desired item. Then we use QuantumBlock::GetModifiableItem to retrieve the actual item and return it to the caller.

The MainObjectArray::PutElement **Function**

The next function we'll cover, MainObjectArray::PutElement, shown in Figure 5.32, is used to store a ModifiableElement value into a main object.

Figure 5.32: The MainObjectArray::PutElement function (from quantum\newquant.cpp)

```
int MainObjectArrayPtr::MainObjectArray::PutElement(
    ObjectNumber p_MainObjectNumber, ArrayIndex p_ElementIndex,
    ModifiableElement p_Element)
{
    MainObjectEntry BPAQuantumNumber;
    BigPointerBlockPtr BigPointerBlock;
    LittlePointerBlockPtr LittlePointerBlock;
    LeafBlockPtr ElementBlock;
    ArrayIndex BigPointerIndex;
    ArrayIndex LittlePointerIndex;
    QuantumNumber LPAQuantumNumber;
    ItemReference ElementRef;
    ItemReference NewElementRef;
    ModifiableElement Element;
    QFreeSpaceEntry SpaceAvailable;
```

```
QuantumNumber NewQuantum;
QuantumNumber PossibleQuantum;
LeafBlockPtr NewElementBlock;
ArrayIndex FreeSpace;
ArrayIndex ActualFreeSpace;
ArrayIndex NewItemNumber;
ObjectNumber LeafObjectNumber;

qfassert (p_Element.GetSize() < MaxItemSize);

BigPointerIndex = p_ElementIndex / ItemReferencesPerBlock;

BPAQuantumNumber = Get(p_MainObjectNumber);

BigPointerBlock = m_QuantumFile->MakeBigPointerBlockPtr(BPAQuantumNumber);

LPAQuantumNumber = BigPointerBlock->GetBigArrayElement(BigPointerIndex);

LittlePointerBlock =
    m_QuantumFile->MakeLittlePointerBlockPtr(LPAQuantumNumber);

LittlePointerIndex = p_ElementIndex % ItemReferencesPerBlock;
ElementRef = LittlePointerBlock->GetLittleArrayElement(LittlePointerIndex);

if (ElementRef.IsReference())
    {
    ElementBlock =
        m_QuantumFile->MakeLeafBlockPtr(ElementRef.GetQuantumNumber());
    ElementBlock->DeleteItem(ElementRef.GetItemNumber());
    }

if (p_Element.GetSize() == 0) // nothing to store
    {
    ElementRef.SetQuantumNumber(NoQuantum);
    ElementRef.SetItemNumber(NoItem);
    LittlePointerBlock->SetLittleArrayElement(LittlePointerIndex,ElementRef);
    return 0;
    }

NewQuantum = NoQuantum;
PossibleQuantum = BigPointerBlock->GetLastQuantumAddedTo();
if (PossibleQuantum != NoQuantum)
    {
    SpaceAvailable = m_QuantumFile->QGetFreeSpace(PossibleQuantum);
    FreeSpace = SpaceAvailable.m_FreeSpaceCode * FreeSpaceConversion;
    if (SpaceAvailable.m_FreeSpaceCode != AvailableQuantum &&
      FreeSpace > p_Element.GetSize())
      {
```

```
        NewElementBlock = m_QuantumFile->MakeLeafBlockPtr(PossibleQuantum);
        ActualFreeSpace = NewElementBlock->CalculateFreeSpace();
        if (ActualFreeSpace > p_Element.GetSize())
            NewQuantum = PossibleQuantum;
        }
    }

if (NewQuantum == NoQuantum)
    {
    NewQuantum = m_QuantumFile->FindSpaceForItem(p_MainObjectNumber,
        p_Element.GetSize());
    NewElementBlock = m_QuantumFile->MakeLeafBlockPtr(NewQuantum);
    LeafObjectNumber = NewElementBlock->GetMainObjectNumber();
    qfassert(LeafObjectNumber == p_MainObjectNumber);
    }

BigPointerBlock->SetLastQuantumAddedTo(NewQuantum);
NewElementRef.SetQuantumNumber(NewQuantum);

NewItemNumber = NewElementBlock->AddItem(p_Element,
    VARIABLE_LENGTH_STRING, p_ElementIndex);
NewElementRef.SetItemNumber(NewItemNumber);

LeafObjectNumber = NewElementBlock->GetMainObjectNumber();
qfassert(LeafObjectNumber == p_MainObjectNumber);

NewElementBlock->UpdateFreeSpace();

LittlePointerBlock->SetLittleArrayElement(LittlePointerIndex,NewElementRef);

return 0;
}
```

This starts out by using a preprocessor macro called qfassert to
check whether the size of the item to be stored is legal, i.e., that it is
less than the maximum allowable item size.[26] After that, the code is
very similar to its counterpart, GetModifiableElement, until we retrieve
the item reference from the little pointer array. Then, if the item
reference is not null, we call QuantumBlock::DeleteItem to delete the
current contents of that element. Then we check whether the size of

---

26. If a preprocessor variable called DEBUG is defined, then the action of this macro will be to
terminate the program if the condition is not met; otherwise, it will do nothing. You can find
the implementation of this macro and its underlying function in qfassert.h and qfassert.cpp.

the element to be stored is zero; if so, we store a null reference in the little pointer array (as noted previously).

On the other hand, if we have some data to be stored, we have to find a place to store it. The most logical place to look is in the quantum that we have most recently used to store something for this object, and this information is therefore maintained by the big pointer block access code in the BigPointerBlock class.[27] Therefore, we check whether there may be enough free space in that quantum by calling QuantumFile::QGetFreeSpace.[28]

Because a free space code is only one byte (to reduce the size of the free space list), it cannot exactly represent the amount of free space in a quantum. Therefore, if the free space list entry indicates that this quantum may have enough space for the item, we have to retrieve the quantum via QuantumFile::MakeLeafBlockPtr and then call QuantumBlock::CalculateFreeSpace to calculate its free space more precisely. If the actual free space is larger than the size of the item, then we have found the quantum we will use to store the item.

However, if that quantum does not have enough space to store the item, then we will have to search for one that does. That is handled by QuantumFile::FindSpaceForItem, which returns the number of the first quantum that fits the bill.

At this point, we have a quantum in which to store the item. Therefore, after setting the "last quantum added to" member variable, we set the quantum number in the element reference to that quantum number. Then we call QuantumBlock::AddItem to add the item to that quantum, and set the item number in the element reference to the value returned from that function. Finally, we update the little array pointer that points to the newly added element.

---

27. We often will step through an array assigning values to each element in turn, for example when importing data from an ASCII file; since we are not modifying previously stored values, the quantum we used last is the most likely to have room to add another item. In such a case, the most recently written-to quantum is half full on the average; this makes it a good place to look for some free space. In addition, it is very likely to be already in memory, so we won't have to do any disk accesses to get at it.

28. By the way, this function was originally named GetFreeSpace, and its return type was called FreeSpaceEntry, but I had to change the name of the return type to avoid a conflict with a name that Microsoft had used once upon a time in their MFC classes and still had some claim on; I changed the name of the function to match. This is a good illustration of the need to avoid polluting the global name space; using the namespace construct in the new C++ standard would be a good solution to such a problem.

The MainObjectArray::GetMainObjectElementCount Function

The next function, MainObjectArray::GetMainObjectElementCount (Figure 5.33), is used to retrieve the number of elements that a main object currently contains.

Figure 5.33: The MainObjectArray::GetMainObjectElementCount function (from quantum\newquant.cpp)

```
ArrayIndex MainObjectArrayPtr::MainObjectArray::GetMainObjectElementCount(
    ArrayIndex p_MainObjectNumber)
{
    MainObjectEntry BPAQuantumNumber;
    BigPointerBlockPtr BigPointerBlock;

    BPAQuantumNumber = Get(p_MainObjectNumber);
    BigPointerBlock = m_QuantumFile->MakeBigPointerBlockPtr(BPAQuantumNumber);
    return BigPointerBlock->GetBigArrayElementCount();
}
```

You might think that this would be a trivial "get" function that merely returns the value of a member variable, but that is not the case. The reason is that this information is stored in the quantum file itself, as part of the big pointer array, because it needs to be maintained between executions of this program (or any other program that might want to use the file).

However, it's not too complicated. After using the Get function to retrieve the quantum number of the big pointer array for the object, it uses QuantumFile::MakeBigPointerBlockPtr to provide access to the big pointer array. Then it calls BigPointerBlock::GetBigArrayElementCount to retrieve the value to be returned.

The MainObjectArray::GetMainObjectMaxElementCount Function

The next function, MainObjectArray::GetMainObjectMaxElementCount (Figure 5.34), is used to retrieve the maximum number of elements that a main object is permitted to contain. Because it is exactly like the previous function except for the function it calls in the BigPointerBlock class, I'll just list it without further comment.

Figure 5.34: The MainObjectArray::GetMainObjectMaxElementCount function (from quantum\newquant.cpp)

```
ArrayIndex MainObjectArrayPtr::MainObjectArray::GetMainObjectMaxElementCount(
    ArrayIndex p_MainObjectNumber)
{

    MainObjectEntry BPAQuantumNumber;
    BigPointerBlockPtr BigPointerBlock;

    BPAQuantumNumber = Get(p_MainObjectNumber);
    BigPointerBlock = m_QuantumFile->MakeBigPointerBlockPtr(BPAQuantumNumber);
    return BigPointerBlock->GetBigArrayMaxElementCount();
}
```

The MainObjectArray::CreateMainObject **Function**

The next function we'll cover, MainObjectArray::CreateMainObject, shown in Figure 5.35, is used to create a new main object.

Figure 5.35: The MainObjectArray::CreateMainObject function (from quantum\newquant.cpp)

```
void MainObjectArrayPtr::MainObjectArray::CreateMainObject(
    ModifiableElement p_ObjectName, ObjectNumber p_ObjectNumber,
    ArrayIndex p_ElementCount, ArrayIndex p_MaxElementCount)
{
    QuantumNumber NewBigPointerQuantum;
    BigArrayHeader NewBigArrayHeader;
    SVector<QuantumNumber> NewBigPointerArray;
    SVector<ItemReference> NewLittlePointerArray;
    ArrayIndex LittlePointerBlockCount;
    ArrayIndex i;
    ArrayIndex NewQuantum;
    QFreeSpaceEntry TempFreeSpaceEntry;

    if (p_ElementCount == 0)
        p_ElementCount = 1;  // this is the simplest handling for 0-length arrays

    TempFreeSpaceEntry.m_ObjectNumber = p_ObjectNumber;
    TempFreeSpaceEntry.m_FreeSpaceCode = 0;
    NewBigPointerQuantum = m_QuantumFile->FindEmptyBlock();
```

```
BigPointerBlockPtr NewBigPointerBlock =
    m_QuantumFile->MakeBigPointerBlockPtr(NewBigPointerQuantum);
NewBigPointerBlock->Clear();
NewBigPointerBlock->SetQuantumType(BIG_POINTER_ARRAY);
NewBigPointerBlock->SetMainObjectNumber(p_ObjectNumber);
NewBigArrayHeader.m_ElementCount = p_ElementCount;
NewBigArrayHeader.m_MaxElementCount = p_MaxElementCount;
NewBigArrayHeader.m_LastQuantumAddedTo = NoQuantum;

NewBigPointerBlock->AddItem(&NewBigArrayHeader,
    sizeof(BigArrayHeader), BIG_ARRAY_HEADER, 0);

LittlePointerBlockCount = (p_ElementCount-1)/ItemReferencesPerBlock + 1;
NewBigPointerArray = SVector<QuantumNumber>(LittlePointerBlockCount);
NewLittlePointerArray = SVector<ItemReference>(ItemReferencesPerBlock);

for (i = 0; i < LittlePointerBlockCount; i ++)
    {
    NewQuantum = m_QuantumFile->FindEmptyBlock();
    m_QuantumFile->SetFreeSpace(NewQuantum,TempFreeSpaceEntry);
    NewBigPointerArray[i] = NewQuantum;

    LittlePointerBlockPtr NewLittlePointerBlock =
        m_QuantumFile->MakeLittlePointerBlockPtr(NewQuantum);
    NewLittlePointerBlock->Clear();
    NewLittlePointerBlock->SetQuantumType(LITTLE_POINTER_ARRAY);
    NewLittlePointerBlock->SetMainObjectNumber(p_ObjectNumber);
    NewLittlePointerBlock->AddItem(NewLittlePointerArray.GetDataAddress(),
        NewLittlePointerArray.GetSize()*sizeof(ItemReference),
        LITTLE_POINTER_ARRAY,0);
    NewLittlePointerBlock->ClearLittleArray();
    m_QuantumFile->SetFreeSpace(NewQuantum,TempFreeSpaceEntry);
    }

NewBigPointerBlock->AddItem(NewBigPointerArray.GetDataAddress(),
    NewBigPointerArray.GetSize()*sizeof(QuantumNumber),
    BIG_POINTER_ARRAY,0);

m_QuantumFile->SetFreeSpace(NewBigPointerQuantum,TempFreeSpaceEntry);
Set(p_ObjectNumber,NewBigPointerQuantum);
PutElement(MainObjectDirectory, p_ObjectNumber, p_ObjectName);
}
```

This function is somewhat complex, but that should be understandable because it takes quite a bit of work to create a new main object. We start off by checking whether the user has asked to create a zero-length object. Such an object would cause complications in the way that the size of the little pointer array is calculated; namely, the calculation of the number of blocks needed to hold the little pointer arrays (LittlePointerBlockCount) produces correct results for all values of the element count that are greater than 0 but produces a nonsensical result when the element count is 0. Because arrays can grow in size, a zero-element array may be a reasonable thing to create, so I didn't want to disallow them; the simplest solution, and the one I adopted, was to treat a request to create a zero-element array as a request for a one-element array. Because a zero-length object isn't very useful until it has been resized, this isn't likely to surprise the user.

Once that detail has been handled, we compute a free space entry indicating that this block is no longer available for use. Then we continue by calling QuantumFile::FindEmptyBlock to find a block for the big pointer array, then calling QuantumFile::MakeBigPointerBlockPtr to allow access to that block as a big pointer block.

Now we are ready to begin setting up the big pointer block for use. We start by calling BigPointerBlock::Clear to erase any previous data in the block.[29] Next, we call BigPointerBlock::SetQuantumType to set the type of the quantum to indicate that it contains a big pointer array; this information is used for consistency checking when accessing a quantum that is supposed to be a big pointer array quantum.[30] Then we call BigPointerBlock::SetMainObjectNumber to set the entry in the big pointer block that indicates which main object it belongs to. This is needed when we are updating the free space list, because each free space entry includes the number of the main object for that quantum. This is relevant because we do not share a quantum among several main objects, to simplify the task of programs that recover as much data as possible from a quantum file that has become corrupted.

The next step is to set up the header for the big pointer array. This contains the current element count, the maximum element count, and the last quantum that we've added an element to; of course, the latter

---

29. The alert reader will notice that the type of the NewBigPointerBlock variable is BigPointerBlockPtr, not BigPointerBlock. However, the functions that we call through that variable via the operator-> are from the BigPointerBlock class, because that is the type of the pointer that operator-> returns, as explained in the section on overloading operator->.

30. Another possible use is to implement variant arrays, in which the structure of the array is variable. In that case, we might use the type to determine whether we have the item we want or some kind of intermediate structure requiring further processing to extract the actual data.

variable is initialized to NoQuantum, as we have not yet added any data to this new object. Once we have set the header up, we call QuantumBlock::AddItem to add it to the big pointer block, so that it will be accessible the next time we use the big pointer array.

Now it's time to initialize the little pointer array for this object and the big pointer array that allows us to access the little pointer array. To start this process, we calculate the number of little pointer blocks that we will need, which is dependent on the number of elements in the object and the number of item references that fit in one block. Once we have determined that number, we can create a big pointer array containing that number of quantum numbers, and a temporary little pointer array that we will use to initialize each block in the little pointer array.

We're up to the loop that initializes all of the blocks in the little pointer array. It begins by calling QuantumFile::FindEmptyBlock to find an empty block that we can use for the little pointer array. Then we call QuantumFile::SetFreeSpace to reserve this quantum for the current main object and mark it as full.[31] Next, we set the current element of the big pointer array to the quantum number of the quantum where we are storing the current little pointer array block.

Now we're ready to initialize the little pointer block. We start by calling QuantumFile::MakeLittlePointerBlockPtr to allow us to treat the current quantum as a little pointer block. Once we have done that, we call LittlePointerBlock::Clear to initialize the quantum to an unused state, LittlePointerBlock::SetQuantumType to set the quantum type to "little pointer array" (for consistency checking while retrieving data), LittlePointerBlock::SetMainObjectNumber to allow us to update the free space list when adding data to this quantum, QuantumBlock::AddItem to add a section of the little pointer array to this quantum, and LittlePointerBlock::ClearLittleArray to initialize that section of the little pointer array to null item references.

One detail that might not be immediately obvious is why we have to call QuantumFile::SetFreeSpace again at the end of the loop. The reason is that the QuantumBlock::AddItem function recalculates the free space for the block to which it adds the item. Since we want to

---

31. The reason we mark this quantum as being full is twofold: first, there won't be very much (if any) space left in this quantum after we have added the little pointer array; and second, we don't want to store any actual data for our new main object in the same quantum as we are using for a section of the little pointer array, to make the reconstruction of a partially corrupted file easier.

prevent any further data from being added to this block, we have to reset the free space manually (to "none available") to indicate that this block is full.

Once we have initialized all of the little pointer array sections, we're ready to finish setting up the big pointer array for use. The first step in that process is to add the big pointer array data we have just filled in to the big pointer quantum, via QuantumBlock::AddItem. Then we use QuantumFile::SetFreeSpace to reserve the big pointer quantum for our new main object and mark it full. Then we use the member function Set to set the big pointer array quantum number for our new main object. Finally, we call the member function PutElement to set up the directory entry for the new main object.

The MainObjectArray::FindObjectByName **Function**

The next function we'll cover, MainObjectArray::FindObjectByName (Figure 5.36), is used to look up a main object in the "directory".

Figure 5.36: The MainObjectArray::FindObjectByName function (from quantum\newquant.cpp)

```
ObjectNumber MainObjectArrayPtr::MainObjectArray::FindObjectByName(
    ModifiableElement p_ObjectName)
{
    ObjectNumber i;
    ModifiableElement TempElement;

// note: there is no object numbered 0
    for (i = 1; i < m_MainObjectCount; i ++)
        {
        TempElement = GetModifiableElement(MainObjectDirectory,i);
        if (p_ObjectName == TempElement)
            return i;
        }
    return NoObject;
}
```

This one is fairly simple. It steps through the elements of the main object directory, looking for an element whose contents are equal to the argument to the function. If it finds such an element, it returns the index of that element, which is the object number of the object with that name. On the other hand, if it gets to the end of the main object directory without finding a match, it returns the value NoObject.

The MainObjectArray::GrowMainObject **Function**

The next function, MainObjectArray::GrowMainObject (Figure 5.37), is used to increase the size of a main object when needed to accommodate more elements.

Figure 5.37: The MainObjectArray::GrowMainObject function (from quantum\newquant.cpp)

```
ArrayIndex MainObjectArrayPtr::MainObjectArray::GrowMainObject(
    ObjectNumber p_ObjectNumber, ArrayIndex p_NewElementCount)
{
    MainObjectEntry BPAQuantumNumber;
    BigPointerBlockPtr BigPointerBlock;
    LittlePointerBlockPtr NewLittlePointerBlock;
    SVector<ItemReference> NewLittlePointerArray;
    BigPointerArray OldBigPointerArray;
    SVector<QuantumNumber> NewBigPointerArray;
    ArrayIndex NewLittlePointerBlockCount;
    ArrayIndex OldLittlePointerBlockCount;
    ArrayIndex i;
    ArrayIndex NewQuantum;
    QFreeSpaceEntry TempFreeSpaceEntry;
    ArrayIndex UpdatedElementCount;

    BPAQuantumNumber = Get(p_ObjectNumber);
    BigPointerBlock = m_QuantumFile->MakeBigPointerBlockPtr(BPAQuantumNumber);
    OldBigPointerArray = BigPointerBlock->GetBigPointerArray(); // big pointer array
    NewBigPointerArray = OldBigPointerArray;

    NewLittlePointerBlockCount = (p_NewElementCount-1)/ItemReferencesPerBlock + 1;
    UpdatedElementCount = NewLittlePointerBlockCount * ItemReferencesPerBlock;
    OldLittlePointerBlockCount = NewBigPointerArray.GetSize();
    if (NewLittlePointerBlockCount == OldLittlePointerBlockCount) // first overflow
        {
        BigPointerBlock->SetBigArrayElementCount(UpdatedElementCount);
        return UpdatedElementCount;
        }
```

```
NewBigPointerArray.SetSize(NewLittlePointerBlockCount);
BigPointerBlock->SetBigArrayElementCount(UpdatedElementCount);

TempFreeSpaceEntry.m_ObjectNumber = p_ObjectNumber;
TempFreeSpaceEntry.m_FreeSpaceCode = 0;

NewLittlePointerArray = SVector<ItemReference>(ItemReferencesPerBlock);
for (i = OldLittlePointerBlockCount; i < NewLittlePointerBlockCount; i ++)
    {
    NewQuantum = m_QuantumFile->FindEmptyBlock();
    m_QuantumFile->SetFreeSpace(NewQuantum,TempFreeSpaceEntry);
    NewBigPointerArray[i] = NewQuantum;
    NewLittlePointerBlock =
            m_QuantumFile->MakeLittlePointerBlockPtr(NewQuantum);
    NewLittlePointerBlock->Clear();
    NewLittlePointerBlock->SetQuantumType(LITTLE_POINTER_ARRAY);
    NewLittlePointerBlock->SetMainObjectNumber(p_ObjectNumber);
    NewLittlePointerBlock->AddItem(NewLittlePointerArray.GetDataAddress(),
        NewLittlePointerArray.GetSize()*sizeof(ItemReference),
        LITTLE_POINTER_ARRAY,0);
    NewLittlePointerBlock->ClearLittleArray();
    m_QuantumFile->SetFreeSpace(NewQuantum,TempFreeSpaceEntry);
    }
BigPointerBlock->DeleteItem(2); // big pointer array
BigPointerBlock->AddItem(NewBigPointerArray.GetDataAddress(),
    NewBigPointerArray.GetSize()*sizeof(QuantumNumber),
    BIG_POINTER_ARRAY,0);
m_QuantumFile->SetFreeSpace(BPAQuantumNumber,TempFreeSpaceEntry);
return UpdatedElementCount;
}
```

This is about as complicated as CreateMainObject. However, because it is quite similar to that function, we'll be able to shorten the explanation considerably.

We start by retrieving the existing big pointer block for the object. Then we copy the big pointer array from that block to a new big pointer array. Next, we calculate the size of the new little pointer array needed to hold references to all the elements in the new, enlarged, object.

The next few lines of code might be a little mysterious if I don't explain a few details of the size calculation. To simplify the accounting needed to keep track of the sizes of all of the little pointer arrays, I've decided always to allocate a little pointer array to the largest size that will fit into a quantum. However, setting the accessible size of an array to the actual number of elements allocated for its little pointer arrays has the drawback that the user wouldn't be able to find out when the program accessed an element that is within the allocated size but outside the number of elements specified when creating the array. Therefore, I've crafted a compromise: when an array is created, I set the number of accessible elements to the number the user specifies[32]; however, if the array is increased in size, the new size is always equal to the total allocation for all little pointer arrays. This means that if an array is expanded by a reference to an element that was already allocated but was outside the specified array size, GrowMainObject simply resets the size to the number of elements contained in all little pointer arrays already extant and returns that value. Otherwise, a new little pointer array is allocated, and the big pointer array is updated to reflect the change.

Assuming that we actually do need to allocate some new little pointer blocks, we continue by increasing the size of the big pointer array to accommodate the new number of little pointer blocks. Then we allocate and initialize each of the new little pointer blocks in exactly the same way as we allocated and initialized the original little pointer blocks when we created the object. Then we delete the old big pointer array from the big pointer block, add the new big pointer array to the big pointer block, set the free space entry for the big pointer block to indicate that it is full, and return the new element count to the caller.

Now that we have reached the end of the discussion of the MainObjectArray class, we'll return to the QuantumFile class. This time, we're going to get into the member functions that are used in the implementation, since we've already dealt with those that are used by outside programs.

The QuantumFile class

We'll skip over the QuantumFile member functions that fall in three categories:

---

32. There's one exception to this rule, for reasons described above: if the user specifies 0 elements, I change it to 1.

1. Those that merely compute the number of blocks occupied by a segment of the quantum file (i.e., GetMainObjectBlockCount and QGetFreeSpaceListBlockCount).

2. Those that merely return a block of the appropriate type to be accessed as a little pointer block, big pointer block, and the like (i.e., MakeFreeSpaceBlockPtr, MakeMainObjectBlockPtr, MakeLittlePointerBlockPtr, MakeBigPointerBlockPtr, MakeLeafBlockPtr).

3. Those that merely call member functions of the FreeSpaceArray class (i.e., SetFreeSpace, QGetFreeSpace, FindEmptyBlock, FindSpaceForItem).

We'll see how the functions in the third category work when we examine the underlying functions that they call.

The QuantumFile::SetModified **Function**

However, that still leaves us with several functions to discuss in the QuantumFile class. We'll start with QuantumFile::SetModified, which is shown in Figure 5.38.

Figure 5.38: The QuantumFile::SetModified function (from quantum\block.cpp)

```
void QuantumFile::SetModified(ArrayIndex p_BlockNumber)
{
    ArrayIndex BufferNumber;

    BufferNumber = FindBuffer(p_BlockNumber,
        (ArrayIndex *)m_BlockNumber.GetDataAddress(),
        m_BlockNumber.GetSize());

    qfassert(BufferNumber != BadBlockNumber);

    m_BufferModified[BufferNumber] = TRUE;
}
```

This is actually a fairly simple function. It calls a global function called FindBuffer to look up the specified quantum number in the list of quantum buffers.[33] If the quantum with that quantum number is in fact in one of the quantum buffers, then the "buffer modified" flag for that buffer is set, and the function returns. The only complication is a consistency check in the form of an "assert" that the quantum in question is actually in one of the buffers. If that is not the case, then we have a serious problem, because the program should not be trying to set the modified flag for a quantum that isn't in memory: that indicates that the buffer that contained the quantum has been reused too soon.

The QuantumFile::Position **Function**

The next function we will examine is QuantumFile::Position, which is shown in Figure 5.39.

Figure 5.39: The QuantumFile::Position function (from quantum\block.cpp)

```
void QuantumFile::Position(ArrayIndex p_BlockNumber)
{
    long DesiredPosition;

    DesiredPosition = (p_BlockNumber)*(long)BlockSize;

    fseek(m_DosFilePtr,DesiredPosition,SEEK_SET);
}
```

This function is used by the Read and Write functions to position the file pointer to the correct place for reading or writing a quantum. This is quite simple because every block is the same size. However, it is important to remember that the quantum file contains data other than the quanta themselves, so the block number of a quantum is not the same as its quantum number. To convert between these two numbers is the responsibility of the function that computes the block number supplied to Position.

---

33. It would probably have been better to create a class to contain this function as well as a few others that are global in this implementation.

The QuantumFile::Read **Function**

The next function we will examine is QuantumFile::Read, which is shown in Figure 5.40.

Figure 5.40: The QuantumFile::Read function (from quantum\block.cpp)

```
void QuantumFile::Read(ArrayIndex p_BufferNumber)
{
    Position(m_BlockNumber[p_BufferNumber]); // position the file

    fread((char *)m_Block[p_BufferNumber],1,BlockSize,m_DosFilePtr);

    m_BufferModified[p_BufferNumber] = FALSE;

    m_ReadCount ++;
}
```

After positioning the file pointer to the location in the file where this block is stored, we read it into the buffer. Then we set the modified flag for the buffer to FALSE, indicating that the disk and memory versions of the block are the same. Finally, we increment the read count, which is used for performance analysis.

The QuantumFile::Write **Function**

The next function we will examine is QuantumFile::Write, which is shown in Figure 5.41. This is identical to the Read function, except of course that it writes the data to the file rather than reading it.

Figure 5.41: The QuantumFile::Write function (from quantum\block.cpp)

```
void QuantumFile::Write(ArrayIndex p_BufferNumber)
{
    Position(m_BlockNumber[p_BufferNumber]); // position the file

    fwrite((char *)m_Block[p_BufferNumber],1,BlockSize,m_DosFilePtr);

    m_BufferModified[p_BufferNumber] = FALSE;
```

```
        m_WriteCount ++;
}
```

The QuantumFile::MakeBlockResident **Function**

The last function in this class is QuantumFile::MakeBlockResident. This is where we rejoin the thread of discussion about operator->. You see, MakeBlockResident is called during the execution of operator-> for any of the BlockPtr classes.[34] Figure 5.42 shows an early implementation of this routine.

Figure 5.42: Early MakeBlockResident code

```
BlockBuffer *MRUBlockManager::MakeBlockResident(ArrayIndex p_BlockNumber,
ArrayIndex &p_OldBufferNumber)
{
        ArrayIndex i;
        ArrayIndex EarliestStamp;
        time_t TimeStamp;

        if (m_BlockNumber[p_OldBufferNumber] == p_BlockNumber)
            {
            m_TimeStamp[p_OldBufferNumber] = time(NULL);
            return m_BlockBuffer[p_OldBufferNumber];
            }

        for (i = 0; i < m_BlockNumber.GetSize(); i ++)
            {
            if (m_BlockNumber[i] == p_BlockNumber)
                {
                m_TimeStamp[i] = time(NULL);
                return m_BlockBuffer[i];
                }
            }

        TimeStamp = WayInTheFuture;
        for (i = 0; i < m_TimeStamp.GetSize(); i ++)
            {
            if (m_TimeStamp[i] < TimeStamp) // find the earliest timestamp
```

---

34. These are FreeSpaceBlockPtr, MainObjectBlockPtr, BigPointerBlockPtr, LittlePointerBlockPtr, and LeafBlockPtr.

```
            {
            TimeStamp = m_TimeStamp[i];
            EarliestStamp = i;
            }
        }

    if (m_BufferModified[EarliestStamp]) /* it needs to be written out */
        Write(EarliestStamp);

    // set block number of new occupant
    m_BlockNumber[EarliestStamp] = p_BlockNumber;

    m_BufferModified[EarliestStamp] = FALSE; // not modified yet
    m_TimeStamp[EarliestStamp] = time(NULL);
    Read(EarliestStamp);

    p_OldBufferNumber = EarliestStamp;

    return m_BlockBuffer[EarliestStamp];
}
```

This is a fairly straightforward implementation of a least recently used (LRU) priority algorithm, but there are a few wrinkles to reduce overhead. First, we use the reference parameter p_OldBufferNumber to retrieve the buffer number (if any) in which the searched-for block was located on our last attempt. If the number of the block held in that buffer matches the one we're looking for, we will be able to avoid the overhead of searching the entire buffer list. The reason that p_OldBufferNumber is a reference parameter is so that we can update the caller's copy when we locate the block in a different buffer; that way, the next time that MakeBlockResident is called to retrieve the same block's address, we can check that buffer number first.

In order to make this work, we can't implement the LRU priority list by moving the most recently used block to the front of the block list; the saved buffer number would be useless if the blocks moved around in the list every time a block other than the most recently used one was referenced. Instead, each slot has an attached timestamp, updated by calling the time function every time the corresponding block is referenced. When we need to free up a buffer, we select the one with the lowest (i.e., oldest) timestamp. If that buffer has the "modified" attribute set, then it has been updated in memory and needs to be written back to the disk before being reused, so we do that. Then we read the new block into the buffer, update the caller's p_OldBufferNumber for next time, and return the address of the buffer.

This seems simple enough, without much scope for vast improvements in efficiency; at least, it seemed that way to me, until I ran Turbo Profiler™ on it and discovered that it was horrendously inefficient. The profiler indicated that 73% of the CPU time of my test program was accounted for by calls to the time routine! To add insult to injury, the timing resolution of that routine is quite coarse (approximately 18 msec), with the result that most of the blocks would often get the same timestamp when running the program normally.[35]

Upon consideration, I realized that the best possible "timestamp" would be a simple count of the number of times that MakeBlockResident was called. This would entail almost no overhead and would be of exactly the correct resolution to decide which block was least recently used; this is the mechanism used in the current version.

Punching the Time Clock

One interesting consideration in the original design of this mechanism was what size of counter to use for the timestamp. At first, it seemed necessary (and sufficient) to use a 32-bit type such as an unsigned long, which would allow 4 billion accesses before the counter would "turn over" to 0. However, because the original implementation was compiled with a 16-bit compiler, the natural size to use would be an unsigned (meaning unsigned short) variable. Therefore, I had to decide whether a longer type was necessary.

After some thought, I decided that it wasn't. The question is: what happens when the counter turns over? To figure this out, let's do a thought experiment, using two-byte counters. Suppose that the priority list looks like Figure 5.43, with the latest timestamp being 65535.

---

35. Of course, while stepping through the program at human speeds in Turbo Debugger, the timestamps were nicely distributed; this is a demonstration of Heisenberg's Uncertainty Principle as it applies to debugging.

Figure 5.43: Timestamps before turnover

Block number	Timestamp
14	65533
22	65535
23	65000
9	65100

Let's suppose that the next reference is to block 9, with the counter turning over to 0. The list will now look like Figure 5.44.

Figure 5.44: Timestamps immediately after turnover

Block number	Timestamp
14	65533
22	65535
23	65000
9	0

The next time that a new block has to be loaded, block 9 will be replaced, instead of block 23, which is actually the least recently used block. What effect will this have on performance? At first glance, it doesn't appear that the maximum possible effect could be very large; after all, each turnover would only cause each buffer to be replaced incorrectly once. If we have 100 buffers (a typical number), the worst case would be that the "wrong" buffer is replaced 100 times out of 64K, which is approximately 1.5% of the time; with fewer buffers, the effect is even smaller. There is no danger to the data, since the buffers will be written out if they have changed. I suspected that the cost (under a 16-bit compiler) of handling a unsigned long counter instead of an unsigned short on every call to MakeBlockResident would probably be larger than the cost of this inefficient buffer use, but it didn't appear important either way.

Getting Our Clocks Cleaned

Although the preceding analysis was good enough to convince me not to worry about the counter turning over, unfortunately it wasn't good enough to convince the machine. What actually happened was that after a large number of block references, the program started to run *very* slowly. I was right that the data wasn't in danger, but performance suffered greatly. Why?

Let's go back to our example. Which buffer would be replaced when the next block needed to be read in? The one currently holding block 9, since it has the "lowest" priority. If that block number happened to be 32, for example, that would leave us with the arrangement in Figure 5.45.

Figure 5.45: Timestamps shortly after turnover

Block number	Timestamp
14	65533
22	65535
23	65000
32	1

The problem should now be obvious: the newest block still has the "lowest" priority! The reason that the program started to run very slowly after turnover was that the "fossil" timestamps on the old blocks were preventing them from being reused for more active blocks, so every block that had to be read in had to share buffers with the ones that had been read in after turnover. The solution was fairly simple; on turnover, I set all of the timestamps to 0 to give every buffer the same priority. This isn't really optimal, since it doesn't preserve the relative priority of the blocks already in memory; however, it has the virtue of simplicity, and does reduce the problem to the fairly insignificant level indicated by my first analysis of the turnover problem.

Speed Demon

Is this the end of our concern for the MakeBlockResident routine? Not at all; as befits its central role in the virtual memory mechanism, this routine has undergone quite a few transformations during the development process. One attempt to speed it up took the form of creating a FastResidenceCheck routine that would have the sole purpose of checking whether the old buffer number saved from the previous call to load the same block number was still good; if so, it would return that buffer number after resetting the timestamp. The theoretical advantage of splitting this function off from the more general case was that such a routine might be simple enough to be inlined effectively, which would remove the overhead of one function call from the time needed to make sure that the block in question was memory resident. Unfortunately, this measure turned out to be ineffective; one reason was that the routines that called MakeBlockResident typically didn't reuse the object where the former buffer number was saved, but had to create another one every time they were called by their client routines. Therefore, the attempt to "remember" the previous buffer number wasn't successful in most cases.

While FastResidenceCheck was in use, it suffered from a bug caused by improperly initializing the old buffer number to 0, a valid buffer number. The result of this error was that when a block happened to be loaded into buffer number 0, operator-> didn't initialize the pointer to the ItemIndex array, since the new buffer number "matched" the old buffer number. This problem would have been solved anyway by the new versions of operator->, which always initialize any pointers that might need to be updated; after the attempt to avoid apparently redundant initializations of these pointers caused a couple of bugs, I decided that discretion was the better part of optimization.

As a result of this change, we no longer have to inform the caller of the buffer number that this block contains, so the reference argument to MakeBlockResident for that purpose has been removed.

Virtual Perfection

The acid test of this virtual memory mechanism is to run the program with only one block buffer; unsurprisingly, this test revealed a nasty bug. It seems that I had neglected to initialize the value of the EarliestStamp variable, used to keep track of the buffer with the earliest timestamp. When running with only one buffer, it was possible under some circumstances for a block to be replaced before it was ever used; when this happened, the timestamp on the buffer it had occupied was left set to its initial value of ULONG_MAX. This initial value was significant because the search for the earliest timestamp also starts out by setting the TimeStamp variable to ULONG_MAX, which should be greater than any timestamp found in the search. If there were no blocks in the list with a "real" timestamp, the conditional statement that set the EarliestStamp value in the search loop was never executed. As a result, the EarliestStamp variable was left in an uninitialized state, which caused a wild access to a nonexistent block buffer. The fix was to initialize EarliestStamp to 0, so the first buffer will be selected under these circumstances; you can see this implemented in the current version of MakeBlockResident (Figure 5.46).

The QuantumFile::MakeBlockResident **function**

Figure 5.46: The MakeBlockResident function (from quantum\block.cpp)

```
Block *QuantumFile::MakeBlockResident(ArrayIndex p_BlockNumber)
{
    Ulong TimeStamp;
    ArrayIndex i;
    ArrayIndex EarliestStamp;
    ArrayIndex BufferNumber;

    m_Counter ++;
    if (m_Counter == 0)  // thrash prevention
        {
        for (i = 0; i < m_BlockNumber.GetSize(); i ++)
            m_TimeStamp[i] = 0;
        }

    BufferNumber = FindBuffer(p_BlockNumber,
      (ArrayIndex *)m_BlockNumber.GetDataAddress(),
```

```
        m_BlockNumber.GetSize());

    if (BufferNumber != BadBlockNumber)
        {
        m_TimeStamp[BufferNumber] = m_Counter;
        return m_Block[BufferNumber];
        }

    TimeStamp = ULONG_MAX;
    EarliestStamp = 0; // in case we don't find anything to boot
    for (i = 0; i < m_TimeStamp.GetSize(); i ++)
        {
        if (m_TimeStamp[i] < TimeStamp) // find the earliest timestamp
            {
            TimeStamp = m_TimeStamp[i];
            EarliestStamp = i;
            }
        }

    if (m_BufferModified[EarliestStamp]) /* it needs to be written out */
        Write(EarliestStamp);

    // set block number of new occupant
    m_BlockNumber[EarliestStamp] = p_BlockNumber;

    m_BufferModified[EarliestStamp] = FALSE; // not modified yet
    m_TimeStamp[EarliestStamp] = m_Counter;
    Read(EarliestStamp);

    return m_Block[EarliestStamp];
}
```

We've already covered most of the tricky parts of this function, but let's go over it one more time just to be on the safe side. We begin by incrementing the counter that serves as a timestamp; if it turns over to 0, we set all of the timestamps to 0 to prevent the newest block from being replaced continually.[36] Then we look up the buffer number for the quantum in question, via the FindBuffer global function. If the quantum is found in a buffer, then we merely reset the timestamp on that buffer to indicate that it is the most recently used, and return a pointer to that buffer for use by the operator-> function that called MakeBlockResident.

---

36. In a 32-bit implementation, it's entirely possible that the counter will never turn over, as its maximum value is more than four billion. However, if you let the program run long enough, eventually that will occur; at full tilt, such an event might take a few months.

However, in the event that the quantum we want isn't yet in a buffer, then we have to figure out which buffer it should be read into. We do this by examining the timestamp for each buffer, and selecting the buffer with the earliest timestamp.

Once we have found the buffer that we are going to reuse, we check whether it has been modified; if so, we write it back to the disk. Then we set its block number to the block number of the new quantum that is being read in, set its modified flag to FALSE, set the timestamp on the buffer to the current timestamp, and read the quantum into the buffer. Finally, we return a pointer to the buffer for use by the calling operator-> function.

The Ptr-Patter of Little Blocks

Now that we've seen how MakeBlockResident works, let's see how it is used in one of the "BlockPtr" classes. Because all of these classes work in much the same way, we will examine only one of them in any detail. I've chosen LittlePointerBlockPtr because it made for a better section title, but any of them would have done just as well. First, Figure 5.47 shows the interface for this class.

Figure 5.47: The interface for the LittlePointerBlockPtr class (from quantum\blocki.h)

```
class LittlePointerBlockPtr
{
protected:
LittlePointerBlock m_LittlePointerBlock;
public:
LittlePointerBlockPtr(ArrayIndex p_BlockNumber, QuantumFile *p_BlockManager);
LittlePointerBlockPtr();
LittlePointerBlock *operator->();
};
```

As you can see, this interface isn't very large. In fact, with only one member variable and three functions, it's the smallest one we'll see.[37] However, that doesn't mean that it is completely without interest, as we'll discover. Let's start with the normal constructor, shown in Figure 5.48.

Figure 5.48: The normal constructor for the LittlePointerBlockPtr class (from quantum\block.cpp)

```
LittlePointerBlockPtr::LittlePointerBlockPtr(ArrayIndex p_BlockNumber,
   QuantumFile *p_BlockManager)
{
    m_LittlePointerBlock.m_BlockNumber = p_BlockNumber;
    m_LittlePointerBlock.m_BlockManager = p_BlockManager;
    m_LittlePointerBlock.m_Block = 0;
}
```

This constructor is simple but unrevealing: to see the effects of the variables it is initializing, we will have to wait until we examine the LittlePointerBlock class. For now, let me just say that the block number is the number of the block where the little pointer block is stored, and the block manager is a pointer to the QuantumFile object that controls the quantum file where the little pointer block is stored. The block variable is a pointer to the buffer where the block is stored in memory; it is assigned a value in the next function we will examine, operator-> (Figure 5.49).

The LittlePointerBlockPtr::operator-> **Function**

Figure 5.49: The LittlePointerBlockPtr::operator-> function (from quantum\block.cpp)

```
LittlePointerBlock *LittlePointerBlockPtr::operator->()
{
    m_LittlePointerBlock.m_Block =
    m_LittlePointerBlock.m_BlockManager->MakeBlockResident(
```

---

37. At least, it's the smallest interface for a class that actually does anything. As we'll see, this program contains one class that doesn't contribute either data or functions. I'll explain why that is when we get to it.

```
    m_LittlePointerBlock.m_BlockNumber);

    m_LittlePointerBlock.m_ItemIndex =
    &m_LittlePointerBlock.m_Block->m_QuantumBlockData.m_ItemIndex[0];

    m_LittlePointerBlock.SetLittlePointerArray();

    return &m_LittlePointerBlock;
}
```

As we've seen in the prior discussion of operator->, the return value of this function will be used to point to the object for which the final function will be executed. In this case, that object will be the little pointer block object embedded in this LittlePointerBlockPtr object. The main purpose of this operator-> function is to make sure that the block that the little pointer block object refers to is in memory before we try to do anything with it. That's why QuantumFile::MakeBlockResident exists, and that's why we call it here. Once that function returns, we know that the little pointer block is resident in memory. At that point, we set the item index member variable to the address of the item index in the block, call LittlePointerBlock::SetLittlePointerArray to allow access to the little pointer array in the block, and return the address of our little pointer block object.

When the function that called our operator-> resumes execution, it will reapply the same function call to the pointer that we return. This time, because the return value is in fact a pointer rather than an object, the function call will go through to its final destination.[38]

This would seem to be a logical time to start our examination of how the body class, LittlePointerBlock, works. However, before we get to that class, we have quite a bit of ground to cover. You see, the block classes are arranged in an inheritance tree that begins with a very simple structure called Block, and builds in complexity from there. The best place to start is at the beginning, so that's what we'll do.

Just Up the Block

Figure 5.50 shows the definition of the Block union.

---

38. For a detailed example of how this works, see the section entitled "Polite Pointing".

Figure 5.50: The definition of the Block union (from quantum\blocki.h)

```
union Block
{
    char m_Data[BlockSize];
    char m_QuantumVersionInfo[64];
    QFreeSpaceEntry m_FreeSpaceData[FreeSpaceEntriesPerBlock];
    MainObjectEntry m_MainObjectData[MainObjectEntriesPerBlock];
    QuantumBlockStruct m_QuantumBlockData;
};
```

I don't use the union type very much. In fact, this Block type is the only example of a union in this book. That's because they can be the source of subtle errors if you don't keep track of the actual type of the data in a union very carefully. However, in this case it came in very handy because the different types of blocks have to be identified at run-time anyway; putting the logic that discriminates among the various types of blocks into the various block classes should make it reasonably safe, and in fact I haven't seen any problems from this implementation decision.

So what are all the types of data that can be stored in a Block? The simplest is an array of char taking up the entire block; this low-level type is used when we are copying a block or otherwise treating it as simply a bunch of undifferentiated data. The next possibility, a 64-element array of char, is used in the header block of a quantum file, and consists of a 64 character "version information string". This is used to determine whether the version of the quantum file implementation that wrote the file is the same as the current implementation, as described earlier. The next type is an array of QFreeSpaceEntry elements, which is used in the free space list classes. The next possible type is an array of MainObjectEntry elements, which is used in the main object classes. Finally, a Block can contain a QuantumBlockStruct, which is the data type used to access blocks that contain normal quanta.

The QuantumBlockStruct struct

The last of these types is actually a bit more complicated than it looks, as we'll see when we examine the definition of QuantumBlockStruct, shown in Figure 5.51.

Figure 5.51: The QuantumBlockStruct struct (from quantum\blocki.h)

```
struct QuantumBlockStruct
{
    QuantumBlockHeader m_QuantumBlockHeader;
    ItemIndex m_ItemIndex[1]; // place holder for item index array
};
```

What makes this apparently innocent QuantumBlockStruct data type more mysterious than it looks? The clue is in the comment on the m_ItemIndex variable: this is actually a place holder for a variable-length array of item index elements. Although you cannot directly declare a variable-length array in C or C++, it is possible to use such a place holder to simplify the calculation of the beginning address of a variable-length array that is "mapped" onto a buffer, as we do when accessing data in a quantum block. We'll see how this works when we get to the first of the block classes that is used for accessing data in the normal quantum format rather than as one of the other types (e.g., free space entry or main object entries).

The QuantumBlockHeader struct

We should also take a look at the definition of QuantumBlockHeader, shown in Figure 5.52.

Figure 5.52: The QuantumBlockHeader struct (from quantum\blocki.h)

```
struct QuantumBlockHeader
{
    ObjectType m_QuantumType;
    ObjectNumber m_MainObjectNumber;
```

```
        ArrayIndex m_ItemCount;
};
```

This struct represents the data that is present at the beginning of every block that holds a normal quantum. It consists of three fields: the quantum type field, the object number field, and the item count field.

The quantum type field contains a value indicating the type of the quantum, such as "little pointer array", "big pointer array", or "leaf node". This information could be used to allow a deeper hierarchy of pointer types, but currently it is used only for consistency checking. That is, the top-level quantum pointed to by a main object entry must be a big pointer array quantum, the quantum pointed to by a big pointer array entry must be a little pointer array quantum, and the quantum pointed to by a little pointer entry must be a leaf node (i.e., one that contains user data).

The object number field contains the number of the main object to which this quantum belongs. This is used when we update the free space list, because we do not share a quantum among more than one main object.

The item count field represents the number of data items in this quantum, which is also the number of entries in the variable-length m_ItemIndex array.

The BaseBlockPtr class

Now that we've discussed those data types, we're ready to look at the base class of the block types, BaseBlockPtr, whose interface is shown in Figure 5.53.

We've already discussed the purpose of the Block data type, so I don't have to explain why we have such a variable in this class. The block number variable keeps track of which block in the quantum file this object represents. The block manager variable represents the quantum file object itself, which is used when we are reading or writing the block. As for the implementation of the only member function (Figure 5.54), it merely sets the block number and block manager variable to 0, so I won't bother to discuss it further.

Figure 5.53: The interface for the BaseBlockPtr class (from quantum\blocki.h)

```
class BaseBlockPtr
{
protected:
Block *m_Block;
ArrayIndex m_BlockNumber;
QuantumFile *m_BlockManager;
BaseBlockPtr();
};
```

Figure 5.54: The default constructor for the BaseBlockPtr class (from quantum\block.cpp)

```
BaseBlockPtr::BaseBlockPtr()
{
    m_BlockNumber = 0;
    m_BlockManager = 0;
}
```

Now we're ready to start looking at the derived block classes. I won't bother going over the Ptr handle classes, because they are all essentially identical to LittlePointerBlockPtr, which we've already covered. However, each of the body classes has its own set of member functions appropriate to its specific task, so we'll look at each one in turn, starting with the FreeSpaceBlock class.[39]

The FreeSpaceBlockPtr::FreeSpaceBlock class

The interface for FreeSpaceBlock is shown in Figure 5.55.

---

39. I'm not going to prefix the name of each embedded function or class with the name of its enclosing class, to make the explanations shorter; I'll just include it in the title of the main section discussing the class.

Figure 5.55: The interface for the FreeSpaceBlock class (from quantum\blocki.h)

```
class FreeSpaceBlock : public BaseBlockPtr
{
friend FreeSpaceBlockPtr;
public:
FreeSpaceBlock();
FreeSpaceBlock(ArrayIndex p_BlockNumber, QuantumFile *p_BlockManager);
QFreeSpaceEntry Get(ArrayIndex p_Index);
void Set(ArrayIndex p_Index, QFreeSpaceEntry p_Value);
LeafBlockPtr MakeLeafBlockPtr(ArrayIndex p_Index);
};
```

The default constructor (Figure 5.56) and normal constructor (Figure 5.57) for this class merely initialize the block pointer, block number, and block manager variables for the free space block, exactly as the analogous functions do in the LittlePointerBlockPtr class that we've already examined; we'll see how those variables are used when we get to the other member functions.

Figure 5.56: The default constructor for the FreeSpaceBlock class (from quantum\block.cpp)

```
FreeSpaceBlockPtr::FreeSpaceBlock::FreeSpaceBlock()
{
    m_Block = 0;
}
```

Figure 5.57: The normal constructor for the FreeSpaceBlock class (from quantum\block.cpp)

```
FreeSpaceBlockPtr::FreeSpaceBlock::FreeSpaceBlock(ArrayIndex p_BlockNumber,
QuantumFile *p_BlockManager)
{
    m_BlockNumber = p_BlockNumber;
    m_BlockManager = p_BlockManager;
    m_Block = 0;
}
```

The Get function (Figure 5.58) returns an element of the free space data array in the block, using the m_FreeSpaceData member of the Block union.

Figure 5.58: The FreeSpaceBlock::Get function (from quantum\block.cpp)

```
QFreeSpaceEntry FreeSpaceBlockPtr::FreeSpaceBlock::Get(ArrayIndex p_Index)
{
    return m_Block->m_FreeSpaceData[p_Index];
}
```

The Set function (Figure 5.59) sets the value of an element of the free space data array in the block, also using the m_FreeSpaceData union member.

Figure 5.59: The FreeSpaceBlock::Set function (from quantum\block.cpp)

```
void FreeSpaceBlockPtr::FreeSpaceBlock::Set(ArrayIndex p_Index, QFreeSpaceEntry
p_Value)
{
    m_BlockManager->SetModified(m_BlockNumber);
    m_Block->m_FreeSpaceData[p_Index] = p_Value;
}
```

The MakeLeafBlockPtr function (Figure 5.60) is used in the FreeSpaceArrayPtr::FreeSpaceArray::FindSpaceForItem function to allow that function to access a block as a leaf block so that it can be used to store data. As you can see, this function calls the corresponding function in the QuantumFile class to do the actual work.

Figure 5.60: The FreeSpaceBlock::MakeLeafBlockPtr function (from quantum\block.cpp)

```
LeafBlockPtr FreeSpaceBlockPtr::FreeSpaceBlock::MakeLeafBlockPtr(ArrayIndex p_Index)
{
    return m_BlockManager->MakeLeafBlockPtr(p_Index);
}
```

The MainObjectBlockPtr::MainObjectBlock class

The interface for MainObjectBlock is shown in Figure 5.61.

Figure 5.61: The interface for the MainObjectBlock class (from quantum\blocki.h)

```
class MainObjectBlock : public BaseBlockPtr
{
friend MainObjectBlockPtr;
public:
MainObjectBlock();
MainObjectBlock(ArrayIndex p_BlockNumber, QuantumFile *p_BlockManager);
MainObjectEntry Get(ArrayIndex p_Index);
void Set(ArrayIndex p_Index, MainObjectEntry p_Value);
};
```

As you can see, this interface is exactly the same as the one for FreeSpaceArrayPtr::FreeSpaceArray, except that the MakeLeafBlockPtr function is not included and the types used by the Get and Set functions are different, as is necessary for their proper functioning. Because the default and normal constructors are exactly the same as those in the previous class, I'm not going to waste space reproducing them here, so let's move right along to the Get and Set functions.

The Get function (Figure 5.62) returns an element of the main object array in the block, using the m_MainObjectData union member.

Figure 5.62: The MainObjectBlock::Get function (from quantum\block.cpp)

```
MainObjectEntry MainObjectBlockPtr::MainObjectBlock::Get(ArrayIndex p_Index)
{
    return m_Block->m_MainObjectData[p_Index];
}
```

The Set function (Figure 5.63) sets the value of an element of the main object array in the block, also using the m_MainObjectData union member.

Figure 5.63: The MainObjectBlock::Set function (from quantum\block.cpp)

```
void MainObjectBlockPtr::MainObjectBlock::Set(ArrayIndex p_Index, MainObjectEntry
p_Value)
{
    m_BlockManager->SetModified(m_BlockNumber);
    m_Block->m_MainObjectData[p_Index] = p_Value;
}
```

The QuantumBlock class

The interface for QuantumBlock is shown in Figure 5.64. This is a more interesting class than the previous few we've discussed; it has a number of fairly complicated functions that we will need to go over in detail. Probably the best place to start is with the AddItem function, because that is the function that adds each item to a quantum.

Figure 5.64: The interface for the QuantumBlock class (from quantum\blocki.h)

```
class QuantumBlock : public BaseBlockPtr
{
protected:
  ItemIndex *m_ItemIndex;
public:
  void SetItemCount(ArrayIndex p_NewItemCount);
  void SetQuantumType(ObjectType p_QuantumType);
  ObjectType GetQuantumType();
  void SetMainObjectNumber(ObjectNumber p_MainObjectNumber);
  ObjectNumber GetMainObjectNumber();
  ArrayIndex GetItemCount();
  ModifiableElement GetModifiableItem(ArrayIndex p_ItemNumber);
  ItemIndex GetItemIndexEntry(ArrayIndex p_ItemNumber);
  AccessVector<Ulong> GetAccessVectorUlong(ArrayIndex p_ItemNumber);
  void DeleteItem(ArrayIndex p_ItemNumber);
  ArrayIndex AddItem(ModifiableElement p_Element,
      ObjectType p_Type, ArrayIndex p_Index);
  ArrayIndex AddItem(void *p_Element, ArrayIndex p_ElementSize,
      ObjectType p_Type, ArrayIndex p_Index);
  void UpdateFreeSpace();
  ArrayIndex CalculateFreeSpace();
```

```
void SetModified();
void Clear();
void DumpQuantumBlock(); // for debugging
bool CheckQuantumBlock(); // for debugging
};
```

The QuantumBlock::AddItem Function

Since there are actually two versions of this function, let's start with the simpler one, which takes a ModifiableElement (i.e., String) first argument. The code for this function is shown in Figure 5.65.

Figure 5.65: One overloaded version of the QuantumBlock::AddItem function (from quantum\block.cpp)

```
ArrayIndex QuantumBlock::AddItem(ModifiableElement p_Element, ObjectType p_Type,
    ArrayIndex p_Index)
{
    ArrayIndex ItemSize = p_Element.GetSize();
    void *ItemAddress = p_Element.GetDataAddress();

    return AddItem(ItemAddress, ItemSize, p_Type, p_Index);
}
```

As you can see, this function retrieves the size and data address from its ModifiableElement argument and then calls the other overloaded AddItem function, returning the result of that function to its caller. So let's continue by looking at the other AddItem function, whose code is shown in Figure 5.66.

Figure 5.66: The other overloaded version of the QuantumBlock::AddItem function (from quantum\block.cpp)

```
ArrayIndex QuantumBlock::AddItem(void *p_ItemAddress, ArrayIndex p_ElementSize,
    ObjectType p_Type, ArrayIndex p_Index)
{
    ArrayIndex StartingOffset;
    ArrayIndex LastItemOffset;
    char *DataFrom;
```

```
char *DataTo;
ArrayIndex DataLength;
ItemIndex TempItemIndex;
int ItemFound;
ArrayIndex ItemNumber;
ArrayIndex ItemCount;

SetModified();

ItemFound = FindUnusedItem(&m_ItemIndex[0], GetItemCount());

ArrayIndex FreeSpace = CalculateFreeSpace();

qfassert(FreeSpace > p_ElementSize);

if (ItemFound >= 0) // we can reuse an item
    {
    m_ItemIndex[ItemFound].m_Type = p_Type;
    m_ItemIndex[ItemFound].m_Index = p_Index;

    StartingOffset = m_ItemIndex[ItemFound].m_Offset;
    ItemCount = GetItemCount();
    LastItemOffset = m_ItemIndex[ItemCount-1].m_Offset;
    DataFrom = m_Block->m_Data + BlockSize - LastItemOffset;
    DataTo = DataFrom - p_ElementSize;
    DataLength = LastItemOffset - StartingOffset;
    BlockMove(DataTo,DataFrom,DataLength);

    AdjustOffset(&m_ItemIndex[ItemFound],ItemCount-ItemFound,
        p_ElementSize);

    DataTo = m_Block->m_Data + BlockSize - m_ItemIndex[ItemFound].m_Offset;
    BlockMove(DataTo,p_ItemAddress,p_ElementSize);
    ItemNumber = ItemFound + 1;
    }
else    // must make a new item
    {
    if (GetItemCount() == 0)
        TempItemIndex.m_Offset = p_ElementSize;
    else
        {
        LastItemOffset = m_ItemIndex[GetItemCount()-1].m_Offset;
        TempItemIndex.m_Offset = LastItemOffset + p_ElementSize;
        }
    DataTo = m_Block->m_Data + BlockSize - TempItemIndex.m_Offset;
    BlockMove(DataTo,p_ItemAddress,p_ElementSize);

    TempItemIndex.m_Type = p_Type;
```

```
            TempItemIndex.m_Index = p_Index;
            m_ItemIndex[GetItemCount()] = TempItemIndex;
            SetItemCount(GetItemCount()+1);
            ItemNumber = GetItemCount(); // 1-based
            }
        UpdateFreeSpace();
        return ItemNumber;
}
```

This starts by setting the modified flag for its block; because we are going to modify the block, we want to make sure that the block is written back to disk before the buffer is reused. Then we call a global function called FindUnusedItem to locate an item index entry that we can use for our new item.[40] Then we call CalculateFreeSpace to figure out how much space is available in this block. This is actually a safety measure, as the calling function is responsible for making sure that this block has enough free space before attempting to add an item to the block. But I'd rather be safe than sorry, so I check whether the free space is insufficient; if not, this is an error, which is trapped by the assert that immediately follows.

However, let's assume that we do have sufficient room to store the new item. In that case, we continue by checking whether the item number that was returned by FindUnusedItem is greater than or equal to 0. If so, we are going to reuse an item that has been previously used, so we set its type and index value to the new values supplied as arguments to the AddItem function.

We've referred to the ItemIndex data type a few times in the past, but haven't really looked at what it consists of. I think this would be a good time to do so, so let's take a look at its definition, which is shown in Figure 5.67.

Figure 5.67: The definition of the ItemIndex struct (from quantum\blocki.h)

```
struct ItemIndex
{
        unsigned m_Index:32; // must be size of ArrayIndex
// Note: must consider changing the next two items if increasing block size
        unsigned m_Offset:16;
        unsigned m_Type:16;
```

---

40. I'll cover this and the other global functions in the next chapter.

};

This is a fairly simple data type, consisting of an index entry (which represents the element number of this item in the array of which it is an element), the offset of the beginning of the data for the element from the end of the block, and a type indicator that specifies the type of the element. While the purpose of the offset member variable should be fairly obvious, the purpose of the other two member variables may not be. The purpose of the type indicator is consistency checking; if we're trying to access a little pointer array, we can use this type indicator to make sure that we are getting what we expect. In a similar vein, the purpose of the index entry is to provide information needed by a program that will recover data from a quantum file that has become corrupted.

Now let's continue with our analysis of the AddItem function (Figure 5.66), where we have just updated the type and index of the item index entry that we are reusing to the new values supplied as arguments to this function. Next, we extract the offset field from that item index entry and call GetItemCount to find out how many items are in the index. Now we have to calculate the parameters needed to shift the data already in the quantum so that we have room for our new item. The offset of the last item is equal to the distance in bytes from the beginning of that item to the first byte after the end of the quantum. Therefore, the address of the beginning of the last item in the quantum, DataFrom, can be calculated as the address of the beginning of the buffer in which the quantum resides, plus the size of a quantum, minus the offset of the last item in the quantum. The byte at that address, and all those after it up to the starting address for the new item's data, must be moved down in memory by enough to leave room for the new data.[41] Therefore, the new address of that first byte of the last item's data, DataTo, will be its old address minus p_ElementSize. We want to move all of the items that precede our new item in memory, which means those that have higher item numbers; therefore, the number of bytes we want to move, DataLength, is equal to the distance from the beginning of the last item to the beginning of the area where we will store our new item. Now that we have

---

41. It is important to remember that the last item in a quantum is actually at the lowest address of any item in that quantum, because items are stored in the quantum starting from the end and working back toward the beginning of the quantum.

calculated these parameters, we can call the global BlockMove function to perform the transfer.

Now we have moved the existing data, but the index still refers to the old locations of the data, so we have to call the global AdjustOffset function to adjust the elements of the item index that refer to data that has been moved. Once we have adjusted the item index, we calculate the address where the new data will be stored and call BlockMove again, this time to copy the new data to the correct place in the block. Finally, we calculate the return value from this function, which is the item number of the item we have entered, as one more than the index of the item entry we reused; this adjustment is needed because item numbers start at 1 rather than 0.

I think an example might be very helpful here. Suppose that we want to insert a new field with index number 6 to store the company name ("Chrysalis") in the following quantum, reusing the currently unused fourth item (see Figure 5.68).

Figure 5.68: Item index and data before item insertion

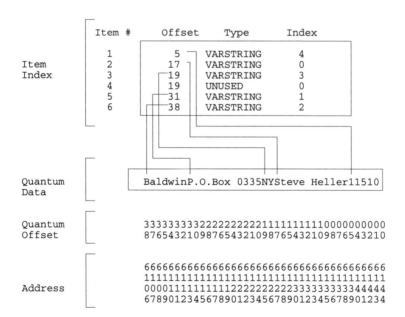

To do this, we have to move items 5 and 6 toward the beginning of the quantum by 9 characters, which is the length of the new item. Assuming that the address of the beginning of the buffer holding the quantum is 4096 and BlockSize is 2048, the address of the beginning of the last item is 4096+2048-38, or 6106, which is the value of DataFrom. The value of DataTo is calculated from DataFrom by subtracting the length of the new item, or 9, resulting in 6097. The value of DataLength is the amount of data to move; we have to move everything from the last item up to but not including the place where we are going to put the new data. We could add up the lengths of all of the items from the last item to the one before which we will insert our new data, but it is easier simply to subtract the offset of that item from the offset of the last item, which produces the same result: 38 - 19, or 19 bytes to be moved.

After the move, the quantum looks like Figure 5.69.

Figure 5.69: Item index and data after move

```
          Item #      Offset    Type           Index

            1            5  ┐ VARSTRING          4
Item        2           17  ┐ VARSTRING          0
Index       3         ┌─19    VARSTRING          3
            4           19    UNUSED             0
            5        ┌─31     VARSTRING          1
            6      ┌─┬─38     VARSTRING          2
```

```
Quantum
Data          │ BaldwinP.O.Box 0335????????NYSteve Heller11510 │
```

```
Quantum       4444444433333333333322222222221111111111110000000000
Offset        7654321098765432109876543210987654321098765432109876543210
```

```
              666666666666666666666666666666666666666666666666666
Address       999111111111111111111111111111111111111111111111111
              999000000000001111111111222222222233333333334444444
              789012345678901234567890123456789012345678901234
```

Of course, all of the item index entries from the one we are inserting to the last one now have the wrong offset; we have to add the size of the new item to these offsets, to account for the move we just did, which we do by calling AdjustOffset.

We're almost done with this insertion. All we have left is to calculate the actual position of the new item in the quantum as the quantum buffer's address + the size of a quantum - the offset of this item, (4096+2048-28, or 6116) and store the result in DataTo. Then we can call BlockMove to copy the new item's data to that position, and finish up by setting the relative item number (which is the return value from this function) to ItemFound + 1 and returning it. The final quantum contents look like Figure 5.70.

Figure 5.70: Item index and data after item insertion

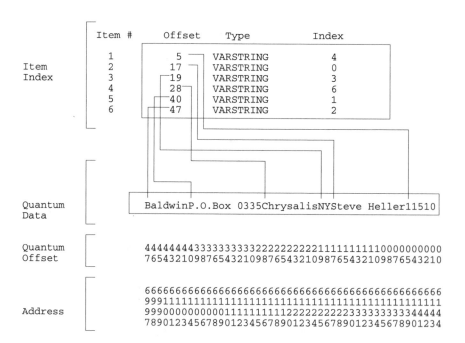

The above scenario handles the case of reusing an item index slot. The code following the comment that says "must make a new item" deals with the case where we have to add a new item index element at the end of the index, which is somewhat simpler, as we don't have to move any preexisting data: our new item is the last in the quantum.

Something New

When adding a new item, there are two subsidiary possibilities: that this is the first element in the item index, or that there are existing elements in the item index and we're adding a new one at the end.

Of course, the simplest case of all is the one where there aren't any items in the quantum as yet. In this case, the offset of the new item is equal to its size. However, if there are some items in the quantum already, then the offset of the new item is equal to the offset of the last item in the quantum added to the size of the new item. Once we have calculated the offset, we can move the new item's data to its position in the quantum. Then we set the type and index of the new item and store it in the last position of the m_ItemIndex array, set the ItemNumber to one more than the number of items that were in the array before, increment the item count, and return the relative item number to the calling routine.

Finally, whether we have reused an existing item or added a new one, we call UpdateFreeSpace to recompute the amount of free space in the quantum, then return the item number of the new item.

The QuantumBlock::GetModifiableItem **Function**

Now that we have seen how to add an item to a quantum, perhaps we should take a look at the function that allows us to get it back: GetModifiableItem (shown in Figure 5.71).

Figure 5.71: The QuantumBlock::GetModifiableItem Function (from quantum\block.cpp)

```
ModifiableElement QuantumBlock::GetModifiableItem(ArrayIndex p_ItemNumber)
{
    ModifiableElement TempItem;
    ArrayIndex StartingOffset;
    ArrayIndex Length;
```

```
    char *StartingLocation;

    qfassert (p_ItemNumber > 0 && p_ItemNumber <= GetItemCount());
    p_ItemNumber --; /* make it zero-based */
    StartingOffset = m_ItemIndex[p_ItemNumber].m_Offset;
    StartingLocation = m_Block->m_Data + BlockSize - StartingOffset;
    if (p_ItemNumber == 0) /* the first one goes to the end of the block */
        Length = StartingOffset;
    else
        Length = StartingOffset - m_ItemIndex[p_ItemNumber-1].m_Offset;
    TempItem = ModifiableElement(Length, StartingLocation);

    return TempItem;
}
```

As you might imagine, retrieving an item is simpler than storing the item in the first place, because we don't have to move anything around. We start with an assert that checks two conditions: that the item number is greater than 0 and that it is less than or equal to the item count. Once we have passed that sanity check, we decrement the item number to convert it to an index into the item index array, then retrieve the offset of the item from its item index entry. Then we calculate its actual starting address and length, which gives us the information necessary to create a ModifiableElement from the data. We do so, and return the result to the caller.

The QuantumBlock::DeleteItem **function**

The third fundamental operation that we can perform on an item is to delete it. This operation is used both when simply deleting an item from the main object and when changing the value of an item; to change an item, we actually delete the previous item and add a new one. So let's take a look at DeleteItem (shown in Figure 5.72).

Figure 5.72: The QuantumBlock::DeleteItem function (from quantum\block.cpp)

```
void QuantumBlock::DeleteItem(ArrayIndex p_ItemNumber)
{
    ArrayIndex StartingOffset;
    int i; // must be signed for termination condition
```

```
ArrayIndex LastItemOffset;
char *DataFrom;
char *DataTo;
ArrayIndex DataLength;
ArrayIndex Length;
SetModified();

qfassert (p_ItemNumber > 0 && p_ItemNumber <= GetItemCount());

p_ItemNumber --; /* make it zero-based */
if (p_ItemNumber == GetItemCount() - 1) // it's the last one
    {
    m_ItemIndex[p_ItemNumber].m_Type = UNUSED_ITEM;
    for (i = GetItemCount() - 1; i >= 0; i --)
        {
        if (m_ItemIndex[i].m_Type == UNUSED_ITEM)
            {
            m_ItemIndex[i].m_Offset = 0;
            m_ItemIndex[i].m_Index = 0;
            m_ItemIndex[i].m_Type = 0;
            }
        else
            break;
        }
    SetItemCount(i+1);
    if (i == -1) // we've cleared out the whole block
        Clear();
    UpdateFreeSpace();
    return;
    }

StartingOffset = m_ItemIndex[p_ItemNumber].m_Offset;
if (p_ItemNumber == 0) /* the first one goes to the end of the block */
    Length = StartingOffset;
else
    Length = StartingOffset - m_ItemIndex[p_ItemNumber-1].m_Offset;

LastItemOffset = m_ItemIndex[GetItemCount()-1].m_Offset;
DataFrom = m_Block->m_Data + BlockSize - LastItemOffset;
DataTo = DataFrom + Length;
DataLength = LastItemOffset - StartingOffset;
BlockMove(DataTo,DataFrom,DataLength);

AdjustOffset(&m_ItemIndex[p_ItemNumber+1],
    GetItemCount()-(p_ItemNumber+1), -1*Length);

m_ItemIndex[p_ItemNumber].m_Type = UNUSED_ITEM;
```

```
//Must set up correct offset for length calculation of next item
if (p_ItemNumber == 0)
    m_ItemIndex[p_ItemNumber].m_Offset = 0;
else
    m_ItemIndex[p_ItemNumber].m_Offset =
        m_ItemIndex[p_ItemNumber-1].m_Offset;

UpdateFreeSpace();
}
```

After checking that the item number is legal and converting it to an index into the item index array, we determine whether the item to be deleted is the last one in the quantum. If so, we set its type to UNUSED_ITEM. While this would be sufficient to allow the reuse of this item index entry, if we stopped there, we would never be able to reduce the size of the item index; eventually, the quantum would fill up with unused item index entries, leaving no room for actual data. To prevent this, we clean up any trailing unused entries in the item index by searching backwards from the end of the item index, clearing any trailing unused entries to zeroes.[42] When we get to an item index entry that is in use, or to the beginning of the item index, we stop searching. At that point, we reset the item count to 1 more than the last value of the index in the loop. If that last loop index value was -1, then we have emptied the quantum, so we call Clear to reset it to an unused state. Finally, we call UpdateFreeSpace to recalculate the amount of free space in the quantum and return the result to the caller.

That takes care of deleting the last item in a quantum, but what if we need to delete some other item? In that case, we extract the starting offset of the item to be deleted and calculate its length. For the first item, the item length is equal to the m_Offset field in the item, because the data for the first item in the quantum is stored at the end of the quantum, as illustrated in Figure 5.2. For other items, the item length is equal to the offset of the previous item subtracted from the offset of the current item. This may seem backward, as the figure shows that the second item is stored before the first, the third before the second, and so on. However, the offset of an item is defined as the distance in bytes from the start of the item to the first byte after the end of the quantum, which is always nonnegative.

---

42. We can't delete unused item index entries that aren't at the end of the index because that would change the item numbers of the following items, rendering them inaccessible.

We also have to set the offset of this item to the offset of the previous item (if there is a previous item), which will indicate that this item's length is zero. For the first item, we can just set the offset to zero, since there is no previous item to worry about.

Now we're ready to compute the offset of the last item, the source and destination addresses for the data to be moved into the deleted item's space, and the length of that data. We calculate the source address (DataFrom) as the address of the last item (m_Block->m_Data+BlockSize-LastItemOffset), the destination address (DataTo) as the source address added to the length of the item we are deleting (DataFrom+item length), and the number of bytes to move (DataLength) as the total length of all the items from the one we are deleting to the last item (LastItemOffset - StartingOffset) Then we call BlockMove to transfer the data and AdjustOffset to update the offsets of the other items. Next, we set the item's type to UNUSED_ITEM and its offset to the same value as the previous entry in the item index (or 0, if it is the first item) so that the length of the next item can be properly calculated. Finally, we call UpdateFreeSpace and return to the calling function.

To make this clearer, let's look at what happens if we delete the item holding the state name from the example in Figure 5.73. Let's suppose the address of the quantum is 4096. The offset of the last item, marked by "^", is 41; substituting values in the expression for DataFrom, m_Block->m_Data+BlockSize-LastItemOffset equals 4096+2048-41, or 6103. The offset of the item we're deleting, marked by the "*", is 19, and the offset of the previous item (marked by the "&") is 17, which makes the item length 2; therefore, the DataTo address is 6103+2, or 6105. This is where the last item will start after the move, since we are removing the 2 bytes of the item being deleted. Finally, DataLength is the amount of data to be moved, which is the length of all the items with higher index numbers than the one being deleted, in this case 41-19, or 22.

Figure 5.73: Sample IRA, etc., before deletion

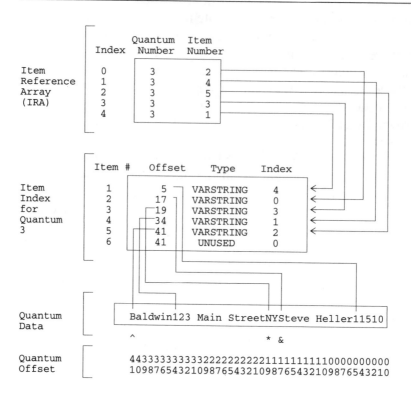

After we do the move, the result looks like Figure 5.74. The data is in the right place now, but the pointers are wrong. Specifically, the m_Offset fields of the items that have higher item numbers than the one we have deleted are off by the length of the deleted field. That's why we have to call AdjustOffset to reduce the m_Offset field of every item after the deleted one by ItemLength, which is the length of the deleted item. Then we set the data type of the deleted item in the item index to UNUSED_ITEM.

Figure 5.74: Sample IRA, etc., during deletion

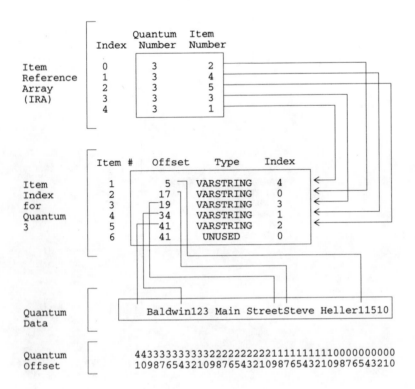

After correcting the index, our quantum looks like Figure 5.75. We can now access the data in the quantum correctly, as long as we use the "official" route through the IRA and the item index.[43]

---

43. Of course, in the real program, we will find the IRA by looking it up in the main object index, but that detail is irrelevant to the current discussion of deleting an element.

Figure 5.75: Sample IRA, etc., after deletion

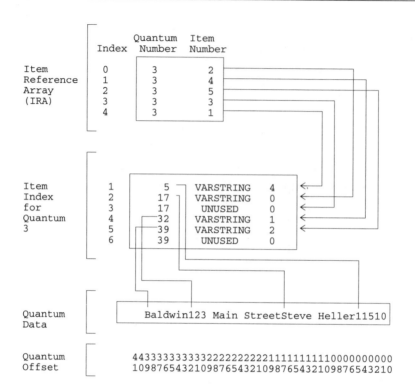

The QuantumBlock::CalculateFreeSpace function

Another interesting function in this class is CalculateFreeSpace. You might think that this would be a very simple function, but it has a few twists, as you will see by looking at its code, shown in Figure 5.76.

Figure 5.76: The QuantumBlock::CalculateFreeSpace function (from quantum\block.cpp)

```
ArrayIndex QuantumBlock::CalculateFreeSpace()
{
    int FreeSpace;
    ArrayIndex LastItemOffset;
    ArrayIndex ItemCount = GetItemCount();
```

```
qfassert (ItemCount < NoItem);

if (ItemCount == NoItem-1) // can't add any new items to this block
    return 0;

FreeSpace = BlockSize - (Margin + sizeof(QuantumBlockHeader));

if (GetItemCount() == 0)
    {
    // Make adjustment to mark this quantum as "available"
    FreeSpace = FreeSpaceConversion * AvailableQuantum;
    return(FreeSpace);
    }

LastItemOffset = m_ItemIndex[GetItemCount()-1].m_Offset;
FreeSpace -= LastItemOffset;
FreeSpace -= sizeof(ItemIndex) * GetItemCount();

if (FreeSpace < 0)
    FreeSpace = 0;

if (FreeSpace >= FreeSpaceConversion * AvailableQuantum)
    return FreeSpaceConversion * AvailableQuantum - 1;

return(FreeSpace);
}
```

As we frequently do, we begin with an assert that tests the validity of the key data used by the function; in this case, that takes the form of checking that the number of items in this quantum is within the legal limit, i.e., that it is less than the NoItem constant used to indicate an invalid item number. Assuming that it passes that test, we then check whether we have already stored the maximum possible number of items in this quantum. If so, we "lie" to the caller by returning the value 0, indicating that there is no space available in this quantum. Of course, this is a white lie, because without an available entry in the item index, we cannot in fact add any new items to this quantum, so the caller needs to look elsewhere.

Assuming that we pass that test, we can calculate the free space in the quantum by a series of steps. First, we subtract the size of the quantum block header (plus a margin of safety) from the size of a block. If the number of items in the block is equal to 0, we have the answer: the quantum should be marked as having the maximum possible free space, so we compute the free space code that indicates this situation and return it to the caller.[44]

On the other hand, if there are some items in the quantum then we calculate the offset of the last item in the quantum and subtract it from the free space. Then we calculate the size of the item index as the number of entries in the item index multiplied by the size of one entry, and subtract it from the free space. If the result comes out to be less than 0, we return 0; otherwise, we return the calculated free space.

The QuantumBlock::UpdateFreeSpace **Function**

As long as we're discussing the intriguing topic of free space, we might as well take a look at UpdateFreeSpace, whose code is shown in Figure 5.77.

Figure 5.77: The QuantumBlock::UpdateFreeSpace function (from quantum\block.cpp)

```
void QuantumBlock::UpdateFreeSpace()
{
    QFreeSpaceEntry SpaceAvailable;

    SpaceAvailable.m_ObjectNumber = GetMainObjectNumber();
    SpaceAvailable.m_FreeSpaceCode =
        FreeSpaceCode(CalculateFreeSpace()/FreeSpaceConversion);
    m_BlockManager->SetFreeSpace(
        m_BlockNumber-m_BlockManager->GetQuantumNumberAdjustment(),
        SpaceAvailable);
    SetModified();
}
```

Why do we need this function, when we already have a function to calculate the amount of free space in a quantum? This is not just another version of the CalculateFreeSpace function, because it actually

---

44. The statement that calculates the value we should return for an empty quantum may be a bit puzzling. The reason it works as it does is that the routine that looks for an empty block compares the available free space code to a specific value, namely AvailableQuantum. If we did not return a value that corresponded to that free space code, a quantum that was ever used for anything would never be considered empty again.

updates the information in the free space list. As you may recall, the free space list stores more than just the amount of free space in a quantum; it also stores the object number of the main object that quantum belongs to. This is so that we can avoid scanning a lot of quanta to find one that has enough free space in it and also belongs to the main object that we need the additional space for. Now that we know what this function does, it shouldn't be too hard to determine how it does it. First, it sets the object number of a newly created free space object to the object number of the block for which the free space is being updated. Then it converts the free space calculated by the CalculateFreeSpace function to a free space code, which occupies only one byte. Finally, it uses the SetFreeSpace function of the quantum file class to update the free space list with the new information for this quantum.

The rest of the functions in the quantum block class aren't particularly interesting or instructive, so we won't bother to go over them. You shouldn't have much trouble understanding how they work by simply looking at the code, which is all on the CD ROM in the back of the book, along with the DJGPP compiler. The next class we will examine is the big pointer block class, which is derived from the quantum block class.

The BigPointerBlock class

The interface for BigPointerBlock is shown in Figure 5.78.

Figure 5.78: The interface for the BigPointerBlock class (from quantum\blocki.h)

```
class BigPointerBlock : public QuantumBlock
{
friend BigPointerBlockPtr;
protected:
BigArrayHeader *m_BigArrayHeader;
BigPointerArray m_BigPointerArray;
public:
  BigPointerArray &GetBigPointerArray(){return m_BigPointerArray;};
  void SetBigArrayHeader();
  void SetBigPointerArray();
```

```
ArrayIndex GetBigArrayElementCount();
void SetBigArrayElementCount(ArrayIndex p_ElementCount);
ArrayIndex GetBigArrayMaxElementCount();
QuantumNumber GetBigArrayElement(ArrayIndex p_Index);
void SetBigArrayElement(ArrayIndex p_Index, QuantumNumber p_Element);
QuantumNumber GetLastQuantumAddedTo();
void SetLastQuantumAddedTo(QuantumNumber p_QuantumNumber);
void DumpQuantumBlock();
};
```

Most of the functions in this class aren't very interesting, so we won't bother to go over them. However, there are a couple that we should take a quick look at, because they contain a few tricks that you should understand if you're going to have to modify the behavior of any of these classes. We'll start with SetBigArrayHeader, whose code is shown in Figure 5.79.

The BigPointerBlock::SetBigArrayHeader Function

Figure 5.79: The BigPointerBlock::SetBigArrayHeader function (from quantum\block.cpp)

```
void BigPointerBlock::SetBigArrayHeader()
{
    ArrayIndex StartingOffset;
    char *StartingLocation;

    StartingOffset = m_ItemIndex[0].m_Offset;
    StartingLocation = m_Block->m_Data + BlockSize - StartingOffset;
    m_BigArrayHeader = (BigArrayHeader *)(StartingLocation);
}
```

The purpose of this function is to allow us to access data that is stored in the big pointer block quantum. To be precise, the data that we are going to access is the "big array header", which includes information about the number of elements in the array, the maximum number of elements in the array, and the last quantum where we added data for this array.[45]

---

45. It is important to note that the number of elements that I'm referring to here is not the number of elements in the big pointer array (i.e., the number of quanta that the small pointer array occupy) but the actual number of elements in the array itself (i.e., the number of data items that the user has stored in the array).

As you can see by looking at the code, the member variable m_BigArrayHeader is a pointer to the data in the quantum. This is not hazardous, because the header consists of several fields, each of which is fixed length; therefore, we don't have to worry about running off the end of the data in the header.

Once we have executed the SetBigArrayHeader function, we can call the various access functions that get and set these values in the array header, where it resides in the big pointer array quantum buffer in memory.[46]

The BigPointerBlock::SetBigPointerArray **Function**

The next function we'll look at is SetBigPointerArray, whose code is shown in Figure 5.80.

Figure 5.80: The BigPointerBlock::SetBigPointerArray function (from quantum\block.cpp)

```
void BigPointerBlock::SetBigPointerArray()
{
    ArrayIndex StartingOffset;
    ArrayIndex Length;
    char *StartingLocation;
    ArrayIndex ElementCount;

    StartingOffset = m_ItemIndex[1].m_Offset;
    StartingLocation = m_Block->m_Data + BlockSize - StartingOffset;
    Length = StartingOffset - m_ItemIndex[0].m_Offset;
    ElementCount = Length/sizeof(QuantumNumber);
    m_BigPointerArray = BigPointerArray(ElementCount,
        (QuantumNumber *)StartingLocation);
}
```

This function is superficially similar to the one that we just discussed; its purpose is to allow us to access data that is in the big pointer array quantum. However, there is a major difference between these two functions: while the previous function could safely provide

---

46. Note that we have to remember to set the modified flag for the big pointer array quantum whenever we change a value in the big pointer array header or the big pointer array itself, so that these changes will be reflected on the disk rather than being lost.

us with a simple pointer to the big array header data structure in the big pointer array quantum, that would be extremely unsafe in the case of the big pointer array itself. The problem is that a big pointer array can have a variable number of elements in it, so it would be all too easy for us to accidentally step off the end of the big pointer array, with potentially disastrous results. To prevent such a possibility, I have created the data type called AccessVector. The purpose of this data type is to combine the safety features of a normal SVector with the ability to specify the address where the data for the SVector should start, rather than relying on the run-time memory allocation library to assign the address. Because this data type is designed to refer to an existing area of memory, the copy constructor is defaulted, as is the assignment operator and the destructor, and there is no SetSize function such as exists for "regular" SVectors. This data type allows us to "map" a predefined structure onto an existing set of data, which is exactly what we need to access a big pointer array safely.

As this suggests, the "big array header" is an AccessVector variable, which we can use just as though it were a normal SVector.[47]

The LittlePointerBlock class

The interface for LittlePointerBlock is shown in Figure 5.81.

Figure 5.81: The interface for the LittlePointerBlock class (from quantum\blocki.h)

```
class LittlePointerBlock : public QuantumBlock
{
friend LittlePointerBlockPtr;
protected:
LittlePointerArray m_LittlePointerArray;
public:
  void SetLittlePointerArray();
  void ClearLittleArray();
```

---

47. Although we will be unable to go into the details of the implementation of the AccessVector type, it is defined in the header file vector.h; if you are familiar with C++ templates, I recommend that you read that header file to understand how this type actually works.

```
ItemReference GetLittleArrayElement(ArrayIndex p_Index);
void SetLittleArrayElement(ArrayIndex p_Index, ItemReference p_ItemReference);
ArrayIndex GetLittleArraySize();
};
```

There's nothing in this class that isn't exactly analogous to the corresponding functions in the big pointer array class. Therefore, I won't waste either your time or mine by repeating the analysis of the big pointer array class here. Instead, let's move along to another class that is somewhat more interesting, if only because it seems to have no purpose for existing.

The LeafBlock class

The interface for LeafBlock is shown in Figure 5.82.

Figure 5.82: The interface for the LeafBlock class (from quantum\blocki.h)

```
class LeafBlock : public QuantumBlock
{
friend LeafBlockPtr;
};
```

This is a real oddity: a class that defines no new member functions or member variables. Of what value could such a class possibly be?

The answer is that it provides a "hook" for attaching a handle class, namely LeafBlockPtr. This allows us to use a leaf block just as we would any of the other quantum classes. If we did not have this class, we could always create another class called QuantumBlockPtr, which would have much the same effect as creating this class. So why did I create this class in the first place?

The answer is that originally it did have some member functions, but they eventually turned out to be superfluous. At this point in the development of this project, it would probably be unwise for me to go through the code to root out all of the references to this class. And after all, a class that defines no new member functions or member variables certainly can't take up too much extra space; in fact, using this class should have absolutely no effect on the size of the program or its execution time, so I think I'll leave it just as it is, at least for now.

The FreeSpaceArray class

Finally, we're finished with the block classes. Our next target of opportunity will be the classes that maintain and provide access to the free space list. We'll start with FreeSpaceArray, whose interface is shown in Figure 5.83.

Figure 5.83: The interface for the FreeSpaceArray class (from quantum\newquant.h)

```
class FreeSpaceArray
{
friend FreeSpaceArrayPtr;
protected:
SVector<FreeSpaceBlockPtr> m_BlockPtr;
ArrayIndex m_FreeSpaceListCount;
ArrayIndex m_FreeSpaceListBlockCount;
ArrayIndex m_CurrentLowestFreeBlock;
ArrayIndex m_QuantumBlockNumberAdjustment;
int m_ReferenceCount;

public:
      FreeSpaceArray();
      FreeSpaceArray(QuantumFile *p_QuantumFile);
      ~FreeSpaceArray();
QFreeSpaceEntry Get(ArrayIndex p_Index);
void Set(ArrayIndex p_Index, QFreeSpaceEntry p_Entry);
QuantumNumber FindEmptyBlock();
QuantumNumber FindSpaceForItem(ObjectNumber p_ObjectNumber, ArrayIndex p_ItemSize);
ArrayIndex QGetFreeSpaceListCount() {return m_FreeSpaceListCount;}
};
```

The Normal Constructor for FreeSpaceArray

The first function we'll look at is the normal constructor for FreeSpaceArray, whose code is shown in Figure 5.84.

Figure 5.84: The normal constructor for FreeSpaceArray (from quantum\newquant.cpp)

```
FreeSpaceArrayPtr::FreeSpaceArray::FreeSpaceArray(QuantumFile *p_MRU)
{
    ArrayIndex i;

    m_CurrentLowestFreeBlock = 0;
    m_FreeSpaceListCount = p_MRU->QGetFreeSpaceListCount();
    m_FreeSpaceListBlockCount = p_MRU->QGetFreeSpaceListBlockCount();
    m_QuantumBlockNumberAdjustment = p_MRU->GetQuantumNumberAdjustment();
    m_BlockPtr.SetSize(p_MRU->QGetFreeSpaceListBlockCount());
    for (i = 0; i < m_BlockPtr.GetSize(); i ++)
        m_BlockPtr[i] = p_MRU->MakeFreeSpaceBlockPtr(i);
}
```

As you can see, all this function does (as is common in the case of constructors) is to initialize a number of member variables. Most of these initializations are fairly straightforward, but we should go over them briefly. First, we set the current lowest free block number to 0, because we have no idea what blocks might be free in the free space list, as we have not looked through it yet. Then we get the free space list count, the number of blocks in the free space list, and the quantum number adjustment from the quantum file object; this last value is used when we need to convert between block numbers and quantum numbers. Next, we resize the block pointer SVector so it can hold block pointers for all of the free space list blocks in the quantum file. Finally, we assign free space block pointers to all the elements of that SVector. Now we are ready to access the free space list.

The FreeSpaceArray::Get **Function**

The next function we'll look at is FreeSpaceArray::Get, whose code is shown in Figure 5.85.

Figure 5.85: The FreeSpaceArray::Get function (from quantum\newquant.cpp)

```
QFreeSpaceEntry FreeSpaceArrayPtr::FreeSpaceArray::Get(ArrayIndex p_Index)
{
    ArrayIndex Block;
    ArrayIndex Element;
    QFreeSpaceEntry Result;

    if (p_Index >= m_FreeSpaceListCount)
        {
        Result.m_ObjectNumber = 0;
        Result.m_FreeSpaceCode = 0;
        return Result;
        }

    Block = p_Index / FreeSpaceEntriesPerBlock;
    Element = p_Index % FreeSpaceEntriesPerBlock;
    Result = m_BlockPtr[Block]->Get(Element);

    return Result;
}
```

The operation of this function is fairly straightforward. First, we check whether we're trying to access something that is off the end of the free space list. If so, we return a value that indicates that there is no free space in the quantum for which information was requested. However, if the input argument is valid, we calculate which block and which element in that block contains the information we need. We then call the Get function of the block pointer to retrieve that element. Finally, we return the result to the caller.

The FreeSpaceArray::Set **Function**

The next function we'll look at is FreeSpaceArray::Set, whose code is shown in Figure 5.86.

Figure 5.86: The FreeSpaceArray::Set function (from quantum\newquant.cpp)

```
void FreeSpaceArrayPtr::FreeSpaceArray::Set(ArrayIndex p_Index,
    QFreeSpaceEntry p_Entry)
```

```
{
    ArrayIndex Block;
    ArrayIndex Element;

    if (p_Index >= m_FreeSpaceListCount)
        return; // can't store off the end

    Block = p_Index / FreeSpaceEntriesPerBlock;
    Element = p_Index % FreeSpaceEntriesPerBlock;
    m_BlockPtr[Block]->Set(Element, p_Entry);
    if ((p_Entry.m_FreeSpaceCode == AvailableQuantum)
        && (p_Index < m_CurrentLowestFreeBlock))
            m_CurrentLowestFreeBlock = p_Index;

    return;
}
```

This function is very similar to its counterpart, the Get function. However, there is one difference that we should look at: if the entry that we have just found in the array indicates that its quantum is completely empty (i.e., has the maximum available space) and this entry has a lower index than the current value of the "lowest free block" variable, then we reset the "lowest free block" variable to indicate that this is the lowest free block.

Free the Quantum 16K!

This is an optimization whose purpose is to avoid searching the entire free list every time we want to find a block that isn't committed to any particular main object. In both the previous C implementation and the current C++ one, we first check the last quantum to which we added an item; if that has enough space to add the new item, we use it.[48] In the old implementation, the free space list contained only a "free space code", indicating how much space was available in the quantum but not which object it belonged to. Therefore, when we

---

48. The "last quantum added to" variable is stored in the big pointer quantum. When first writing the code to update that variable, I had forgotten to update the "modified" flag for the big pointer quantum when the variable actually changed. As a result, every time the buffer used for the big pointer quantum was reused for a new block, that buffer was overwritten without being written out to the disk. When the big pointer quantum was reloaded, the "last quantum added to" variable was reset to an earlier, obsolete value, with the result that a new quantum was started unnecessarily. This error caused the file to grow very rapidly.

wanted to find a quantum belonging to the current object that had enough space to store a new item, we couldn't use the free space list directly. As a substitute, the C code went through the current little pointer array, looking up each quantum referenced in that array in the free space list; if one of them had enough space, we used it. However, this was quite inefficient; since each quantum can hold dozens or hundreds of items, this algorithm might require us to look at the same quantum that many times![49] Although this wasn't too important in the old implementation, where the free space list was held in memory, it could cause serious delays in the current one if we used the standard virtual memory services to access the free space list. The free space list in the old program took up 16K, one byte for each quantum in the maximum quantum file size allowed. In the new implementation, using 16K blocks of virtual memory, that same free space list would occupy only one block, so searching such a list would not require any extra disk accesses. However, the current implementation can handle much larger quantum files that might contain tens or hundreds of thousands of blocks, with correspondingly larger free space lists. Using the old method, searching the free space list from beginning to end could take quite a while, because the search routine would not access the list in a linear manner and therefore might require extra disk accesses to access the same free space list entries several times. At the very least, the free space blocks would be artificially promoted to higher levels of activity and would therefore tend to crowd other quanta out of the buffers.

Even if the free space blocks were already resident, virtual memory accesses are considerably slower than "regular" accesses; it would be much faster to scan the free space list sequentially by quantum number than randomly according to the entries in the little pointer array. Of course, we could make a list of which quanta we had already examined and skip the check in those cases, but I decided to simplify matters by another method.

---

49. For a similar reason, if we were adding an item to a large object with many little pointer arrays, each of which contained only a few distinct quantum number references, we wouldn't be gathering information about very much of the total storage taken up by the object; we might very well start a new quantum when there was plenty of space in another quantum owned by this object.

The FreeSpaceArray::FindSpaceForItem **Function**

In the current implementation, the free space list contains not just the free space for each quantum but also which object it belongs to (if any).[50] This lets us write a FreeSpaceArray::FindSpaceForItem routine that finds a place to store a new item by scanning each block of the free list sequentially in memory, rather than using a virtual memory access to retrieve each free space entry; we stop when we find a quantum that belongs to the current object and has enough free space left to store the item (Figure 5.87).[51]

Figure 5.87: The FreeSpaceArray::FindSpaceForItem function (from quantum\newquant.cpp)

```
QuantumNumber FreeSpaceArrayPtr::FreeSpaceArray::FindSpaceForItem(
    ObjectNumber p_ObjectNumber, ArrayIndex p_ItemSize)
{
    ArrayIndex Block;
    ArrayIndex Element;
    ArrayIndex Result = BadArrayIndex;
    ArrayIndex ItemSizeCode = p_ItemSize / FreeSpaceConversion;
    QFreeSpaceEntry TempFreeSpaceEntry;
    LeafBlockPtr TempLeafBlockPtr;

    for (Block = 0; Block < m_FreeSpaceListBlockCount; Block ++)
        {
        for (Element = 0; Element < FreeSpaceEntriesPerBlock; Element ++)
            {
            TempFreeSpaceEntry = m_BlockPtr[Block]->Get(Element);
            if (TempFreeSpaceEntry.m_FreeSpaceCode == AvailableQuantum)
                {
                TempFreeSpaceEntry.m_ObjectNumber = p_ObjectNumber;
                m_BlockPtr[Block]->Set(Element,TempFreeSpaceEntry);
                Result = Block * FreeSpaceEntriesPerBlock + Element;
```

---

50. In order to reduce the size of the free space list entries, I've also reduced the number of objects in the main object list to 256, so that an object number will fit in one byte.

51. Another possible optimization would be of use when we are loading a large number of items into a quantum file; in that case, we could just start a new quantum whenever we run out of space in the "last added to" quantum. This would eliminate the search of the free space list entirely and might be quite effective in decreasing the time needed to do such a mass load. Of course, this solution would require some way for the class user to inform the quantum file system that a mass load is in progress, as well as when it is over, so that the default behavior could be reestablished.

```
                    TempLeafBlockPtr =
                        m_BlockPtr[Block]->MakeLeafBlockPtr(Result);
                    TempLeafBlockPtr->Clear();
                    TempLeafBlockPtr->SetQuantumType(LEAF_NODE);
                    TempLeafBlockPtr->SetMainObjectNumber(p_ObjectNumber);
                    break;
                    }
              if (TempFreeSpaceEntry.m_ObjectNumber == p_ObjectNumber &&
                  TempFreeSpaceEntry.m_FreeSpaceCode > ItemSizeCode)
                    {
                    Result = Block * FreeSpaceEntriesPerBlock + Element;
                    TempLeafBlockPtr =
                        m_BlockPtr[Block]->MakeLeafBlockPtr(Result);
                    if (TempLeafBlockPtr->CalculateFreeSpace() > p_ItemSize)
                        break;
                    else
                        Result = BadArrayIndex;
                    }
                }
          if (Result != BadArrayIndex)
                break;
            }

       return Result;
}
```

However, if there isn't a quantum in the free space list that belongs to our desired main object and also has enough space left to add the new item, then we have to start a new quantum; how do we decide which one to use?

One way is to keep track of the first free space block we find in our search and use it if we can't find a suitable block already belonging to our object. However, I want to bias the storage mechanism to use blocks as close as possible to the beginning of the file, which should reduce head motion, as well as making it possible to shrink the file's allocated size if the amount of data stored in it decreases. My solution is to take a free block whenever it appears; if that happens to be before a suitable block belonging to the current object, so be it. This appears to be a self-limiting problem, since the next time we want to add to the same object, the newly assigned block will be employed if it has enough free space and is the first suitable block in the list.

This approach solves another problem as well, which is how we determine when to stop scanning the free space list in the first place.

Of course, we could also maintain the block number of the last occupied block in the file and stop there. However, I felt this was unnecessary, since stopping at the first free block provides a natural shortcut, without contributing any obvious problems of its own. However, as with many design decisions, my analysis could be flawed: there's a possibility that using this algorithm with many additions and deletions could reduce the space efficiency of the file, although I haven't seen such an effect in my testing.

This mechanism did not mature without some growing pains. For example, the one-byte FreeSpaceCode code, used to indicate the approximate space available in a quantum, is calculated by dividing the size by a constant (32 in the case of 16K blocks) and discarding the remainder. As a result, the size code calculated for items of less than 32 bytes is 0. Since the original check for sufficient space in a quantum tested whether the space code for the quantum was greater than or equal to the space code for the new item, even blocks with no free space (i.e., those having a free space code of 0) were considered possible storage places for these very small items. This resulted in a large number of unnecessary disk accesses to read those quanta so that their actual free space could be calculated. Changing from ">=" to ">" in the test fixed this; of course, I could also have made the size calculation round up rather than down.

Another problem I encountered with the free space handling in the new algorithm is that blocks and quanta are no longer synonymous, as they were in the old program. That is, the virtual memory system deals not only with quanta (i.e., blocks containing user data) but also with free space blocks and the block(s) occupied by the main object list. At one point, some routines dealing with the free space list were using physical block numbers and others were using logical quantum numbers; however, since only blocks containing user data are controlled by the free space list, the correct solution was to use only logical quantum numbers in all such routines.

The FreeSpaceArray::FindEmptyBlock **Function**

The last function that we will cover in this class is FindEmptyBlock, which is shown in Figure 5.88.

Figure 5.88: The FreeSpaceArray::FindEmptyBlock function (from quantum\newquant.cpp)

```
QuantumNumber FreeSpaceArrayPtr::FreeSpaceArray::FindEmptyBlock()
{
    ArrayIndex Block;
    ArrayIndex Element;
    ArrayIndex Result = BadArrayIndex;

    Block = m_CurrentLowestFreeBlock / FreeSpaceEntriesPerBlock;
    Element = m_CurrentLowestFreeBlock % FreeSpaceEntriesPerBlock;
    for (; Block < m_FreeSpaceListBlockCount; Block ++)
        {
        for (; Element < FreeSpaceEntriesPerBlock; Element ++)
            {
            if (m_BlockPtr[Block]->Get(Element).m_FreeSpaceCode
                == AvailableQuantum)
                {
                Result = Block * FreeSpaceEntriesPerBlock + Element;
                break;
                }
            }
        if (Result != BadArrayIndex)
            break;
        Element = 0;
        }

    m_CurrentLowestFreeBlock = Result;

    return Result;
}
```

As you can see, this code uses the member variable called m_CurrentLowestFreeBlock to reduce the amount of time needed to find a free block as the file fills up. Each time that a free block with a block number less than the current value is created or located, the m_CurrentLowestFreeBlock variable is updated to point to that block, and FindEmptyBlock starts at that location when looking for an empty block. FindEmptyBlock has an understandable resemblance to FindSpaceForItem, since both of them search the free space list looking for a quantum with a certain amount of space available; however, this resemblance misled me into introducing a bug in FindEmptyBlock. The problem came from the fact that I was using m_CurrentLowestFreeBlock to determine the starting block and element for searching the free space list before entering the outer loop, rather than initializing the loop indices in the for statements. This worked properly on the first time through the outer loop that is executed once for each block in the free space list, but when all the elements of the first block had been read and the outer loop index was incremented to refer to the next block, the inner index was left unchanged rather than being reset to 0 to address the first element of the new block. This would have showed itself in some unpleasant way after the blocks controlled by the first block of the free space list were allocated to objects, but luckily I found it by examination before that occurred.

The FreeSpaceArrayPtr class

The last class involved in the maintenance of the free space list is FreeSpaceArrayPtr, whose interface is shown in Figure 5.89.

Figure 5.89: The interface for the FreeSpaceArrayPtr class (from quantum\newquant.h)

```
class FreeSpaceArrayPtr
{
protected:
class FreeSpaceArray //body class
{
friend FreeSpaceArrayPtr;
protected:
SVector<FreeSpaceBlockPtr> m_BlockPtr;
ArrayIndex m_FreeSpaceListCount;
ArrayIndex m_FreeSpaceListBlockCount;
ArrayIndex m_CurrentLowestFreeBlock;
ArrayIndex m_QuantumBlockNumberAdjustment;
int m_ReferenceCount;

public:
    FreeSpaceArray();
    FreeSpaceArray(QuantumFile *p_QuantumFile);
    ~FreeSpaceArray();
QFreeSpaceEntry Get(ArrayIndex p_Index);
void Set(ArrayIndex p_Index, QFreeSpaceEntry p_Entry);
QuantumNumber FindEmptyBlock();
```

```
QuantumNumber FindSpaceForItem(ObjectNumber p_ObjectNumber, ArrayIndex
p_ItemSize);
ArrayIndex QGetFreeSpaceListCount() {return m_FreeSpaceListCount;}
};
```

Because this is a perfectly typical handle class, similar in every way to the ones that we've discussed already, you should be able to figure it out without further explanation.

The Global Functions

There are four functions that we haven't covered yet: BlockMove, AdjustOffset, FindUnusedItem, and FindBuffer. What they have in common is that they're all used quite a few times during the execution of the program and therefore would be good candidates for rewriting in assembly language. In the previous edition of this book I did just that, so why am I not doing it here?

There are actually two reasons. First, in the several years that have elapsed since the publication of the second edition, the use of processors other than Intel's has become much more common in high-end applications. Obviously, any assembly language enhancements would be useless to readers who are using, for example, DEC's Alpha processor.

However, an equally good reason is the lack of a standard for creating assembly language functions that interface with C++ programs or using assembly language in a C++ function, which would limit the utility of any such performance enhancements to those who were using the same compiler as the one for which I developed them.

Raising the Standard

Happily, compatibility among C++ compilers themselves has improved considerably of late. After several decades of development of the C++ language, which led to a number of similar but not identical dialects, ISO and ANSI (the international and American standards bodies, respectively) are on the verge of approving a C++ standard. Once that standard has been officially approved, the compiler manufacturers should be able to produce compilers that comply with it fairly quickly, and in fact most of the features of the draft standard have already been incorporated into a number of commercial compilers.

The similarity among C++ compilers is already sufficient that I was able to compile all the programs in this book using both Microsoft's Visual C++ 5.0 compiler and the DJGPP 2.8.0 compiler on the CD-ROM in the back of the book. They should also compile successfully on any compiler that complies with the new draft standard for C++.[52]

Unfortunately, there is no such standard for assembly language enhancements to C++ programs. Therefore, any such enhancements that I would write would be useful only with one compiler, and I elected to eliminate such enhancements rather than providing them only for one compiler.

However, this does not mean that such enhancements would be useless for you. If you know what machine and compiler you're going to be using, and if the performance of this program is unacceptable on the machine which it must run, then you may very well want to write assembly language functions to replace C++ functions that are heavily used at runtime. The four functions whose declarations appear in Figure 5.90 are excellent candidates for replacement with assembly language equivalents, according to the tests that I ran for the second edition of this book.

Figure 5.90: The declarations of the global functions (quantum\asmfunc.h)

```
void BlockMove(void *dest, const void *src, size_t n);
void AdjustOffset(ItemIndex *Item, int Count, int Adjustment);
int FindUnusedItem(ItemIndex *Item, int Count);
int FindBuffer(ArrayIndex BlockNumber, ArrayIndex *BlockNumberList, int Count);
```

---

52. And they may even work properly after you compile them. Unfortunately, I discovered shortly before sending this book to the publisher that the mailing list program in Chapter 3 doesn't work when compiled under DJGPP 2.8.0, although it runs perfectly when compiled under VC++ 5.0. Apparently the similarity among compilers isn't quite as great as I thought it was.

The BlockMove **Function**

Let's start with the simplest of these functions, BlockMove, shown in Figure 5.91.

Figure 5.91: The BlockMove global function (from quantum\asmfunc.cpp)

```
void BlockMove(void *dest, const void *src, size_t n)
{
      memmove(dest,src,n);
}
```

As you can see, this function consists of nothing more than a call to the standard C library function memmove. It might be hard to imagine that such a basic function could be improved upon, but that's what I found in the previous edition of this book: by re-coding that routine in assembly language I was able to speed it up by a factor of approximately two to one over the version supplied with Borland C++ 3.1. Of course, without doing the same thing for the compilers I'm using in this book, I can't guarantee that such a speedup is possible; however, it is a good place to look for performance improvement because it is used very frequently.

The AdjustOffset **Function**

The next of these functions, AdjustOffset, is shown in Figure 5.92.

Figure 5.92: The AdjustOffset global function (from quantum\asmfunc.cpp)

```
void AdjustOffset(ItemIndex *Item, int Count, int Adjustment)
{
      int i;

      for (i = 0; i < Count; i ++)
            Item[i].m_Offset += Adjustment;
}
```

This one also isn't very complicated. It merely steps through each of the items in an item index, starting from the one whose address is passed as its first argument, for the count provided as the second argument. To each of these items, it adds the adjustment provided as the third argument, which can be either positive or negative, depending on the reason that we're calling this function. If we have deleted something, then the adjustment will be negative because the items referred to by the item index will be moving closer to the end of the quantum. On the other hand, if we've inserted new data into the quantum, then the adjustment will be positive because those items will be moving farther from the end of the quantum.

The FindUnusedItem **Function**

The next of these functions, FindUnusedItem, is shown in Figure 5.93.

Figure 5.93: The FindUnusedItem global function (from quantum\asmfunc.cpp)

```
int FindUnusedItem(ItemIndex *Item, int Count)
{
    int i;
    ItemIndex TempItemIndex;
    int ItemFound;

    ItemFound = -1;

    for (i = 0; i < Count; i ++)
        {
        TempItemIndex = Item[i];
        if (TempItemIndex.m_Type == UNUSED_ITEM)
            {
            ItemFound = i;
            break;
            }
        }

    return ItemFound;

}
```

This function is slightly more complicated than the previous two, but it's still pretty simple. It steps through the item index of a quantum, checking for an entry whose type is UNUSED_ITEM. If it finds such an entry, it returns the index of that entry; otherwise, it returns the value -1 to indicate that there are no unused entries. We use this function when we want to insert a new item in a quantum and need to find an available item index entry for that item.

The FindBuffer **Function**

The last of these functions, FindBuffer, is shown in Figure 5.94.

Figure 5.94: The FindBuffer global function (from quantum\asmfunc.cpp)

```
int FindBuffer(ArrayIndex BlockNumber, ArrayIndex *BlockNumberList, int Count)
{
    int i;
    int ItemFound;

    ItemFound = -1;

    for (i = 0; i < Count; i ++)
        {
        if (BlockNumber == BlockNumberList[i])
            {
            ItemFound = i;
            break;
            }
        }

    return ItemFound;
}
```

This function steps through the block number list that keeps track of which block is in each buffer, looking for a particular block number. If it finds that the desired block is in one of the buffers, it returns the index of that buffer in the block number list. If the block isn't in any of the buffers, it returns the special value -1 to indicate that the search failed.

Summary

In this chapter, we have seen how quantum files allow us to gain efficient random access to a large volume of variable-length textual data. In the next chapter, we will use this algorithm as a building block to provide random access by key to large quantities of variable-length data.

Problems

1. What modifications to the quantum file implementation would be needed to add the following capabilities?

   a. Shrinking the file when deleting records.

   b. Adding a "mass load mode" to facilitate the addition of large numbers of records by reducing the free space list search time.

2. What changes to the "Directory" facility would make it more generally useful?

3. Write a QFIX program that employs the redundant information in the block headers and item index to reconstruct as much as possible of the logical structure of a quantum file that has become corrupted: i.e., in which at least one of the blocks is unreadable or logically inconsistent.

(You can find suggested approaches to problems in Chapter 8).

Chapter 6

Heavenly Hash: A Dynamic Hashing Algorithm

Introduction

It's time to revisit the topic of hash coding, or "hashing" for short, which we previously discussed in Chapter 2.

Algorithm Discussed

Dynamic Hashing

Problems with Standard Hashing

Hashing is a way to store and retrieve large numbers of records rapidly, by calculating an address close to the one where the record is actually stored. However, traditional disk-based methods of hashing have several deficiencies:

1. Variable-length records cannot be stored in the hash table.
2. Deleting records and reusing the space is difficult.
3. The time needed to store and retrieve a record in a file increases greatly as the file fills up, due to overflows between previously separated areas of the file.

4.   Most serious of all, the maximum capacity of the file cannot be
      changed after its creation.

The first of these problems can be handled by having fixed-length
hash records pointing to variable-length records in another file,
although this increases the access time. The second problem can be
overcome with some extra work in the implementation to mark
deleted records for later reuse. The third problem can be alleviated
significantly by the use of "last-come, first-served" hashing, as I
mentioned in a footnote in Chapter 2. However, until relatively
recently, the fourth problem, a fixed maximum capacity for a given
file, seemed intractable.

Of course, nothing stops us from creating a new, bigger, hash table
and copying the records from the old file into it, rehashing them as
we go along. In fact, one of the questions at the end of Chapter 2 asks
how we could handle a file that becomes full, as an off-line process,
and the "suggested approaches" section in Chapter 8 proposes that
exact answer.

However, this solution to the problem of a full hash table has two
serious drawbacks. For one thing, we have to have two copies of the
file (one old and one new) while we're doing this update, which can
take up a large amount of disk space temporarily. More important in
many applications, this "big bang" file maintenance approach won't
work for a file that has to be available all of the time. Without doing
a lot of extra work, we can't update the data during this operation,
which might take a long time (perhaps several hours or even days) if
the file is big. Is it possible to increase the size of the file after its
creation without incurring these penalties, and still gain the
traditional advantages of hashing, i.e., extremely fast access to large
amounts of data by key?

Until shortly before I wrote the second edition of this book, I
would have said that it wasn't possible. Therefore, I was quite
intrigued when I ran across an article describing a hashing algorithm
that can dynamically resize the hash table as needed during
execution, without any long pauses in execution.[1] Unfortunately, the
implementation described in the article relies on the use of linked

---

1. William G. Griswold and Gregg M. Townsend, "The Design and Implementation of Dynamic
   Hashing for Sets and Tables in Icon". *Software Practice and Experience*, 23(April 1993),
   351-367.

lists to hold the records pointed to by the hash slots. While this is acceptable for in-memory hash tables, such an implementation is not appropriate for disk-based hash tables, where minimizing the number of disk seeks is critical to achieving good performance.[2]

Nonetheless, it was obviously a fascinating algorithm, so I decided to investigate it to see whether it could be adapted to disk-based uses.

Just Another Link in the Chain

According to the the Griswold and Townsend article, Per-Ake Larson adapted an algorithm called "linear dynamic hashing", previously limited to accessing external files, to make it practical for use with in-memory tables.[3] The result, appropriately enough, is called "Larson's algorithm". How does it work?

First, let's look at the "slot" method of handling overflow used by many in-memory hash table algorithms, including Larson's algorithm. To store an element in the hash table, we might proceed as follows, assuming the element to be stored contains a "next" pointer to point to another such element:

1. The key of each element to be stored is translated into a slot number to which the element should be attached, via the hashing algorithm.
2. The "next" pointer of the element to be attached to the slot is set to the current contents of the slot's "first" pointer, which is initialized to a null pointer when the table is created.
3. The slot's "first" pointer is set to the address of the element being attached to the slot.

The result of this procedure is that the new element is linked into the chain attached to the slot, as its first element.

To retrieve an element, given its key, we simply use the hashing algorithm to get the slot number, and then follow the chain from that

---

2. In case you're thinking that the availability of virtual memory will solve this problem by allowing us to pretend that we have enough memory to hold the lists no matter how large they get, you may be surprised to discover that the performance of such an algorithm in virtual memory is likely to be extremely poor. I provide an example of this phenomenon in my previously cited article "Galloping Algorithms".

3. P.-A. Larson, "Dynamic Hash Tables". *Communications of the ACM*, 31(1988).

slot until we find the element. If the element isn't found by the time we get to a null pointer, it's not in the table.

This algorithm is easy to implement, but as written it has a performance problem: namely, with a fixed number of slots, the chains attached to each slot get longer in proportion to the number of elements in the table, which means that the retrieval time increases proportionately to the number of elements added. However, if we could increase the number of slots in proportion to the number of elements added, then the average time to find an element wouldn't change, no matter how many elements were added to the table. The problem is how we can find elements we've already added to the table if we increase the number of slots. It may not be obvious why this is a problem; for example, can't we just leave them where they are and add the new elements into the new slots?

Unfortunately, this won't work. The reason is that when we want to look up an element, we don't generally know when the element was added, so as to tell what "section" of the hash file it resides in. The only piece of information we're guaranteed to have available is the key of the element, so we had better be able to find an element given only its key. Of course, we could always rehash every element in the table to fit the new number of slots, but we've already seen that this can cause serious delays in file availability. Larson's contribution was to find an efficient way to increase the number of slots in the table without having to relocate every element when we do it.

Relocation Assistance

The basic idea is reasonably simple, as are most great ideas, once you understand them.[4] For our example, let's assume that the key is an unsigned value; we start out with 8 slots, all marked "active"; and we want to limit the average number of elements per slot to 6.

This means that in order to store an element in the table, we have to generate a number between 0 and 7, representing the number of the slot to which we will chain the new element being stored. For purposes of illustration, we'll simply divide the key by the number of

---

4. Of course, thinking them up in the first place is a little harder!

slots and take the remainder.[5] For reasons which will become apparent shortly, the actual algorithm looks like this:

1. Divide the key by the number of slots (8), taking the remainder. This will result in a number from 0 to the number of slots - 1, i.e., 0-7 in this case.
2. If the remainder is greater than or equal to the number of "active" slots (8), subtract one-half the number of slots (4).

You will notice that the way the parameters are currently set, the second rule will never be activated, since the remainder can't be greater than or equal to 8; we'll see the reason for the second rule shortly.

Now we're set up to handle up to 48 elements. On the 49th element, we should add another slot to keep the average number per slot from exceeding 6. What do we do to the hash function to allow us to access those elements we have already stored?

We double the number of slots, making it 16, recording that new number of slots allocated; then we increase the number of "active" slots, bringing that number to 9. The hash calculation now acts like this:

1. Divide the key by the number of slots (16), taking the remainder; the result will be between 0 and 15 inclusive.
2. If the remainder is more than the number of active slots (9), subtract one-half the number of slots (8).

This modified hashing algorithm will spread newly added elements over nine slots rather than eight, since the possible slot values now range from 0 to 8 rather than 0 to 7. This keeps the number of elements per slot from increasing as we add new elements, but how do we retrieve elements that were already in the table?

Here is where we see the stroke of genius in this new algorithm. Only one slot has elements that might have to be moved under the new hashing algorithm, and that is the first slot in the table! Why is this so?

---

5. This step alone will probably not provide a good distribution of records with a number of slots that is a power of two; in such cases, it effectively discards all the high-order bits of the key. In our actual test program, in order to improve the distribution, we precede this step by one that uses all of the bits in the input value. However, the principle is the same.

The analysis isn't really very difficult. Let's look at the elements in the second slot (i.e., slot number 1). We know that their hash codes under the old algorithm were all equal to 1, or they wouldn't be in that slot. That is, the remainder after dividing their keys by 8 was always 1, which means that the binary value of the remainder always ended in 001. Now let's see what the possible hash values are under the new algorithm. We divide the key by 16 and take the remainder. This is equivalent to taking the last four bits of the remainder. However, the last three bits of the remainder after dividing by 16 and the last three bits of the remainder after dividing by 8 have to be the same.[6] Therefore, we have to examine only the fourth bit (the 8's place) of the remainder to calculate the new hash code. There are only two possible values of that bit, 0 and 1. If the value of that bit is 0, we have the same hash code as we had previously, so we obviously can look up the element successfully even with the additional slot in the table. However, if the value is 1, the second rule tells us to compare the hash code, which is 1001 binary or 9 decimal against the number of active slots (9). Since the first is greater than or equal to the second, we subtract 8, getting 1 again; therefore, the lookup will always succeed. The same considerations apply to all the other slots previously occupied in the range 2-7. There's only one where this analysis breaks down, and that's slot 0. Why is this one different?

Because slot 8 is actually available; therefore, the second rule won't apply. In this case, we do have to know whether an element is in slot 0 or 8. While this will be taken care of automatically for newly added elements using the new hash code parameters, we still have the old elements in slot 0 to contend with; on the average, half of them will need to be moved to slot 8. This is easy to fix; all we have to do is to retrieve each element from slot 0 and recalculate its hash value with the new parameters. If the result is 0, we put it back in slot 0; if the result is 8, we move it to slot 8.

Now we're okay until we have to add the 57th element to the hash table, at which point we need to add another slot to keep the average

---

6. This may be obvious, but if it's not, the following demonstration might make it so:
   1. Let's call the value to be hashed x.
   2. $y = x \gg 4$ [divide by 16]
   3. $z = y \ll 4$ [multiply result by 16; result must have low four bits = 0]
   4. $x \% 16 = x - z$ [definition of "remainder"; result is low four bits of x]
   Obviously, an analogous result holds true for the remainder after dividing by 8; therefore, the low three bits of these two values must be the same.

chain length to 6. Happily, all we have to do is to increase the number of active slots by 1 (to 10) and rehash the elements in slot 1. It works just like the example above; none of the slots 2-7 is affected by the change, because the second rule "folds" all of their hash calculations into their current slots.

When we have added a total of 96 elements, the number of "active" slots and the total number of slots will both be 16, so we will be back to a situation similar to the one we were in before we added our first expansion slot. What do we do when we have to add the 97th element? We double the total number of slots again and start over as before.[7] This can go on until the number of slots gets to be too big to fit in the size of integer in which we maintain it, or until we run out of memory, whichever comes first.

Of course, if we want to handle a lot of data, we will probably run out of memory before we run out of slot numbers. Since the ability to retrieve any record in any size table in constant time, on the average, would certainly be very valuable when dealing with very large databases, I considered that it was worth trying to adapt this algorithm to disk-based hash tables. All that was missing was a way to store the chains of records using a storage method appropriate for disk files.

Making a Quantum Leap

Upon further consideration, I realized that the quantum file access method could be used to store a variable-length "storage element" pointed to by each hash slot, with the rest of the algorithm implemented pretty much as it was in the article. This would make it possible to store a very large number of strings by key and get back any of them with an average of a little more than one disk access, without having to know how big the file would be when we created it. This algorithm also has the pleasant effect of making deletions fairly simple to implement, with the file storage of deleted elements automatically reclaimed as they are removed.

---

7. As it turns out, there's no reason to actually allocate storage for all the new slots when we double the current maximum count, because the only one that's immediately needed is the first new one created. Accordingly, Larson's algorithm allocates them in blocks of a fixed size as they're needed, which is effectively the way my adaptation works as well.

Contrary to my usual practice elsewhere in this book, I have not developed a sample "application" program, but have instead opted to write a test program to validate the algorithm. This was very useful to me during the development of the algorithm; after all, this implementation of dynamic hashing is supposed to be able to handle hundreds of thousands of records while maintaining rapid access, so it is very helpful to be able to demonstrate that it can indeed do that. The test program is hashtest.cpp (Figure 6.1).

Figure 6.1: The test program for the dynamic hashing algorithm (quantum\hashtest.cpp)

```
/*TITLE test program for block classes*/

/****keyword-flag*** "%v %f %n" */
/* "18 9-May-98,15:11:08 HASHTEST.CPP" */

/****keyword-flag*** "%v %f %n" */
char HashtestVersionInfo[] = "18 9-May-98,15:11:08 HASHTEST.CPP";

#include "common.h"
extern "C" {
#include <time.h>
}

int main(int argc, char *argv[])
{
        QuantumFile QF;
        MainObjectArrayPtr MOA;
        ModifiableElement Element;
        FILE *infile;
        ofstream ofs;
        long ilong;
        int i;
        char *result;
        ModifiableElement TestName;
        String Command;
        clock_t StartAdd;
        clock_t StartRead;
        clock_t StartDelete;
        clock_t End;
        clock_t CurrentTicks;
        clock_t PreviousTicks;
        AccountNumber AcctNum;
```

```
ModifiableElement TempElement;
long Dup = 0;
char buf[4000];
char *KeyPtr = &buf[0];
char *DataPtr = &buf[10];
long TotalKeys = 100000L;
ArrayIndex nbuf = 20;
long CurrentReadCount;
long PreviousReadCount;
long ReadCount;
long DeleteCount;
long CurrentWriteCount;
long PreviousWriteCount;
String TestFile = "testx.qnt";
ModifiableElement Key;
const int KeyOffset = 10;
long CurrentTotalKeys;
long PreviousTotalKeys;
long StartingElement = 0;
int NewKeyAdded;
PrintStat Statistics;
DynamicHashArray DHArray;
FlexArray SaveKeys;

if (argc == 1)
    {
    printf("Syntax: hashtest command buffers qfile total-keys [starting-element] \n");
    printf("Where 'command' is one of the following:\n");
    printf("%s\n%s\n%s\n",
    "a (add elements to existing file)",
    "i (import new file)",
    "r (read and export elements from existing file)",
    "d (delete records from file)\n");
    printf("'buffers' is the number of buffers to allocate;\n");
    printf("'qfile' is the name of the quantum file;\n");
    printf("for 'a' or 'i' commands,\n"
    "'total-keys' is the number of keys the file should contain after the run;\n");
    printf("for 'r' commands, 'total-keys' is the number of keys to read\n"
        "and 'starting-element' is the key number to start with.\n");
    printf("for 'd' commands, 'total-keys' is the number of keys to delete\n"
        "and 'starting-element' is the key number to start with.\n");
    exit(1);
    }

Command = argv[1];
if (Command.GetSize() > 2)
    {
    printf("Only one command at a time, please!\n");
```

```
                    exit(1);
                    }

        if (argc > 2)
                nbuf = atoi(argv[2]);

        if (argc > 3)
                TestFile = argv[3];

        if (argc > 4)
                TotalKeys = atol(argv[4]);

        if (argc > 5)
                StartingElement = atol(argv[5]);

        strcpy(buf," ");
        for (i = 1; i < argc; i ++)
                {
                strcat(buf,argv[i]);
                strcat(buf," ");
                }

        Statistics.Init("stats.out");
        Statistics.Write("\n\n%s\nArguments:%s\n",HashtestVersionInfo,buf);
        Statistics.Write("\nBlockSize: %lu\n\n",BlockSize);

        if (Command == "i")
                remove(TestFile);

        TestName = ModifiableElement("Test");

        infile = fopen("names.in","rb");
        setvbuf(infile,NULL,_IOFBF,16384);

        ofs.open("names.out",ios::outlios::binary);

        QF.Open(TestFile,nbuf);

        PersistentArrayUlong Save(&QF,"Save");

        SaveKeys.Open(&QF,"SaveKeys");

        DHArray.Open(&QF,"DHArray");

        Element = "";

        Statistics.Write("\nSetup\n");
        CurrentReadCount = QF.GetReadCount();
        CurrentWriteCount = QF.GetWriteCount();
```

```
CurrentTicks = clock();
Statistics.Write("%lu:%lu:%lu\n",
CurrentTicks,
CurrentReadCount,
CurrentWriteCount);
PreviousTicks = CurrentTicks;
PreviousReadCount = CurrentReadCount;
PreviousWriteCount = CurrentWriteCount;

StartAdd = clock();

if (Command == "i")
    {
    Save[0] = KeyOffset; // start storing keys here
    Save[1] = 0; // offset in input file
    Command = "a"; // now it's the same as appending
    }


CurrentTotalKeys = Save[0] - KeyOffset;
PreviousTotalKeys = CurrentTotalKeys;
Statistics.Write("\nPrevious keys stored: %lu",CurrentTotalKeys);

if (Command == "a")
    {
    Statistics.Write("\nWrite");

    fseek(infile,Save[1],SEEK_SET); // skip used input lines

    Statistics.Write("\n%6lu: ",CurrentTotalKeys);

    NewKeyAdded = FALSE;
    while (CurrentTotalKeys < TotalKeys)
        {
        if (CurrentTotalKeys % 4000 == 0 && NewKeyAdded == TRUE)
            {
            NewKeyAdded = FALSE;
            Statistics.Write("\n%6lu: ",CurrentTotalKeys);
            }
        if (CurrentTotalKeys % 1000 == 999 && NewKeyAdded == TRUE)
            {
            NewKeyAdded = FALSE;
            CurrentReadCount = QF.GetReadCount();
            CurrentWriteCount = QF.GetWriteCount();
            CurrentTicks = clock();
            Statistics.Write("%lu:%lu:%lu ",
            CurrentTicks-PreviousTicks,
            CurrentReadCount-PreviousReadCount,
```

```
                         CurrentWriteCount-PreviousWriteCount);
                         PreviousTicks = CurrentTicks;
                         PreviousReadCount = CurrentReadCount;
                         PreviousWriteCount = CurrentWriteCount;
                         }
                   memset(buf,0,4000);
                   result = fgets(buf, 4000, infile);
                   if (result == NULL)
                         break;

                   Key = ModifiableElement(9,KeyPtr); // get account number
                   AcctNum = Key;

                   ArrayIndex DataLength = strlen(DataPtr);
                   if (DataLength == 1)
                         DataLength = 0; //get rid of cr/lf
                   Element = ModifiableElement(DataLength,DataPtr);
                   TempElement = DHArray[AcctNum];
                   DHArray[AcctNum] = Element;
                   if (TempElement != "")
                         Dup++;
                   else
                         {
                         SaveKeys[CurrentTotalKeys] = AcctNum;
                         CurrentTotalKeys++;
                         NewKeyAdded = TRUE;
                         }

             }
      Save[0] = CurrentTotalKeys+KeyOffset; // set to next available place
      Save[1] = ftell(infile); // where to start the next time we add stuff
      }

StartRead = clock();
PreviousTicks = StartRead;

if (Command == "r")
      {
      Statistics.Write("\nRead");
      if (StartingElement % 4000 != 0)
            Statistics.Write("\n%6lu: ", StartingElement);

      for (ilong = StartingElement; ilong < TotalKeys; ilong ++)
            {
            if (ilong % 4000 == 0)
                  Statistics.Write("\n%6lu: ",ilong);
            if (ilong % 1000 == 999)
                  {
                  CurrentReadCount = QF.GetReadCount();
```

```
                    CurrentWriteCount = QF.GetWriteCount();
                    CurrentTicks = clock();
                    Statistics.Write("%lu:%lu:%lu ",
                    CurrentTicks-PreviousTicks,
                    CurrentReadCount-PreviousReadCount,
                    CurrentWriteCount-PreviousWriteCount);
                    PreviousTicks = CurrentTicks;
                    PreviousReadCount = CurrentReadCount;
                    PreviousWriteCount = CurrentWriteCount;
                    }
            AcctNum = SaveKeys[ilong];
            if (AcctNum == "")
                    break;

            Element = DHArray[AcctNum];

            if (Element == "")
                    ofs << "Key " << AcctNum << " not found." << endl;
            else
                    ofs << AcctNum << ' ' << Element;


            }
        ReadCount = ilong - StartingElement;
        }

StartDelete = clock();
PreviousTicks = StartDelete;

if (Command == "d")
        {
        Statistics.Write("\nDelete");
        if (StartingElement % 4000 != 0)
            Statistics.Write("\n%6lu: ", StartingElement);

        for (ilong = StartingElement; ilong < TotalKeys; ilong ++)
                {
                if (ilong % 4000 == 0)
                        Statistics.Write("\n%6lu: ",ilong);
                if (ilong % 1000 == 999)
                        {
                        CurrentReadCount = QF.GetReadCount();
                        CurrentWriteCount = QF.GetWriteCount();
                        CurrentTicks = clock();
                        Statistics.Write("%lu:%lu:%lu ",
                        CurrentTicks-PreviousTicks,
                        CurrentReadCount-PreviousReadCount,
                        CurrentWriteCount-PreviousWriteCount);
                        PreviousTicks = CurrentTicks;
```

```
                        PreviousReadCount = CurrentReadCount;
                        PreviousWriteCount = CurrentWriteCount;
                        }
                AcctNum = SaveKeys[ilong];
                if (AcctNum == "")
                        break;

                Element = DHArray[AcctNum];
                DHArray[AcctNum] = "";

                if (Element == "")
                        ofs << "Key " << AcctNum << " not found" << endl;
                }
        DeleteCount = ilong - StartingElement;
        }

QF.Flush();
Statistics.Write("\n");
CurrentReadCount = QF.GetReadCount();
CurrentWriteCount = QF.GetWriteCount();

End = clock();

fclose(infile);

if (Command == "a")
        {
        Statistics.Write("\nTimer ticks to add %lu elements: %lu\n",
                CurrentTotalKeys-PreviousTotalKeys,StartRead-StartAdd);
        Statistics.Write("%lu duplicates found\n",Dup);
        Statistics.Write("Number of chain overflows: %lu\n",
                DynamicHashString::GetChainCount());
        }

if (Command == "r")
        Statistics.Write("\nTimer ticks to read %lu elements: %lu\n",
                ReadCount,End-StartRead);

if (Command == "d")
        Statistics.Write("\nTimer ticks to delete %lu elements: %lu\n",
                DeleteCount,End-StartDelete);

Statistics.Write("\nTotal ticks: %lu, total reads: %lu, total writes: %lu\n",
        End,CurrentReadCount, CurrentWriteCount);

if (Command == "a" || Command == "i")
        Statistics.Write("\nTotal number of keys stored: %lu\n",CurrentTotalKeys);
```

```
        return(0);
}
```

This program stores and retrieves strings by a nine-digit key, stored as a String value. To reduce the overhead of storing each entry as a separate object in the quantum file, all strings having the same hash code are combined into one "storage element" in the quantum file system; each storage element is addressed by one "hash slot". The current version of the dynamic hashing algorithm used by hashtest.cpp allocates one hash slot for every six strings in the file; since the average individual string length is about 60 characters, and there are 18 bytes of overhead for each string in a storage element (four bytes for the key length, four bytes for the data length, and 10 bytes for the key value including its null further), this means that the average storage element will be a bit under 500 bytes long. A larger element packing factor than six strings per element would produce a smaller hash table and would therefore be more space efficient. However, the choice of this value is not critical with the current implementation of this algorithm, because any storage elements that become too long to fit into quantum will be broken up and stored separately by a mechanism which I will get to later.

Of course, in order to run meaningful tests, we have to do more than store records in the hash file; we also have to retrieve what has been stored, which means that we have to store the keys someplace so that we can use them again to retrieve records corresponding to those keys. In the current version of this algorithm, I use a FlexArray (i.e., a persistent array of strings, such as we examined in the previous chapter) to store the values of the keys. However, in the original version of this algorithm, I was storing the key as an unsigned long value, so I decided to use the quantum file storage to implement a persistent array of unsigned long values, and store the keys in such an array.

Persistence Pays Off

It was surprisingly easy to implement a persistent array of unsigned long values,[8] for which I defined a typedef of Ulong, mostly to save typing. The header file for this data type is persist.h (Figure 6.2).

Figure 6.2: The interface for the PersistentArrayUlong class (quantum\persist.h)

```
/*TITLE Persistent array class declarations */

/****keyword-flag*** "%v %f %n" */
/* "3 28-Mar-98,21:21:24 PERSIST.H" */

#include "blocki.h"

const ArrayIndex UlongEntriesPerBlock = MaxItemSize / sizeof(Ulong) - 1;

class PersistentArrayUlong;

class PersistentArrayUlongRef
{
private:
     PersistentArrayUlong &m_PAU;
     Ulong m_Index;

private: //prevent compiler warnings
     PersistentArrayUlongRef& operator=(const PersistentArrayUlongRef&);

public:
     PersistentArrayUlongRef(PersistentArrayUlong &p_PAU, Ulong p_Index);
     PersistentArrayUlongRef& operator=(Ulong p_Element);
     operator Ulong();
};

class PersistentArrayUlong
{
protected:
     ModifiableElement m_ArrayName;
     QuantumFile *m_QF;
     MainObjectArrayPtr m_MOA;
     ObjectNumber m_ObjectNumber;
public:
     PersistentArrayUlong();
     ~PersistentArrayUlong();
```

---

8. Given the quantum file access method, that is!

```
PersistentArrayUlong(QuantumFile *p_QF, ModifiableElement p_ArrayName);
void StoreElement(Ulong p_Index, Ulong p_Element);
Ulong GetElement(Ulong p_Index);
PersistentArrayUlongRef operator[](Ulong p_Index);
};
```

As you can see, this class isn't very complex, and most of the implementation code is also fairly straightforward. However, we get a lot out of those relatively few lines of code; these arrays are not only persistent, but they also automatically expand to any size up to and including the maximum size of a quantum file; with the current maximum of 10000 16K blocks, a maximum size PersistentArrayUlong could contain approximately 40,000,000 elements! Of course, we don't store each element directly in a separate addressable entry within a main object, as this would be inappropriate because the space overhead per item would be larger than the Ulongs we want to store! Instead, we employ a two-level system similar to the one used in the dynamic hashing algorithm; the quantum file system stores "segments" of data, each one containing as many Ulongs as will fit in a quantum. To store or retrieve an element, we determine which segment the element belongs to and access the element by its offset in that segment.

However, before we can use a PersistentArrayUlong, we have to construct it, which we can do via the default constructor (Figure 6.3).

Figure 6.3: The default constructor for the PersistentArrayUlong class (from quantum\persist.cpp)

```
PersistentArrayUlong::PersistentArrayUlong()
{
    m_ObjectNumber = 0;
}
```

This constructor doesn't actually create a usable array; it is only there to allow us to declare a PersistentArrayUlong before we want to use it. When we really want to construct a usable array, we use the normal constructor shown in Figure 6.4.

Figure 6.4: The normal constructor for the PersistentArrayUlong class (from quantum\persist.cpp)

```
PersistentArrayUlong::PersistentArrayUlong(QuantumFile *p_QF, ModifiableElement
p_ArrayName)
{
    m_ArrayName = p_ArrayName;
    m_QF = p_QF;
    m_MOA = MainObjectArrayPtr(m_QF);

    m_ObjectNumber = m_MOA->FindObjectByName(m_ArrayName);
    if (m_ObjectNumber == NoObject)
        {
        m_ObjectNumber = m_MOA->FindAvailableObject();
        m_MOA->CreateMainObject(m_ArrayName,m_ObjectNumber,1,
            MaxFileQuantumCount);
        }
}
```

As you can see, to construct a real usable array, we provide a pointer to the quantum file in which it is to be stored, along with a name for the array. The object directory of that quantum file is searched for a main object with the name specified in the constructor; if it is found, the construction is complete. Otherwise, a new object is created with one element, expandable to fill up the entire file system if necessary.

To store an element in the array we have created, we can use StoreElement (Figure 6.5).

Figure 6.5: The PersistentArrayUlong::StoreElement function (from quantum\persist.cpp)

```
void PersistentArrayUlong::StoreElement(Ulong p_Index, Ulong p_Element)
{
    ArrayIndex SegmentNumber;
    ArrayIndex ElementNumber;
    ModifiableElement TempVector;
    AccessVector<Ulong> TempUlongVector;
    ArrayIndex OldSegmentCount;
    ArrayIndex RequiredSegmentCount;

    SegmentNumber = ArrayIndex(p_Index / UlongEntriesPerBlock);
    ElementNumber = ArrayIndex(p_Index % UlongEntriesPerBlock);
```

```
qfassert(SegmentNumber <
     m_MOA->GetMainObjectMaxElementCount(m_ObjectNumber));
OldSegmentCount = m_MOA->GetMainObjectElementCount(m_ObjectNumber);
RequiredSegmentCount = SegmentNumber+1;
if (RequiredSegmentCount > OldSegmentCount)
     m_MOA->GrowMainObject(m_ObjectNumber,RequiredSegmentCount);

TempVector = m_MOA->GetModifiableElement(m_ObjectNumber,SegmentNumber);
if (TempVector.GetSize() == 0)
     {
     TempVector = ModifiableElement(UlongEntriesPerBlock*sizeof(Ulong));
     memset(TempVector.GetDataAddress(),0,TempVector.GetSize());
     }

TempUlongVector = AccessVector<Ulong>(UlongEntriesPerBlock,
     (Ulong *)TempVector.GetDataAddress());
TempUlongVector[ElementNumber] = p_Element;

m_MOA->PutElement(m_ObjectNumber,SegmentNumber,TempVector);
}
```

This routine first calculates which segment of the array contains the element we need to retrieve, and the element number within that segment. Then, if we are running the "debugging" version (i.e., asserts are enabled), it checks whether the segment number is within the maximum range we set up when we created the array. This test should never fail unless there is something wrong with the calling routine (or its callers), so that the element number passed in is absurdly large. As discussed above, with all such conditional checks, we have to try to make sure that our testing is good enough to find any errors that might cause this to happen; with a "release" version of the program, this would be a fatal error.

Next, we check whether the segment number we need is already allocated to the array; if not, we increase the number of segments as needed by calling GrowMainObject, but don't actually initialize any new segments until they're accessed, so that "sparse" arrays won't take up as much room as ones that are filled in completely. Next, we get a copy of the segment containing the element to be updated; if it's of zero length, that means we haven't initialized it yet, so we have to allocate memory for the new segment and fill it with zeros. At this point, we are ready to create an AccessVector called TempUlongVector of type Ulong and use it as a "template" (no pun intended) to allow access to the element we want to modify. Since AccessVector has the semantics of an array, we can simply set the ElementNumberth element of TempUlongVector to the value of the input argument p_Element; the result of this is to place the new element value into the correct place in the TempVector array. Finally, we store TempVector back into the main object, replacing the old copy of the segment.

To retrieve an element from an array, we can use GetElement (Figure 6.6).

Figure 6.6: The PersistentArrayUlong::GetElement function (from quantum\persist.cpp)

```
Ulong PersistentArrayUlong::GetElement(Ulong p_Index)
{
        ArrayIndex SegmentNumber;
        ArrayIndex ElementNumber;
        ModifiableElement TempVector;
        AccessVector<Ulong> TempUlongVector;

        SegmentNumber = ArrayIndex(p_Index / UlongEntriesPerBlock);
        ElementNumber = ArrayIndex(p_Index % UlongEntriesPerBlock);

        qfassert (SegmentNumber <
                m_MOA->GetMainObjectElementCount(m_ObjectNumber));
        TempVector = m_MOA->GetModifiableElement(m_ObjectNumber,SegmentNumber);
        TempUlongVector = AccessVector<Ulong>(UlongEntriesPerBlock,
                (Ulong *)TempVector.GetDataAddress());
        return TempUlongVector[ElementNumber];
}
```

First, we calculate the segment number and element number, and check (via qfassert) whether the segment number is within the range of allocated segments; if it isn't, we have committed the programming error of accessing an uninitialized value. Assuming this test is passed, we retrieve the segment, set up the temporary Vector TempUlongVector to allow access to the segment as an SVector of Ulongs, and return the value from the ElementNumberth element of the array.

All this is very well if we want to write things like "Y.Put(100,100000L);" or "X = Y.Get(100);", to store or retrieve the 100th element of the Y "array", respectively. But wouldn't it be much nicer to be able to write "Y[100] = 100000L;" or "X = Y[100];" instead?

In Resplendent Array

Clearly, that would be a big improvement in the syntax; as it happens, it's not hard to make such references possible, with the addition of only a few lines of code.[9] Unfortunately, this code is not the most straightforward, but the syntactic improvement that it provides is worth the trouble. The key is operator[ ] (Figure 6.7).

Figure 6.7: The PersistentArrayUlong::operator[ ] function (from quantum\persist.cpp)

```
PersistentArrayUlongRef PersistentArrayUlong::operator[ ](Ulong p_Index)
{
        return PersistentArrayUlongRef(*this, p_Index);
}
```

This function returns a temporary value of a type that behaves differently in the context of an "lvalue" reference (i.e., a "write") than it does when referenced as an "rvalue" (i.e, a "read"). In order to follow how this process works, let's use the example in Figure 6.8.

Figure 6.8: Persistent array example

```
/*TITLE persistent array example program*/

#include "common.h"

main()
{
        PersistentArrayUlong Save;
        QuantumFile QF;
        Ulong TestValue;

        QF.Open("testx.qnt",100);
        Save = PersistentArrayUlong(&QF,"Save");
        Save[1000000L] = 1234567L;
        TestValue = Save[1000000L];
        printf("%lu\n",TestValue);
}
```

---

9. This is also from James Coplien's book, mentioned earlier.

The first question to be answered is how the compiler decodes the following line:

```
Save[1000000L] = 1234567L;
```

According to the definition of PersistentArrayUlong::operator[ ], this operator returns a PersistentArrayUlongRef that is constructed with the two parameters *this and p_Index, where the former is the PersistentArrayUlong object for which operator[ ] was called (i.e., Save), and the latter is the value inside the [ ], which in this case is 1000000L. What is this return value? To answer this question, we have to look at the normal constructor for the PersistentArrayUlongRef class (Figure 6.9).

Figure 6.9: The normal constructor for the PersistentArrayUlongRef class (from quantum\persist.cpp)

```
PersistentArrayUlongRef::PersistentArrayUlongRef(PersistentArrayUlong &p_PAU,
Ulong p_Index) : m_PAU(p_PAU), m_Index(p_Index)
{
}
```

This constructor sets m_PAU to a reference to p_PAU and m_Index to the value of p_Index, so the object returned from the operator[ ] call will be a PersistentArrayUlongRef with those values. Therefore, the compiler-generated code looks something like this, so far:

```
PersistentArrayUlongRef T(Save,1000000L);
T = 1234567L;
```

where T is an arbitrary name for a temporary object.

The second of these lines is then translated into a call to PersistentArrayUlongRef::operator = (Figure 6.10), to do the assignment.

Figure 6.10: The PersistentArrayUlongRef::operator = function (from quantum\persist.cpp)

```
PersistentArrayUlongRef &PersistentArrayUlongRef::operator =(Ulong p_Element)
{
    m_PAU.StoreElement(m_Index,p_Element);
    return *this;
}
```

The generated code now looks something like this:

```
PersistentArrayUlongRef T(Save,1000000L);
T.operator =(1234567L);
```

The operator = code, as you can see from the figure, calls the
StoreElement operation for the object m_PAU, which as we noted above
is a reference to the original object Save; the arguments to that call
are m_Index, a copy of the index supplied in the original operator[ ] call,
and p_Element, which is the value specified in the operator = call. Thus,
the result is the same as that of the statement
Save.StoreElement(1000000L,1234567L);, while the notation is that of a
"normal" array access.

However, we've only handled the case where we're updating an
element of the array. We also need to be able to retrieve values once
they've been stored. To see how that works, let's follow the
translation of the following line:

```
TestValue = Save[1000000L];
```

The process is fairly similar to what we've already done. The
definition of PersistentArrayUlong::operator[] causes the compiler to
generate code somewhat like the following:

```
PersistentArrayUlongRef T(Save,1000000L);
TestValue = T;
```

This time, however, rather than translating the second line into a call
to PersistentArrayUlongRef::operator=, the compiler translates it into a call
to PersistentArrayUlongRef::operator Ulong, a "conversion function" that
allows a PersistentArrayUlongRef to be used where a Ulong is expected
(Figure 6.11).

Figure 6.11: The PersistentArrayUlongRef::operator Ulong function (from
quantum\persist.cpp)

```
PersistentArrayUlongRef::operator Ulong()
{
        return m_PAU.GetElement(m_Index);
}
```

Therefore, the final generated code comes out something like this:

```
PersistentArrayUlongRef T(Save,1000000L);
TestValue = Ulong(T);
```

As should be evident by looking at the code for that conversion function, it merely calls the GetElement operation of the object m_PAU, which as we noted above is a reference to the original object Save, with the argument m_Index, which is a copy of the original element index. Thus, the result is the same as the statement TestValue = Save.GetElement(1000000L);, while the notation is that of a "normal" array access.

Before we move on to our next topic, I have a word of warning for you. If you use these "synthetic arrays" frequently, you may be tempted to inline the definitions of these auxiliary functions that make the array notation possible. I recommend that you don't do it, at least not without a lot of testing to make sure it works correctly. When I tried this with Borland C++ 3.1, the result appeared to work but generated terrible memory leaks; as far as I could determine, the memory that wasn't being freed was that belonging to the temporary objects that were created during the operation of these functions.

Some Fine Details

Now let's look at some of the other implementation details and problems I encountered in the process of getting the dynamic hashing algorithm and the hashtest.cpp test program to work.

During development of the test program, I discovered that running the tests on large numbers of records took a fairly large amount of time; to generate a quantum file with 500,000 records in it takes about 45 minutes, doing almost continual disk accesses the whole time.[10] Although this is actually very fast when one considers the amount of data being processed, I still didn't want to have to execute such a program more often than I had to. Therefore, the test program needed the capability of incrementally adding records to an existing quantum file. However, this meant that the test program had to be

---

10. As an illustration of the immense improvements in computer speeds in a few years, creating a new file containing 250,000 records took about four hours with the computer I had in 1995 and about 15 minutes with the computer I have in 1998.

able to start somewhere in the middle of the input file; adding the same records again and again wouldn't work because the algorithm isn't designed to handle records with duplicate keys.

As the test program is implemented, only two pieces of information need to be saved between runs in order to allow the addition of previously unused records to the quantum file: the index number in the SaveKeys array where the next key should be saved, and the offset into the input file where the next record begins. We don't have to save the name of the input file or the ASCII output file, since those are compiled into the program; of course, this would not be appropriate for a real application program, but in our test program we don't want to change the name of the input file between runs. Clearly, if the input file could change from one run to the next, the information as to where we stopped when reading records wouldn't be of much use. Since both of the data items that need to be preserved happen to be representable by an unsigned long value, I decided to use a PersistentArrayUlong named Save to save them between runs. As a result, the only difference between starting a new quantum file and adding records to an existing file is that when we start a new quantum file, the offset in the input file and the starting position for keys to be added to the SaveKeys array have to be reset to their initial values.

This ability to build on a previously created quantum file turned out to be quite useful in fixing an interesting bug that I ran into during capacity testing of the 16-bit version of this program. The theoretical capacity of a quantum file with the original size parameters, when used to support the dynamic hashing algorithm, could be calculated as 64K (maximum hash slots in the 16-bit implementation) * 6 (average records per hash slot), or 393,216. Although I didn't necessarily need to demonstrate that this exact number of records could actually be stored and retrieved successfully, especially in view of the number of hours that my machine would be doing continual random disk accesses, I felt that it was important to check that a very large number of records could be accommodated. I selected 250,000 as a nice round number that wouldn't take quite so long to test, and started to run tests for every multiple of 50,000 records up to 250,000.[11] As each test was finished, I copied the resulting quantum file to a new name to continue the testing to the next higher multiple of 50,000 records.

Everything went along very nicely through the test that created a 150,000 record quantum file. Since adding 50,000 records to a file that already contained 150,000 records should have taken about 45 minutes, I started the next test, which should have generated a 200,000 record file, and went away to do some chores. Imagine my surprise when I came back and found that the program had aborted somewhere between elements 196,000 and 197,000 due to the failure of an assert that checks that all the records in a hash slot that is being split have the correct hash code to be put into either the old slot or the new slot. Upon investigating the reason for this bug, I discovered that the problem was that m_CurrentMaxSlotCount, which is used in DynamicHashArray::CalculateHash to calculate the hash code according to Larson's algorithm, was an unsigned rather than an unsigned long. As a result, when 32K slots were occupied and it was time to double the value of m_CurrentMaxSlotCount, its new value, which should have been 64K, was 0. This caused the hashing function to generate incorrect values and thus caused the assert to fail. Changing the type of m_CurrentMaxSlotCount to unsigned long solved the problem.

However, there was one other place where the code had to change to implement this solution, and that was in the destructor for DynamicHashArray. The reason for this change is that the dynamic hashing algorithm needs to store some state information in a persistent form. To be specific, we need to keep track of the number of active slots, the current maximum slot number, and the number of elements remaining before the next slot is to be activated. With these data items saved in the file, the next time we open the file, we're ready to add more records while keeping the previously stored ones accessible.

Unfortunately, we don't have a convenient persistent numeric array to save these values in, and it doesn't make much sense to create one just for three values. However, we do have a persistent string array, which we're using to store the hashed records, and we can use the first element of that array to store ASCII representations

---

11. You may wonder where I got such a large number of records to test with. They are extracted from a telephone directory on CD-ROM; unfortunately, I can't distribute them for your use, since I don't have permission to do so.

of the three values that must be maintained in the file.[12] This is handled during the normal constructor for the DynamicHashArray type (Figure 6.12), which calls the Open function to do the actual work (Figure 6.13).[13]

Figure 6.12: The normal constructor for the DynamicHashArray class (from quantum\dynhash.cpp)

```
DynamicHashArray::DynamicHashArray(QuantumFile *p_QF, ModifiableElement
p_ArrayName)
{
        Open(p_QF, p_ArrayName);
}
```

Figure 6.13: The DynamicHashArray::Open function (from quantum\dynhash.cpp)

```
void DynamicHashArray::Open(QuantumFile *p_QF, ModifiableElement p_ArrayName)
{
        ArrayIndex i;
        ModifiableElement TempString;

        m_ArrayName = p_ArrayName;
        m_QF = p_QF;
        m_MOA = MainObjectArrayPtr(m_QF);

        m_ObjectNumber = m_MOA->FindObjectByName(m_ArrayName);
        if (m_ObjectNumber == NoObject)
                {
                m_ObjectNumber = m_MOA->FindAvailableObject();
                m_MOA->CreateMainObject(m_ArrayName,m_ObjectNumber);
                m_CurrentSlotCount = InitCurrentSlotCount;
                m_CurrentMaxSlotCount = InitCurrentMaxSlotCount;
                m_ElementsBeforeExpansion = ElementsPerSlot * InitCurrentSlotCount;
                for (i = 0; i < m_CurrentSlotCount; i ++)
```

12. In order to hide this implementation detail from the rest of the dynamic hashing algorithm, the GetString and PutString functions of the DynamicHashArray class increment the element index before using it. Thus, the request to read or update element 0 is translated into an operation on element 1, and so forth. To access element 0, the index is specified as -1.

13. In case you're wondering why we need two functions here instead of one, it's because sometimes we want to create a dynamic hash array before we know what file it's going to be attached to. In such a case, we can use the default constructor and then call the Open function once we know the actual parameters; without separating construction and initialization, we would not have that capability.

```
            PutString(i,TempString);
        PutString((unsigned long)-1,""); // clear parameter string
        }
    else
        {
        TempString = GetString((unsigned long)-1); // get parameter string
        m_CurrentSlotCount = (ArrayIndex)atol(TempString);
        m_CurrentMaxSlotCount = (Ulong)atol(TempString.Mid(7,7));
        m_ElementsBeforeExpansion = (ArrayIndex)atol(TempString.Mid(14,7));
        }
}
```

The Open function retrieves these values from the first element of the array if it has already been created, and the destructor (Figure 6.14) stores them into the first element of the array.

Figure 6.14: The destructor for the DynamicHashArray class (from quantum\dynhash.cpp)

```
ModifiableElement DynamicHashArray::GetString(ArrayIndex p_Index)
{
    p_Index ++;
    qfassert(p_Index < m_MOA->GetMainObjectElementCount(m_ObjectNumber));
    return m_MOA->GetModifiableElement(m_ObjectNumber,p_Index);
}
```

After the change to the type of m_CurrentMaxSlotCount, the sprintf format parameter for that type also had to change, to "%6lu" from "%6u", so that the whole value of the variable would be used. If I hadn't made this change, the data would have been written to the parameter string incorrectly, and the parameters wouldn't have been read back in correctly the next time the file was opened.

Overflow Handling

The previous version of this program, in the second edition of this book, did not have any means of handling the situation where the total size of the records with the same hash code is so large that the element used to store those records will no longer fit into a quantum. Therefore, in the event that too many records were put into a particular element, the program would fail. While this is acceptable in a program that is intended only to demonstrate the dynamic hashing algorithm, it is unacceptable for commercial use and therefore should really be addressed in a book intended for use in the real world.

I've thought about this problem off and on for some time without coming up with a really good solution. However, a few months ago I did figure out how to solve it in a reasonably easy and efficient way, which is illustrated in the code for DynamicHashArray::StoreElement (Figure 6.15).

Figure 6.15: The DynamicHashArray::StoreElement function (from quantum\dynhash.cpp)

```
void DynamicHashArray::StoreElement(AccountNumber p_Key, ModifiableElement
p_Element)
{
        ArrayIndex SlotNumber;
        DynamicHashString DHString;
        DynamicHashString BuddyString;
        DynamicHashString NewSlotString;
        ArrayIndex i;
        ArrayIndex BuddySlotNumber;
        ArrayIndex NewSlotNumber;
        AccountNumber AcctNumber;
        ModifiableElement Data;
        DynamicHashString TempString;
        bool Status = false;

        if (m_ElementsBeforeExpansion == 0)
            {
            if (m_CurrentSlotCount == UINT_MAX)
                exit(1); // should be an exception, but not yet
            if (m_CurrentSlotCount == m_CurrentMaxSlotCount)
                m_CurrentMaxSlotCount *= 2;
            BuddySlotNumber =
                (ArrayIndex)(m_CurrentSlotCount - m_CurrentMaxSlotCount/2);
            NewSlotNumber = m_CurrentSlotCount;
            m_CurrentSlotCount ++;
            TempString = DynamicHashString(GetString(BuddySlotNumber));
            for (i = 0; i < TempString.m_Count; i ++)
                {
                AcctNumber = TempString.m_Key[i];
                SlotNumber = CalculateHash(AcctNumber);
                if (SlotNumber == BuddySlotNumber)
```

```
                        BuddyString.
                             AddElement(AcctNumber, TempString.GetSubString(i));
                   else if (SlotNumber == NewSlotNumber)
                        NewSlotString.
                             AddElement(AcctNumber, TempString.GetSubString(i));
                   else
                        qfassert(0); // should never happen
                   }
              if (TempString.GetChain())
                   {
                   NewSlotString.SetChain();
                   BuddyString.SetChain();
                   BuddyString.BumpChainCount();
                   }
              PutString(NewSlotNumber,NewSlotString);
              PutString(BuddySlotNumber,BuddyString);
              m_ElementsBeforeExpansion = ElementsPerSlot;
              }

     m_ElementsBeforeExpansion --;

     ArrayIndex Size;
     AccountNumber p_Temp = p_Key;
     char buf[10];

     Status = DeleteElement(p_Key); // get rid of old element
     if (p_Element == "") // if new element null, we are done
          return;

     for (i = 0; ; i ++)
          {
          SlotNumber = CalculateHash(p_Temp);
          DHString = DynamicHashString(GetString(SlotNumber));
          Size = ModifiableElement(DHString).GetSize();
          if (Size + p_Element.GetSize() < MaxItemSize)
               {
               DHString.AddElement(p_Temp, p_Element);
               PutString(SlotNumber,DHString);
               break;
               }
          else
               {
               DHString.SetChain();
               DHString.BumpChainCount();
               PutString(SlotNumber,DHString);
               sprintf(buf,"\f%d",i);
               p_Temp = p_Key + buf;
               p_Temp = p_Temp.Mid(0,p_Temp.GetSize()-1);
```

```
            }
        }
}
```

The basic idea is that whenever a particular element that we are trying to store in the hash array is about to exceed the size of a quantum, we create a new element in which we'll store the records that wouldn't fit in the previous element. The question, of course, is how we find the records stored in this new element, when they will not be stored in the location in the hash array where we expect to find it.

The answer is that we modify the keys of the stored records in a way that we can do again when we're trying to find a particular record. Then we set a "chain" flag in the original element in the hash array indicating that it has overflowed, so that we don't mistakenly tell the user that the record in question is not in the file.

Exactly how do we modify the key of the record? By appending a character sequence to it that consists of a form feed character followed by an ASCII representation of the number of times that we've had an overflow in this particular chain. For example, if the original key was "ABC", the first overflow key would be "ABC\f0", where "\f" represents the form feed character, and "0" is the ASCII digit 0.

Of course, it's also possible that even the second element in which we're storing records with a particular hash key will overflow. However, the same algorithm will work in that case as well; in this case, the second record will have its "chain" flag set to indicate that the program should continue looking for the record in question if it is not found in the current element and the key will be modified again to make it unique; to continue our previous example, if the original key was "ABC", the second overflow key would be "ABC\f1", where "\f" represents the form feed character, and "1" is the ASCII digit 1.

How did I choose this particular way of modifying the keys? Because it would not limit the users' choice of keys in a way that they would object to. Of course, I did have to inform the users that they should use only printable ASCII characters in their keys, but they did not consider that a serious limitation. If your users object to this limitation, then you'll have to come up with another way of constructing unique keys that won't collide with any keys that the users actually want to use.

As this suggests, there were a few tricky parts to this solution, but overall it really wasn't that difficult to implement. I haven't done any serious performance testing on its effects, but I don't expect them to be significant; after all, assuming that we select our original parameters properly, overflows should be a rare event.

I should also explain how we find a record that has overflowed. That is the job of DynamicHashArray::FindElement (Figure 6.16).

Figure 6.16: The DynamicHashArray::FindElement function (from quantum\dynhash.cpp)

```
ModifiableElement DynamicHashArray::FindElement(AccountNumber p_Key)
{
        ArrayIndex SlotNumber;
        DynamicHashString DHString;
        ModifiableElement Result;

        AccountNumber p_Temp = p_Key;
        char buf[10];

        for (int i = 0; ; i ++)
                {
                SlotNumber = CalculateHash(p_Temp);
                DHString = DynamicHashString(GetString(SlotNumber));
                Result = DHString.FindElement(p_Temp);
                if (Result != "")
                        break;
                else if (DHString.GetChain() == 0)
                        break;
                else
                        {
                        sprintf(buf,"\f%d",i);
                        p_Temp = p_Key + buf;
                        p_Temp = p_Temp.Mid(0,p_Temp.GetSize()-1);
                        }
                }

        return Result;
}
```

As you can see, the code to look up a record is not complicated very much by the possibility of an overflow. First, we calculate a slot number based on the key that we are given by the user. Then we check whether that key is found in the element for that slot. If it is, we are done, so we break out of the loop. However, if we haven't found the record we're looking for yet, we check to see whether the particular element that we are looking in has its chain flag set. If not, the record must not be in the file, so we break out of the loop.

On the other hand, if the chain flag is set in the element that we were looking at, then we have to keep looking. Therefore, we calculate what the key for that record would be if it were in the next element and continue processing at the top of the loop.

On the next pass through the loop, we'll retrieve the next element that the record might be in, based on its modified key. We'll continue through this loop until we either find the record we're looking for or get to an element whose chain flag is not set; the latter situation, of course, means that the desired record is not in the file.

Settling Our Hash

I've recently had the opportunity to use this algorithm in a commercial setting, and have discovered (once again) that how the hash code is calculated is critical to its performance. In this case, the keys were very poorly suited to the simple (if not simple-minded) calculation used in the version of DynamicHashArray::CalculateHash in Figure 6.17.

Figure 6.17: The DynamicHashArray::CalculateHash function (from quantum\dynhash.cpp)

```
ArrayIndex DynamicHashArray::CalculateHash(AccountNumber p_Key)
{
    unsigned long Result;
    unsigned long HashNumber = 0;
    unsigned long TempHash = 0;
    ArrayIndex AccountNumberLength;
    AccountNumberLength = p_Key.GetSize();

    for (ArrayIndex i = 0; i < AccountNumberLength; i ++)
        {
        HashNumber <<= 3;
        HashNumber += p_Key[i] & 7;
        }

    HashNumber %= 1048583L;
```

```
Result = HashNumber & (m_CurrentMaxSlotCount-1);
if (Result >= m_CurrentSlotCount)
        Result -= m_CurrentMaxSlotCount/2;

    return (ArrayIndex)Result;
}
```

The problem was that the keys used in the application were all very similar to one another. In particular, the last seven or eight characters in each key were likely to differ from the other keys in only one or two places. This caused tremendous overloading of the hash slots devoted to those keys, with corresponding performance deterioration.

Luckily, I was able to provide a solution to this problem in short order by using an algorithm that produced much better hash codes. Interestingly enough, the algorithm that I substituted for my poorly performing hash code wasn't even designed to be a hash code algorithm at all. Instead, it was a cyclical redundancy check (CRC) function whose purpose was to calculate a value based on a block of data so that when the data was later read again, the reading program could determine whether it had been corrupted.

One second thought, perhaps it wasn't so strange that a CRC algorithm would serve as a good hash code. After all, for it to do its job properly, any change to the data should be very likely to produce a different CRC. Therefore, even if two keys differed by only one or two bytes, their CRC's would almost certainly be different, which of course is exactly what we want for a hash code. As it happens, this substitution greatly improved the performance of the program, so apparently my choice of a new hash algorithm was appropriate.

Fortunately, I came up with this solution just in time to include the new code on the CD-ROM in the back of this book. It is shown in Figure 6.18.

Figure 6.18: The DynamicHashArray::CalculateHash function (from quantum\dynhash.cpp)

```
ArrayIndex DynamicHashArray::CalculateHash(AccountNumber p_Key)
{
        crc32 CRC;

        unsigned long Result;
```

```
    unsigned long HashNumber = 0;
    unsigned long TempHash = 0;
    ArrayIndex KeyLength;
    KeyLength = p_Key.GetSize();

    CRC.processBuffer((unsigned char*)p_Key.GetDataAddress(),KeyLength);
    HashNumber = CRC.get_result().crc;

    Result = HashNumber & (m_CurrentMaxSlotCount-1);
    if (Result >= m_CurrentSlotCount)
        Result -= m_CurrentMaxSlotCount/2;

    return (ArrayIndex)Result;
}
```

As for the CRC class, its interface is shown in Figure 6.19.

Figure 6.19: The interface for the CRC32 class (from quantum\dynhash.cpp)

```
/* \td\g\util\crc.h */

#ifndef TD_G_UTIL_CRC_H // {
#define TD_G_UTIL_CRC_H


/* Crc - 32 BIT ANSI X3.66 CRC checksum files */

typedef unsigned int UINT4;
typedef unsigned char UBYTE;
typedef unsigned short UINT2;

class       crc32
{
    public:
    struct      result
    {
        UINT4           crc;
        UINT4           nChars;

        void
        printMe();
    };

    private:
    result              result_;
```

```
public:

crc32();
~crc32();

void
init();

result& get_result();

void
processBuffer(
        UBYTE*                          buffer,
        UINT4                           nBytesInBuffer);
}; /* class          crc32 */
#endif
```

And its implementation, which also includes a brief description of the algorithm, is shown in Figure 6.20.

Figure 6.20: The implementation for the CRC32 class (from
quantum\dynhash.cpp)

```
/* Crc - 32 BIT ANSI X3.66 CRC checksum files */

#include "crc32.h"
#include <stdio.h>

/************************************************************************\
|* Program to compute the 32-bit CRC used as the frame
|* check sequence in ADCCP (ANSI X3.66, also known as FIPS PUB 71
|* and FED-STD-1003, the U.S. versions of CCITT's X.25 link-level
|* protocol).  The 32-bit FCS was added via the Federal Register,
|* 1 June 1982, p.23798.  I presume but don't know for certain that
|* this polynomial is or will be included in CCITT V.41, which
|* defines the 16-bit CRC (often called CRC-CCITT) polynomial.  FIPS
|* PUB 78 says that the 32-bit FCS reduces otherwise undetected
|* errors by a factor of 10^-5 over 16-bit FCS.
\************************************************************************/


/* Copyright (C) 1986 Gary S. Brown.  You may use this program, or
        code or tables extracted from it, as desired without restriction.*/

/* First, the polynomial itself and its table of feedback terms.  The */
/* polynomial is                                          */
```

```
/* X^32+X^26+X^23+X^22+X^16+X^12+X^11+X^10+X^8+X^7+X^5+X^4+X^2+X^1+X^0 */
/* Note that we take it "backwards" and put the highest-order term in */
/* the lowest-order bit.  The X^32 term is "implied"; the LSB is the  */
/* X^31 term, etc.  The X^0 term (usually shown as "+1") results in   */
/* the MSB being 1.                                          */

/* Note that the usual hardware shift register implementation, which  */
/* is what we're using (we're merely optimizing it by doing eight-bit */
/* chunks at a time) shifts bits into the lowest-order term.  In our  */
/* implementation, that means shifting towards the right.  Why do we  */
/* do it this way?  Because the calculated CRC must be transmitted in */
/* order from highest-order term to lowest-order term.  UARTs transmit */
/* characters in order from LSB to MSB.  By storing the CRC this way, */
/* we hand it to the UART in the order low-byte to high-byte; the UART */
/* sends each low-bit to hight-bit; and the result is transmission bit */
/* by bit from highest- to lowest-order term without requiring any bit */
/* shuffling on our part.  Reception works similarly.            */

/* The feedback terms table consists of 256, 32-bit entries.  Notes:  */
/*                                                          */
/* 1. The table can be generated at runtime if desired; code to do so */
/*    is shown later.  It might not be obvious, but the feedback    */
/*    terms simply represent the results of eight shift/xor opera-  */
/*    tions for all combinations of data and CRC register values.   */
/*                                                          */
/* 2. The CRC accumulation logic is the same for all CRC polynomials, */
/*    be they sixteen or thirty-two bits wide.  You simply choose the */
/*    appropriate table.  Alternatively, because the table can be    */
/*    generated at runtime, you can start by generating the table for */
/*    the polynomial in question and use exactly the same "updcrc",  */
/*    if your application needn't simultaneously handle two CRC     */
/*    polynomials.  (Note, however, that XMODEM is strange.)       */
/*                                                          */
/* 3. For 16-bit CRCs, the table entries need be only 16 bits wide;  */
/*    of course, 32-bit entries work OK if the high 16 bits are zero. */
/*                                                          */
/* 4. The values must be right-shifted by eight bits by the "updcrc" */
/*    logic; the shift must be unsigned (bring in zeroes).  On some  */
/*    hardware you could probably optimize the shift in assembler by */
/*    using byte-swap instructions.                            */

static UINT4 crc_32_tab[] = { /* CRC polynomial 0xedb88320 */
0x00000000UL, 0x77073096UL, 0xee0e612cUL,
0x990951baUL, 0x076dc419UL, 0x706af48fUL,
0xe963a535UL, 0x9e6495a3UL, 0x0edb8832UL,
0x79dcb8a4UL, 0xe0d5e91eUL, 0x97d2d988UL,
0x09b64c2bUL, 0x7eb17cbdUL, 0xe7b82d07UL,
0x90bf1d91UL, 0x1db71064UL, 0x6ab020f2UL,
```

0xf3b97148UL, 0x84be41deUL, 0x1adad47dUL,
0x6ddde4ebUL, 0xf4d4b551UL, 0x83d385c7UL,
0x136c9856UL, 0x646ba8c0UL, 0xfd62f97aUL,
0x8a65c9ecUL, 0x14015c4fUL, 0x63066cd9UL,
0xfa0f3d63UL, 0x8d080df5UL, 0x3b6e20c8UL,
0x4c69105eUL, 0xd56041e4UL, 0xa2677172UL,
0x3c03e4d1UL, 0x4b04d447UL, 0xd20d85fdUL,
0xa50ab56bUL, 0x35b5a8faUL, 0x42b2986cUL,
0xdbbbc9d6UL, 0xacbcf940UL, 0x32d86ce3UL,
0x45df5c75UL, 0xdcd60dcfUL, 0xabd13d59UL,
0x26d930acUL, 0x51de003aUL, 0xc8d75180UL,
0xbfd06116UL, 0x21b4f4b5UL, 0x56b3c423UL,
0xcfba9599UL, 0xb8bda50fUL, 0x2802b89eUL,
0x5f058808UL, 0xc60cd9b2UL, 0xb10be924UL,
0x2f6f7c87UL, 0x58684c11UL, 0xc1611dabUL,
0xb6662d3dUL, 0x76dc4190UL, 0x01db7106UL,
0x98d220bcUL, 0xefd5102aUL, 0x71b18589UL,
0x06b6b51fUL, 0x9fbfe4a5UL, 0xe8b8d433UL,
0x7807c9a2UL, 0x0f00f934UL, 0x9609a88eUL,
0xe10e9818UL, 0x7f6a0dbbUL, 0x086d3d2dUL,
0x91646c97UL, 0xe6635c01UL, 0x6b6b51f4UL,
0x1c6c6162UL, 0x856530d8UL, 0xf262004eUL,
0x6c0695edUL, 0x1b01a57bUL, 0x8208f4c1UL,
0xf50fc457UL, 0x65b0d9c6UL, 0x12b7e950UL,
0x8bbeb8eaUL, 0xfcb9887cUL, 0x62dd1ddfUL,
0x15da2d49UL, 0x8cd37cf3UL, 0xfbd44c65UL,
0x4db26158UL, 0x3ab551ceUL, 0xa3bc0074UL,
0xd4bb30e2UL, 0x4adfa541UL, 0x3dd895d7UL,
0xa4d1c46dUL, 0xd3d6f4fbUL, 0x4369e96aUL,
0x346ed9fcUL, 0xad678846UL, 0xda60b8d0UL,
0x44042d73UL, 0x33031de5UL, 0xaa0a4c5fUL,
0xdd0d7cc9UL, 0x5005713cUL, 0x270241aaUL,
0xbe0b1010UL, 0xc90c2086UL, 0x5768b525UL,
0x206f85b3UL, 0xb966d409UL, 0xce61e49fUL,
0x5edef90eUL, 0x29d9c998UL, 0xb0d09822UL,
0xc7d7a8b4UL, 0x59b33d17UL, 0x2eb40d81UL,
0xb7bd5c3bUL, 0xc0ba6cadUL, 0xedb88320UL,
0x9abfb3b6UL, 0x03b6e20cUL, 0x74b1d29aUL,
0xead54739UL, 0x9dd277afUL, 0x04db2615UL,
0x73dc1683UL, 0xe3630b12UL, 0x94643b84UL,
0x0d6d6a3eUL, 0x7a6a5aa8UL, 0xe40ecf0bUL,
0x9309ff9dUL, 0x0a00ae27UL, 0x7d079eb1UL,
0xf00f9344UL, 0x8708a3d2UL, 0x1e01f268UL,
0x6906c2feUL, 0xf762575dUL, 0x806567cbUL,
0x196c3671UL, 0x6e6b06e7UL, 0xfed41b76UL,
0x89d32be0UL, 0x10da7a5aUL, 0x67dd4accUL,
0xf9b9df6fUL, 0x8ebeeff9UL, 0x17b7be43UL,

```
    0x60b08ed5UL, 0xd6d6a3e8UL, 0xa1d1937eUL,
    0x38d8c2c4UL, 0x4fdff252UL, 0xd1bb67f1UL,
    0xa6bc5767UL, 0x3fb506ddUL, 0x48b2364bUL,
    0xd80d2bdaUL, 0xaf0a1b4cUL, 0x36034af6UL,
    0x41047a60UL, 0xdf60efc3UL, 0xa867df55UL,
    0x316e8eefUL, 0x4669be79UL, 0xcb61b38cUL,
    0xbc66831aUL, 0x256fd2a0UL, 0x5268e236UL,
    0xcc0c7795UL, 0xbb0b4703UL, 0x220216b9UL,
    0x5505262fUL, 0xc5ba3bbeUL, 0xb2bd0b28UL,
    0x2bb45a92UL, 0x5cb36a04UL, 0xc2d7ffa7UL,
    0xb5d0cf31UL, 0x2cd99e8bUL, 0x5bdeae1dUL,
    0x9b64c2b0UL, 0xec63f226UL, 0x756aa39cUL,
    0x026d930aUL, 0x9c0906a9UL, 0xeb0e363fUL,
    0x72076785UL, 0x05005713UL, 0x95bf4a82UL,
    0xe2b87a14UL, 0x7bb12baeUL, 0x0cb61b38UL,
    0x92d28e9bUL, 0xe5d5be0dUL, 0x7cdcefb7UL,
    0x0bdbdf21UL, 0x86d3d2d4UL, 0xf1d4e242UL,
    0x68ddb3f8UL, 0x1fda836eUL, 0x81be16cdUL,
    0xf6b9265bUL, 0x6fb077e1UL, 0x18b74777UL,
    0x88085ae6UL, 0xff0f6a70UL, 0x66063bcaUL,
    0x11010b5cUL, 0x8f659effUL, 0xf862ae69UL,
    0x616bffd3UL, 0x166ccf45UL, 0xa00ae278UL,
    0xd70dd2eeUL, 0x4e048354UL, 0x3903b3c2UL,
    0xa7672661UL, 0xd06016f7UL, 0x4969474dUL,
    0x3e6e77dbUL, 0xaed16a4aUL, 0xd9d65adcUL,
    0x40df0b66UL, 0x37d83bf0UL, 0xa9bcae53UL,
    0xdebb9ec5UL, 0x47b2cf7fUL, 0x30b5ffe9UL,
    0xbdbdf21cUL, 0xcabac28aUL, 0x53b39330UL,
    0x24b4a3a6UL, 0xbad03605UL, 0xcdd70693UL,
    0x54de5729UL, 0x23d967bfUL, 0xb3667a2eUL,
    0xc4614ab8UL, 0x5d681b02UL, 0x2a6f2b94UL,
    0xb40bbe37UL, 0xc30c8ea1UL, 0x5a05df1bUL,
    0x2d02ef8dUL,
    };



    inline       UINT4
    UPDC32(
            UBYTE                         octet,
            UINT4                         crc)
    {
        return      crc_32_tab[(UINT2)((crc ^ octet) & 0xFFUL)] ^ (crc >> 8);
    }



    crc32::crc32()
```

```
{
    init();
} /* crc32::crc32() */


crc32::~crc32()
{
    /* nada */
} /* crc32::~crc32() */




void
crc32::init()
{
    result_.crc                    = 0xFFFFFFFFUL;
    result_.nChars                 = 0;
} /* crc32::init() */




void
crc32::processBuffer(
            UBYTE*                          buffer,
            UINT4                           nBytesInBuffer)
{
    register    UINT4    oldcrc32    = result_.crc;

    register    UINT4    i;
    UBYTE*          p_buffer;
    for(    i=0,
            p_buffer=buffer
            ;
            i<nBytesInBuffer
            ;
            ++i, ++p_buffer
        )
    {
        oldcrc32 = UPDC32(*p_buffer, oldcrc32);
    } /* for(    i=0 */

    result_.nChars    += nBytesInBuffer;
    result_.crc       = oldcrc32;
}
```

```
crc32::result&
crc32::get_result()
{
        register    UINT4    oldcrc32    = result_.crc;
        result_.crc = ~oldcrc32;

        return      result_;
} /* crc32::get_result() */
```

Bigger and Better

What are the limits on the maximum capacity of a dynamic hashing array? As it happens, there are two capacity parameters of the quantum file access method that we can adjust without affecting the implementation very much: BlockSize, which specifies how large each quantum is, and the maximum number of blocks allowed in the file, set by the MaxFileQuantumCount const in blocki.h. In the current implementation, BlockSize is set to 16K, which means we need 14 bits to specify the location of an item in a quantum. Since an ItemIndex (Figure 5.67) uses a 16-bit word to hold the offset, we could increase the BlockSize to as much as 64K bytes. Let's take a look at the advantages and disadvantages of increasing the quantum size.

Suppose we increase the size of each quantum, for example, to 32K bytes from 16K. It's easy to see that this would double the maximum capacity of the file. What may not be so obvious is that this change would also decrease the memory requirements for efficient file access via dynamic hashing, for a given number of records in the file. To see why this is so, we have to look at the typical usage of disk buffers when looking up a string by key in the dynamic hashing algorithm.

Suppose we want to find the record that has the key 609643342. The algorithm calculates which hash slot points to the storage element in which a record with that key would be stored. It then calls the quantum file access routine GetModifiableElement to retrieve that storage element. GetModifiableElement retrieves the big pointer array block for the array that the storage elements are kept in; then it retrieves the little pointer array block for the correct storage element; and finally it gets the block where the storage element is stored, retrieves it from the block, and returns it. The dynamic hashing algorithm then searches the storage element to find the key we specified and, if it is found, extracts the record we want.[14]

So a total of three blocks are accessed for each retrieval of a string: the big pointer array block, a little pointer array block, and the final "leaf" block. The first of these blocks is referenced on every string retrieval, so it is almost certain to be in memory. The "leaf" block, on the other hand, is not very likely to be in memory, since the purpose of the hashing algorithm is to distribute the data as evenly as possible over the file: with a reasonably large file, most "leaf" accesses aren't going to be to one of the relatively few blocks we can keep in memory.

Fortunately, this pessimistic outlook does not apply to the second block retrieved, the little pointer array block. If we have 500,000 strings in our file, there are 83,333 storage elements that the quantum file algorithm has to deal with. With a 16K-byte block, approximately 4000 little pointer elements fit in each little pointer block, so the little pointer blocks would occupy 21 buffers.

Let's look at the situation if we go to 32K-byte blocks. If we double the number of strings in the average storage element to 12 so that the likelihood of an overflow would remain approximately the same as before, then the number of little pointer array elements needed to access a given number of records is halved; in addition, the number of little pointer array elements that fit in each little pointer block is doubled.[15] This means that to be fairly sure that the little pointer block we need will be present in memory, instead of 21 blocks taking up almost 700K of memory, we need only 6 blocks taking up about 200K of memory.

In the case of dynamic hashing, this effect greatly alleviates the primary drawback of increasing the block size, which is that the number of blocks that can be held in a given amount of memory is inversely proportional to the size of each block. In the general case, however, this reduction in the number of buffers can hurt the performance of the program; the system can "thrash" if the working

---

14. This is actually somewhat of an over-simplification, as it ignores the possibility of overflow of a storage element; if that occurs, then the whole process of looking up the storage element by key has to be repeated, doubling the number of block accesses. However, if we've chosen the parameters properly, overflows will be rare and therefore will not affect this analysis significantly.

15. Of course, having a larger block size also makes the algorithm more suitable to other applications with larger data items.

set of data needed at any given time needs more buffers than are available.

The only other apparent drawback of increasing the size of the quanta is that the free space codes become less accurate, since the code remains fixed in size at one byte; with a 32K block, each increment in the size code represents 128 bytes. However, I doubt that this will cause any significant problems with space utilization.

The More, the Merrier

The other fairly simple way to increase the capacity of the system is to increase the number of blocks that can be addressed. The ItemReference class (Figure 6.21) defines objects that take up four bytes each, 20 bits for the m_QuantumNumber field and 12 bits for the m_RelativeItemNumber field.

Figure 6.21: The ItemReference class (from quantum\blocki.h)

```
class ItemReference
{
protected:
// The size of the m_QuantumNumber field limits the number
// of quanta that can exist in one file.  If we don't want
// to increase the size of an ItemReference object, then
// we can't increase this number without simultaneously
// lowering the number of items in a block.
      unsigned m_QuantumNumber:20;
      unsigned m_RelativeItemNumber:12;
public:
int    IsReference() { return m_RelativeItemNumber != NoItem; }
int    GetItemNumber() {return m_RelativeItemNumber;}
int    GetQuantumNumber() {return m_QuantumNumber;}
      void SetItemNumber(ArrayIndex p_ItemNumber)
            {
            m_RelativeItemNumber = p_ItemNumber;
            }
      void SetQuantumNumber(QuantumNumber p_QuantumNumber)
            {
            m_QuantumNumber = p_QuantumNumber;
            }
};
```

If we wanted to increase the number of quanta from its current maximum of 10,000 (set by the MaxFileQuantumCount const in blocki.h), we could increase it up to 1024K without changing the size of the m_QuantumNumber field.

The main drawback of increasing the maximum block count is that the free space list gets bigger; in fact, that's the reason that I've set the maximum file quantum count to 10,000 despite the fact that the quantum number field in the item reference class can handle a file with far more quanta. However, if our application needs so much data that a 160-MB maximum file size is too small, the extra space taken up by a larger free space list probably isn't an obstacle.

Summary

In this chapter, we have used the quantum file access method as the base for a disk-based variant of Larson's dynamic hashing. This algorithm provides efficient hash-coded access by key to a very large amount of variable-length textual data, while eliminating the traditional drawbacks of hashing, especially the need to specify the maximum size of the file in advance.

In the final chapter, we will summarize the algorithms we have covered in this book and discuss some other resources we can use to improve the efficiency of our programs.

Problems

1. What modifications to the dynamic hashing implementation would be needed to add the following capabilities?

   a. Shrinking the file when deleting records;
   b. Storing and retrieving records with duplicate keys.

2. How could the PersistentArrayUlong class be generalized to other data types?

(You can find suggested approaches to problems in Chapter 8).

Chapter 7

Zensort: A Sorting Algorithm for Limited Memory

Introduction

This chapter will explain how to get around the major limitation of the otherwise very efficient distribution counting sort algorithm: its poor performance with limited available memory.

Algorithms Discussed

Zensort: A version of the distribution counting sort for use with limited available memory

Virtual Impossibility

For many years, I've been a very big fan of the "distribution counting sort", which is described in Chapter 3. However, it does have one fairly serious drawback: it doesn't work very well in virtual memory. The problem with the distribution counting sort in virtual memory is that it has very poor locality of reference: that is, rather than stepping through memory in a predictable and linear way, it jumps all over the place. Although this is not optimal even when we are dealing with programs that access data solely in memory, because it makes poor use of the processor cache, it is disastrous when we are dealing with virtual memory. The difficulty is that random accesses to various areas of the disk are much, much slower than sequential accesses: in some cases, the difference may be a factor of 1,000 or more. I discovered this fact (not that I should have had to discover it by experimentation) when I ran some comparison tests between Quicksort and the distribution counting sort for very large files, where the data would not even remotely fit in memory. However, I didn't believe that this was an insuperable obstacle, and I have made a number of attempts to do something about it. Finally, after some years of on-and-off experimentation, I have found the solution.

The Urge to Merge

The solution to this problem is really very simple, when you look at it the right way. If the problem is that we're moving data in a random fashion all over the disk, and thereby incurring massive numbers of positioning operations, perhaps we would do much better if we were to write the data out to intermediate buffers in memory and write those buffers out to disk only when they became full. In this way, we would reduce the number of random disk accesses by a large factor.

Up to this point, I hadn't invented anything new. It has been known for many years that it is possible to sort very large files — by dividing them into blocks each of which will fit into memory, sorting each block, and then merging the results into the final output file. The difficulty with this method of sorting is the merge phase, which requires a great deal of disk I/O in itself and can be a major contributor to the entire time taken to sort the file. However, I discovered that there was a way to avoid this merge phase.

The key (no pun intended) is that by accumulating the data for the keys over the entire file, we could determine exactly where each output record should go in the entire file, even though we were buffering only a small percentage of the data.

The Initial Implementation

This is probably easier to show in code than it is to explain in English, although of course I'll do both before we are finished. However, let's start with the code, which is shown in Figure 7.1.

Figure 7.1: Initial implementation of Zensort (Zensort\zen01.cpp)

```
#include <stdio.h>
#include <stdlib.h>
#include <string.h>
#include <iostream.h>
#include <fstream.h>

#include "e:\opt\common\timings.h"

int main(int argc, char *argv[])
{
    const int BUFSIZE = 16384;
    const int BUFCOUNT = 256;
    const int INPUTLINESIZE = 1024;
    char InputLine[INPUTLINESIZE];
    char *Buffer[BUFCOUNT];
    int Displacement[BUFCOUNT];
    int TotalDisplacement[BUFCOUNT];
    char CurrentChar;
    char* InputFileName;
    char* OutputFileName;
    ifstream InputFile;
    ofstream OutputFile;
    int PassCount;
    int CurrentLength;
    int NewLength;
    int LineLength;
    char* OriginalInputFileName;
    char* OriginalOutputFileName;
    int TotalKeys = 0;
    int TotalData = 0;
    bool StatisticsDisplayed = false;
    int TotalWrites = 0;
    int i;

    if (argc < 4)
        {
```

```
          printf("Usage: zensort passcount infile outfile\n");
          exit(1);
          }
     else
          {
          PassCount = atoi(argv[1]);
          OriginalInputFileName = argv[2];
          OriginalOutputFileName = argv[3];
          }

char temp[100];
start_timing();

     for (i = 0; i < BUFCOUNT; i ++)
          {
          Buffer[i] = new char[BUFSIZE];
          }

     for (int Pass = PassCount - 1; Pass >= 0; Pass --)
          {

          if ((PassCount - Pass) % 2 == 1)
               {
               InputFileName = OriginalInputFileName;
               OutputFileName = OriginalOutputFileName;
               }
          else
               {
               InputFileName = OriginalOutputFileName;
               OutputFileName = OriginalInputFileName;
               }

          InputFile.open(InputFileName,ios::inlios::binary);
          OutputFile.open(OutputFileName,ios::outlios::binary);

          for (i = 0; i < BUFCOUNT; i ++)
               {
               memset(Buffer[i],0,BUFSIZE);
               Displacement[i] = 0;
               TotalDisplacement[i] = 0;
               }

          while (true)
               {
               InputFile.getline(InputLine,INPUTLINESIZE);
               if (!InputFile)
                    break;
               TotalKeys ++;
```

```
            LineLength = strlen(InputLine);
            TotalData += LineLength + 1;
            if (Pass >= LineLength)
                CurrentChar = 0;
            else
                CurrentChar = InputLine[Pass];
            Displacement[CurrentChar] += LineLength + 1;
            }
        InputFile.close();

        for (i = 1; i < BUFCOUNT; i ++)
            {
            TotalDisplacement[i] = TotalDisplacement[i-1] + Displacement[i-1];
            }

if ((Pass == PassCount - 1) && StatisticsDisplayed == false)
    {
    printf("Total keys: %d\n", TotalKeys);
    printf("Total data: %d\n", TotalData);
    StatisticsDisplayed = true;
    }

sprintf(temp,"Finished counting on pass %d",PassCount-Pass);
timing(temp);

        InputFile.open(InputFileName,ios::in|ios::binary);

        while (true)
            {
            InputFile.getline(InputLine,INPUTLINESIZE);
            if (!InputFile)
                break;
            strcat(InputLine,"\n");
            LineLength = strlen(InputLine);
            if (Pass >= LineLength-1)
                CurrentChar = 0;
            else
                CurrentChar = InputLine[Pass];
            CurrentLength = strlen(Buffer[CurrentChar]);
            NewLength = CurrentLength + LineLength;
            if (NewLength >= BUFSIZE)
                {
                OutputFile.seekp(TotalDisplacement[CurrentChar]);
                TotalDisplacement[CurrentChar] += CurrentLength;
                OutputFile.write(Buffer[CurrentChar],CurrentLength);
                TotalWrites ++;
                memset(Buffer[CurrentChar],0,BUFSIZE);
                }
```

```
            strcat(Buffer[CurrentChar],InputLine);
            }

        for (i = 0; i < BUFCOUNT; i ++)
            {
            CurrentLength = strlen(Buffer[i]);
            if (CurrentLength > 0)
                {
                OutputFile.seekp(TotalDisplacement[i]);
                OutputFile.write(Buffer[i],CurrentLength);
                TotalWrites ++;
                }
            }
        InputFile.close();
        OutputFile.close();

sprintf(temp,"Finished distributing on pass %d",PassCount-Pass);
timing(temp);
    }

    printf("Total writes: %d\n", TotalWrites);

    for (i = 0; i < BUFCOUNT; i ++)
        {
        delete [] Buffer[i];
        }

    end_timing();

    return 0;
}
```

We start out reasonably enough by extracting the size of the keys, the input file name, and the output file name from the command line. After initializing the timing routine, we allocate space for the buffers that will be used to hold the data on its way to the disk. As you may recall from Chapter 3, the distribution counting sort moves data from the input file to the output file based on the value of the current character of the key being sorted. Therefore, we need one buffer for each possible character in the key being sorted, so that we can keep the data for each character value separate from the data for every other character value.

Now we are ready to start the main body of the algorithm. For each pass through the data, we have to read from one file and write to the other. On the first pass, of course, we will read from the original input file and write to the original output file. However, on the second pass we'll read from the original output file and write back to the original input file, because after the first pass, the output file is sorted on only the last character of the key. In the distribution counting sort algorithm, we sort on each character of the key separately, in reverse order of their positions in the key. After the first pass, the original output file contains exactly the information we need as input for the second pass.

That's the reason we use the modulus operator in the if statement that determines which filenames to use for which files: on every odd numbered pass, we use the original input file name for the input file, and on every even numbered pass, we use the original output file name for the input file. Of course, the reverse is true for the output file.

Once we figure out which file will be used for input and which will be used for output, we open them. Then we initialize all of the buffers by clearing them to 0, initialize the displacement values for each buffer to 0, and initialize the total displacement values for each buffer to 0.

The displacement array keeps track of the amount of data in the input file for each possible value of the current key character. That is, the entry in the displacement array that has the index 65 (the ASCII value for 'A') represents the total size of all the records seen so far in the current pass that have the letter A in the current position in their key. The total displacement array, on the other hand, is used to accumulate the total amount of data in the input file that has a key character less than the ASCII value of the index in the total displacement array. For example, the entry in the total displacement array that has the index 65 represents the total size of all the records whose key character was less than the letter A, which is the same as the displacement into the output file of the first record whose key character is A. Of course, we cannot fill in the values of this array until we are finished with the pass through the file, because until then we do not know the total sizes of all records with a given key character.[1]

But we are getting a little ahead of ourselves here. Before we can calculate the total size of all the records for a given key character, we

---

1. The displacement and total displacement arrays play the same roles in this program as the bucket count and bucket position arrays did in the distribution counting program in Chapter 3.

have to read all the records in the file, so let's continue by looking at the loop that does that. This "endless" loop starts by reading a line from the input file and checking whether it was successful. If the status of the input file indicates that the read did not work, then we break out of the loop. Otherwise, we increment the total number of keys read (for statistical purposes), calculate the length of the record, and increment the total amount of data read (also for statistical purposes). Next, we determine whether the record is long enough for us to extract the character of the key that we need; if it is, we do so, and otherwise we treat as though it were 0 so that such a record will sort to the beginning of the file.[2] Once we have found (or substituted for) the character on which we are sorting, we add the length of the line (plus one for the new-line character that the getline function discards) to the displacement for that character. Then we continue with the next iteration of the loop.

Once we get to the end of the input file, we close it. Then we compute the total displacement values for each character, by adding the total displacement value for the previous character to the displacement value for the previous character. At this point, having read all of the data from the input file, we can display the statistics on the total number of keys and total amount of data in the file, if this is the first pass. This is also the point where we display the time taken to do the counting pass.

Now we're ready for the second, distribution, pass for this character position. This is another "endless" loop, very similar to the previous one. As before, we read a line from the input file and break out of the loop if the read fails. Next, we concatenate a new-line character to the end of the input line. This is necessary because the getline function discards that character from lines that it reads; therefore, if we did not take this step, our output file would have no new-line characters in it, which would undoubtedly be disconcerting to our users.

Next, we extract the current key character from the line, or substitute a null byte for it if it is not present. The next operation is to calculate the current amount of data in the buffer used to store data for this key character. Then we add the length of the current line to

---

2. This special handling for short records is required so that we don't accidentally pick up garbage characters past the end of the key if the record we are handling is shorter than the number of characters on which we wish to sort.

the amount of existing data in the buffer. If adding the new line to the buffer would cause it to overflow its bounds, then we have to write out the current data and clear the buffer before storing our new data in it.

To do this, we seek to the position in the output file corresponding to the current value of the total displacement array for the current character value. As we have already seen, the initial value of the total displacement array entry for each character is equal to the number of characters in the file for all records whose key character precedes this character. For example, if the current key character is a capital 'A', then element 65 in the total displacement array starts out at the beginning of the distribution loop with the offset into the output file where we want to write the first record whose key character is a capital 'A'. If this is the first time that we are writing the buffer corresponding to the letter 'A', we need to position the output file to the first place where records whose keys contain the key character 'A' should be written, so the initial value of the total displacement array element is what we need in this situation.

However, once we have written that first batch of records whose keys contain the letter 'A', we have to update the total displacement element for that character so that the next batch of records whose keys contain the letter 'A' will be written immediately after the first batch. That's the purpose of the next statement in the source code.

Now we have positioned the file properly and have updated the next output position, so we write the data in the buffer to the file. Then we update the total number of writes for statistical purposes, and clear the buffer in preparation for its next use to hold more records with the corresponding key character.

At this point, we are ready to rejoin the regular flow of the program, where we append the input line we have just read to the buffer that corresponds to its key character. That's the end of the second "endless" loop, so we return to the top of that loop to continue processing the rest of the lines in the file.

Once we've processed all the lines in the input file, there's one more task we have to handle before finishing this pass through the data: writing out whatever remains in the various buffers. This is the task of the for loop that follows the second "endless" loop. Of course, there's no reason to write out data from a buffer that doesn't contain anything, so we check whether the current length of the buffer is greater than 0 before writing it out to the file.

After displaying a message telling the user how long it took to do this distribution pass, we return to the top of the outer loop and begin again with the next pass through the file to handle the next character position in the key. When we get through with all the characters in the key, we are finished with the processing, so we display a final message indicating the total number of writes that we have performed, free the memory for the buffers, terminate the timing routines, and exit.

Performance: Baseline

So how does this initial version of the program actually perform? While I was working on the answer to this question, it occurred to me that perhaps it would be a good idea to run tests on machines of various amounts of physical memory. After all, even if this algorithm works well with limited physical memory, that doesn't mean that having additional memory wouldn't help its performance. In particular, when we are reading and writing a lot of data, the availability of memory to use as a disk cache can make a lot of difference. Therefore, I ran the tests twice, once with 64 MB of RAM in my machine and once with 192 MB. The amount of available memory did make a substantial difference, as you'll see when we discuss the various performance results.

Figure 7.2 illustrates how this initial version works with files of various sizes, starting with 100,000 records of approximately 60 bytes apiece and ending with one million similar records.[3]

---

3. Notes on performance tables:
  1. All times are in seconds.
  2. All tests were run on a machine with a Pentium II processor running at 233 MHz with either 64 or 192 MB of RAM and a Western Digital model 35100 5.1 GB Ultra DMA hard drive. The disk partition on which the tests were run was defragmented before each test was run.
  3. The programs were run in a DOS session under Windows 95.
  4. I know that the entries in some of the figures look suspicious, as the timing for the small and large memory configurations are sometimes identical on the 100000 record case. However, the entries are correct; I guess it's just a fluke of testing.

Figure 7.2: Performance of Zensort version 1 (Zensort\timings.01)

```
Sorting variable-length records

Record     Total      64MB RAM   192MB RAM   64MB RAM   192MB RAM
Count      Data       Time       Time        Kb/Sec     KB/Sec

100000     6348151    203.08     203.74      31.26      31.16
250000     15971969   512.03     512.58      31.19      31.16
500000     31930988   1125.66    1030.88     28.37      30.97
1000000    63754674   2435.16    2090.55     26.18      30.50
```

According to these figures, this is in fact a linear sort, or close enough to make no difference, at least on the larger machine. An *n log n* sort would take exactly 1.2 times as long per element when sorting one million records as when sorting 100,000 records. While this sort takes almost exactly that much longer per element for the one million record file on the smaller machine, the difference is only three percent on the larger machine, so obviously the algorithm itself has the capability of achieving linear scaling.

But linear performance only matters if the performance is good enough in the region in which we are interested. Since this is a book on optimization, let's see if we can speed this up significantly.

The Initial Improvements

One of the most obvious areas where we could improve the efficiency of this algorithm is in the use of the buffer space. The particular input file that we are sorting has keys that consist entirely of digits, which means that allocating 256 buffers of equal size, one for each possible ASCII character, is extremely wasteful, because only 10 of those buffers will ever be used. Although not all keys consist only of digits, that is a very common key composition; similarly, many keys consist solely of alphabetic characters, and of course there are keys that combine both. In any of these cases, we would do much better to allocate more memory to buffers that are actually going to be used; in fact, we should not bother to allocate any memory for buffers that are not used at all. Luckily, we can determine this on the counting pass with very little additional effort, as you can see in Figure 7.3.

Figure 7.3: Zensort version 2 (Zensort\zen02.cpp)

```
#include <stdio.h>
#include <stdlib.h>
#include <string.h>
#include <iostream.h>
#include <fstream.h>

#include "e:\opt\common\timings.h"

int main(int argc, char *argv[])
{
    const int BUFCOUNT = 256;
    const int TOTAL_BUFFER = 4*1048576;
    const int INPUTLINESIZE = 1024;
    char InputLine[INPUTLINESIZE];
    char *Buffer[BUFCOUNT];
    int BufferSize[BUFCOUNT];
    int BufferCharCount[BUFCOUNT];
    int Displacement[BUFCOUNT];
    int TotalDisplacement[BUFCOUNT];
    char CurrentChar;
    char* InputFileName;
    char* OutputFileName;
    ifstream InputFile;
    ofstream OutputFile;
    int PassCount;
    int CurrentLength;
    int NewLength;
    int LineLength;
    char* OriginalInputFileName;
    char* OriginalOutputFileName;
    int TotalKeys = 0;
    int TotalData = 0;
    bool StatisticsDisplayed = false;
    int TotalWrites = 0;
    int i;
    double BufferRatio;

    if (argc < 4)
        {
        printf("Usage: zensort passcount infile outfile\n");
        exit(1);
        }
    else
        {
```

```
        PassCount = atoi(argv[1]);
        OriginalInputFileName = argv[2];
        OriginalOutputFileName = argv[3];
        }

char temp[100];
start_timing();

    for (int Pass = PassCount - 1; Pass >= 0; Pass --)
        {

        if ((PassCount - Pass) % 2 == 1)
            {
            InputFileName = OriginalInputFileName;
            OutputFileName = OriginalOutputFileName;
            }
        else
            {
            InputFileName = OriginalOutputFileName;
            OutputFileName = OriginalInputFileName;
            }

        InputFile.open(InputFileName,ios::inlios::binary);
        OutputFile.open(OutputFileName,ios::outlios::binary);

        for (i = 0; i < BUFCOUNT; i ++)
            {
            Displacement[i] = 0;
            TotalDisplacement[i] = 0;
            }

        while (true)
            {
            InputFile.getline(InputLine,INPUTLINESIZE);
            if (!InputFile)
                break;
            TotalKeys ++;
            LineLength = strlen(InputLine);
            if (Pass >= LineLength)
                CurrentChar = 0;
            else
                CurrentChar = InputLine[Pass];
            Displacement[CurrentChar] += LineLength + 1;
            }
        InputFile.close();

        for (i = 1; i < BUFCOUNT; i ++)
            {
```

```
                              TotalDisplacement[i] = TotalDisplacement[i-1] + Displacement[i-1];
                              }

                 if (TotalData == 0)
                     {
                     for (i = 0; i < BUFCOUNT; i ++)
                         {
                         TotalData += Displacement[i];
                         }
                     BufferRatio = (double) TOTAL_BUFFER / TotalData;
                     }

                 for (i = 0; i < BUFCOUNT; i ++)
                     {
                     BufferSize[i] = (int) (BufferRatio*Displacement[i]);
                     if (BufferSize[i] == 0)
                         Buffer[i] = 0;
                     else
                         {
                         Buffer[i] = new char[BufferSize[i]];
                         memset(Buffer[i],0,BufferSize[i]);
                         }
                     BufferCharCount[i] = 0;
                     }

if ((Pass == PassCount - 1) && StatisticsDisplayed == false)
    {
    printf("Total keys: %d\n", TotalKeys);
    printf("Total data: %d\n", TotalData);
    StatisticsDisplayed = true;
    }

sprintf(temp,"Finished counting on pass %d",PassCount-Pass);
timing(temp);

                 InputFile.open(InputFileName,ios::in|ios::binary);

                 while (true)
                     {
                     InputFile.getline(InputLine,INPUTLINESIZE);
                     if (!InputFile)
                         break;
                     LineLength = strlen(InputLine)+1;
                     strcpy(InputLine+LineLength-1,"\n");
                     if (Pass >= LineLength-1)
                         CurrentChar = 0;
                     else
                         CurrentChar = InputLine[Pass];
```

```
            CurrentLength = BufferCharCount[CurrentChar];
            NewLength = CurrentLength + LineLength;
            if (NewLength >= BufferSize[CurrentChar])
                {
                OutputFile.seekp(TotalDisplacement[CurrentChar]);
                TotalDisplacement[CurrentChar] += CurrentLength;
                OutputFile.write(Buffer[CurrentChar],CurrentLength);
                TotalWrites ++;
                memset(Buffer[CurrentChar],0,BufferSize[CurrentChar]);
                BufferCharCount[CurrentChar] = 0;
                }
            strcpy(Buffer[CurrentChar]+BufferCharCount[CurrentChar],InputLine);
            BufferCharCount[CurrentChar] += strlen(InputLine);
            }

        for (i = 0; i < BUFCOUNT; i ++)
            {
            if (Buffer[i])
                {
                CurrentLength = BufferCharCount[i];
                if (CurrentLength > 0)
                    {
                    OutputFile.seekp(TotalDisplacement[i]);
                    OutputFile.write(Buffer[i],CurrentLength);
                    TotalWrites ++;
                    }
                }
            }
        InputFile.close();
        OutputFile.close();

        for (i = 0; i < BUFCOUNT; i ++)
            {
            delete [] Buffer[i];
            }

sprintf(temp,"Finished distributing on pass %d",PassCount-Pass);
timing(temp);
        }

    printf("Total writes: %d\n", TotalWrites);

    end_timing();

    return 0;
}
```

The first changes of any significance in this program are the addition of two new arrays that we will use to keep track of the buffer size for each possible key character and the total number of characters stored in each buffer. Of course, because we are assigning memory to buffers in a dynamic fashion, we can't allocate those buffers until we know how much memory we want to devote to each buffer. Therefore, the allocation has to be inside the main loop rather than preceding it. By the same token, we have to delete each buffer before the end of the main loop so that they can be re-allocated for the next pass.

The next question, of course, is how we decide how much space to devote to each buffer. It seemed to me that the best way to approach this would be to calculate the proportion of the entire file that the records for each key character correspond to, and allocate that proportion of the entire buffer space to the buffer for that key character, so that's how I did it.

First, we add up all of the record length totals; then we compute the ratio of the total amount of space available for buffers to the total amount of data in the file. Then we step through all the different key characters and compute the appropriate size of the buffer for each key character. If the result comes out to be zero, then we don't allocate any space for that buffer; instead, we assign a null pointer to that buffer address, as that is much more efficient than allocating a zero-length buffer. However, if the buffer size comes out to be greater than zero, we allocate the computed amount of space for that buffer, then clear it to zeros. Finally, we clear the buffer character count for that buffer, as we haven't stored anything in it yet.

When it's time to store some data in the buffer, we use the buffer character count array rather than calling strlen to find out how much data is currently in the buffer. I decided to track the count myself because when I first changed the buffer allocation strategy from fixed to variable, the program ran much more slowly than it had previously. This didn't make much sense to me at first, but upon reflection I realized that the longer the buffers are, the longer it would take strlen to find the end of each buffer. To prevent this undesirable effect, I decided to keep track of the size of buffers myself rather than relying on strlen to do it. Of course, that means that we have to add the length of each record to the total count for each buffer as we add the record to the buffer, so I added a line to handle this task.

The Second Version

So how does this second version of the program actually perform? Figure 7.4 illustrates how it works with files of various sizes.[4]

Figure 7.4: Performance of Zensort version 2 (Zensort\timings.02)

```
Sorting variable-length records

 Record      Total    64MB RAM  192MB RAM  64MB RAM  192MB RAM
 Count       Data     Time      Time       Kb/Sec    KB/Sec

 100000     6348151    27.20      27.20     233.39    233.39
 250000    15971969    74.95      69.12     213.10    231.08
 500000    31930988   194.23     149.84     164.40    213.10
1000000    63754674   542.58     315.71     117.50    201.94
```

If you compare the performance of this second version of the program to the previous version on the small file, you'll notice that it is over 7.5 times as fast in the 64 MB machine and almost 7.5 times as fast on the 192 MB machine as was the previous version. However, what is more important is how well it performs when we have a lot of data to sort. While we haven't achieved quite as much of a speed-up on larger files as on the smallest one, we have still sped up the one million record sort by a factor of almost 4.5 to one when running the sort on a machine with "only" 64 MB of RAM and more than 6.5 to 1 on the more generously equipped machine with 192 MB of RAM, which is not an insignificant improvement.[5]

---

4. All times are in seconds.

5. You may be wondering how much of the improvement in performance was due to the better buffer allocation strategy and how much to the other minor improvements such as keeping track of the buffer contents ourselves rather than calling strlen. Unfortunately, I can't give you that information because I did not run tests with each of those factors isolated; there are just too many combinations for me to test in a reasonable amount of time. However, because you have the source code for all the different versions of this program, you can find that out for yourself. I would be interested in receiving the results of any comparative tests you might run.

Is this the best we can do? Not at all, as you'll see in the analysis of the other versions of the program. Let's continue with a very simple change that provided some improvement without any particular effort.

The Third Version

At this point in the development of the sorting algorithm, I decided that although saving memory is nice, we don't have to go overboard. On the assumption that anyone who wants to sort gigantic files has a reasonably capable computer, I decided to increase the amount of memory allocated to the buffers from 4 MB to 16 MB. As you might imagine, this improved performance significantly on larger files, although not nearly as much proportionally as our previous change did.

Originally, I wasn't planning to make any changes to the program from the previous version to this one other than increasing the buffer size. However, when running tests with the 64 MB memory configuration, I discovered that making just that one change caused the program to fail with a message telling me I was out of memory. This was hard to understand at first, because I was allocating only 16 MB at any one time; surely a 64 MB machine, even one running Windows 95, should be able to handle that without difficulty!

However, the program was crashing at the same place every time I ran it with the same data, after a number of passes through the main loop, so I had to figure out what the cause might be. At first, I didn't see anything questionable about the program. On further examination, however, I did notice something that was cause for concern: I was allocating and freeing those memory buffers every time through the main loop. While it seems reasonable to me that allocating a number of buffers and then freeing all of them should return the memory allocation map to its original state, apparently this was not the case. At least, that's the only explanation I can find for why the available memory displayed by the debugger should drop suddenly after a number of passes through the main loop in which it remained nearly constant.

Actually, even if allocating and freeing the buffers every time through the loop did work properly, it really isn't the right way to handle the memory allocation task. It's much more efficient to allocate one large buffer and just keep pointers to the places in that buffer where our smaller, logically distinct, buffers reside. Once I made those changes to the program, the crashes went away, so I apparently identified the problem correctly. The new, improved version is shown in Figure 7.5.

Figure 7.5: Zensort version 3 (Zensort\zen03.cpp)

```
#include <stdio.h>
#include <stdlib.h>
#include <string.h>
#include <iostream.h>
#include <fstream.h>

#include "e:\opt\common\timings.h"

int main(int argc, char *argv[])
{
        const int BUFCOUNT = 256;
        const int TOTAL_BUFFER = 16*1048576;
        const int INPUTLINESIZE = 1024;
        char InputLine[INPUTLINESIZE];
        char* BigBuffer = new char [TOTAL_BUFFER];
        char** Buffer = new char* [BUFCOUNT];
        int* BufferSize = new int[BUFCOUNT];
        int* BufferCharCount = new int[BUFCOUNT];
        int* Displacement = new int[BUFCOUNT];
        int* TotalDisplacement = new int[BUFCOUNT];
        char CurrentChar;
        char* InputFileName;
        char* OutputFileName;
        ifstream InputFile;
        ofstream OutputFile;
        int PassCount;
        int CurrentLength;
        int NewLength;
        int LineLength;
        char* OriginalInputFileName;
        char* OriginalOutputFileName;
        int TotalKeys = 0;
        int TotalData = 0;
        bool StatisticsDisplayed = false;
        int TotalWrites = 0;
```

```
        int i;
        double BufferRatio;
        int TotalBufferSize;

        if (argc < 4)
            {
            printf("Usage: zensort passcount infile outfile\n");
            exit(1);
            }
        else
            {
            PassCount = atoi(argv[1]);
            OriginalInputFileName = argv[2];
            OriginalOutputFileName = argv[3];
            }

char temp[100];
start_timing();

        for (int Pass = PassCount - 1; Pass >= 0; Pass --)
            {

            if ((PassCount - Pass) % 2 == 1)
                {
                InputFileName = OriginalInputFileName;
                OutputFileName = OriginalOutputFileName;
                }
            else
                {
                InputFileName = OriginalOutputFileName;
                OutputFileName = OriginalInputFileName;
                }

            InputFile.open(InputFileName,ios::inlios::binary);
            OutputFile.open(OutputFileName,ios::outlios::binary);

            for (i = 0; i < BUFCOUNT; i ++)
                {
                Displacement[i] = 0;
                TotalDisplacement[i] = 0;
                }

            while (true)
                {
                InputFile.getline(InputLine,INPUTLINESIZE);
                if (!InputFile)
                        break;
                TotalKeys ++;
```

```
            LineLength = strlen(InputLine);
            if (Pass >= LineLength)
                 CurrentChar = 0;
            else
                 CurrentChar = InputLine[Pass];
            Displacement[CurrentChar] += LineLength + 1;
            }
        InputFile.close();

        for (i = 1; i < BUFCOUNT; i ++)
            TotalDisplacement[i] = TotalDisplacement[i-1] + Displacement[i-1];

        if (TotalData == 0)
            {
            for (i = 0; i < BUFCOUNT; i ++)
                TotalData += Displacement[i];
            BufferRatio = (double) TOTAL_BUFFER / TotalData;
            }

        TotalBufferSize = 0;
        for (i = 0; i < BUFCOUNT; i ++)
            {
            BufferSize[i] = (int) (BufferRatio*Displacement[i]);
            if (BufferSize[i] == 0)
                Buffer[i] = 0;
            else
                {
                Buffer[i] = BigBuffer + TotalBufferSize;
                TotalBufferSize += BufferSize[i];
                }
            BufferCharCount[i] = 0;
            }

    memset(BigBuffer,0,TOTAL_BUFFER);

if ((Pass == PassCount - 1) && StatisticsDisplayed == false)
    {
    printf("Total buffer space: %d\n",TOTAL_BUFFER);
    printf("Total keys: %d\n", TotalKeys);
    printf("Total data: %d\n", TotalData);
    StatisticsDisplayed = true;
    }

sprintf(temp,"Finished counting on pass %d",PassCount-Pass);
timing(temp);

        InputFile.open(InputFileName,ios::in|ios::binary);
```

```
                 while (true)
                     {
                     InputFile.getline(InputLine,INPUTLINESIZE);
                     if (!InputFile)
                         break;
                     LineLength = strlen(InputLine)+1;
                     strcpy(InputLine+LineLength-1,"\n");
                     if (Pass >= LineLength-1)
                         CurrentChar = 0;
                     else
                         CurrentChar = InputLine[Pass];
                     CurrentLength = BufferCharCount[CurrentChar];
                     NewLength =  CurrentLength + LineLength;
                     if (NewLength >= BufferSize[CurrentChar])
                             {
                             OutputFile.seekp(TotalDisplacement[CurrentChar]);
                             TotalDisplacement[CurrentChar] += CurrentLength;
                             OutputFile.write(Buffer[CurrentChar],CurrentLength);
                             TotalWrites ++;
                             memset(Buffer[CurrentChar],0,BufferSize[CurrentChar]);
                             BufferCharCount[CurrentChar] = 0;
                             }
                     strcpy(Buffer[CurrentChar]+BufferCharCount[CurrentChar],InputLine);
                     BufferCharCount[CurrentChar] += strlen(InputLine);
                     }

             for (i = 0; i < BUFCOUNT; i ++)
                 {
                 if (Buffer[i])
                     {
                     CurrentLength = BufferCharCount[i];
                     if (CurrentLength > 0)
                         {
                         OutputFile.seekp(TotalDisplacement[i]);
                         OutputFile.write(Buffer[i],CurrentLength);
                         TotalWrites ++;
                         }
                     }
                 }
             InputFile.close();
             OutputFile.close();


sprintf(temp,"Finished distributing on pass %d",PassCount-Pass);
timing(temp);
     }

   printf("Total writes: %d\n", TotalWrites);
```

```
    end_timing();

    return 0;
}
```

I think the changes in the program are relatively self-explanatory. Basically, the only changes are the allocation of a new variable called BigBuffer which is used to hold all the data for the records being sorted, and the change of the previously existing Buffer variable to an array of char* rather than an array of char. Rather than allocating and deleting the individual buffers on every pass through the main loop, we merely recalculate the position in the large buffer where the logical buffer for each character begins. The performance results for this version of the program are shown in Figure 7.6.

Figure 7.6: Performance of Zensort version 3 (Zensort\timings.03)

Sorting variable-length records

Record Count	Total Data	64MB RAM Time	192MB RAM Time	64MB RAM Kb/Sec	192MB RAM KB/Sec
100000	6348151	13.68	13.85	464.05	458.35
250000	15971969	53.63	47.69	297.82	334.91
500000	31930988	176.54	118.68	180.87	269.05
1000000	63754674	481.87	269.34	132.31	236.71

While we didn't get as much of an increase in performance from making more room available for the buffers as we did from improving the algorithm in the previous stage, we did get about a 13 percent increase in throughput on the largest file with a 64 MB system, and about 17 percent on the 192 MB system, which isn't negligible.[6]

Now let's take a look at another way of speeding up this algorithm that will have considerably more effect: sorting on two characters at a time.

---

6. In case you were wondering how much of the performance improvement was due to using one large buffer rather than many small buffers, there was little or no performance improvement from that change. However, according to the first law of optimization, that doesn't make any difference because the program didn't work properly until I made that change.

The Fourth Version

Every pass we make through the file requires a significant amount of disk activity, both reading and writing. Therefore, anything that reduces the number of passes should help speed the program up noticeably. The simplest way of accomplishing this goal in a general way is to sort on two characters at a time rather than one as we have been doing previously.

This requires a number of changes to the program, none of which is particularly complicated. The new version is shown in Figure 7.7.

Figure 7.7: Zensort version 4 (Zensort\zen04.cpp)

```cpp
#include <stdio.h>
#include <stdlib.h>
#include <string.h>
#include <iostream.h>
#include <fstream.h>

#include "e:\opt\common\timings.h"

int CalculateKeySegment(int Pass, char* InputLine, int LineLength)
{
    int KeySegment;
    unsigned char HighChar;
    unsigned char LowChar;

    if (LineLength < Pass)
        KeySegment = 0;
    else if (LineLength == Pass)
        KeySegment = 256 * InputLine[Pass-1];
    else
        {
        HighChar = 0;
        LowChar = InputLine[Pass];
        if (Pass > 0)
            HighChar = InputLine[Pass-1];
        KeySegment = HighChar * 256 + LowChar;
        }

    return KeySegment;
}
```

```
int main(int argc, char *argv[])
{
    const int BUFCOUNT = 65536;
    const int TOTAL_BUFFER = 16*1048576;
    const int INPUTLINESIZE = 1024;
    char InputLine[INPUTLINESIZE];
    char* BigBuffer = new char [TOTAL_BUFFER];
    char** Buffer = new char* [BUFCOUNT];
    int* BufferSize = new int[BUFCOUNT];
    int* BufferCharCount = new int[BUFCOUNT];
    int* Displacement = new int[BUFCOUNT];
    int* TotalDisplacement = new int[BUFCOUNT];
    int KeySegment;
    char* InputFileName;
    char* OutputFileName;
    ifstream InputFile;
    ofstream OutputFile;
    int PassCount;
    int CurrentLength;
    int NewLength;
    int LineLength;
    char* OriginalInputFileName;
    char* OriginalOutputFileName;
    int TotalKeys = 0;
    int TotalData = 0;
    bool StatisticsDisplayed = false;
    int TotalWrites = 0;
    int i;
    double BufferRatio;
    int NumberOfPasses = 0;
    int PartialLength;
    int TotalBufferSize;

    if (argc < 4)
        {
        printf("Usage: zensort passcount infile outfile\n");
        exit(1);
        }
    else
        {
        PassCount = atoi(argv[1]);
        OriginalInputFileName = argv[2];
        OriginalOutputFileName = argv[3];
        }

char temp[100];
start_timing();
```

```
for (int Pass = PassCount - 1; Pass >= 0; Pass -=2)
  {

  if ((NumberOfPasses % 2) == 0)
    {
    InputFileName = OriginalInputFileName;
    OutputFileName = OriginalOutputFileName;
    }
  else
    {
    InputFileName = OriginalOutputFileName;
    OutputFileName = OriginalInputFileName;
    }

  NumberOfPasses ++;

  InputFile.open(InputFileName,ios::inlios::binary);
  OutputFile.open(OutputFileName,ios::outlios::binary);

  for (i = 0; i < BUFCOUNT; i ++)
    {
    Displacement[i] = 0;
    TotalDisplacement[i] = 0;
    }

  for (i = 0; ; i ++)
    {
    InputFile.getline(InputLine,INPUTLINESIZE);
    if (!InputFile)
      break;
    TotalKeys ++;
    LineLength = strlen(InputLine) + 1;
    strcpy(InputLine+LineLength-1,"\n");
    KeySegment = CalculateKeySegment(Pass,InputLine,LineLength);
    Displacement[KeySegment] += LineLength;
    }
  InputFile.close();

  for (i = 1; i < BUFCOUNT; i ++)
    TotalDisplacement[i] = TotalDisplacement[i-1] + Displacement[i-1];

  if (TotalData == 0)
    {
    for (i = 0; i < BUFCOUNT; i ++)
      TotalData += Displacement[i];
    BufferRatio = (double) TOTAL_BUFFER / TotalData;
    }
```

```
    TotalBufferSize = 0;
    for (i = 0; i < BUFCOUNT; i ++)
        {
        BufferSize[i] = (int) (BufferRatio*Displacement[i]);
        Buffer[i] = BigBuffer + TotalBufferSize;
        TotalBufferSize += BufferSize[i];
        BufferCharCount[i] = 0;
        }

    memset(BigBuffer,0,TOTAL_BUFFER);

if ((Pass == PassCount - 1) && StatisticsDisplayed == false)
    {
    printf("Total buffer space: %d\n",TOTAL_BUFFER);
    printf("Total keys: %d\n", TotalKeys);
    printf("Total data: %d\n", TotalData);

    StatisticsDisplayed = true;
    }
sprintf(temp,"Finished counting on pass %d",PassCount-Pass);
timing(temp);

    InputFile.open(InputFileName,ios::inlios::binary);

    for (i = 0; ; i ++)
        {
        InputFile.getline(InputLine,INPUTLINESIZE);
        if (!InputFile)
          break;
        LineLength = strlen(InputLine)+1;
        strcpy(InputLine+LineLength-1,"\n");
        KeySegment = CalculateKeySegment(Pass,InputLine,LineLength);
        CurrentLength = BufferCharCount[KeySegment];
        if (LineLength > BufferSize[KeySegment])
            {
            OutputFile.seekp(TotalDisplacement[KeySegment]);
            if (CurrentLength > 0)
              OutputFile.write(Buffer[KeySegment],CurrentLength);
            BufferCharCount[KeySegment] = 0;
            OutputFile.write(InputLine,LineLength);
            TotalDisplacement[KeySegment] += CurrentLength + LineLength;
            TotalWrites ++;
            continue;
            }
        NewLength = CurrentLength + LineLength;
        if (NewLength >= BufferSize[KeySegment])
            {
```

```
                PartialLength = BufferSize[KeySegment] - CurrentLength;
                memcpy(Buffer[KeySegment]+CurrentLength,
                    InputLine,PartialLength);
                CurrentLength = BufferSize[KeySegment];
                OutputFile.seekp(TotalDisplacement[KeySegment]);
                OutputFile.write(Buffer[KeySegment],CurrentLength);
                TotalDisplacement[KeySegment] += CurrentLength;
                TotalWrites ++;
                memset(Buffer[KeySegment],0,CurrentLength);
                memcpy(Buffer[KeySegment],InputLine+PartialLength,
                    LineLength-PartialLength);
                BufferCharCount[KeySegment] = LineLength - PartialLength;
                }
            else
                {
                memcpy(Buffer[KeySegment]+BufferCharCount[KeySegment],
                    InputLine,LineLength);
                BufferCharCount[KeySegment] += LineLength;
                }
            }

        for (i = 0; i < BUFCOUNT; i ++)
            {
            if (Buffer[i])
                {
                CurrentLength = BufferCharCount[i];
                if (CurrentLength > 0)
                    {
                    OutputFile.seekp(TotalDisplacement[i]);
                    OutputFile.write(Buffer[i],CurrentLength);
                    TotalWrites ++;
                    }
                }
            }
        InputFile.close();
        OutputFile.close();

sprintf(temp,"Finished distributing on pass %d",PassCount-Pass);
timing(temp);
    }

    printf("Total writes: %d\n", TotalWrites);

    end_timing();

    return 0;
}
```

We'll start by examining a new function called CalculateKeySegment, which, as its name suggests, calculates the segment of the key that we're going to use for sorting. In this case, because we're going to be sorting on two characters at a time, this function calculates a key segment value by combining two characters of the input key, with the more significant character contributing more to the resulting value than the less significant character.

A simple way to think of this optimization is that we're going to sort on an alphabet consisting of 65536 characters, each of which is composed of two characters from the regular ASCII set. Because the maximum possible value of a character is 256, we can calculate the buffer in which we will store a particular record according to two characters of its key by multiplying the first character of the key by 256 and adding the second character of the key. This value will never be more than 65535 or less than 0, so we will allocate 65536 buffers, one for each possible combination of two characters.

Besides the substitution of the key segment for the individual character of the key, the other major change to the program is in the handling of a full buffer. In the old program, whenever a new record would cause the output buffer to overflow, we would write out the previous contents of the buffer and then store the new record at the beginning of the buffer. However, this approach has the drawback that it is possible in some cases to have a record that is larger than the allocated buffer, in which case the program will fail if we attempt to store the record in that buffer.

This wasn't too much of a problem in the previous version of the program, because with only 256 buffers, each of them would be big enough to hold any reasonably-sized record. However, now that we have 65536 buffers, this is a real possibility. With the current implementation, as long as the record isn't more than twice the size of the buffer, the program will work correctly. If we're worried about records that are larger than that, we can change the code to handle the record in any number of segments by using a while loop that will continue to store segments of the record in the buffer and write them out until the remaining segment will fit in the buffer.

So how does this fourth version of the program actually perform? Figure 7.8 answers that question.

Figure 7.8: Performance of Zensort version 4 (Zensort\timings.04)

Sorting variable-length records

Record Count	Total Data	64MB RAM Time	192MB RAM Time	64MB RAM Kb/Sec	192MB RAM KB/Sec
100000	6348151	7.31	7.42	868.42	855.55
250000	15971969	29.78	25.16	536.33	634.82
500000	31930988	112.86	83.30	282.93	383.33
1000000	63754674	302.20	175.11	210.97	364.08

If you compare the performance of this fourth version of the program to the previous version on the small file, you'll notice that it has nearly doubled on both memory configurations. As usual, however, what is more important is how well it performs when we have a lot of data to sort. As you can see from the performance results, the throughput when sorting the large file has improved by over 50 percent on both the small and large memory configurations.

We've just about reached the end of the line with incremental changes to the implementation. To get any further significant increases in performance, we'll need a radically different approach, and that's what the next version of this program provides.

The Fifth Version

Before we get to this change in the program, though, it might be instructive if I explain how I arrived at the conclusion that such a change was either necessary or even possible.

Unlike some well-known authors who shall remain nameless, I take technical writing very seriously. I test my code before publishing it, I typeset my books myself to reduce the likelihood of typesetting errors, and I even create my master CDs myself, to minimize the chance that errors will creep in somewhere in between my development system and your computer. Of course, this doesn't guarantee that there aren't any bugs in my programs; if major software development companies can't guarantee that, my one-man development and quality assurance organization certainly can't! However, I do a pretty good job, and when I miss something, I usually hear from readers right away and can get the correction into the next printing of the book in question.

You may be wondering what this has to do with the changes to the implementation of this sorting algorithm. The answer is that, although I thought I had discovered something important when I broke through the limited memory problem with distribution sorting, I decided it would be a good idea to see how its performance compares with other available sorts. Therefore, I asked a friend if he knew of any resources on sorting performance. After he found a page about sorting on the Internet, I followed up and found a page referring to a sorting contest.

Before I could tell how my implementation would compare to those in the contest, I had to generate some performance figures. Although the page about the contest was somewhat out of date, it gave me enough information so that I was able to generate a test file similar to the one described in the contest. The description was "one million 100-byte records, with a 10-byte random key". I wasn't sure what they meant by "random": was it a string of ten random digits, or 10 random binary bytes, or 10 random ASCII values? I decided to assume that 10 random decimal digits would be close enough to start with, so that's how I created an initial version of a test file. When I ran my latest, greatest version on this file, I was pretty happy when I discovered I could sort about 500,000 records in a minute, because the figures on the contest page indicated that this was quite cost-competitive in the "minute sort" category, which was based on the number of records sorted in a minute; although I was certainly not breaking any speed records as such, my system was much cheaper than the one that had set the record, so on a cost-performance basis I was doing quite well. However, I did need some more recent information to see how the latest competition was going.

So I contacted Jim Gray, who was listed on that page as a member of the contest committee, and heard back from him the next day. Imagine my surprise when I discovered that my "fast" sorting algorithm wasn't even in the ball park. My best throughput of approximately 800 KB/sec or so was less than one third of the leading competitors. Obviously, I had a lot more work to do if I wanted to compete in any serious way.

The first priority was to find out exactly why these other programs were so much faster than my program was. My discussion with Jim

Gray gave me the clue when he told me that all of the best programs were limited by their disk I/O throughput. Obviously, if we have to make five passes through the file, reading and writing all of the data on each pass, we aren't going to be competitive with programs that do much less disk I/O, if that is the limiting factor on sorting speed.

Obviously, any possible sorting algorithm must read the entire input file at least once and write an output file of the same size. Is there any way to reduce the amount of I/O that our sorting algorithm uses so that it can approach that ideal?

Although we can't get to that limiting case, it is possible to do much better than we have done. However, doing so requires more attention to the makeup of the keys that we are sorting. Until now, we haven't cared very much about the distribution of the keys, except that we would get larger buffers if there were fewer different characters in the keys, which would reduce the number of disk write operations needed to create the output file and thereby improve performance.

However, if the keys were composed of reasonably uniformly distributed characters (or sets of characters) that we could use to divide up the input file into a number of segments of similar size based on their key values, then we could use a "divide and conquer" approach to sorting that can improve performance significantly. That's what the next version of this program, shown in Figure 7.9, does.

Figure 7.9: Zensort version 5 (Zensort\zen05.cpp)

```
#include <stdio.h>
#include <stdlib.h>
#include <string.h>
#include <iostream.h>
#include <fstream.h>

#include "e:\opt\common\timings.h"

int CalculateKeySegment(char* InputLine)
{
    int KeySegment = 0;

    for (int i = 0; i < 6; i ++)
```

```
        {
        KeySegment *= 10;
        KeySegment += InputLine[i]-'0';
        }

    return KeySegment;
}

int main(int argc, char *argv[])
{
    const int KEY_PREFIX_LENGTH = 2;
    const int MAXPASSCOUNT = 100;
    const int BUFCOUNT = 1000000;
    const int TOTAL_BUFFER = 16*1048576;
    const int INPUTLINESIZE = 1024;
    char InputLine[INPUTLINESIZE];
    int* BufferOffset = new int [BUFCOUNT+1];
    int* BufferCharCount = new int[BUFCOUNT];
    int KeySegment;
    char* InputFileName;
    char* OutputFileName;
    ifstream InputFile;
    ofstream OutputFile;
    int PassCount;
    int CurrentLength;
    int NewLength;
    int LineLength;
    int TotalKeys = 0;
    bool StatisticsDisplayed = false;
    int TotalWrites = 0;
    int i;
    int j;
    double BufferRatio;
    int PartialLength;
    int TotalBufferSize;
    int KeyLength;

    if (argc < 4)
        {
        printf("Usage: zen05 keylength infile outfile\n");
        exit(1);
        }
    else
        {
        KeyLength = atoi(argv[1]);
        InputFileName = argv[2];
        OutputFileName = argv[3];
        }
```

```
char temp[100];
start_timing();

   InputFile.open(InputFileName,ios::inlios::binary);

//start counting pass

   int* BufferCapacity = new int[BUFCOUNT];
   for (i = 0; i < BUFCOUNT; i ++)
      BufferCapacity[i] = 0;

   for (i = 0; ; i ++)
      {
      InputFile.getline(InputLine,INPUTLINESIZE);
      if (!InputFile)
         break;
      TotalKeys ++;
      LineLength = strlen(InputLine);
      if (LineLength < KeyLength)
         {
         printf("Illegal record: %s",InputLine);
         exit(1);
         }
      KeySegment = CalculateKeySegment(InputLine);
      BufferCapacity[KeySegment] += LineLength + 1;
      }


   int Split[MAXPASSCOUNT]; // possible number of passes
   int SplitTotalSize[MAXPASSCOUNT]; // bytes per pass
   int SplitData;
   int ThisDisplacement;
   int TotalData = 0;
   Split[0] = 0;

   i = 0;
   for (j = 1; j < MAXPASSCOUNT; j ++)
      {
      SplitData = 0;
      BufferOffset[i] = 0;
      for (; i < BUFCOUNT; i ++)
         {
         ThisDisplacement = BufferCapacity[i];
         if (SplitData + ThisDisplacement > TOTAL_BUFFER)
            break;
         SplitData += ThisDisplacement;
         BufferOffset[i+1] = SplitData;
         }
```

```
      Split[j] = i;
      SplitTotalSize[j-1] = SplitData;
      TotalData += SplitData;
      if (i == BUFCOUNT)
        break;
      }

   delete [] BufferCapacity;

   PassCount = j;

printf("Total buffer space: %d\n",TOTAL_BUFFER);
printf("Total keys: %d\n", TotalKeys);
printf("Total data: %d\n", TotalData);

sprintf(temp,"Finished counting");
timing(temp);

   OutputFile.open(OutputFileName,ios::outlios::binary);

   char* BigBuffer = new char [TOTAL_BUFFER];

   for (int Pass = 0; Pass < PassCount ; Pass ++)
      {
      for (i = Split[Pass]; i < Split[Pass+1]; i ++)
         {
         BufferCharCount[i] = 0;
         }

      InputFile.clear();
      InputFile.seekg(0);

      memset(BigBuffer,0,TOTAL_BUFFER);

      int CompareResult;
      for (i = 0; ; i ++)
         {
         InputFile.getline(InputLine,INPUTLINESIZE);
         if (!InputFile)
            break;
         LineLength = strlen(InputLine)+1;
         strcpy(InputLine+LineLength-1,"\n");
         KeySegment = CalculateKeySegment(InputLine);
         char* Where;
         if (KeySegment >= Split[Pass] && KeySegment < Split[Pass+1])
            {
            CurrentLength = BufferCharCount[KeySegment];
            char* CurrentPosition = BufferOffset[KeySegment]+BigBuffer;
```

```
        char* EndOfBuffer = CurrentPosition + CurrentLength;
        for (Where = CurrentPosition; Where < EndOfBuffer;)
          {
          CompareResult = memcmp(InputLine,Where,KeyLength);
          if (CompareResult < 0)
            {
            break;
            }
          else
            {
            while (*(Where++) != '\n')
              ;
            }
          }
        memmove(Where+LineLength,Where,EndOfBuffer-Where);
        memcpy(Where,InputLine,LineLength);
        BufferCharCount[KeySegment] += LineLength;
        }
      }

    OutputFile.write(BigBuffer,SplitTotalSize[Pass]);
    TotalWrites ++;


sprintf(temp,"Finished distributing on pass %d",PassCount-Pass);
timing(temp);
  }

  InputFile.close();
  OutputFile.close();

  printf("Total writes: %d\n", TotalWrites);

  end_timing();

  return 0;
}
```

This new version of the algorithm works in a different way from the ones we've seen before. Instead of moving from right to left through the keys, sorting on the less significant positions to prepare the way for the more significant positions, we use the leftmost part of the key to decide which logical buffer the record will be put in. Once we have decided which logical buffer the record will go into, we use an insertion sort to stick it into the appropriate place in the buffer, i.e., after any record in that buffer with a lower key and ahead of any record in that buffer with a higher key.

Our use of the insertion sort to arrange the records in each buffer is the reason that we need a reasonably uniform distribution of keys to get good performance. As we have seen in previous versions of the program, if the keys are very non-uniform in their distribution, then each logical buffer will be very large. However, in contrast to our previous experience, with this version of the algorithm big logical buffers are a major impediment to good performance. The problem is that insertion sort is extremely time-consuming when used with large numbers of keys. Therefore, if we have a few big logical buffers, the insertion sort will dominate the time required to execute the algorithm. However, if the keys are reasonably uniformly distributed, then each logical buffer will be small and the insertion sort will not take very long to execute.

If we had enough memory to hold the entire input file, this version of the algorithm would be very simple to implement: we would examine the key for each record, decide which buffer it goes into, then put it into that buffer in the appropriate place via the insertion sort.

However, we may not have enough memory to hold a 100 MB file, and even if we do, using that much memory for our buffer is likely to be counterproductive because it will prevent that memory from being used for disk caching by the operating system, thus reducing the speed of our disk I/O. In addition, this solution is not scalable to larger files. Therefore, we need another approach.

Luckily, there is one that is not too difficult to implement: we make several passes through the input file, selecting the records that will fit in the buffer according to their keys. At the end of each pass, we write the entire buffer out to disk with one disk I/O operation. On each pass, we select successively higher key values, until we have handled all the records in the input file.

Let's see exactly how this works with our usual variable-length record input file. One fairly obvious change to the program is that we no longer are copying data from the input file to the output file and back again, which means we don't have to switch the filenames for the input and output files. Another change I've made, to reduce the amount of memory the program requires, is to eliminate several of the auxiliary arrays: Buffer, BufferSize, and TotalDisplacement. Instead of the Buffer array, I'm using a new array called BufferOffset that keeps track of the position in the one large buffer where each logical buffer starts. The TotalDisplacement array isn't really necessary, because it was only used during the calculations of the positions of the logical buffers and of the total data for all the records in the file; both of these functions have been replaced in the new implementation by a loop that calculates exactly how many records will fit in the big buffer and where they will go.

As for the BufferSize array, that turns out to be unnecessary in the new implementation of the algorithm. Because we will be precalculating the exact amount of space that will be occupied by the records in that buffer, we don't have to worry about whether any particular record will fit in the buffer: if it belongs in that buffer, it will fit.

Before we get to the major changes in the algorithm, I should explain the reason for the new version of CalculateKeySegment. As I've already mentioned, with this new version of the algorithm, it is extremely important to make each logical buffer as small as possible, to reduce the time needed to insert each record into its logical buffer. Therefore, because we want to be able to handle a one million record input file in an efficient manner, we will allocate one million logical buffers within our large physical buffer.

But how do we decide which logical buffer each record should be stored in? Because the keys in this file are composed of numeric digits, we can use the first six digits of the key to determine the appropriate logical buffer for each record. Although this is not theoretically optimal, because the keys in the file are not random, the performance results indicate that it is sufficient to give us a significant increase in speed over the previous version of the program, at least for large files.

Now let's get to the more complicated changes in this version of the algorithm, which are in the calculation of which data we will actually store in the big buffer. That's the responsibility of the code that starts with the line int Split[MAXPASSCOUNT] and ends with the line PassCount = j;. Let's go over this in some detail.

First, we have the declaration of the variable Split, which is used to keep track of which keys we are handling on this pass. This variable is an array of a number of elements sufficient to handle any file of reasonable size: to be exact, we need one element in this array for every possible pass through the input file, so 100 elements would suffice for a file of about 1.6 GB if we're using a 16 MB buffer for each pass.

Next, we have an array called SplitTotalSize, of the same number of elements, which is used to keep track of the total amount of data to be handled in each pass through the input file. We need this information to determine exactly how many bytes we're going to write from the big buffer at the end of each pass.

After declaring a couple of auxiliary variables, we get to the actual code. First, we initialize the value of the first element of the Split array to 0, because we know that on the first pass through the file, we will start handling records from the lowest possible key value, which of course is 0.

Now we're ready to start counting the keys and records that will be stored in the big buffer during each pass through the input file. To calculate the splits, we start by initializing the data count for each split to 0 and the offset of the first logical buffer to zero as well. Then we step through the array of buffer capacities, adding up the capacity of all the logical buffers that we encounter.

As long as we've not yet exceeded the size of the big buffer, we add the size of each logical buffer to the previous total size and set the offset of the next logical buffer to that total size. Once we get to a buffer whose size would cause an overflow of the big buffer capacity, we break out of the loop without updating the total size or the next logical buffer's offset.

Once we've exited from that inner loop, we know what segment of keys we're going to handle on this pass, so we set the next element of the Split array to the number of the last buffer that will fit in the big buffer on this pass. We also know the total size of the data that will be handled on this pass, so we set the value of the SplitTotalSize array element for this pass to that value. Next, we add the amount of data for this pass to the total data in the file so that we can report this information to the user. Finally, if we've reached the end of all the buffers, we break out of the outer loop, delete the BufferCapacity array, and set the PassCount variable to the number of passes that we will need to handle all the data.

Once we know how we are going to split up the input file, the rest of the changes are pretty simple. After opening the output file, we allocate the big buffer, then start the main loop that will execute once for each pass through the input file.

On each pass through the main loop, we handle the records whose keys fall in the range allocated to that pass. This requires changes in several areas of the code. First, at the beginning of the main loop, we clear the buffer character counts for each of the buffers that will be active during this pass. Then we reset the status of the input file, reposition it to its beginning, and clear the big buffer to all zeros.

The next set of changes occur when we have found the key segment for the current record from the input file. If that key segment falls within the current pass, then we have to put the record into the appropriate buffer. However, unlike our previous implementations, we have to be careful exactly where we put the record in the buffer, rather than just appending it at the end. This is because we're going to be writing the records into their final position in the file rather than merely copying them to an output file in partial order by a segment of the key. Therefore, we have to insert each record into the buffer in the precise relative position where it should go in the file. To do this, we compare the key of this record to the key of each record already in the buffer. When we find a record whose key is greater than the key of the record that we're trying to put in the buffer, we shift that record and all the following records toward the end of the buffer to make room for the new record. If the key of the record that we're looking at in the buffer is less than or equal to the key of the record that we want to put in the buffer, we have to locate the next record in the buffer to see if its key is greater than the new record. To do this, we increment our pointer into the buffer until we find a new-line character, which signals the end of the record whose key we have just examined, then continue our key comparison with the next record's key, which follows immediately after. Of course, if we don't find a record with a greater key by the time we get to the end of the buffer, then the new record goes at the end of the buffer.

Each time we reach the end of the outer loop, we have a big buffer filled with data that needs to be written to the file. Therefore, we call the write function to write the exact number of bytes that that pass has handled, which is stored in the SplitTotalSize variable for the particular pass that we are executing.

So how does this fifth version of the program actually perform? Figure 7.10 answers that question.

Figure 7.10: Performance of Zensort version 5 (Zensort\timings.05)

```
Sorting variable-length records
```

Record Count	Total Data	64MB RAM Time	192MB RAM Time	64MB RAM Kb/Sec	192MB RAM KB/Sec
100000	6348151	2.91	3.41	2181.50	1861.63
250000	15971969	11.59	9.95	1378.08	1605.22
500000	31930988	44.62	30.22	715.62	1056.62
1000000	63754674	128.19	82.80	497.35	769.98

As in our previous comparison, we have improved performance radically on the smallest file, producing a 2.5 to 1 increase in speed with the smaller memory configuration and more than doubling it with the larger configuration. As usual, however, what is more important is how well it performs when we have a lot of data to sort. As you can see from the performance results, the throughput when sorting the large file has more than doubled on both the small and large memory configurations.

The Key Requirement

However, unlike our previous improvements, this one carries a fairly hefty price tag: if the keys are not reasonably evenly distributed, the program will run extremely slowly, and in some extreme cases may fail to work at all. The former problem results from the fact that as the number of keys in each logical buffer increases, the time taken to insert a key in that logical buffer increases as well. If the file is too big to fit in memory and a very large proportion of the keys are identical, then the program as currently written may fail to execute: this will happen if the size of one logical buffer exceeds the amount of memory allocated for all buffers.

Does this mean that this new version of the program is useless? Not at all: it means that we have to be prepared for the eventuality that this version of the algorithm may behave badly on certain data and handle that eventuality should it occur. This is the subject of a problem at the end of this chapter.

The Sixth Version

The previous version marks the end of our performance improvements on the original input file, mostly because I couldn't think of any other improvements to implement. However, even after increasing the performance significantly on that file, I was still very interested in seeing how well an adaptation of the same algorithm could be made to perform on an input file like the ones specified in the sorting contest.

It turned out that the changes needed to sort one of those files reasonably efficiently were not terribly complex, as you can see by looking at the next version of the program, shown in Figure 7.11.

Figure 7.11: Zensort version 6 (Zensort\zen06.cpp)

```
#include <stdio.h>
#include <stdlib.h>
#include <string.h>
#include <iostream.h>
#include <fstream.h>

#include "e:\opt\common\timings.h"

int CalculateKeySegment(char* InputLine)
{
    int KeySegment = 0;

    unsigned char LowChar = (InputLine[2] - ' ');
    unsigned char MiddleChar = InputLine[1] - ' ';
    unsigned char HighChar = InputLine[0] - ' ';
    KeySegment = HighChar * 96 * 96 + MiddleChar * 96 + LowChar;

    return KeySegment;
}

int main(int argc, char *argv[])
{
    const int KEY_PREFIX_LENGTH = 2;
    const int MAXPASSCOUNT = 100;
    const int BUFCOUNT = 96*96*96;
    const int TOTAL_BUFFER = 16*1048576;
    const int INPUTLINESIZE = 1024;
    char InputLine[INPUTLINESIZE];
```

```
int* BufferOffset = new int [BUFCOUNT+1];
int* BufferCharCount = new int[BUFCOUNT];
int KeySegment;
char* InputFileName;
char* OutputFileName;
ifstream InputFile;
ofstream OutputFile;
int PassCount;
int CurrentLength;
int NewLength;
int LineLength;
int TotalKeys = 0;
bool StatisticsDisplayed = false;
int TotalWrites = 0;
int i;
int j;
double BufferRatio;
int PartialLength;
int TotalBufferSize;
int KeyLength;

if (argc < 4)
    {
    printf("Usage: zen06 keylength infile outfile\n");
    exit(1);
    }
else
    {
    KeyLength = atoi(argv[1]);
    InputFileName = argv[2];
    OutputFileName = argv[3];
    }

char temp[100];
start_timing();

    InputFile.open(InputFileName,ios::inlios::binary);

//start counting pass

    int* BufferCapacity = new int[BUFCOUNT];
    for (i = 0; i < BUFCOUNT; i ++)

    {
    BufferCapacity[i] = 0;
    }

    for (i = 0; ; i ++)
```

```
    {
    InputFile.getline(InputLine,INPUTLINESIZE);
    if (!InputFile)
       break;
    TotalKeys ++;
    LineLength = strlen(InputLine);
    if (LineLength < KeyLength)
       {
       printf("Illegal record: %s",InputLine);
       exit(1);
       }
    KeySegment = CalculateKeySegment(InputLine);
    BufferCapacity[KeySegment] += LineLength + 1;
    }


    int Split[MAXPASSCOUNT]; // possible number of passes
    int SplitTotalSize[MAXPASSCOUNT]; // bytes per pass
    int SplitData;
    int ThisDisplacement;
    int TotalData = 0;
    Split[0] = 0;

    i = 0;
    for (j = 1; j < MAXPASSCOUNT; j ++)
       {
       SplitData = 0;
       BufferOffset[i] = 0;
       for (; i < BUFCOUNT; i ++)
          {
          ThisDisplacement = BufferCapacity[i];
          if (SplitData + ThisDisplacement > TOTAL_BUFFER)
             break;
          SplitData += ThisDisplacement;
          BufferOffset[i+1] = SplitData;
          }
       Split[j] = i;
       SplitTotalSize[j-1] = SplitData;
       TotalData += SplitData;
       if (i == BUFCOUNT)
          break;
       }

    delete [] BufferCapacity;

    PassCount = j;

 printf("Total buffer space: %d\n",TOTAL_BUFFER);
```

```
printf("Total keys: %d\n", TotalKeys);
printf("Total data: %d\n", TotalData);

sprintf(temp,"Finished counting");
timing(temp);

  OutputFile.open(OutputFileName,ios::outlios::binary);

  char* BigBuffer = new char [TOTAL_BUFFER];

  for (int Pass = 0; Pass < PassCount ; Pass ++)
    {
    for (i = Split[Pass]; i < Split[Pass+1]; i ++)
      {
      BufferCharCount[i] = 0;
      }

    InputFile.clear();
    InputFile.seekg(0);

    memset(BigBuffer,0,TOTAL_BUFFER);

    int CompareResult;
    for (i = 0; ; i ++)
      {
      InputFile.getline(InputLine,INPUTLINESIZE);
      if (!InputFile)
        break;
      LineLength = strlen(InputLine)+1;
      strcpy(InputLine+LineLength-1,"\n");
      KeySegment = CalculateKeySegment(InputLine);
      char* Where;
      if (KeySegment >= Split[Pass] && KeySegment < Split[Pass+1])
        {
        CurrentLength = BufferCharCount[KeySegment];
        char* CurrentPosition = BufferOffset[KeySegment]+BigBuffer;
        char* EndOfBuffer = CurrentPosition + CurrentLength;
        for (Where = CurrentPosition; Where < EndOfBuffer;)
          {
          CompareResult = memcmp(InputLine,Where,KeyLength);
          if (CompareResult < 0)
            {
            break;
            }
          else
            {
            while (*(Where++) != '\n')
              ;
```

```
            }
          }
        memmove(Where+LineLength,Where,EndOfBuffer-Where);
        memcpy(Where,InputLine,LineLength);
        BufferCharCount[KeySegment] += LineLength;
          }
        }

    OutputFile.write(BigBuffer,SplitTotalSize[Pass]);
    TotalWrites ++;


sprintf(temp,"Finished distributing on pass %d",PassCount-Pass);
timing(temp);
    }

    InputFile.close();
    OutputFile.close();

    printf("Total writes: %d\n", TotalWrites);

    end_timing();

    return 0;
}
```

In fact, all I had to do was change the calculation of the key segment to combine values from the first three ASCII characters in the input line rather than the first six digits of the numeric key in the previous input file, and change the number of logical buffers to correspond to this modification.

So how does this sixth version of the program actually perform? Figure 7.12 answers that question.

Figure 7.12: Performance of Zensort version 6 (Zensort\timings.06)

```
Sorting 100-byte records with 10-byte keys
```

Record Count	Total Data	64MB RAM Time	192MB RAM Time	64MB RAM Kb/Sec	192MB RAM KB/Sec
100000	10000000	2.36	2.42	4237.29	4132.23
250000	25000000	21.98	9.29	1137.40	2691.07
500000	50000000	70.11	24.34	713.17	2054.23
1000000	100000000	185.88	71.48	537.98	1398.99

Unfortunately, we can't directly compare the results of this series of tests with the previous one because the file sizes are different. However, we can establish a lower bound on our improvements if we compare the throughput on the one million record file: because throughput generally decreases as the size of the file increases, we can be fairly sure that the throughput figures on the 100 MB file would be lower with the old algorithm than the throughput figures on the 63 MB file with that same algorithm.

As usual, the relative improvement is greatest on the smallest file, being almost twice as fast as the previous program on the smaller memory configuration and over twice as fast on the larger configuration. However, the improvement in throughput on the larger files with the larger memory configuration is also quite substantial. The better key distribution has enabled us to improve performance on the large file under the large memory configuration by 80 percent over our previous best with minimal code changes.

The Final Version

There's one more change we can make that will improve performance significantly on a file with fixed-length records, such as the one used in the sorting contest. Of course, if that were the only "application" using such records, they wouldn't be worth our attention. However, this is far from the case; in fact, most traditional data processing systems rely heavily on files with fixed-length records, which is a main reason they were chosen for the sorting contest in the first place. Therefore, optimizing the code for such records is worthwhile.

It turned out that the changes needed to handle fixed-length records more efficiently were not very difficult, as you can see by looking at the next version of the program, shown in Figure 7.13.

Figure 7.13: Zensort version 7 (Zensort\zen07.cpp)

```
#include <stdio.h>
#include <stdlib.h>
#include <string.h>
```

```cpp
#include <iostream.h>
#include <fstream.h>

#include "e:\opt\common\timings.h"

int CalculateKeySegment(char* InputLine)
{
    int KeySegment = 0;

    unsigned char LowChar = (InputLine[2] - ' ');
    unsigned char MiddleChar = InputLine[1] - ' ';
    unsigned char HighChar = InputLine[0] - ' ';
    KeySegment = HighChar * 96 * 96 + MiddleChar * 96 + LowChar;

    return KeySegment;
}

int main(int argc, char *argv[])
{
    const int KEY_PREFIX_LENGTH = 2;
    const int MAXPASSCOUNT = 100;
    const int BUFCOUNT = 96*96*96;
    const int TOTAL_BUFFER = 16*1048576;
    const int INPUTLINESIZE = 100;
    char InputLine[INPUTLINESIZE];
    int* BufferOffset = new int [BUFCOUNT+1];
    int* BufferCharCount = new int[BUFCOUNT];
    int KeySegment;
    char* InputFileName;
    char* OutputFileName;
    ifstream InputFile;
    ofstream OutputFile;
    int PassCount;
    int CurrentLength;
    int NewLength;
    int LineLength;
    int TotalKeys = 0;
    bool StatisticsDisplayed = false;
    int TotalWrites = 0;
    int i;
    int j;
    double BufferRatio;
    int PartialLength;
    int TotalBufferSize;
    int KeyLength;

    if (argc < 4)
        {
```

```
         printf("Usage: zen07 keylength infile outfile\n");
         exit(1);
         }
      else
         {
         KeyLength = atoi(argv[1]);
         InputFileName = argv[2];
         OutputFileName = argv[3];
         }

char temp[100];
start_timing();

   InputFile.open(InputFileName,ios::inlios::binary);

//start counting pass

   int* BufferCapacity = new int[BUFCOUNT];
   for (i = 0; i < BUFCOUNT; i ++)

      {
      BufferCapacity[i] = 0;
      }

   for (i = 0; ; i ++)
      {
      InputFile.read(InputLine,INPUTLINESIZE);
      if (!InputFile)
         break;
      TotalKeys ++;
      LineLength = INPUTLINESIZE;
      if (LineLength < KeyLength)
         {
         printf("Illegal record: %s",InputLine);
         exit(1);
         }
      KeySegment = CalculateKeySegment(InputLine);
      BufferCapacity[KeySegment] += LineLength;
      }

   int Split[MAXPASSCOUNT]; // possible number of passes
   int SplitTotalSize[MAXPASSCOUNT]; // bytes per pass
   int SplitData;
   int ThisDisplacement;
   int TotalData = 0;
   Split[0] = 0;

   i = 0;
```

```
    for (j = 1; j < MAXPASSCOUNT; j ++)
      {
      SplitData = 0;
      BufferOffset[i] = 0;
      for (; i < BUFCOUNT; i ++)
        {
        ThisDisplacement = BufferCapacity[i];
        if (SplitData + ThisDisplacement > TOTAL_BUFFER)
          break;
        SplitData += ThisDisplacement;
        BufferOffset[i+1] = SplitData;
        }
      Split[j] = i;
      SplitTotalSize[j-1] = SplitData;
      TotalData += SplitData;
      if (i == BUFCOUNT)
        break;
      }

  delete [] BufferCapacity;

  PassCount = j;

printf("Total buffer space: %d\n",TOTAL_BUFFER);
printf("Total keys: %d\n", TotalKeys);
printf("Total data: %d\n", TotalData);

sprintf(temp,"Finished counting");
timing(temp);

  OutputFile.open(OutputFileName,ios::outlios::binary);

  char* BigBuffer = new char [TOTAL_BUFFER];

  memset(BigBuffer,0,TOTAL_BUFFER);

  for (int Pass = 0; Pass < PassCount ; Pass ++)
    {
    for (i = Split[Pass]; i < Split[Pass+1]; i ++)
      {
      BufferCharCount[i] = 0;
      }

    InputFile.clear();
    InputFile.seekg(0);

    int CompareResult;
    for (i = 0; ; i ++)
```

```
{
InputFile.read(InputLine,INPUTLINESIZE);
if (!InputFile)
   break;
TotalKeys ++;
LineLength = INPUTLINESIZE;
KeySegment = CalculateKeySegment(InputLine);
char* Where;
if (KeySegment >= Split[Pass] && KeySegment < Split[Pass+1])
   {
   CurrentLength = BufferCharCount[KeySegment];
   char* CurrentPosition = BufferOffset[KeySegment]+BigBuffer;
   char* EndOfBuffer = CurrentPosition + CurrentLength;
      for (Where = CurrentPosition; Where < EndOfBuffer; Where += LineLength)
      {
      CompareResult = memcmp(InputLine,Where,KeyLength);
      if (CompareResult < 0)
         break;
      }
   memmove(Where+LineLength,Where,EndOfBuffer-Where);
   memcpy(Where,InputLine,LineLength);
   BufferCharCount[KeySegment] += LineLength;
   }
}

OutputFile.write(BigBuffer,SplitTotalSize[Pass]);
TotalWrites ++;

sprintf(temp,"Finished distributing on pass %d",PassCount-Pass);
timing(temp);
}

InputFile.close();
OutputFile.close();

printf("Total writes: %d\n", TotalWrites);

end_timing();

return 0;
}
```

Basically these changes consisted of: using the read function rather than the getline function to read a fixed-length record into an input buffer; changing the calculation of the record length to use the fixed length; and stepping through the buffer in units of the fixed record length when searching for the next record rather than searching for

the next new-line character as the end-of-record marker. I also took
advantage of the fixed-length records to avoid clearing the big buffer
on all passes after the first one: since I know exactly where each
record (and therefore key) starts in the buffer, as well as how many
records are in the buffer, records left over from the previous pass can
safely be ignored.

So how does this final version of the program actually perform?
Figure 7.14 answers that question.

Figure 7.14: Performance of Zensort version 7 (Zensort\timings.07)

```
Sorting 100-byte records with 10-byte keys
```

Record Count	Total Data	64MB RAM Time	192MB RAM Time	64MB RAM Kb/Sec	192MB RAM KB/Sec
100000	10000000	1.76	1.65	5681.82	6060.61
250000	25000000	18.85	4.62	1326.26	5411.26
500000	50000000	64.29	16.04	777.73	3117.21
1000000	100000000	162.09	49.67	616.94	2013.29

I'm pretty happy with these figures, especially the ones for the 10
and 25 million byte files with the large memory configuration!
However, even at the 100 million byte mark, the large memory
configuration results are quite good, exceeding our previous mark by
more than 40%.

As for the contest: Although the commercial sorting programs that
have been entered in the sorting contest are noticeably faster than this
one on the largest file, somehow I doubt that their authors will give
you the source code. Therefore, if you need an algorithm that you can
tinker with yourself, and whose inner workings are explained in
detail, I don't think you'll find anything faster than this program.

Summary

In this chapter, we have developed an algorithm for sorting large files
from rather humble beginnings to quite respectable performance by a
series of small, incremental steps. This is a good example of how
such algorithm development occurs in the real world, in addition to
being potentially useful in its own right.

In all, we have improved performance on large files by more than 65 to 1 in the large memory configuration, and by a factor of over 20 even in a relatively small 64 MB machine, compared to our first attempt.

Problems

1. How would you modify the "divide-and-conquer" version of the sorting program so that it would handle uneven key distributions in a reasonable manner rather than running extremely slowly or failing to execute at all?

(You can find suggested approaches to problems in Chapter 8).

Chapter 8

Mozart, No. Would You Believe Gershwin?

Introduction

In this final chapter we will summarize the characteristics of the algorithms we have encountered in previous chapters (Figures 8.1-8.4), discuss the future of the art of optimization, and examine approaches to the problems posed in previous chapters.

Summary of Characteristics

Figure 8.1: Characteristics of file access time reduction techniques

---

■ Standard disk-based hashing[1] (Chapter 2)
   o   Excellent time efficiency

   o   Extra storage needed to handle collisions (usually 25% extra is enough)

   o   Appropriate for tables of a few hundred or more entries

---

1. Hash coding can also be used to eliminate binary or linear searches through tables in memory.

363

o   Data can be accessed by a unique key which can be assigned arbitrarily

■ Dynamic hashing (Chapter 6)
   o   Excellent time efficiency

   o   Table expands as needed

   o   Appropriate for tables of almost unlimited size

   o   Data can be accessed by a unique key which can be assigned arbitrarily

■ Caching[2] (Chapter 2)
   o   Excellent time efficiency

   o   Memory utilization can be adjusted according to availability

   o   Useful when the same data are read repeatedly

Figure 8.2: Characteristics of quantum file access method

■ Quantum file access method (Chapters 5 and 6)
   o   Excellent time efficiency

   o   Memory utilization can be adjusted according to availability

   o   Allows random access to records whose length can vary dynamically

   o   Provides array notation for ease of integration

---

2. Caching can also be used to reduce processor time during searches of tables in memory, as the most recently or most frequently referenced items from the table can be kept in a cache.

Figure 8.3: Characteristics of data compression techniques

- Radix40 (Chapters 1 and 2)
  - o   Predictable output size

  - o   Good time efficiency

  - o   Moderate compression ratio: output size = .67 * input size

  - o   Character set limited to 40 distinct characters

- BCD (Chapter 2)
  - o   Predictable output size

  - o   Good time efficiency

  - o   Good compression ratio: output size = .5 * input size

  - o   Character set limited to 16 distinct characters

- Bitmaps (Chapter 3)
  - o   Predictable output size

  - o   Good time efficiency

  - o   Excellent compression ratio: output size = .125 * input size

  - o   Character set limited to two distinct characters

- Arithmetic coding (Chapter 4)
  - o   Unpredictable output size

  - o   Fair time efficiency

  - o   Very good compression ratio: output size typically ranges from .3 to .5 * input size

  - o   Character set not artificially restricted

Figure 8.4: Characteristics of processor time reduction techniques

---

- Hash coding (Chapter 2)
  - o   See entry in Figure 8.1

- Lookup tables (Chapters 1 and 4)
  - o   Excellent time efficiency

  - o   May use somewhat more memory than searching a list

  - o   Appropriate for tables of a few hundred or thousand items

  - o   Data can be accessed only by a unique index number, not an arbitrary key

- The distribution counting sort (Chapter 3 and 7)
  - o   Excellent time efficiency, proportional to number of keys

  - o   Predictable timing

  - o   Extra memory needed for copy of pointer or data, depending on implementation

  - o   Appropriate for sorting a few hundred or more keys

  - o   Each type of key to be sorted must be handled separately

- Caching (Chapter 2)
  - o   See entry in Figure 8.1

Some Thoughts on the Future

Although many managers might wish it otherwise, the writing of efficient computer programs will always be an art, not a science. This may appear to be a rash statement, but I think time will prove me correct. Of course, if I am wrong, I am following a rich tradition: according to (Arthur C.) Clarke's Law, if a distinguished elderly scientist [defined as over 30 years old] says that something is possible, he is almost always right; if he says that something is impossible, he is almost always wrong.[3]

However, I feel I am on reasonably firm ground. The main reason is that, as demonstrated by Goedel's Proof, no automatic procedure can discover all of the true statements in a consistent axiomatic system such as the behavior of a programmable computer.[4] This implies that the development of new algorithms will always be an adventure. A fine example of this is the optimization in Chapter 4, in which I discovered that I could replace 16-bit occurrence counts with 4-bit indexes and actually speed up the operation of the program at the same time; I'd like to see the optimizing compiler that could figure that out!

O'viously, such unpredictability can be quite expensive. While other engineering professionals, such as structural engineers, routinely estimate the time and money required for their projects to within a few percent, software engineers are not nearly so accurate. In fact, overruns of hundreds of percent are not uncommon. Why is this so?

Why Johnny Can't Estimate

The answer is quite simple: once a structural engineer has built a dozen bridges (for example), the thirteenth is mostly an application of the knowledge he has already acquired. Of course, this is not to say that the expertise of the engineer is unimportant; far from it. However, experience is a great teacher, and experience gained in such a specialty is extremely valuable.

We software engineers, however, face a fundamentally different situation: once we have solved a given problem, we should never need to solve it again, as we can reuse the solution already developed. Therefore, in our development projects, we are always

---

3. A remarkable example of such hyperconservatism is the following statement, from an otherwise fine book by Edward Yourdon: "*As a programmer, you will always be working for an employer. Unless you are very rich and very eccentric, you will not enjoy the luxury of having a computer in your own home...*". (emphasis in the original) Yourdon, E. *Techniques of Program Structure and Design*. Englewood Cliffs, New Jersey: Prentice-Hall, Inc., 1975, pp. 2-3. This clearly ranks with the worst predictions of all time.

4. An excellent explanation of this important mathematical discovery can be found in Douglas Hofstadter's book *Goedel, Escher, Bach*. New York: Vintage Books, 1979.

venturing into unexplored territory, and we all know how to identify pioneers.[5]

Actually, I find it enjoyable to have a new set of challenges with each new project. We should take pride in our work; it is fairly clear to me, at least, that large software systems are the most complex of human creations. They combine the characteristics of art and engineering: first, we conceive of and build something out of sheer thought, the most evanescent material any artist has ever used, and then it actually performs a useful function![6]

Goodbye for Now

We have reached the end of this book. I hope you have learned as much from reading this volume as I have while writing it.

Suggested Approaches to Problems

Chapter 2

1. Modifications to add capabilities to the program:
    a. To delete records, we need to invent another flag value (for example, 14 or 0xe for the first digit) indicating that the record has been used in the past, but currently is unused. This allows us to continue looking for a record that might be after the current position in the file; however, we should remember the position of this "previously owned" record, so that if the record we are seeking turns out not to be in the file, we can reuse this record rather than taking up an unused one. Of course, this solution will not prevent the

---

5. They're the ones with the arrows in their backs.

6. Interestingly enough, the previously cited passage in Yourdon's book goes on to say: "In short, you cannot be an artist, separate and aloof; it is highly unlikely that the programming community will ever generate a Michaelangelo or a Rembrandt". This is quite a difficult standard to meet: how many artists of this stature have come from any field, including sculpture and painting? While the jury is still out on this prediction, I think we will see a great artist of programming one of these days, although his or her work might be inaccessible to the lay public.

file from gradually being filled up with previously used records, which will result in slower and slower access times, particularly when looking for records which are not in the file; clearly, if every record has been used at least once, we would have to search the entire file to determine that a particular record is not in the file. This can be taken care of by periodic maintenance such as that described in the answer to the next question.

b.   In order to handle the case of a full file, or a file which has become nearly filled with deleted records, we can copy the records in the file to a larger one. This requires opening both the old new file and a new one, with the initialization of the new file set to create a larger file. Then we read every valid record in the old file and write it to the new one; since we don't copy any deleted records, the new file starts out with a clean slate. This situation illustrates one reason for using a PriceFile structure to keep track of the data for each file; this is what allows us to have both the new and old file open at once.

c.   Keeping track of the inventory of each item requires an inventory field to the ItemRecord structure and updating this information whenever items are sold or added to inventory.

2.   Hash coding could be applied to tables in memory in much the same way as we have applied it to disk files: the main difference is that since memory is almost a true random-access device, we could use a different method of selecting which slot to use for overflow records, rather than having to use the next sequential slot.[7]

---

7. Why is memory only "almost" a true random access device? Because the processor is much faster than the main memory of the computer; therefore, frequently used memory locations are copied into much faster memory either on or very close to the processor itself. This means that accessing locations in widely scattered parts of memory is likely to be noticeably slower than sequential access to memory. However, the difference in speed may be a factor of three or four rather than the relative speed difference of hundreds or thousands of times that we see between sequential and random disk accesses, so optimizing memory accesses is not as great a concern to us as the latter problem.

3.   If we wish to reduce the time needed to look up an entry in a table in memory by a key, we can maintain a cache of the most recently seen entries, employing a hash code based on the key to be looked up. Each time we find an entry, we store its key and record number in the cache entry corresponding to its hash code. Then, when we want to find a record, the first place we look is in the cache entry corresponding to its key's hash code. If the key in that cache entry matches the key of the record we are looking for, we use the record number in the cache entry to access the record; if the key doesn't match, we have to search the table as we otherwise would have to do anyway. Since the amount of time needed to check the cache entry is small compared to the time needed to search the table, we should come out ahead in most cases.

Chapter 3

1.   One way to produce output in descending rather than ascending order is to subtract each character from 255 before using it as an index.

2.   In order to make only one pass through the data for each character position, rather than two as at present, we have to add the pointer for each key to the end of a linked list for characters having the ASCII code of the character at the current position in the key. For example, if the current character in the key we are processing is 'A', then the pointer to that key would be added to the 'A' list; similarly for 'B', 'C', and any other character that might occur in the key. When the pointers for all the keys have been added to the appropriate lists, the lists are concatenated into one big list, with the 'B' list attached to the end of the 'A' list, the 'C' list attached to the end of the 'B' list, and so on. Then the process starts again for the next character position.

3.   In order to sort integer or floating-point data rather than character data, we have to know the internal structure of the data. For example, on the Intel 80x86 machines, the low byte of a two-byte unsigned value has a lower memory address than the high byte. We can view this as a two-byte key, with the less

significant part lower in memory. Since we have to sort by the less significant portion first, our outer loop index must count up from 0 to 1, rather than the other way around as it would with a two-byte string. Of course, on a Motorola or other "high end first" machine, such unsigned values would be sorted in the same order as strings. Signed values pose additional difficulty, as the high-order byte of a negative value has a greater character value than the high-order byte of a positive value: one way around this is to negate all the keys both before and after the sort. Applying the distribution sort or any other noncomparison sort to floating-point values is even more complex, as the internal representation of a floating-point value is composed of several parts with differing functions; for this reason, the algorithm must be tailored to the individual circumstances. However, the performance of the resulting algorithm makes this effort worthwhile if the number of values to be sorted is reasonably large.

4. Probably the easiest way to handle variable-length strings as keys is to make one pass through the key array, calling strlen to identify the length of each key, and then saving the result in a temporary array. Then, whenever we are ready to extract a character from the key, we first determine whether we are past the end of the key, in which case we substitute a null byte.
    Another possible way to sort variable-length strings is to ignore the fact that they differ in length. Since a C string is normally terminated by a null byte, two strings that are identical up to the end of the shorter one will sort correctly if both are treated as having the length of the longer one; the null byte will make the shorter one sort before the longer one. However, this approach will not work if you are using a protected-mode operating system and you try to access bytes following the end of a short string when these bytes have not been allocated to your program; you will get a protection violation. Another aspect of this approach is that the garbage after the end of a string that is shorter than the key being sorted will be used to rearrange identical keys that should remain in the same relative position in the file. This may cause problems in applications that rely on identical keys keeping their relative orders.

Chapter 4

1. In order to use arithmetic coding where each of a number of blocks of text must be decompressed without reference to the other blocks, we must generate a table of probabilities by analyzing a file or files which have characteristics similar to those to be compressed. Then, rather than compute the probabilities on the fly when compressing or decompressing one of our text blocks, we use the precomputed probability table. This also increases the speed of compressing and decompressing, as the table does not need to be updated.

2. If the data to be compressed consists entirely of characters with ASCII codes 0 through 127 (or any other subset of the ASCII range), we can eliminate a significant amount of the storage for the probability tables by allocating only those tables needed to encode or decode the characters that can occur in the data. In the example given, we need only 128 tables of 128 elements, rather than 256 tables of 256 elements; the resulting memory requirement is approximately 8 Kbytes rather than approximately 32 Kbytes, saving about 24 Kbytes.

3. There are two excellent places to apply assembly language enhancements to the Megasort routine from Chapter 3: the instructions in the loop that counts the number of occurrences of each character; and the instructions in the loop that copies the pointers to the temporary array are executed for each character of the data to be sorted. Replacing those two loops with assembly language equivalents can increase the speed of the sort by a factor of about six on a 486 machine, and probably will result in similar savings on other processors.

Chapter 5

1. To provide a "mass load mode", you'll have to add a function to change the behavior of PutElement, so that it will start a new block when the current "last added to" block doesn't have enough space. Of course, you'll also have to add a

complementary function to reset its behavior when you're done with the mass load.

2. The directory utility will have to be able to add and delete array names randomly. A hash-coded lookup would probably be the best solution for large numbers of arrays, although this is not critical in the current implementation, which is limited to 256 arrays per file.

3. The QFIX program has the following general description. The first phase starts from the main object index, checking the validity of each main object. The big pointer array quantum is checked to see that it belongs to the object in question. Then each of the small pointer arrays is similarly checked, and then each small pointer array entry is checked as well, along with the element to which it points. If all is well so far, the next main object is checked in the same manner. Any object that checks out completely is added to a list of valid objects; all other objects are noted as being incomplete or erroneous.

When all entries in the main object table have been checked, we report the results to the user. Assuming that the user wants us to rebuild the file, we start phase two. After opening a new quantum file where we will store the rebuilt file, we examine each quantum containing actual user data, skipping any quanta containing the main object table, big pointer arrays, and little pointer arrays. For each such user-data quantum, we extract the object number to which that quantum belongs, and add the elements in that quantum to the appropriate element of the corresponding object in the new quantum file, using the index number of each element as stored with the element.

Chapter 6

1. Modifications to add capabilities to the dynamic hashing implementation:
   a. Deleting records is almost exactly the inverse of adding records. Every time the number of records decreases by the average number of records per slot, we take the storage element from the highest-numbered slot and combine it

with the one from its buddy slot, placing the result back in the buddy slot. Then we decrease the active slot count by one. If the active slot count becomes equal to one-half of the allocated slot count, we halve the allocated count.

b. The main problem with duplicate keys is that since records with the same key will always wind up in the same storage element, they make it imperative to handle the overflow problem. Once that is solved, handling duplicate keys is easy: once you have located all storage elements that might contain records with that key, search each of them to the end, rather than stopping when you get a match. Of course, you then have to decide which record you want to use, but that's an application-specific problem.

2. This is a wonderful application for templates. Even the name of the class is intended to suggest that it could very easily be changed to PersistentArray<type>.

Chapter 7

1. One fairly obvious way to handle the problem of improper key distributions for the "divide-and-conquer" versions of the program is to use the information gained in the first pass to determine which algorithm to use. If the keys are reasonably uniformly distributed, then the "divide-and-conquer" version will have the best performance and should be used; however, if the keys are not uniformly distributed, the program should fall back to an earlier version of the algorithm that will work properly and efficiently with a skewed distribution of keys.

Glossary

Special Characters

& has a number of distinct meanings. When it precedes the name of a *variable* without following a *type* name, it means "the address of the following variable". For example, &Str means "the address of the variable Str". When & follows a type name and precedes a variable name, it means that the variable which is being declared is a *reference*; that is, another name for a preexisting variable. In this book, references are used only in argument lists, where they indicate that the variable being defined is a new name for the caller's variable rather than a new local variable.

< is the "less than" operator, which returns the value true if the expression on its left has a lower value than the expression on its right; otherwise, it returns the value false. Also see operator < in the index.

= is the *assignment* operator, which assigns the value on its right to the *variable* on its left. Also see operator = in the index.

> is the "greater than" operator, which returns the value true if the expression on its left has a greater value than the expression on its right; otherwise, it returns the value false. Also see operator > in the index.

. is the "object member access" operator. It separates an object name, on its left, from the member variable or member function on its right.

:: is the class membership operator. See class *membership* for usage.

[is the left square bracket; see *square brackets* for usage.

] is the right square bracket; see *square brackets* for usage.

{ is the left curly brace; see *curly braces* for usage.

} is the right curly brace; see *curly braces* for usage.

!= is the "not equals" operator, which returns the value true if the expression on its left has a value different from the expression on its right; otherwise, it returns the value false. Also see operator != in the index.

&& is the "logical AND" operator. It produces the result true if both of the expressions on its right and left are true; if either of those expressions is false, it produces the result false. However, this isn't the whole story. There is a special rule in C++ governing the execution of the && operator: If the expression on the left is false, then the answer must be false and the expression on the right is not executed at all. The reason for this *short-circuit evaluation* rule is that in some cases you may want to write a right-hand expression that will only be legal if the left-hand expression is false.

++ is the *increment* operator, which adds 1 to the variable to which it is affixed.

+= is the *add to variable* operator, which adds the value on its right to the variable on its left.

-= is the *subtract from variable* operator, which subtracts the value on its right from the variable on its left.

-> is the "object pointer member access" operator. It separates a pointer to an object name, on its left, from the member variable or member function on its right.

// is the comment operator; see *comment* for usage.

<< is the "stream output" operator, used to write data to an ostream. Also see operator << in the index.

<= is the "less than or equal to" operator, which returns the value true if the expression on its left has the same value or a lower value than

the expression on its right; otherwise, it returns the value false. Also see operator <= in the index.

== is the "equals" operator, which returns the value true if the expression on its left has the same value as the expression on its right; otherwise, it returns the value false. Also see operator == in the index.

>= is the "greater than or equal to" operator, which returns the value true if the expression on its left has the same value or a greater value than the expression on its right; otherwise, it returns the value false. Also see operator >= in the index.

>> is the "stream input" operator, used to read data from an istream. Also see operator >> in the index.

[ ] is used after the delete operator to tell the compiler that the *pointer* for which delete was called refers to a group of elements rather than just one data item. This is one of the few times when we have to make that distinction explicitly, rather than leaving it to context.

|| is the "logical OR" operator. It produces the result true if at least one of the two expressions on its right and left is true; if both of those expressions are false, it produces the result false. However, this isn't the whole story. There is a special rule in C++ governing the execution of the || operator: If the expression on the left is true, then the answer must be true and the expression on the right is not executed at all. The reason for this *short-circuit evaluation* rule is that in some cases you may want to write a right-hand expression that will only be legal if the left-hand expression is false.

A **#include statement** has the same effect as copying all of the code from a specified file into another file at the point where the #include statement is written. For example, if we wanted to use definitions contained in a file called iostream.h in the implementation file test.cc, we could insert the include statement #include <iostream.h> in test.cc rather than physically copying the lines from the file iostream.h into test.cc.

A

An **access specifier** controls the access of nonmember functions to the member functions and variables of a class. The C++ access specifiers are public, private, and protected. See public, private, and protected for details. Also see friend.

Access time is a measure of how long it takes to retrieve data from a storage device, such as a hard disk or *RAM*.

Address; see *memory address*.

An **algorithm** is a set of precisely defined steps guaranteed to arrive at an answer to a problem or set of problems. As this implies, a set of steps that might never end is *not* an algorithm.

An **application program** is a program that actually accomplishes some useful or interesting task. Examples include inventory control, payroll, and game programs.

An **application programmer** (or *user*) is a programmer who uses native and class variables to write an application program. Also see *library designer*.

An **argument** is a value that is supplied by one function (the *calling function*) that wishes to make use of the services of another function (the *called function*). There are two main types of *arguments*: *value arguments*, which are copies of the values from the *calling function*, and *reference arguments*, which are not copies but actually refer to *variables* in the calling function.

An **argument list** is a set of *argument* definitions specified in a *function declaration*. The argument list describes the types and names of all the *variables* that the *function* receives when it is called by a *calling function*.

An **array** is a group of *elements* of the same type; for example, we can create an array of chars. The array name corresponds to the address of the first of these elements; the other elements follow the first one immediately in memory. As with a vector, we can refer to the individual elements by their indexes. Thus, if we have an array of chars called m_Data, m_Data[i] refers to the ith char in the array. Also see *pointer*.

The **ASCII code** is a standardized representation of characters by binary or hexadecimal values. For example, the letter *A* is represented as a char with the *hexadecimal* value 41, and the digit *0* is represented as a char with the *hexadecimal* value 30. All other printable characters also have representations in the ASCII code.

An **assembler** is a program that translates *assembly language* instructions into *machine instructions*.

An **assembly language** instruction is the human-readable representation of a *machine instruction*.

Assignment is the operation of setting a *variable* to a value. The operator that indicates assignment is the equal sign, =.

An **assignment operator** is a function that sets a preexisting variable to a value of the same type. There are three varieties of assignment operators:

1. For a variable of a native type, the compiler supplies a native assignment operator.
2. For a variable of a class type, the compiler will generate its own version of an assignment operator (a *compiler-generated* assignment operator), if the class writer does not write one.
3. The class writer can write a *member function* to do the assignment; see operator = in the index.

An **assignment statement** such as x = 5; is *not* an algebraic equality, no matter how much it may resemble one. It is a command telling the compiler to assign a value to a variable. In the example, the variable is x and the value is 5.

The **auto storage class** is the default storage class for *variables* declared within C++ *functions*. When we define a variable of the auto storage class, its *memory address* is assigned *auto*matically upon entry to the function where it is defined; the memory address is valid for the duration of that function.

B

Base class: see *inheritance*.

A **base class initializer** specifies which base class constructor we want to use to initialize the base class part of a *derived* class object. It is one of the two types of expressions allowed in a *member initialization list*. Also see *inheritance*.

The **base class part** of a *derived* class object is an unnamed component of the derived class object whose member variables and functions are accessible as though they were defined in the derived class, so long as they are either public or protected.

A **batch file** is a text file that directs the execution of a number of programs, one after the other, without manual intervention. A similar facility is available in most operating systems.

A **binary** number system uses only two digits, 0 and 1.

A **bit** is the fundamental unit of storage in a modern computer; the word *bit* is derived from the phrase *bi*nary digi*t*. Each bit, as this suggests, can have one of two states: 0 and 1.

A **block** is a group of *statements* that are considered one logical statement. A block is delimited by the "curly braces", { and }. The first of these symbols starts a block, and the second one ends the block. A block can be used anywhere that a statement can be used and is treated in exactly the same way as if it were one statement. For example, if a block is the *controlled block* of an if statement, then all of the statements in the block are executed if the condition in the if is true and none is executed if the condition in the if is false.

A **bool** (short for *Boolean*) is a type of variable whose range of values is limited to true or false. This is the most appropriate return type for a function that uses its return value to report whether some condition exists, such as operator <. In that particular case, the return value true indicates that the first argument is less than the second, while false indicates that the first argument is not less than the second.

Brace; see *curly braces*.

A **break statement** is a loop control device that interrupts processing of a *loop* whenever it is executed within the *controlled block* of a *loop control statement*. When a break statement is executed, the flow of control passes to the next statement after the end of the *controlled block*.

A **byte** is the unit in which data capacities are stated, whether in *RAM* or on a disk. In modern computers, a byte consists of eight *bits*.

C

A **C string** is a literal value representing a variable number of characters. An example is "This is a test.". C strings are surrounded by double quotes ("). Please note that this is *not* the same as a C++ string.

A **cache** is a small amount of fast memory where frequently used data is stored temporarily.

Call; see *function call* or call *instruction*.

A **call instruction** is an *assembly language* instruction that is used to implement a *function call*. It saves the *program counter* on the *stack*, and then transfers execution from the *calling function* to the *called function*.

A **called function** is a *function* that starts execution as the result of a *function call*. Normally, it will return to the *calling function* via a return *statement* when finished.

A **calling function** is a *function* that suspends execution as a result of a *function call*; the *called function* begins execution at the point of the function call.

A **char** is an *integer variable* type that can represent either one character of text or a small whole number. Both signed and unsigned chars are available for use as "really short" integer variables; a signed char can represent a number from −128 to +127, whereas an unsigned char can represent a number from 0 to 255.

   (In case you were wondering how to pronounce this term, the most common pronunciation has an *a* like the *a* in "married", while the *ch* sounds like *k*. Other pronunciations include the standard English pronunciation of "char", as in overcooking meat, and even "car", as in "automobile".)

A **char*** (pronounced "char star") is a *pointer* to (i.e., the *memory address* of) a char or the first of a group of chars.

Child class: see *inheritance*.

cin (pronounced "see in") is a predefined istream; it gets its characters from the keyboard.

A **class** is a user-defined type; for example, string is a class.

A **class implementation** tells the compiler how to implement the facilities defined in the class interface. A class implementation is usually found in a *implementation file*, which the compiler on the CD-ROM in the back of this book assumes has the extension .cc.

A **class interface** tells the user of the class what facilities the class provides by specifying the public member functions of the class. It also tells the compiler what data elements are included in objects of the class, but this is not logically part of the interface. A class interface is usually found in a *header file*; that is, one with the extension .h.

The **class membership** operator, ::, indicates which class a function belongs to. For example, the full name of the default constructor for the string class is string::string().

class scope describes the visibility of *member variables*; that is, those that are defined within a class. These *variables* can be accessed by any *member function* of that class; their accessibility to other *functions* is controlled by the *access specifier* in effect when they were defined in the class *interface*.

A **comment** is a note to yourself or another programmer; it is ignored by the compiler. The symbol // marks the beginning of a comment; the comment continues until the end of the line containing the //. For those of you with BASIC experience, this is just like REM (the "remark" keyword); anything after it on a line is ignored by the compiler.

Compilation is the process of translating *source code* into an *object program*, which is composed of *machine instructions* along with the data needed by those instructions. Virtually all of the *software* on your computer was created by this process.

A **compiler** is a program that performs the process of compilation.

A **compiler-generated** function is supplied by the compiler because the existence of that function is fundamental to the notion of a concrete data type. The compiler will automatically generate its own version of any of the following functions if they are not provided by the creator of the class: the *assignment operator*, the *copy constructor*, the *default constructor*, and the *destructor*.

Compile time means "while the compiler is compiling the source code of a program".

A **concrete data type** is a class whose objects behave like variables of native data types. That is, the class gives the compiler enough information that *objects* of that class can be created, copied, assigned, and automatically destroyed just as native variables are.

The keyword **const** has two distinct meanings as employed in this book. The first is as a modifier to an *argument* of a function. In this context, it means that we are promising not to modify the value of that argument in the function. An example of this use might be the function declaration string& operator = (const string& Str);.

The second use of const in this book is to define a data item similar to a *variable*, except that its value cannot be changed once it has been initialized. For this reason, it is mandatory to supply an initial value when creating a const. An example of this use is const short x = 5;.

A **constructor** is a *member function* that creates new *objects* of a (particular) class type. All constructors have the same name as the class for which they are constructors; for example, the constructors for the string class have the name string.

A **continuation expression** is the part of a for statement computed before every execution of the *controlled block*. The block controlled by the for will be executed if the result of the computation is true, but not if it is false. See for *statement* for an example.

A **controlled block** is a *block* under the control of a *loop control statement* or an if or else statement. The controlled block of a loop control statement can be executed a variable number of times, whereas the controlled block of an if or else statement is executed either once or not at all.

Controlled statement; see *controlled block*.

A **copy constructor** makes a new *object* with the same contents as an existing object of the same type.

cout (pronounced "see out") is a predefined ostream; characters sent to it are displayed on the screen.

CPU is an abbreviation for Central Processing Unit. This is the "active" part of your computer, which executes all the *machine instructions* that make the computer do useful work.

The **curly brace**s { and } are used to surround a *block*. The *compiler* treats the *statements* in the block as one statement.

D

Data are the pieces of information that are operated on by programs. Originally, "data" was the plural of "datum"; however, the form "data" is now commonly used as both singular and plural.

A **debugger** is a program that controls the execution of another program, so that you can see what the latter program is doing. The CD-ROM in the back of this book contains the gdb debugger, which works with the DJGPP compiler on the CD-ROM.

A **dedicated register** is a *register* such as the *stack pointer* whose usage is predefined, rather than being determined by the programmer. Compare with *general registers* such as eax.

A **default constructor** is a *member function* that is used to create an *object* when no initial value is specified for that object. For example, string::string() is the default constructor for the string class.

The **delete** operator is used to free memory that was previously used for *variables* of the *dynamic storage class*. This allows the memory no longer needed for those variables to be reused for other variables.

Derived class: see *inheritance*.

A **destructor** is a *member function* that cleans up when an *object* expires; for an object of the auto *storage class*, the destructor is called automatically at the end of the *function* where that object is defined.

A **digit** is one of the characters used in any positional numbering system to represent all numbers starting at 0 and ending at one less than the base of the numbering system. In the decimal system, there are ten digits, 0 through 9, and in the hexadecimal system there are sixteen digits, 0 through 9 and a through f.

A **double** is a type of *floating-point variable* that can represent a range of positive and negative numbers including fractional values. With most current C++ compilers including DJGPP, these numbers can vary from approximately 4.940656e–324 to approximately 1.79769e+308 (and 0), with approximately 16 digits of precision.

The **dynamic storage class** is used for *variables* whose size is not known until *run time*. Variables of this storage class are assigned *memory addresses* at the programmer's explicit request.

Dynamic type checking refers to the practice of checking the correct usage of *variables* of different types during execution of a program rather than during *compilation*; see *type system* for further discussion.

Dynamic typing means delaying the determination of the exact type of a variable until run time rather than fixing that type at compile time as in *static typing*. Please note that dynamic typing is not the same as *dynamic type checking*; C++ has the former but not the latter. See *type system* for further discussion.

E

An **element** is one of the *variables* that makes up a vector or an array.

The keyword **else** causes its *controlled block* to be executed if the condition in its matching *if* statement turns out to be false at run time.

An **empty stack** is a *stack* that currently contains no values.

Encapsulation is the concept of hiding the details of a class inside the implementation of that class rather than exposing them in the interface. This is one of the primary organizing principles that characterize object-oriented programming.

An **end user** is the person who actually uses an *application program* to perform some useful or interesting task. Also see *application programmer, library designer*.

Envelope class; see *manager/worker idiom*.

Executable; see *executable program*.

An **executable program** is a program in a form suitable for running on a computer; it is composed of *machine instructions* along with data needed by those instructions.

F

The keyword **false** is a predefined value, representing the result of a conditional expression whose condition is not satisfied. For example, in the conditional expression x < y, if x is not less than y, the result of the expression will be false. Also see bool.

A **fencepost error** is a logical error that causes a loop to be executed one more or one less time than the correct count. A common cause of this error is confusing the number of *elements* in a vector or *array* with the *index* of the last *element*. The derivation of this term is by analogy with the problem of calculating the number of fence sections and fenceposts that you need for a given fence. For example, if you have to put up a fence 100 feet long and each section of the fence is 10 feet long, how many sections of fence do you need? Obviously, the answer is 10. Now, how many fenceposts do you need? 11. The confusion caused by counting fenceposts when you should be counting segments of the fence (and vice-versa) is the cause of a fencepost error.

To return to a programming example, if you have a vector with 11 elements, the index of the last element is 10, not 11. Thus, confusing the number of elements with the highest index has much the same effect as the fencepost problem.

This sort of problem is also known, less colorfully, as an *off-by-one* error.

Field; see *manipulator*.

A **float** is a type of *floating-point variable* that can represent a range of positive and negative numbers including fractional values. With most current C++ compilers including DJGPP, these numbers can vary from approximately 1.401298e−45 to approximately 3.40282e+38 (and 0), with approximately 6 digits of precision.

A **floating-point variable** is a C++ approximation of a mathematical "real number". Unlike mathematical real numbers, C++ floating-point variables have a limited range and precision, depending on their types. See the individual types float and double for details.

A **for statement** is a *loop control statement* that causes its *controlled block* to be executed while a specified logical expression (the *continuation expression*) is true. It also provides for a *starting expression* to be executed before the first execution of the controlled block, and a *modification expression* to be executed after every execution of the controlled block. For example, in the for statement for (i = 0; i < 10; i ++), the initialization expression is i = 0, the continuation expression is i < 10, and the modification expression is i ++.

The keyword **friend** allows access by a specified class or *function* to private or protected members of a particular class.

A **function** is a section of code having a name, optional *arguments*, and a *return type*. The name makes it possible for one function to start execution of another one via a *function call*; the arguments are used to provide input for the function, and the return type allows the function to provide output to its *calling function* when the return *statement* causes the calling function to resume execution.

A **function call** (or *call* for short) causes execution to be transferred temporarily from the current *function* (the *calling function*) to the one named in the function call (the *called function*). Normally, when a called function is finished with its task, it will return to the calling function, which will pick up execution at the statement after the function call.

A **function declaration** tells the compiler some vital statistics of the function: its name, its *arguments*, and its *return type*. Before we can use a *function*, the compiler must have already seen its function declaration. The most common way to arrange for this is to use a #include *statement* to insert the function declaration from the header file where it exists into our implementation file.

Function header; see *function declaration*.

Function overloading is the C++ facility that allows us to create more than one *function* with the same name. So long as all such functions have different *signatures*, we can write as many of them as we wish and the compiler will be able to figure out which one we mean.

G

A **general register** is a *register* whose usage is determined by the programmer, rather than being predefined as with *dedicated registers* such as the *stack pointer*. On an Intel CPU such as the 486 or Pentium, the 16-bit general registers are ax, bx, cx, dx, si, di, and bp; the 32-bit general registers are eax, ebx, ecx, edx, esi, edi, and ebp.

Global scope describes the visibility of *variables* that are defined outside any *function*; such variables can be accessed by code in any function. It also describes the visibility of *functions* that are defined outside any class.

H

Hardware refers to the physical components of a computer, the ones you can touch. Examples include the keyboard, the monitor, and the printer.

A **header file** is a file that contains class *interface* definitions and/or global *function declarations*. By convention, header files have the extension .h.

The **heap** is the area of memory where *variables* of the *dynamic storage class* store their data.

Hex is an abbreviation for *hexadecimal*.

A **hexadecimal** number system has 16 digits, 0–9 and a–f.

I

An **identifier** is a user-defined name; both *function* names and *variable* names are identifiers. Identifiers must not conflict with *keywords* such as if and for; for example, you cannot create a function or a variable with the name for.

An **if statement** is a *statement* that causes its *controlled block* to be executed if the *logical expression* specified in the if statement is true.

An **ifstream** (pronounced "i f stream") is a stream used for input from a file.

Implementation; see class *implementation*.

An **implementation file** contains source code statements that are turned into executable code by a compiler. In this book, implementation files have the extension *.cc*.

Include; see #include statement.

Inheritance is the definition of one class as a more specific version of another class that has been previously defined. The newly defined class is called the *derived* (or sometimes the *child*) class, while the previously defined class is called the *base* (or sometimes the *parent*) class. In this book, we use the terms *base* and *derived*. The derived class inherits all of the *member variables* and *regular member functions* from the base class. Inheritance is one of the primary organizing principles of object-oriented programming.

To **increment a variable** means to add 1 to its value. This can be done in C++ by using the increment operator, ++.

An **index** is an expression used to select one of a number of *elements* of a vector or an *array*. It is enclosed in *square brackets* ([ ]). For example, in the expression a[i+1], the index is the expression i+1.

An **index variable** is a *variable* used to hold an index into a vector or an *array*.

Initialization is the process of setting the initial value of a *variable* or const. It is very similar to *assignment* but is not identical. Initialization is done only when a variable or const is created, whereas a variable can be assigned to as many times as desired. A const, however, cannot be assigned to at all, so it must be initialized when it is created.

Input is the process of reading data into the computer from the outside world. A very commonly used source of input for simple programs is the keyboard.

Instruction; see *machine instruction*.

An **int** (short for *integer*) is a type of *integer variable*. While the C++ language definition requires only that an int be at least as long as a short and no longer than a long, with most current C++ compilers this type is equivalent to either a short or a long, depending on the compiler you are using. A 16-bit compiler such as Borland C++ 3.1 has 16-bit (2-byte) ints that are the same size as shorts. A 32-bit compiler such as DJGPP (the compiler on the CD-ROM that comes with this book) has 32-bit (4-byte) ints that are the same size as longs.

An **integer variable** is a C++ representation of a whole number. Unlike mathematical integers, C++ integers have a limited range, which varies depending on their types. See the individual types char, short, int, and long for details. The type bool is sometimes also considered an integer variable type.

Interface; see class *interface*.

I/O is an abbreviation for "input/output". This refers to the process of getting information into and out of the computer. See *input* and *output* for more details.

iostream.h is the name of the *header file* that tells the *compiler* how to compile code that uses predefined stream *variables* like cout and operators like <<.

An **istream** is a stream used for input. For example, cin is a predefined istream that reads characters from the keyboard.

K

A **keyword** is a word defined in the C++ language, such as if and for. It is illegal to define an *identifier* such as a *variable* or *function* name that conflicts with a keyword; for example, you cannot create a function or a variable with the name for.

L

Letter class; see *manager/worker idiom*.

A **library** (or library module) contains the *object code* generated from several *implementation files*, in a form that the *linker* can search when it needs to find general-purpose functions.

A **library designer** is a programmer who creates classes for *application programmers* to use in writing *application programs*.

The **linker** is a program that combines information from all of the *object files* for our program, along with some previously prepared files called *libraries*, to produce an *executable program*.

Linking is the process of creating an *executable program* from *object files* and *libraries*.

A **literal** value doesn't have a name, but represents itself in a literal manner. Some examples are 'x' (a char literal having the ASCII value that represents the letter x) and 5 (a numeric literal with the value 5).

Local scope describes the visibility of *variables* that are defined within a *function*; such variables can be accessed only by code in that function.[1]

A **logical expression** is an expression that takes on the value true or false, rather than a numeric value. Some examples of such expressions are x > y (which will be true if x has a greater value than y and false otherwise) and a == b (which will be true if a has the same value as b, and false otherwise). Also see bool.

---

1. In fact, a variable can be declared in any *block*, not just in a *function*. In that case, its scope is from the point where it is declared until the end of the block where it is defined. However, in this book all local variables have function scope, so this distinction is not critical here and omitting it simplifies the discussion.

A **long** is a type of *integer variable* that can represent a whole number. With most current C++ compilers, including DJGPP, a long occupies 4 bytes of storage and therefore can represent a number in either the range –2147483648 to 2147483647 (if signed) or the range 0 to 4294967295 (if unsigned).

A **loop** is a means of executing a *controlled block* a variable number of times, depending on some condition. The statement that controls the controlled block is called a *loop control statement*. This book covers the while and for loop control statements. See while and for for details.

A **loop control statement** is a *statement* that controls the *controlled block* in a *loop*.

M

Machine address; see *memory address*.

Machine code is the combination of *machine instructions* with the data used by those instructions. A synonym is *object code*.

A **machine instruction** is one of the fundamental operations that a *CPU* can perform. Some examples of these operations are addition, subtraction, or other arithmetic operations; other possibilities include operations that control what instruction will be executed next. All C++ programs must be converted into machine instructions before they can be executed by the *CPU*.

A **machine language** program is a program composed of *machine instructions*.

A **manipulator** is a member function of one of the iostreams classes that controls how output will be formatted without necessarily producing any output of its own. Manipulators operate on *fields*; a field could be defined as the result of one << operator.

The **manager/worker** idiom (also known as the envelope/letter idiom) is a mechanism that allows the effective type of an object to be determined at run-time without requiring the user of the object to be concerned with pointers. It is used to implement *polymorphic objects* in C++.

A **member function** is a *function* defined in a class interface. It is viewed as "belonging" to the class, which is the reason for the adjective *member*.

A **member initialization expression** is the preferred method of specifies how a member variable is to be initialized in a constructor. Also see *inheritance*.

A **member initialization list** specifies how member variables are to be initialized in a constructor. It includes two types of expressions: *base class initializers* and *member initialization expressions*. Also see *inheritance*.

A **member variable** is a *variable* defined in a class interface. It is viewed as "belonging" to the class, which is the reason for the adjective *member*.

Memberwise copy means to copy every *member variable* from the source *object* to the destination object. If we don't define our own *copy constructor* or *assignment operator* for a particular class, the *compiler-generated* versions will use memberwise copy.

A **memory address** is a unique number identifying a particular *byte* of *RAM*.

A **memory hierarchy** is the particular arrangement of the different kinds of storage devices in a given computer. The purpose of using various kinds of storage devices having different performance characteristics is to provide the best overall performance at the lowest cost.

A **memory leak** is a programming error in which the programmer forgot to delete something that had been dynamically allocated. Such an error is very insidious, because the program appears to work correctly when tested casually. The usual way to find these errors is to notice that the program runs apparently correctly for a (possibly long) time and then fails due to running out of available memory.

A **modification expression** is the part of a for statement executed after every execution of the *controlled block*. It is often used to *increment* an *index variable* to refer to the next *element* of an *array* or a vector; see for *statement* for an example.

N

A **nanosecond** is one-billionth of a second.

A **native** data type is one that is defined in the C++ language, as opposed to a *user-defined* data type (class).

The **new** operator is used to allocate memory for *variables* of the *dynamic storage class*; these are usually variables whose storage requirements may not be known until the program is executing.

Nondisplay character; see *nonprinting* character.

A **nonmember function** is one that is not a member of a particular class being discussed, although it may be a *member function* of another class.

A **nonnumeric variable** is a *variable* that is not used in calculations like adding, multiplying, or subtracting. Such variables might represent names, addresses, telephone numbers, Social Security numbers, bank account numbers, or drivers license numbers. Note that just because something is called a *number* or even is composed entirely of the digits 0–9, does not make it a *numeric variable* by our standards; the question is how the item is used. No one adds, multiplies, or subtracts drivers license numbers, for example; they serve solely as identifiers and could just as easily have letters in them, as indeed some of them do.

A **nonprinting character** is used to control the format of our displayed or printed information, rather than to represent a particular letter, digit, or other special character. The *space* ( ) is one of the more important nonprinting characters.

A **normal constructor** is a *constructor* whose arguments supply enough information to initialize all of the member fields in the object being created. Also see *constructor*.

A **null byte** is a byte with the value 0, commonly used to indicate the end of a *C string*. Note that this is not the same as the character '0', which is a normal printable character having the *ASCII* code 48.

A **null object** is an *object* of some (specified) class whose purpose is to indicate that a "real" object of that class does not exist, analogously to a *null pointer*. One common use for a null object is as a *return value* from a *member function* that is supposed to return an object with some specified properties but cannot find such an object. For example, a null StockItem object might be used to indicate that an item with a specified UPC cannot be found in the inventory of a store.

A **null pointer** is a *pointer* with the value 0. This value is particularly suited to indicate that a pointer isn't pointing to anything at the moment, due to some special treatment of zero-valued pointers built into the C++ language.

A **numeric variable** is a *variable* representing a quantity that can be expressed as a number, whether a whole number (an *integer variable*) or a number with a fractional part (a *floating-point variable*), and that can be used in calculations such as addition, subtraction, multiplication, or division. The integer variable types in C++ are char, short, int, and long. Each of these integer types can be further subdivided into signed and unsigned versions. The former of these can represent both negative and positive values (and 0), whereas the latter can represent only positive values (and 0) but provides a greater range of positive values than the corresponding signed version does.

The floating-point variable types are float and double, which differ in their range and precision. Unlike the integer variable types, the floating-point types are not divided into signed and unsigned versions; all floating-point variables can represent either positive or negative numbers as well as 0. See float and double for details on range and precision.

O

An **object** is a *variable* of a class type, as distinct from a *variable* of a *native* type. The behavior of an object is defined by the code that implements the class to which the object belongs. For example, a variable of type string is an object whose behavior is controlled by the definition of the string class.

Object code; see *machine code*. This term is unrelated to C++ *objects*.

An **object code module** is the result of compiling a *implementation file* into *object code*. A number of object code modules are combined to form an *executable program*. This term is unrelated to C++ *objects*.

Object file; see *object code module*. This term is unrelated to C++ *objects*.

Object-oriented programming is an approach to solving programming problems by creating *objects* to represent the entities being handled by the program, rather than relying solely on *native* data types. This approach has the advantage that you can match the language to the needs of the problem you're trying to solve. For example, if you were writing a nurse's station program in C++, you would want to have objects that represented nurses, doctors, patients, various sorts of equipment, and so on. Each of these objects would display the behavior appropriate to the thing or person it was representing.

Off-by-one error; see *fencepost error*.

An **ofstream** (pronounced "o f stream") is a stream used for output to a file.

An **op code** is the part of a *machine instruction* that tells the *CPU* what kind of instruction it is and sometimes also specifies a *register* to be operated on.

An **operating system** is a program that deals with the actual hardware of your computer. It supplies the lowest level of the software infrastructure needed to run a program. By far the most common operating system for Intel CPUs, at present, is MS-DOS (which is also the basis for Windows 95), followed by OS/2 and Windows NT.

The keyword **operator** is used to indicate that the following symbol is the name of a C++ operator that we are redefining, either globally or for a particular class. For example, to redefine =, we have to specify operator = as the name of the function we are writing, rather than just =, so that the *compiler* does not object to seeing an operator when it expects an *identifier*.

An **ostream** is a stream used for output. For example, cout is a predefined ostream that displays characters on the screen.

Output is the process of sending data from the computer to the outside world. The most commonly used source of output for most programs is the screen.

A member function in a derived class is said to **override** the base class member function if the derived class function has the same *signature* (name and argument types) as the base class member function. The derived class member function will be called instead of the base class member function when the member function is referred to via an object of the derived class.

A member function in a derived class with the same name but a different signature from a member function in the base class does *not* override the base class member function. Instead, it "hides" that base class member function, which is no longer accessible as a member function in the derived class.

P

Parent class; see *inheritance*.

A **pointer** is essentially the same as a *memory address*. The main difference between these two concepts is that a memory address is "untyped" (i.e., it can refer to any sort of *variable*), but a pointer always has an associated data type. For example, char* (pronounced "char star") means "pointer to a char".

To say "a variable points to a memory location" is almost exactly the same as saying "a variable's value is the address of a memory location". In the specific case of a variable of type char*, to say "the char* x points to a C string" is equivalent to saying "x contains the address of the first byte of the C string". Also see *array*.

A **polymorphic object** is a C++ object that presents the appearance of a simple object that behaves polymorphically without the hazards of exposing pointers to the user of the polymorphic object. The user does not have to know about any of the details of the implementation, but merely instantiates an object of the single visible class (the *manager* class). That object does what the user wants with the help of an object of a *worker* class, which is derived from the *manager* class. Also see *manager/worker idiom*.

Polymorphism is the major organizing principle in C++ that allows us to implement several classes with the same interface and treat objects of all these classes as though they were of the same class. This is the C++ mechanism for *dynamic typing*. The word *polymorphism* is derived from the Greek words *poly*, meaning "many", and *morph*, meaning "form". In other words, the same behavior is implemented in different forms.

Pop means to remove the top value from a *stack*.

The keyword **private** is an *access specifier* that denies *nonmember functions* access to *member functions* and *member variables* of its class.

A **program** is a set of instructions specifying the solution to a set of problems, along with the data used by those instructions.

The **program counter** is a *dedicated register* that holds the address of the next instruction to be executed. During a *function call*, a call *instruction* pushes the contents of the program counter on the *stack*. This enables the *called function* to return to the *calling function* when finished.

Programming is the art and science of solving problems by the following procedure:

1. Find or invent a general solution to a set of problems.
2. Express this solution as an *algorithm* or set of algorithms.
3. Translate the algorithm(s) into terms so simple that a stupid machine like a computer can follow them to calculate the specific answer for any specific problem in the set.

Warning: This definition may be somewhat misleading since it implies that the development of a program is straightforward and linear, with no revision. This is known as the "waterfall model" of programming, since water going over a waterfall follows a preordained course in one direction. However, real-life programming doesn't usually work this way; rather, most programs are written in an incremental process as assumptions are changed and errors are found and corrected.

The keyword **protected** is an *access specifier*. When present in a base class definition, it allows derived class functions access to member variables and functions in the base class part of a derived class object, while preventing access by other functions outside the base class.

The keyword **public** is an *access specifier* that allows *nonmember functions* access to *member functions* and *member variables* of its class.

Specifying **public inheritance** means that we are going to let outside functions treat an object of the derived class as an object of the base class. That is, any function that takes a base class object as a parameter will accept a derived class object in its place. All of the public member functions and public data items (if there are any) in the base class are accessible in a derived class object as well.

Push means to add another value to a *stack*.

A **put** pointer holds the address of the next byte in the output area of an ostream; i.e., where the next byte will be stored if we use << to write data into the stream.

R

RAM is an acronym for Random Access Memory. This is the working storage of a computer, where data and programs are stored while we're using them.

A **reference argument** is another name for a *variable* from a *calling function*, rather than an independent variable in the *called function*. Changing a reference argument therefore affects the corresponding *variable* in the calling function. Compare with *value argument*.

The **reference-counting** idiom is a mechanism that allows one object (the "reference-counted object") to be shared by several other objects (the "client objects") rather than requiring a copy to be made for each of the client objects.

A **register** is a storage area that is on the same chip as the *CPU* itself. Programs use registers to hold data items that are actively in use; data in registers can be accessed within the time allocated to instruction execution, rather than the much longer times needed to access data in *RAM*.

A **regular member function** is any *member function* that is not in any of the following categories:
1. *Constructor*
2. *Destructor*
3. The *assignment operator*, operator =.
   A *derived* class inherits all regular member functions from its *base* class.

A **retrieval function** is a *function* that retrieves data, which may have been previously stored by a *storage function* or may be generated when needed by some other method such as calculation according to a formula.

A **return address** is the *memory address* of the next *machine instruction* in a *calling function*. It is used during execution of a return *statement* in a *called function* to transfer execution back to the correct place in the calling function.

A **return statement** is used by a *called function* to transfer execution back to the *calling function*. The return statement can also specify a value of the correct *return type* for the called function. This value is made available to the calling function to be used for further calculation. An example of a return statement is return 0;, which returns the value 0 to the calling function.

A **return type** tells the *compiler* what sort of data a *called function* returns to the *calling function* when the called function finishes executing. The *return value* from main is a special case; it can be used to determine what action a batch file should take next.

ROM is an abbreviation for Read-Only Memory. This is the permanent internal storage of a computer, where the programs needed to start up the computer are stored. As this suggests, ROM does not lose its contents when the power is turned off, as contrasted with *RAM*.

Run time means "while a (previously compiled) program is being executed".

S

A **scalar variable** has a single value (at any one time); this is contrasted with a vector or an *array*, which contains a number of values each of which is referred to by its *index*.

The **scope** of a *variable* is the part of the program in which the variable can be accessed. The scopes with which we are concerned are *local*, *global*, and class; see *local scope*, *global scope*, and class *scope* for more details.

A **selection sort** is a sorting algorithm that selects the highest (or lowest) *element* from a set of elements (the "input list") and moves that selected element to another set of elements (the "output list"). The next highest (or lowest) element is then treated in the same manner; this operation is repeated until as many elements as desired have been moved to the output list.

A **short** is a type of *integer variable* that can represent a whole number. With most current C++ compilers including DJGPP, a short occupies 2 bytes of storage and therefore can represent a number in either the range –32768 to 32767 (if signed) or the range 0 to 65535 (if unsigned).

The **short-circuit evaluation rule** governs the execution of the || and the && operators. See || and && for details.

A **side effect** is any result of calling a *function* that persists beyond the execution of that function, other than its returning a *return value*. For example, writing data to a file is a side effect.

The **signature** of a *function* consists of its name and the types of its *arguments*. In the case of a *member function*, the class to which the function belongs is also part of its signature. Every function is uniquely identified by its signature, which is what makes it possible to have more than one function with the same name; this is called *function overloading*.

A **signed char** is a type of *integer variable*. See char for details.

A **signed int** is a type of *integer variable*. See int for details.

A **signed long** is a type of *integer variable*. See long for details.

A **signed short** is a type of *integer variable*. See short for details.

A **signed variable** can represent either negative or positive values. See char, short, int, or long for details.

Software refers to the nonphysical components of a computer, the ones you cannot touch. If you can install it on your hard disk, it's software. Examples include a spreadsheet, a word processor, and a database program.

Source code is a program in a form suitable for reading and writing by a human being.

Source code file; see *implementation file*.

Source code module; see *implementation file*.

The **space** character ( ) is one of the *nonprinting characters* (or *nondisplay characters*) that controls the format of displayed or printed information.

The **square bracket**s, [and], are used to enclose an *array* or vector *index*, which selects an individual *element* of the *array* or vector. Also see [ ].

A **stack** is a data structure with characteristics similar to a spring-loaded plate holder such as you might see in a cafeteria. The last plate deposited on the stack of plates will be the first one to be removed when a customer needs a fresh plate; similarly, the last value deposited (*pushed*) onto a stack is the first value retrieved (*popped*).

The **stack pointer** is a *dedicated register*. The stack pointer is used to keep track of the address of the most recently *pushed* value on the *stack*.

A **starting expression** is the part of a for statement that is executed once before the *controlled block* of the for statement is first executed. It is often used to initialize an *index variable* to 0, so that the index variable can be used to refer to the first element of an *array* or vector. See for *statement* for an example.

A **statement** is a complete operation understood by the C++ compiler. Each statement is ended with a semicolon (;).

A **static member function** is a member function of a class that can be called without reference to an object of that class. Such a function has no this pointer passed to it on entry, and therefore cannot refer to member variables of the class.

The **static storage class** is the simplest of the three *storage classes* in C++; *variables* of this storage class are assigned *memory addresses* in the *executable program* when the program is *linked*.

Static type checking refers to the practice of checking the correct usage of variables of different types during compilation of a program rather than during execution. C++ uses static type checking. See *type system* for further discussion. Note that this has no particular relation to the keyword static.

Static typing means determining the exact type of a variable when the program is compiled. It is the default typing mechanism in C++. Note that this has no particular relation to the keyword static, nor is it exactly the same as *static type checking*. See *type system* for further discussion.

Stepwise refinement is the process of developing an *algorithm* by starting out with a "coarse" solution and "refining" it until the steps are within the capability of the C++ language.

Storage; synonym for *memory*.

A **storage class** is the characteristic of a *variable* that determines how and when a *memory address* is assigned to that variable. C++ has three different storage classes: static, auto, and *dynamic*. Please note that the term *storage class* has nothing to do with the C++ term class. See static storage class, auto storage class, and *dynamic* storage class for more details.

A **storage function** is a *function* that stores data for later retrieval by a *retrieval function*.

A **stream** is a place to put (in the case of an ostream) or get (in the case of an istream) characters. Some predefined streams are cin and cout.

A **stream buffer** is the area of memory where the characters put into the stream are stored.

The **string class** defines a type of *object* that contains a group of chars; the chars in a string can be treated as one unit for purposes of *assignment, I/O,* and comparison.

T

Temporary; see *temporary variable*.

A **temporary variable** is automatically created by the *compiler* for use during a particular operation, such as a *function call* with an *argument* that has to be converted to a different type.

The keyword **this** represents a hidden *argument* automatically supplied by the compiler in every *member function* call. Its value during the execution of any member function is the address of the class object for which the member function call was made.

A **token** is a part of a program that the *compiler* treats as a separate unit. It's analogous to a word in English; a *statement* is more like a sentence. For example, string is a token, as are :: and (. On the other hand, x = 5; is a statement.

The keyword **true** is a predefined value representing the result of a conditional expression whose condition is satisfied. For example, in the conditional expression x < y, if x is less than y the result of the expression will be true.

The **type** of an *object* is the class to which it belongs. The type of a native *variable* is one of the predefined variable types in C++. See *integer variable, floating-point variable,* and bool for details on the native types.

The **type system** refers to the set of rules that the compiler uses to decide how a variable of a given *type* may legally be employed. In C++, these determinations are made by the compiler (*static type checking*). This makes it easier to prevent type errors than it is in languages where type checking is done during execution of the program (*dynamic type checking*).

Please note that C++ has both *static type checking* and *dynamic typing*. This is possible because the set of types that is acceptable in any given situation can be determined at compile time, even though the exact type of a given variable may not be known until run time.

U

An **uninitialized variable** is one that has never been set to a known value. Attempting to use such a *variable* is a logical error that can cause a program to act very oddly.

An **unqualified name** is a reference to a *member variable* that doesn't specify which *object* the member variable belongs to. When we use an unqualified name in a *member function*, the compiler assumes that the object we are referring to is the object for which that member function has been called.

An **unsigned char** is a type of *integer variable*. See char for details.

An **unsigned int** is a type of *integer variable*. See int for details.

An **unsigned long** is a type of *integer variable*. See long for details.

An **unsigned short** is a type of *integer variable*. See short for details.

An **unsigned variable** is an *integer variable* that represents only positive values (and 0). See char, short, int, and long for details.

The term **user** has several meanings in programming. The primary usage in this book is *application programmer*. However, it can also mean *library designer* (in the phrase *user-defined data type*) or even *end user*.

A **user-defined** data type is one that is defined by the user. In this context, *user* means "someone using language facilities to extend the range of variable types in the language", i.e., *library designer*. The primary mechanism used to define a user-defined type is the class.

V

A **value argument** is a *variable* of *local scope* created when a *function* begins execution. Its initial value is set to the value of the corresponding *argument* in the *calling function*. Changing a value argument does not affect any variable in the calling function. Compare with *reference argument*.

A **variable** is a programming construct that uses a certain part of *RAM* to represent a specific item of data that we wish to keep track of in a program. Some examples are the weight of a pumpkin or the number of cartons of milk in the inventory of a store.

A **vector** is a group of *variables* that can be addressed by their position in the group; each of these variables is called an *element*. A vector has a name, just as a regular variable does, but the elements do not. Instead, each element has an *index* which represents its position in the vector.

Declaring a function to be **virtual** means that it is a member of a set of *functions* having the same *signatures* and belonging to classes related by *inheritance*. The actual function to be executed as the result of a given *function call* is selected from the set dynamically (i.e., at run time) based on the actual type of an *object* referred to via a base class pointer (or base class reference). This is the C++ mechanism used to implement *dynamic typing*, in contrast to the *static typing* used for non-virtual functions.

A **void** return type specifier in a *function* declaration indicates that the function in question does not return any value when it finishes executing.

The term **vtable** is an abbreviation for "virtual *function* address table". This is the table where the addresses of all of the virtual *functions* for a given class are stored; every object of that class contains the address of the vtable for that class.

W

A **while statement** is a *loop control statement* that causes its *controlled block* to be executed while a specified logical expression is true.

Z

Zero-based indexing refers to the practice of numbering the *elements* of an *array* or vector starting at 0 rather than 1.

About the Author

Steve Heller had always been fascinated by writing. In his childhood days in the 1950s and 1960s, he often stayed up far past his bedtime reading science fiction. Even in adulthood, if you came across him in his off-hours, he was more likely to be found reading a book than doing virtually anything else.

After college, Steve got into programming more or less by accident; he was working at an actuarial consulting firm and was selected to take charge of programming on their time-sharing terminal, because he was making much less than most of the other employees. Finding the programming itself to be more interesting than the actuarial calculations, he decided to become a professional programmer.

Until 1984, Steve remained on the consuming side of the writing craft. Then one day he was reading a magazine article on some programming-related topic and said to himself, "I could do better than that". With encouragement from his wife of the time, he decided to try his hand at technical writing. Steve's first article submission — to the late lamented *Computer Language Magazine* — was published, as were a dozen more over the next ten years.

But although writing magazine articles is an interesting pastime, writing a book is something entirely different. Steve got his chance at this new level of commitment when Harry Helms, then an editor for Academic Press, read one of his articles in *Dr. Dobb's Journal* and wrote him a letter asking whether he would be interested in writing a book for AP. He answered, "Sure, why not?", not having the faintest idea of how much work he was letting himself in for.

The resulting book, *Large Problems, Small Machines* received favorable reviews for its careful explanation of a number of facets of program optimization, and sold a total of about 20,000 copies within a year after publication of the second edition, entitled *Efficient C/C++ Programming*.

By that time, Steve was hard at work on his next book, *Who's Afraid of C++*, which is designed to make object-oriented programming intelligible to anyone from the sheerest novice to the programmer with years of experience in languages other than C++. To make sure that his exposition was clear enough for the novice, he posted a message on CompuServe requesting the help of someone new to programming. The responses included one from a woman named Susan, who ended up contributing a great deal to the book; in fact, about 100 pages of the book consist of email between Steve and Susan. Her contribution was wonderful, but not completely unexpected.

What *was* unexpected was that Steve and Susan would fall in love during the course of this project, but that's what happened. Since she lived in Texas and he lived in New York, this posed some logistic difficulties. The success of his previous book now became extremely important, as it was the key to Steve's becoming a full-time writer. Writers have been "telecommuting" since before the invention of the telephone, so his conversion from "programmer who writes" to "writer" made it possible for him to relocate to her area, which he promptly did.

Since his move to Texas, Steve has been hard at work on his writing projects, including *Introduction to C++*, a classroom text that covers more material in the same space as *Who's Afraid of C++?* at the expense of the email exchanges in the latter book, followed by *Who's Afraid of Java?*. Their latest project is *Who's Afraid of More C++?*, which should be out in the Spring of 1998.

Steve and Susan were married in 1997.

Index

Back | Forward | Home | Reload | Images | Open | Print | Find | Stop

http://www.phptr.com/

What's New? | What's Cool? | Destinations | Net Search | People | Software

PRENTICE HALL

Professional Technical Reference

Tomorrow's Solutions for Today's Professionals.

Keep Up-to-Date with
PH PTR Online!

We strive to stay on the cutting-edge of what's happening in professional computer science and engineering. Here's a bit of what you'll find when you stop by **www.phptr.com**:

@ Special interest areas offering our latest books, book series, software, features of the month, related links and other useful information to help you get the job done.

Deals, deals, deals! Come to our promotions section for the latest bargains offered to you exclusively from our retailers.

$ Need to find a bookstore? Chances are, there's a bookseller near you that carries a broad selection of PTR titles. Locate a Magnet bookstore near you at www.phptr.com.

! What's New at PH PTR? We don't just publish books for the professional community, we're a part of it. Check out our convention schedule, join an author chat, get the latest reviews and press releases on topics of interest to you.

✉ Subscribe Today! Join PH PTR's monthly email newsletter!

Want to be kept up-to-date on your area of interest? Choose a targeted category on our website, and we'll keep you informed of the latest PH PTR products, author events, reviews and conferences in your interest area.

Visit our mailroom to subscribe today! **http://www.phptr.com/mail_lists**

LICENSE AGREEMENT AND LIMITED WARRANTY

READ THE FOLLOWING TERMS AND CONDITIONS CAREFULLY BEFORE OPENING THIS CD PACKAGE. THIS LEGAL DOCUMENT IS AN AGREEMENT BETWEEN YOU AND PRENTICE-HALL, INC. (THE "COMPANY"). BY OPENING THIS SEALED CD PACKAGE, YOU ARE AGREEING TO BE BOUND BY THESE TERMS AND CONDITIONS. IF YOU DO NOT AGREE WITH THESE TERMS AND CONDITIONS, DO NOT OPEN THE CD PACKAGE. PROMPTLY RETURN THE UNOPENED CD PACKAGE AND ALL ACCOMPANYING ITEMS TO THE PLACE YOU OBTAINED THEM FOR A FULL REFUND OF ANY SUMS YOU HAVE PAID.

1.   **GRANT OF LICENSE:** In consideration of your purchase of this book, and your agreement to abide by the terms and conditions of this Agreement, the Company grants to you a nonexclusive right to use and display the copy of the enclosed software program (hereinafter the "SOFTWARE") on a single computer (i.e., with a single CPU) at a single location so long as you comply with the terms of this Agreement. The Company reserves all rights not expressly granted to you under this Agreement.

2.   **OWNERSHIP OF SOFTWARE:** You own only the magnetic or physical media (the enclosed CD) on which the SOFTWARE is recorded or fixed, but the Company and the software developers retain all the rights, title, and ownership to the SOFTWARE recorded on the original CD copy(ies) and all subsequent copies of the SOFTWARE, regardless of the form or media on which the original or other copies may exist. This license is not a sale of the original SOFTWARE or any copy to you.

3.   **COPY RESTRICTIONS:** This SOFTWARE and the accompanying printed materials and user manual (the "Documentation") are the subject of copyright. The individual programs on the CD are copyrighted by the authors of each program. Some of the programs on the CD include separate licensing agreements. If you intend to use one of these programs, you must read and follow its accompanying license agreement. If you intend to use the trial version of Internet Chameleon, you must read and agree to the terms of the notice regarding fees on the back cover of this book. You may not copy the Documentation or the SOFTWARE, except that you may make a single copy of the SOFTWARE for backup or archival purposes only. You may be held legally responsible for any copying or copyright infringement which is caused or encouraged by your failure to abide by the terms of this restriction.

4.   **USE RESTRICTIONS:** You may not network the SOFTWARE or otherwise use it on more than one computer or computer terminal at the same time. You may physically transfer the SOFTWARE from one computer to another provided that the SOFTWARE is used on only one computer at a time. You may not distribute copies of the SOFTWARE or Documentation to others. You may not reverse engineer, disassemble, decompile, modify, adapt, translate, or create derivative works based on the SOFTWARE or the Documentation without the prior written consent of the Company.

5.   **TRANSFER RESTRICTIONS:** The enclosed SOFTWARE is licensed only to you and may not be transferred to any one else without the prior written consent of the Company. Any unauthorized transfer of the SOFTWARE shall result in the immediate termination of this Agreement.

6.   **TERMINATION:** This license is effective until terminated. This license will terminate automatically without notice from the Company and become null and void if you fail to comply with any provisions or limitations of this license. Upon termination, you shall destroy the Documentation and all copies of the SOFTWARE. All provisions of this Agreement as to warranties, limitation of liability, remedies or damages, and our ownership rights shall survive termination.

7.   **MISCELLANEOUS:** This Agreement shall be construed in accordance with the laws of the United States of America and the State of New York and shall benefit the Company, its affiliates, and assignees.

8. **LIMITED WARRANTY AND DISCLAIMER OF WARRANTY:** The Company warrants that the SOFTWARE, when properly used in accordance with the Documentation, will operate in substantial conformity with the description of the SOFTWARE set forth in the Documentation. The Company does not warrant that the SOFTWARE will meet your requirements or that the operation of the SOFTWARE will be uninterrupted or error-free. The Company warrants that the media on which the SOFTWARE is delivered shall be free from defects in materials and workmanship under normal use for a period of thirty (30) days from the date of your purchase. Your only remedy and the Company's only obligation under these limited warranties is, at the Company's option, return of the warranted item for a refund of any amounts paid by you or replacement of the item. Any replacement of SOFTWARE or media under the warranties shall not extend the original warranty period. The limited warranty set forth above shall not apply to any SOFTWARE which the Company determines in good faith has been subject to misuse, neglect, improper installation, repair, alteration, or damage by you. EXCEPT FOR THE EXPRESSED WARRANTIES SET FORTH ABOVE, THE COMPANY DISCLAIMS ALL WARRANTIES, EXPRESS OR IMPLIED, INCLUDING WITHOUT LIMITATION, THE IMPLIED WARRANTIES OF MERCHANTABILITY AND FITNESS FOR A PARTICULAR PURPOSE. EXCEPT FOR THE EXPRESS WARRANTY SET FORTH ABOVE, THE COMPANY DOES NOT WARRANT, GUARANTEE, OR MAKE ANY REPRESENTATION REGARDING THE USE OR THE RESULTS OF THE USE OF THE SOFTWARE IN TERMS OF ITS CORRECTNESS, ACCURACY, RELIABILITY, CURRENTNESS, OR OTHERWISE.

IN NO EVENT, SHALL THE COMPANY OR ITS EMPLOYEES, AGENTS, SUPPLIERS, OR CONTRACTORS BE LIABLE FOR ANY INCIDENTAL, INDIRECT, SPECIAL, OR CONSEQUENTIAL DAMAGES ARISING OUT OF OR IN CONNECTION WITH THE LICENSE GRANTED UNDER THIS AGREEMENT, OR FOR LOSS OF USE, LOSS OF DATA, LOSS OF INCOME OR PROFIT, OR OTHER LOSSES, SUSTAINED AS A RESULT OF INJURY TO ANY PERSON, OR LOSS OF OR DAMAGE TO PROPERTY, OR CLAIMS OF THIRD PARTIES, EVEN IF THE COMPANY OR AN AUTHORIZED REPRESENTATIVE OF THE COMPANY HAS BEEN ADVISED OF THE POSSIBILITY OF SUCH DAMAGES. IN NO EVENT SHALL LIABILITY OF THE COMPANY FOR DAMAGES WITH RESPECT TO THE SOFTWARE EXCEED THE AMOUNTS ACTUALLY PAID BY YOU, IF ANY, FOR THE SOFTWARE.

SOME JURISDICTIONS DO NOT ALLOW THE LIMITATION OF IMPLIED WARRANTIES OR LIABILITY FOR INCIDENTAL, INDIRECT, SPECIAL, OR CONSEQUENTIAL DAMAGES, SO THE ABOVE LIMITATIONS MAY NOT ALWAYS APPLY. THE WARRANTIES IN THIS AGREEMENT GIVE YOU SPECIFIC LEGAL RIGHTS AND YOU MAY ALSO HAVE OTHER RIGHTS WHICH VARY IN ACCORDANCE WITH LOCAL LAW.

ACKNOWLEDGMENT

YOU ACKNOWLEDGE THAT YOU HAVE READ THIS AGREEMENT, UNDERSTAND IT, AND AGREE TO BE BOUND BY ITS TERMS AND CONDITIONS. YOU ALSO AGREE THAT THIS AGREEMENT IS THE COMPLETE AND EXCLUSIVE STATEMENT OF THE AGREEMENT BETWEEN YOU AND THE COMPANY AND SUPERSEDES ALL PROPOSALS OR PRIOR AGREEMENTS, ORAL, OR WRITTEN, AND ANY OTHER COMMUNICATIONS BETWEEN YOU AND THE COMPANY OR ANY REPRESENTATIVE OF THE COMPANY RELATING TO THE SUBJECT MATTER OF THIS AGREEMENT.

Should you have any questions concerning this Agreement or if you wish to contact the Company for any reason, please contact in writing at the address below.

Robin Short
Prentice Hall PTR
One Lake Street
Upper Saddle River, New Jersey 07458

About the CD

The DJGPP compiler and RHIDE front-end on the CD have been tested and will run under MS-DOS or in an MS-DOS window under Windows 95. They should also work under Windows 3.1x, but have not been tested in that environment. I have heard that DJGPP will work under Windows NT, but cannot supply installation instructions for that platform. The resource requirements are likely to be higher for NT.

The hardware requirements are:

    Intel 386 or compatible (Cyrix, AMD) or higher

    16 MB of memory

    50 MB of disk space

The installation instructions are in the file "README.TXT" in the root directory on the CD.

Please note: Prentice Hall does not offer technical support for this software. However, if there is a problem with the media, you may obtain a replacement copy by emailing us with the problem at discexchange@phptr.com